Cambridge Imperial and Postcolonial Stud

General Editors: **Megan Vaughan**, King's Co
King's College London

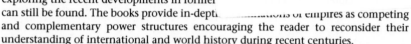

This informative series covers the broad spa
exploring the recent developments in former
can still be found. The books provide in-depth .... ui empires as competing
and complementary power structures encouraging the reader to reconsider their
understanding of international and world history during recent centuries.

Titles include:

Sunil S. Amrith
DECOLONIZING INTERNATIONAL HEALTH
India and Southeast Asia, 1930–65

Tony Ballantyne
ORIENTALISM AND RACE
Aryanism in the British Empire

Peter Fibiger Bang and C. A. Bayly (editors)
TRIBUTARY EMPIRES IN GLOBAL HISTORY

James Beattie
EMPIRE AND ENVIRONMENTAL ANXIETY
Health, Science, Art and Conservation in South Asia and Australasia, 1800–1920

L.J. Butler
COPPER EMPIRE
Mining and the Colonial State in Northern Rhodesia, c. 1930–64

Nandini Chatterjee
THE MAKING OF INDIAN SECULARISM
Empire, Law and Christianity, 1830–1960

Andrew Dilley
FINANCE, POLITICS, AND IMPERIALISM
Australia, Canada and the City of London, c. 1896–1914

Michael S. Dodson
ORIENTALISM, EMPIRE AND NATIONAL CULTURE
India, 1770–1880

Jost Dülffer and Marc Frey (editors)
ELITES AND DECOLONIZATION IN THE TWENTIETH CENTURY

Hilary M. Carey (editor)
EMPIRES OF RELIGION

Ulrike Hillemann
ASIAN EMPIRE AND BRITISH KNOWLEDGE
China and the Networks of British Imperial Expansion

B.D. Hopkins
THE MAKING OF MODERN AFGHANISTAN

Ronald Hyam
BRITAIN'S IMPERIAL CENTURY, 1815–1914: A STUDY OF EMPIRE AND EXPANSION
Third Edition

Iftekhar Iqbal
THE BENGAL DELTA
Ecology, State and Social Change, 1840–1943

Brian Ireland
THE US MILITARY IN HAWAI'I
Colonialism, Memory and Resistance

Sloan Mahone and Megan Vaughan (editors)
PSYCHIATRY AND EMPIRE

Javed Majeed
AUTOBIOGRAPHY, TRAVEL AND POST-NATIONAL IDENTITY

Gabriel Paquette
ENLIGHTENMENT, GOVERNANCE AND REFORM IN SPAIN AND ITS EMPIRE, 1739–1808

Jennifer Regan-Lefebvre
IRISH AND INDIAN
The Cosmopolitan Politics of Alfred Webb

Ricardo Roque
HEADHUNTING AND COLONIALISM
Anthropology and the Circulation of Human Skulls in the Portuguese Empire, 1870–1930

Ricardo Roque and Kim A. Wagner (editors)
ENGAGING COLONIAL KNOWLEDGE
Reading European Archives in World History

Michael Silvestri
IRELAND AND INDIA
Nationalism, Empire and Memory

John Singleton and Paul Robertson
ECONOMIC RELATIONS BETWEEN BRITAIN AND AUSTRALASIA, 1945–70

Aparna Vaidik
IMPERIAL ANDAMANS
Colonial Encounter and Island History

Kim A. Wagner (editor)
THUGGEE
Banditry and the British in Early Nineteenth-Century India

Jon E. Wilson
THE DOMINATION OF STRANGERS
Modern Governance in Eastern India, 1780–1835

Cambridge Imperial and Postcolonial Studies Series
Series Standing Order ISBN 0–333–91908–4 (Hardback) 0–333–91909–2 (Paperback)
(*outside North America only*)

You can receive future titles in this series as they are published by placing a standing order. Please contact your bookseller or, in case of difficulty, write to us at the address below with your name and address, the title of the series and the ISBN quoted above.

Customer Services Department, Macmillan Distribution Ltd, Houndmills, Basingstoke, Hampshire RG21 6XS, England

The Making of Modern Afghanistan

B. D. Hopkins

Assistant Professor of History and International Affairs, The George Washington University, USA

First published in hardback 2008
This paperback edition published 2012 by
PALGRAVE MACMILLAN

Palgrave Macmillan in the UK is an imprint of Macmillan Publishers Limited,
registered in England, company number 785998, of Houndmills, Basingstoke,
Hampshire RG21 6XS.

Palgrave Macmillan in the US is a division of St Martin's Press LLC,
175 Fifth Avenue, New York, NY 10010.

Palgrave Macmillan is the global academic imprint of the above companies
and has companies and representatives throughout the world.

Palgrave® and Macmillan® are registered trademarks in the United States,
the United Kingdom, Europe and other countries.

ISBN 978–0–230–55421–4 hardback
ISBN 978–0–230–30237–2 paperback

This book is printed on paper suitable for recycling and made from fully
managed and sustained forest sources. Logging, pulping and manufacturing
processes are expected to conform to the environmental regulations of the
country of origin.

A catalogue record for this book is available from the British Library.

Library of Congress Cataloging-in-Publication Data
Hopkins, B. D., 1978–
    The making of modern Afghanistan / B. D. Hopkins.
        p.   cm. — (Cambridge imperial and post-colonial studies series)
    Based on the author's doctoral dissertation, University of Cambridge.
    Includes bibliographical references.
    ISBN-13: 978–0–230–55421–4 (hbk. : alk. paper)
    ISBN-10: 0–230–55421–0 (hbk. : alk. paper)
    1. Afghanistan—History—19th century.   2. East India Company—History.
    I. Title.
    DS361.H67 2008
    958.1'03—dc22   2008021575

10   9   8   7   6   5   4   3   2   1
21   20   19   18   17   16   15   14   13   12

Printed and bound in Great Britain by
CPI Antony Rowe, Chippenham and Eastbourne

Contents

Note on Transliteration   vii

Acknowledgements   viii

List of Maps   xi

Introduction   1
  I.   Afghanistan imagined   1
  II. Situating Afghanistan   2
  III. The argument   6

1 The Power of Colonial Knowledge   11
  I.   Introduction   11
  II. British imaginings   13
  III. Elphinstone's legacy   23
  IV. Conclusion   32

2 The Myth of the 'Great Game'   34
  I.   Introduction   34
  II. The 'Great Game'   35
  III. The Indus Scheme   47
  IV. British policy west of the Indus   50
  V. Conclusion   59

3 Anglo-Sikh Relations and South Asian Warfare   61
  I.   Introduction   61
  II. The failure of British strategy   62
  III. The Punjab and the 'military labour market'   70
  IV. The Afghan-Sikh conflict   75
  V. Conclusion   78

4 Ontology of the Afghan Political Community   82
  I.   Introduction   82
  II. The contours of Afghanistan's social ecology 84
  III. A tribal kingdom: The evolution of the Afghan
      proto-state   87
  IV. Afghanistan's plundering polity model   90
  V. Afghanistan's Islamic moral landscape   98
  VI. 'Royalism' in an egalitarian society   102
  VII. Conclusion   107

5 Camels, Caravans and Corridor Cities: The Afghan Economy   **110**
    I.   Introduction   110
    II.   The Afghan transit economy   113
    III.   Exogenous factors affecting the Afghan economy   123
    IV.   Conclusion   133

6 The Afghan Trade Corridor   **136**
    I.   Introduction   136
    II.   Typology of caravan corridor cities   137
    III.   Corridor cities of Central Asian caravan commerce   139
    IV.   Conclusion   159

Conclusion: The 'Failure' of the Afghan Political Project   **163**
    I.   The creation of 'Afghanistan'   163
    II.   The argument revisited   165
    III.   Implications   167
    IV.   The colonial legacy   170

Epilogue   **174**

Notes   177

Glossary of Foreign Terms   229

Unpublished Sources   231

Bibliography   234

Index   250

Note on Transliteration

In the main, I have employed the most common transliteration of well-known terms where possible. For those less commonly used, I have loosely followed the transliteration standard of the Encyclopaedia of Islam.

Acknowledgements

My interest in Afghanistan was, at its inception, a bit of an accident. Looking for a graduate research topic which encapsulated the various themes which interested me, I was inexorably drawn to the North West Frontier of British India. No doubt, the stories of intrigue and spies best encapsulated by *Kim* initially captured my attention. I had little inclination, however, that on the Frontier, fact is stranger, and indeed more interesting than fiction. When I began examining the literature on the Frontier and Afghanistan, I found that there was relatively little of recent vintage, especially with regard to earlier part of the nineteenth century. That Afghanistan and the Frontier were the subject of such spartan attention was not in itself surprising. These were, after all, the days before September 11, 2001. Yet since that time, despite the amount of money, men and material spent on this once forgotten corner of the world, the scholarship remains thin, particularly regarding its history before 1980. This is surprising, and sadly telling. Though not the intent of this book, I can only hope that it will inform those who read it of the canvas upon which present efforts are being painted. Afghanistan, in spite of our short collective memory, is not a land without history. The West has been there time and time again over the past 200 years, and invariably it is the Afghans who come off worse for the encounter.

The seeds of this project were planted one rainy spring afternoon in London during a conversation with one of my professors while I was an undergraduate. Over the years, they took root, matured and in the end, I hope, flowered. Without the support of a number of people, literally around the world, this project would never have seen the light of day. This work, like any good piece of scholarship, is the product of selfless investment by a number of individuals. It falls on me here to name but a few. The omission of others in print is reflective of neither my lack of gratitude nor ignorance that outstanding debts – intellectual and otherwise – remain.

This book initially took shape as my doctoral dissertation at the University of Cambridge. I could not have produced this without the intellectual mentorship and support of my supervisor, Professor Sir C. A. Bayly. He continually challenged me throughout the progress of my thesis, and has proved no less dogged as I have turned that work into the present book. My intellectual debt and personal gratitude to him are understandably substantial. The conversation on that rainy spring afternoon was with Dr Joya Chatterji, without whose constant encouragement and support I would have never undertaken this study, nor likely pursued graduate work. My debt to Joya has grown over the years as our friendship has deepened. I hope this work stands as a small testament to her investment in my intellectual development. The support of the friends who have seen me through this while working on their own dissertations and books has been incalculable. Magnus, Justin, Taylor, Rachel and others – thank you for listening to my ramblings with good humour. Sadly, Raj Chandavakar, the man who planted a nagging question in my mind about what my work says about the colonial state, did not live to see my answer. The work is undoubtedly poorer because of this. The suggestions of my doctoral examiners, Professors B. R. Tomlinson and David Washbrook, were invaluable, as has been their continuing support. Thanks are due as well to my old friend and mentor Sylla Cousineau, who has long shared and encouraged my love of history.

The production of this book owes much to the assistance rendered by countless librarians and archivists at a number of institutions in the UK, as well as in South Asia. The staffs in the Oriental and African Collections at the British Library as well as at the National Library of Scotland, the Cambridge University Library, the Centre for South Asian Studies and the Royal Asiatic Society in London were simply brilliant. Likewise, their counterparts in South Asia, at the National Archives of India in New Delhi and the Punjab Provincial Archives in Lahore, were extremely helpful. I received financial support from a number of bodies during the research and writing of this book. My doctorate was supported by the Cambridge Commonwealth and Overseas Trust as well as Trinity College, Cambridge. Anil Seal was instrumental in securing this support on my behalf. Trinity supported the transformation of my dissertation into the present book with the Rouse Ball Prize. I have also received support from my present home, Corpus Christi College, Cambridge.

None of this would have been possible without the love and support of my family. Though not always sure of what, exactly, I have been doing with myself, they have been unrelenting in their support and unquestioning in their faith in the final outcome. Had my parents not initially encouraged and subsequently nurtured an intellectual curiosity about the world in general, and a love of history in particular, I would not have taken the path I have. My debt to them is greatest of all. Finally, the patience, love and support of my beautiful wife Lila has been unsurpassed through all of this. To her, this book is dedicated.

Cambridge 2007

List of Maps

1. Macartney's map: Punjab and countries Westward of the Indus   xii
2. Lt. Macartney's map, reproduced in the 1815 edition of
   Elphinstone's *Account*   xiv
3. Gerard's map: Route of J. G. Gerard, Esq., from Herat to
   Peshawur, 1833   xvi
4. Burnes' map: 'Sketch of caravan routes west of the Indus'   xviii

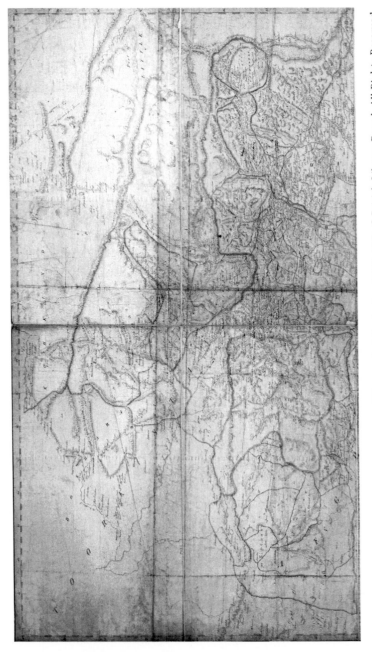

Map 1 Macartney's map: Punjab and countries Westward of the Indus, 1809, IOR. C British Library Board. All Rights Reserved, X/9972.

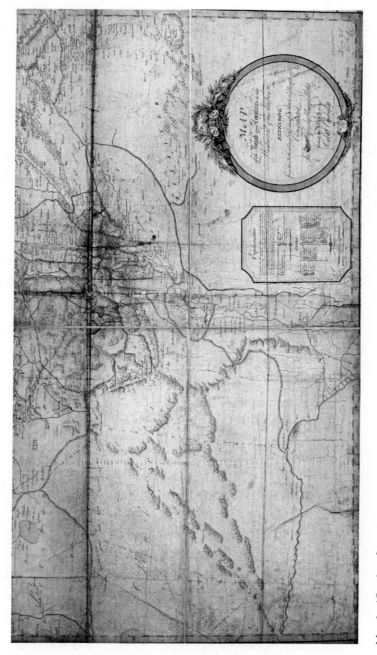

Map 1 (Continued)

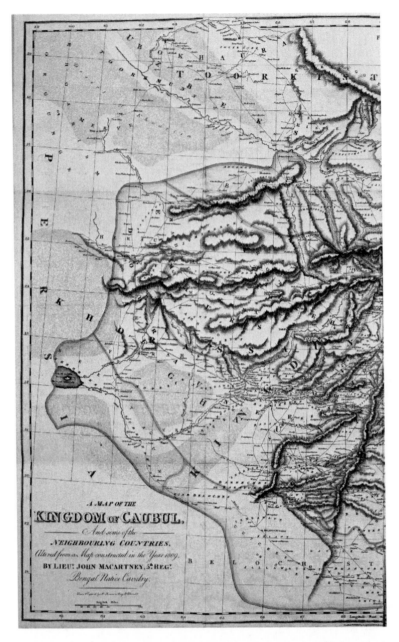

Map 2 Lt. Macartney's map, reproduced in the 1815 edition of Elphinstone's *Account.* By permission of the Master and Fellows of Trinity College Cambridge.

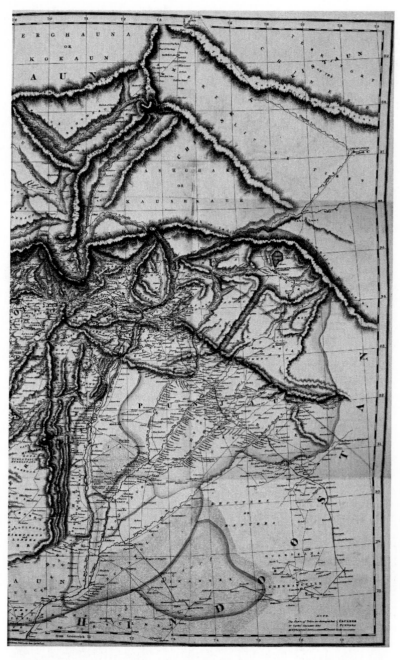

Map 2   (Continued)

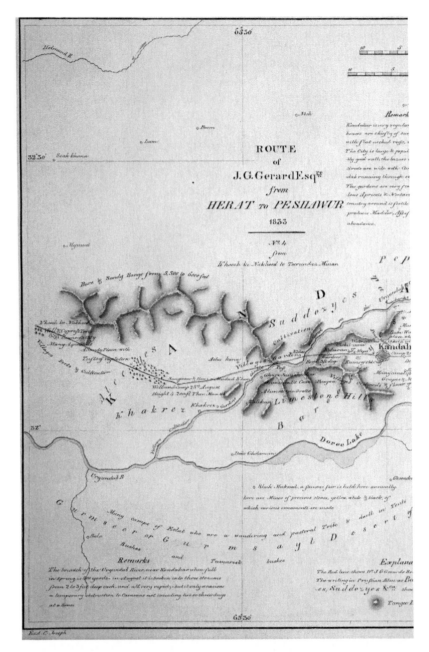

Map 3 Gerard's map: Route of J. G. Gerard, Esq., from Herat to Peshawur, 1833, IOR. C British Library Board. All Rights Reserved, X/3031/4.

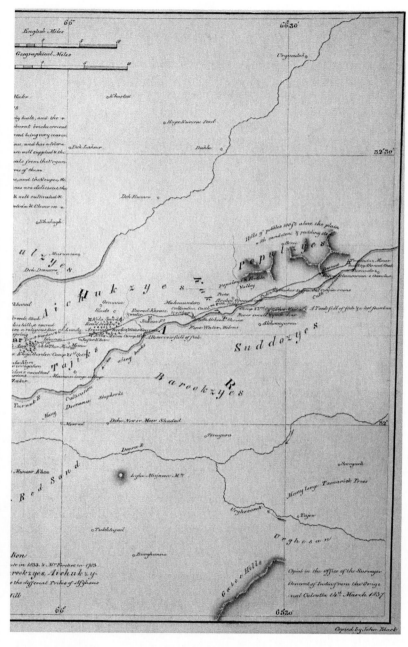

Map 3   (Continued)

xviii

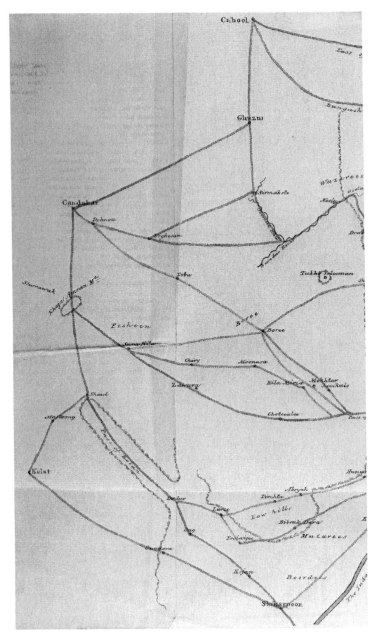

Map 4 Burnes' map: 'Sketch of caravan routes west of the Indus', in *Reports and Papers, Political, Geographical, & Commercial, Submitted to Government*, 1838, IOR. C British Library Board. All Rights Reserved, V3322.

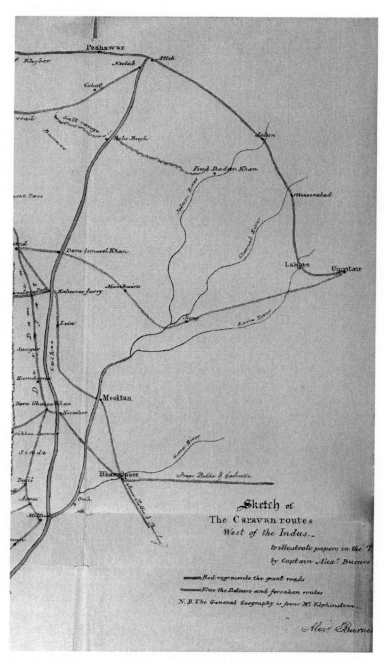

Map 4   (Continued)

Introduction

I. Afghanistan imagined

Today, Afghanistan is popularly thought of as a largely 'failed' state, inhabited by 'wild tribesmen' and harbouring international terrorists who seek to rain disorder on world civilization. Only the forces of international order, incarnate in NATO's International Security Assistance Force (ISAF), keep chaos at bay. The image of Afghanistan as a kind of 'barbarian beyond', residing in an epoch long since outgrown by the rest of the modern world, has its origins in an earlier time. British colonial officials in the latter part of the nineteenth century similarly saw Afghanistan as a land of 'tribal' disorder, as did its own rulers who referred to the tribal outlands as *yaghistan* ('land of rebellion'). Yet the central component of this image, Afghan societies' 'tribal' character, did not always carry with it the pejorative baggage it now entails. Rather, the Afghans simply lagged behind on the scale of civilization, occupying a pre-modern space Europeans too had once inhabited and out of which, like them, the Afghans would progress.

This book is about how the English East India Company (EIC) framed and understood the Afghan political entity and how the subsequent conceptualization affected the formation of the Afghan state. The Company's conceptual framework was the intellectual discourse with which it defined the Afghans for the purposes of its own comprehension. This was not an uncontested monolith of imperial intellectual hegemony constructed overnight. Instead, it was continually challenged and contested both by the Afghans as well as by the British themselves, giving rise to multiple understandings and misunderstandings about what, exactly, lay beyond the realms of British administration. While this framework was first constructed in the early nineteenth century, beginning with the Elphinstone mission to the Kingdom of Kabul in 1808–1809, it would be another 80 years until it held much purchase in the Afghan lands. The absence of colonial personnel, much less authority during the first half of the nineteenth century, meant

1

that the way the British understood the peoples of Afghanistan primarily influenced themselves.

The pages that follow examine the early interactions between the Company and the Afghans through the first four decades of the nineteenth century. For the Company, those interactions produced a particular understanding of the Afghan political entity upon which it predicated its subsequent policies and actions towards the lands beyond the Khyber Pass. Yet this understanding, shaped by contemporary intellectual values and political imperatives, proved deeply flawed. The Company's servants constructed an understanding of the Afghans based on their own memories of home society, as well as the Company's South Asian experiences of rule. As a consequence, the actions of the colonial state, culminating in the invasion of what the British were coming to define as 'Afghanistan' in the First Afghan War (1839–1842), ended in spectacular failure. But the legacy of the conceptual framework producing that flawed understanding remains with us still.

Over time, as the British Indian state, harbinger of a global order constructed by European empires, more firmly established its influence in the Afghan lands, the more the inhabitants of those lands came to resemble the imperial conceptualization of them. As the colonial state's understanding became manifest in its palpable authority, and that authority penetrated more convincingly and deeply into the territories inhabited by the Afghan tribesmen, its expectations of those tribesmen began to shape the reality on the ground. The Afghans began to behave in ways they were expected to, either in conformity with or in resistance to the dictates of the colonial order.

This book is about both the ways in which British colonial authorities constructed their understandings of 'Afghanistan', and more palpably how those understandings shaped colonial actions towards the Afghan lands. The British Indian government in Calcutta predicated their actions protecting the northwest frontier on their knowledge of the area's peoples. But the dissonance between these understandings and the 'reality' on the ground proved disastrous for the colonial regime and had a destabilizing effect on the Afghan political order. These actions, moreover, took place in a changing political and economic environment being transformed by dislocations and re-alignments in the world economy. The book thus looks at the context and effects of the British vision of Afghanistan as it was realized.

II.   Situating Afghanistan

The meaning and making of 'Afghanistan'

The area now known as 'Afghanistan' did not assume its present form until the end of the nineteenth century when its political borders were delineated by neighbouring British and Russian imperial powers. While important dynasties previously emerged from the area, including the eleventh-century

Ghaznavids and the fifteenth-century Timurids of Herat, as well as the Lodhi rulers of Delhi, its recent history has been rather less central to the region. Formerly, the Mughals of north India and the Safavids of Persia shared its southern reaches, while its northern marches lay within the orbit of the Tuqay-Timurid dynasty of Central Asia. The collapse of these empires in the early 1700s threw the areas they ruled over into a process of political re-alignment. In South Asia, this led to the emergence of post-Mughal successor states through the eighteenth century. The Tuqay-Timurids survived, in much contracted form, until 1785, when another dynasty, the Manghits assumed control. Persia faced a period of turmoil, briefly arrested by the rise of Nadir Shah who conquered both Afghanistan and north India. His recruitment of the Abdali Afghans into the ranks of his army secured his Afghan conquests.

Under the leadership of Ahmad Shah Abdali, these Afghans served as his personal bodyguard. With Nadir's assassination in 1747, they seized their opportunity. Looting the Persian treasury, Ahmad Shah returned to the Pashtun heartland around Kandahar, where he was elected the first Afghan shah, establishing the Durrani Empire. Under his leadership, the Afghans exploited north India's instability to finance their 'plundering polity', based on extracting treasure from richer neighbours. But the window of opportunity securing his rule closed with Ahmad Shah's death, and his less able heirs presided over the contraction, and the eventual collapse of the Durrani Empire by the early nineteenth century. The empire Ahmad Shah Abdali founded in the mid-eighteenth century more closely resembled the great Muslim 'gunpowder empires' out of which it arose than the European-constructed state system into which its successors were forced to fit.[1]

The period following the collapse of the Durrani Empire examined in this book is important for a number of reasons. This period marked the beginnings of the colonial encounter between the Afghans and the British which largely shaped the region's subsequent history. The story starts in 1808 with the dispatch of the first British diplomatic mission to the court of the Afghan shah, and concludes in 1842 with the British defeat at the end of the First Afghan War. During the first half of the nineteenth century, 'Afghanistan' was an extremely fluid political environment which the interventions of and interactions with British India made even more so. The collapse of the Durrani Empire makes it historically inaccurate to conceive of a unified Afghan political entity during this period. At most some British colonial administrators thought of the area as 'Afghanistan', while most informed individuals continued to conceive it in terms of multiple, often overlapping centres of suzerain authority. Nonetheless, I employ the term as one of convenience, with the understanding that 'Afghanistan' was in the process of formation at this time, rather than an established reality.

It was during this interval, the first four decades of the nineteenth century, that the British incubated an understanding of 'Afghanistan' which formed the foundation for their later actions and policies. More importantly, the global order into which 'Afghanistan' was to fit was being constructed. That order, based upon the burgeoning European colonial empires, brought about massive re-alignments in social, cultural, political and economic patterns throughout the world. It integrated those patterns on a truly global scale, connecting distant lands through technology, imperialism and trade. But while new linkages were being formed, at the same time older ones atrophied and dissolved. The Afghan lands, once central to the regional order, suffered this fate as British political paramountcy in India rendered them redundant. Yet it was precisely the exclusion from the emerging world order which made the realization of the colonially conceived 'Afghanistan' impossible.

By the time the first British mission under the leadership of Mountstuart Elphinstone, then a relatively young Company administrator, visited Ahmad Shah's grandson Shah Shuja in 1808–1809, his domains had contracted to include modern Afghanistan, Pakistan's North West Frontier Province, Baluchistan and more tenuously Sind. This considerably smaller political entity survived until 1818, when the often-violent competition for the Afghan throne turned into a civil war between competing Durrani tribes. Although the civil war effectively reached a stalemate by 1823, the British continued to view the complicated in-fighting of Afghan *sardārs* as little more than anarchy. Their view of Afghanistan was largely limited to its violence, which they neither understood nor cared to.

British involvement with Afghanistan during the 1820s and 1830s is a rather tragic story marked by imperial hubris. Their fears of European overland incursions into their Indian prize, initially by the French and later by the Russians, awakened their attention. By the late 1820s, the British understood Afghanistan to be the 'highway of conquest' through which the gathering Russian menace would launch its inevitable invasion of India.[2] This great power Anglo-Russian rivalry became known as the 'Great Game', entering the popular imagination most memorably through Rudyard Kipling's' *Kim*. But such utilitarian interests necessarily engendered a skewed view of the region. British threat perceptions moved to the rhythm of European politics and were reinforced by an unease regarding the alien society over which they ruled in South Asia.

The British wanted to establish their paramountcy in the Afghan lands as cheaply as possible, by 'opening' the Indus River to trade in order to flood the Afghan market with British manufactures. They even dispatched a Company officer, Alexander Burnes, as a commercial agent to Kabul to establish friendly trade relations on a firmer footing in 1837. When these measures failed to bring the then ruler of Kabul into the British imperial fold, however, more drastic action was needed. The reception of a Russian agent at Kabul, as well as a Persian siege of Herat then on the verge of success, threatened the political equilibrium on the Company's northwest frontier. The British decided to invade Afghanistan, involving themselves in an imbroglio turned fiasco without equal in the annals of imperial history. With their defeat in 1842, the British decided to abandon, for the moment, attempts to integrate the Afghan political entity into their imperial framework and instead concentrated on isolating the chaos they left behind from their own territories. This decision had profound ramifications on the erection of the proto-colonial state under Abdur Rahman Khan in the late nineteenth century.[3]

Afghanistan's social ecology

Encompassing a large area at the geographical heart of Asia, Afghanistan is both ecologically and socially diverse. Its northern part includes the rugged valleys of Badakhshan and the harsh Pamir knot, as well as the arid deserts of Turkmenistan. The River Oxus serves as the area's lifeblood, allowing the cultivation of irrigated cropland and supporting urban centres on its north and south banks. Southwards, the Hindu Kush, the western reaches of the Himalaya range, dominate its mountainous centre. In eastern Afghanistan, these mountains run to the Indus Plain. Western Afghanistan is marked by arid desert tracks punctuated by mountains and fertile river valleys. Populating this terrain are multiplicity of discrete social constituencies, now referred to as 'ethnic' groups, which compose Afghanistan's unique social ecology.

The area encompassing modern Afghanistan was a patchwork of social and political authority dispersed amongst various leaders vying for paramountcy over one another during the first half of the nineteenth century. The country's relatively barren environment, impoverishing it agriculturally, shaped both the chances and limitations faced by Afghanistan's many disparate groups. While its mountains, deserts and steppes have been regularly penetrated by caravans and plundering conquerors, they have also reinforced the autonomy of discrete groups. Afghanistan's ecological poverty and difficult terrain have created opportunities for centrifugal forces, making the construction of a unified political community difficult. This difficulty has been further compounded by the heterogeneity of Afghanistan's populace, throwing together diverse communities by the force of external circumstances to create an Afghan nation and state.

The heterogeneity of its social ecology makes the use of the term 'Afghan' as problematic as the term 'Afghanistan'. In its proper sense, 'Afghan' refers only to the Pashtun, the largest ethnic group inhabiting the territory of 'Afghanistan', 'land of the Afghans'.[4] As the name indicates, the Pashtuns have dominated the independent history of Afghanistan, often to the detriment of the other ethnic groups such as the Hazaras, Tajiks, Uzbeks and Nuristanees (formerly known as *Kāfirs*). Much of the British colonial interaction with the inhabitants of the area centred on the Pashtuns, who receive an arguably disproportionate amount of attention both in the colonial archives as well as in the subsequent historiography. While the following argument focuses largely on Anglo-Pashtun interactions, it also encompasses for the role played by Afghanistan's other ethnic groups. Thus when the term 'Afghan' is used in the text, it is meant in a broad sense to include all the inhabitants of the area under examination – Pashtun, Tajik, Hazara and others. When reference is made to the Pashtun in particular, they are referred to as such. The use of Afghan, like that of Afghanistan, is one of convenience and acknowledged as such.

III.   The argument

The argument presented in the following pages is two-fold. First, it examines the interactions between the British Indian colonial state and various elements of Afghanistan's diverse social ecology. Chapters One through Three look at how the British structured their understandings of Afghanistan during this period, and how those understandings then affected their actions towards it. These actions and understandings, however, took shape in a historical environment minimally shaped by conscious British design and agency. Second, the argument situates British attitudes and actions in this broader historical moment. Chapters Four through Six discuss the crisis which the Afghan political entity found itself in at the beginning of the nineteenth century due to global changes which disrupted previous patterns of political and economic power, as well as social and cultural exchange.

While the British initially sought to integrate the Afghans into their imperial order, Afghan resistance led the Company to follow a policy of containment, designed to isolate and exclude the perceived chaos of Afghanistan on the far side of the Khyber Pass. The Company's containment strategy ultimately marginalized Afghanistan not only from the British imperial system, but also from the larger global network of trade and political intercourse based on that system. The study of the emergence of the Afghan state is therefore a study of its exclusion from the new patterns of global intercourse and the dissolution of patterns it had previously been integral to. This experience of exclusion was not unique to Afghanistan, one of the first such areas to undergo it. Consequently, Afghanistan's 'failed' colonial encounter serves as a case study informing the experiences of other areas, such as the Balkans, the Levant and the Sudan, which later faced similar experiences. As such, it addresses the larger regional history and the broader forces constructing the international order during this period.

The book draws upon three strands of literature concerning Afghanistan, South Asian colonial history, and newer histories engaging the historical processes of globalization. First, it examines literature on the modern history of the Afghan state, particularly the role of the imperial powers in its formation.[5] Much of this literature follows and reinforces the discourse of the Great Game, although more recent histories of Afghanistan have begun to complexify this narrative.[6] I hope to add to regional studies of Afghanistan by situating the developing Afghan state in the larger history of a region undergoing profound transformation. Second, the book engages with the sophisticated literature on the British colonial experience in South Asia under Company rule.[7] It uses this literature not only for historical context, but also for theoretical structure, most especially in discussing the role of colonial knowledge in the construction of state institutions and structures.[8] Finally, it employs literature on the development of the global imperial order which emerged in the first half of the nineteenth century.[9] Newer works on globalization and transnational history have served to historically ground the integrating processes on which that order was founded. By combining these different genres, this book offers an argument situating the evolution of the Afghan state at the centre of processes taking place across the world at this time.

Contrary to those who argue the colonial state was a kind of monolithic hegemon whose power over those it ruled was absolute, I do not think this the case for the Afghans.[10] It was not as if the Company state imagined and it was. The colonial state's power was simply too ephemeral and fleeting in the area now known as Afghanistan. Nor do I think that simply because the British 'imagined' the Afghan political entity, their understanding had little basis in observed reality. On the contrary, the authors of that vision were keen and sympathetic observers who did not suspend their critical faculties when writing about the Afghans. They were, though, like ourselves, subject to the intellectual and practical constraints of the world in which they lived. They did not produce a single understanding of the Afghan political entity within the colonial order, but rather multiple competing ones which fought for the attentions of decision-makers. The story that follows is about what those understandings were, how they came about, and which ultimately won those attentions and with what consequences.

The book's argument is presented in six chapters examining the colonial imagination of Afghanistan, its implications for Company actions, and the political entity onto which that imagination was projected. The first chapter outlines Company understandings, and misunderstandings, of the Afghans, focusing on the original author of the colonial state's imaginative framework, Mountstuart Elphinstone. When the British first officially encountered the Afghan political entity during the Elphinstone mission in 1808–1809, they had little knowledge of either the land or its peoples. Most of what they did know came from the ancient histories, such as Tacitus, which many officials encountered during their public school educations. They also garnered some information from indigenous sources, both textual and personnel, with the occasional report of bazaar gossip reaching Company ears.

All this changed with the dispatch of Elphinstone's mission. The mission generated a voluminous archive of information about the Afghans which first conceived and then defined Afghanistan for subsequent generations of colonial officials. Yet as time passed, the nuance of Elphinstone's portrait blurred without totally losing shape. The detail was filled in for a later generation of Company policy-makers, championing imperatives of an empire radically changed, by a later generation of Company servants whose intellectual and professional values differed markedly from Elphinstone's.

Those intellectual values and strategic imperatives generated an understanding of the world in which the Afghans were little more than pawns in an imperial rivalry with the Russian Tsarist Empire. That rivalry, popularly known as the 'Great Game', is the focus of Chapters Two and Three. The Game has shaped Afghanistan's place in the eyes of the Western world for the last 150 years. Yet it was largely a fiction for this period, serving as an idiom of confrontation which rendered the still alien Afghans into familiar auxiliaries of European great powers. More importantly, it also disguised the Company's growing unease with indigenous South Asian states which had the potential to severely disrupt its rule, most especially Ranjit Singh's Punjab kingdom. The Great Game was thus the framework in which the Afghans were conceived from the 1820s onwards. But the dominance of this discourse conceals the competing understandings and misunderstandings within the Company's official mind, as well as the Afghan's own contestation of British colonial conceptions of them.

Chapter Two challenges the hegemony of the Great Game, arguing its prominence in both the colonial archives and the subsequent historiography was a consequence of a narrowing of the British Indian official mindset over the colonial empire it ruled. Diversity gave way to uniformity as the Company bureaucratized and professionalized its ranks. Organizational values emphasized utility and civilization as the norms of a new generation assumed pride of place. In this conformity, the Company lost its ability to converse in the languages of South Asian politics. While this was compensated for within its lands by the overpowering preponderance of its military and political might, outside EIC territory such shortcomings proved a great handicap. And in the case of Afghanistan, it proved fatal for the members of the Army of the Indus.

Complementing Chapter Two, Chapter Three argues that the Company's conceptualization of Afghanistan predicated both its actions and expectations when dealing with the tribesmen inhabiting the mountainous land beyond the River Indus. The Company conceived an Afghan state which resembled the other indigenous kingdoms it had dealt with before on the subcontinent. Many of those states, such as the Punjab kingdom, were political hybrids, conversant in both South Asian and European languages of politics. Yet they increasingly fit the patterns of political authority commonly associated with Weberian states fast becoming the norm in the European political universe.[11] The Afghans, however, did not fit this model of statehood, where centralized political authority was sovereign rather than paramount over a defined territory.

The disruptive penetration of the East India Company, however, accounts for only part of the Afghan story. As important was the nature of the Afghan political community, or rather communities, which is the subject of Chapter Four. As a complex patchwork of cultural groupings and units of communal identity, Afghanistan has always been far from socially homogeneous. This social heterogeneity was muted in its political manifestation as long as the Afghans remained ruled by others. The disintegration of the regional political order, with the collapse of the Mughal and Safavid Empires and consequent implosion of the wider Islamic political universe, gave the Afghans control of their own political destiny for the first time. Propelled from being subjects to being sovereigns, the Afghans had to grapple with the ideological and practical implications of self-rule. The Afghans had to construct their own political entity, secured either through consent or force.

As the Durrani Empire failed at the beginning of the nineteenth century, its Pashtun rulers looked for ways to solidify their authority. The establishment of Company power and concurrent rise of Ranjit's Punjab kingdom prevented the Afghans from raiding north India, forcing Afghan rulers to internalize the processes of plunder. This only served to undermine their legitimacy, and contestants for the Afghan throne increasingly attempted to justify themselves through appeal to Afghanistan's competing normative orders of tribe, Islam and royalism. Chapter Four looks at this process, outlining the contours of those orders and the efforts in particular of Dost Muhammad Khan. Yet simply to view the efforts of Afghan rulers as resulting in the 'failure' of the central Afghan state is to ignore the vitality and viability of alternate forms of political order within Afghanistan. The Afghans created a multilayered political order composed of a variety of social and communal forms, such as *qaum*, *khel* and *ṭarīqat*, constructed in the face of immense external pressures. While these social formations often challenged and ultimately subverted the state's legitimacy, they succeeded in constructing a viable political order which survived the adversities of the modern world.

The 'failure' of the Afghan state was inversely related to the success of alternative forms of political community embodied by these social groupings. But these forms of community found themselves increasingly undermined by growing linkages to the emerging modern global order, which are the focus of the book's final two chapters. Those linkages upset the social ecology of Afghanistan, confronting indigenous social systems with alien challenges. The profound disruption of the Afghan social fabric caused by the East India Company and the Sikh kingdom propelled the various social formations into competition to redefine the landscape of their socio-political universe. But this universe was also moulded by changes beyond the control of the Afghans, British or Sikhs.

The final two chapters enrich the preceding analysis of Afghan political community with a discussion of the nature of the Afghan economy. The

Afghan economy of the early nineteenth century represents a type of 'transit economy' seen throughout much of the pre-imperial world. Its central location meant Afghanistan linked West, North, East and South Asia together in a regional trade network which previously supplied European luxury demand. Afghanistan also fed the sumptuary patterns of neighbouring consumer markets with some of its own products, exporting fruits, horses and mercenaries to India. The disruptions caused to those patterns by the ascendancy of the Company, however, helped undermine Afghan political authority.

The internalization of plunder and weakening of rulers' legitimacy meant Afghan shahs relied on taxing the caravan trade which supplied neighbouring markets. They therefore concentrated their authority in cities, which only served to further erode their status in the eyes of their tribal subjects. Chapter Five discusses the Afghan transit economy as a model representative of other marginalized economies on the periphery of the European imperial systems. Chapter Six offers a detailed description of how that model was realized on the ground in Afghanistan, examining the caravan cities of the Afghan trade corridor. The Afghan experience of exclusion, though uniquely conditioned by the congruence of its internal character with external circumstances, presents both a profound moment in the evolution of the modern Afghan state and a case study with which to examine the later stories of similarly marginalized frontiers.

The argument presented here contends that the formation of the Afghan state had important repercussions not only for the Afghans themselves, but also for the wider region as well as the British imperial order. The failures of colonial conceptions and policies in the first half of the nineteenth century would be felt for many years to come, and are arguably visible, if only faintly, even today. Considering the complex intellectual, political and economic relationship between the British Indian state and the emerging Afghan political entity opens a broader set of questions not only about state formation, but also about the impact of imperialism and globalization. The following chapters reflect on those questions by interrogating the history of Anglo-Afghan relations in the early nineteenth century.

1
The Power of Colonial Knowledge

I. Introduction

By the turn of the nineteenth century, the Durrani Empire established by
Ahmad Shah Abdali in 1747 had fallen into definitive disarray. The Afghans,
who had long terrorized the north Indian plain as marauders and helped
sack Delhi on more than one occasion, could no longer mount raids into this
once rich reservoir of plunder. Their fall from political grace coincided with
the rise of a new power whose growing influence over the Gangetic Plain was
to be the story of the new century – the English East India Company (EIC).
As the Company filled the vacuum of authority created by the decline, and
in some cases defeat of South Asia's post-Mughal successor states, it found
itself coming into more regular contact with the political entities inhabiting
the lands beyond the Sutlej and the Indus rivers. When these forces began
to intrude into the Company's conceptual universe, Company servants
recognized the need to construct a framework within which these newly
encountered entities could be understood and dealt with. This framework
would transform the raw information the Company was beginning to
accumulate about these powers into knowledge of the colonial state. Such
colonial knowledge could then be deployed to relate with, if not directly
influence, indigenous powers to the advantage of the Company state. Yet
more profound than the exercise of power through the deployment of
information, the colonial state was in the process of conceptualizing, and
thus defining those with whom it dealt.

In inception, 'Afghanistan' is largely a product of the colonial
conceptualization given form through imperialism. The area we now know
as Afghanistan had no previous existence as a united, independent political
unit. Indeed, it did not convincingly achieve this status until the reign of
Abdur Rahman Khan in the late nineteenth century. However, in the early
nineteenth century the conceptual framework in which Afghanistan could
come into being was constructed. Despite their pretence to epistemological

power though, colonial understandings of Afghanistan had little purchase in Afghan lands. Colonial authority did not yet penetrate beyond the Indus, nor would it establish its palpable authority over territories inhabited by Afghan tribesmen until the latter half of the nineteenth century, and then only partially. Moreover, the conceptual framework being constructed was mediated by indigenous ideas and understandings of Afghanistan, as the British relied on native informants for much of their information. Partly as a consequence, understandings of the Afghans within the 'official mind' during this period were multiple and contested. The story of the conceptual framework the British authored during this period is therefore more about themselves than it is about the Afghans.

Eventually, however, beginning in the late nineteenth century, the power of definition the British claimed in the early 1800s assumed a more palpable form with the establishment of colonial authority in the area. The European colonial powers, and more specifically the British Indian Empire, delineated the Afghan state beginning in the 1870s. Their delimitation of the form of the future Afghan political community had a more lasting effect than their imaginings of its substance. On more than one occasion, the British attempted to assert their control more directly over the Afghan body politic and erect a client state with the trappings expected of native polities existing within the colonial framework. These attempts repeatedly failed, however, and instead the British satisfied themselves with the formal erection of the state's boundaries, leaving the Afghans to figure out its constitution. The British continued, however, to affect that internal debate obliquely through the continued policy of subsidies and support of specific candidates for leadership.

This chapter examines the conceptualization of Afghanistan in the British official mind, and how the image they constructed was subsequently buttressed by the erection of a corpus of colonial knowledge which continues to define Afghanistan. It first looks at the central players in the definition of 'Afghanistan' and the Afghans for the British, particularly Mountstuart Elphinstone. The conceptual framework the British constructed during the early nineteenth century, what I term the 'Elphinstonian episteme', in subtle ways went on to shape Afghan society into a reality fitting British understandings of it. This was not achieved through conquest, though it was certainly attempted, but rather through the slow penetration of the imperial global order personified by the British Indian Empire into the lives of the tribesmen. The chapter goes on to discuss the subsequent and continuing legacy of these authors on contemporary anthropology and the focus on the Pashtun as key players in the Afghan body politic. This chapter informs the work's overall argument by emphasizing the centrality of the Company's conceptualization of 'Afghanistan' and how that conceptualization not only shaped British actions, but also permeated both indigenous and exogenous expectations.

II. British imaginings

Few people have had as much influence upon the subsequent definition of knowledge of a place as Mountstuart Elphinstone retains over Afghanistan. Elphinstone was the first British Ambassador dispatched to the court of the Kingdom of Kabul in 1808–1809, charged with negotiating a treaty with Shah Shuja, then ruler of the kingdom.[1] Although successful in his brief, the political objects of his mission proved fleeting as Shuja was dethroned shortly after Elphinstone's departure and the political situation originally prompting the mission subsided. Yet Elphinstone's most important contribution was not the treaty of defensive alliance, effectively a dead letter by the time he returned to Calcutta, but rather the masses of information he accumulated and catalogued about the kingdom. His collection of private papers, deposited at the India Office, house at least nine volumes dedicated to his Afghan mission alone. This mass does not includes his official correspondence, found elsewhere in the EIC archives.

Elphinstone, along with later Company servants, laid the foundations of the colonial knowledge which came to define Afghanistan not only for the British imperial state, but also for both the wider public as well as later for the Afghans themselves. Colonial knowledge was the accepted corpus of information which shaped and informed the 'official mind' of the colonial state.[2] This knowledge was constructed in the colonial archive, where facts and information were related to one another in order to produce knowledge.[3] The facts from which colonial knowledge was composed in the archive were channelled through the Company's information order.[4] This order prized certain forms of information, in keeping with both the intellectual and bureaucratic values then prevalent amongst colonial administrators. Thus, the Company's, and later colonial state's information order acted as a filter regarding what was knowable about Afghanistan. Information which did not fit this order, such as rumour, was largely disregarded, or rather it was recorded as information, but not related to other facts in the archive and thus constructed as knowledge.

Elphinstone transformed the information collected during his mission into knowledge first for the use of the colonial state, and later for the digestion of the wider educated public with the publication of his *An Account of the Kingdom of Caubul* in 1815, based, ironically enough, on his time in Peshawar. This work, reprinted in 1838, is an encyclopaedic compendium of all there was to know about Afghanistan and its inhabitants.[5] For its European audience, including Company officials, it set the bounds of what could be known about the Afghans. *An Account* includes ethnographic descriptions of the diverse people making up the kingdom, as well as lengthy discussions of the geography, flora, fauna, trade and government. Accompanying the work was a map of the kingdom marking the area inhabited by each of the Afghan tribes Elphinstone documents in his work. Elphinstone's *Account* is undeniably, in the words of Ronald Inden, a 'hegemonic text'.[6]

The power of Elphinstone's text persists today, not only in terms of the vast information included in it, but more profoundly in its conceptualization and understanding of Afghan society. Elphinstone's *Account*, as well as his archived reports and notes, constructed an image of Afghanistan later rendered into being, albeit incompletely, by the penetration of the colonial state. The production of subsequent knowledge about Afghanistan conformed with and continues to adhere to that image. The continuing power of Elphinstone's episteme lay in the fact it remained unchallenged and thus unaltered for a considerable period. No other similarly comprehensive piece of work about the Afghans competed with either official or public attentions. By the time colonial knowledge began 'to emerge as authoritative, official wisdom' in the 1820s, Elphinstone's compendium effectively was the colonial archive of Afghanistan.[7]

When subsequent narratives were produced, beginning in the early 1830s, they incorporated different genres of writing for a different generation of public, as well as Company officialdom.[8] Thus not only the foundations, but in many ways the corpus of colonial knowledge of Afghanistan was laid at a time when the authoritative power of knowledge was being firmly established within the colonial state itself. This body of knowledge about Afghanistan was also authored at a time British political power did not penetrate that which it was defining. While in other areas of South Asia, such a disjuncture would be ameliorated by the establishment of the power of the colonial state, this never happened in Afghanistan.

The new corpus of knowledge about Afghanistan was presented in a form familiar to most of the reading public, especially the Scottish members of the reading public, of the late eighteenth and early nineteenth centuries. Elphinstone's *Account* presented a philosophical history of Afghan society, concerned with explaining the Afghans' place in the hierarchy of civilizations. Referring to 'the similarity of manners in countries in the same state of civilization, though far removed from each other both in place and time', Elphinstone compared early nineteenth-century Afghanistan to Chaucer's England.[9] This didactic form of historical writing, popular amongst Scots, was used as a means of disseminating 'the precepts of contemporary moral philosophy'.[10] It was best epitomized by David Hume's and Adam Smith's writings, the latter of which Elphinstone read while authoring his section on the political and social ordering of Afghan society.[11] Elphinstone's was an intellectual universe formed by the Scottish Enlightenment, and both his conceptualization and understanding of Afghan society were mediated by that universe.[12] Yet the publication of his *Account* was not simply an exercise in esoteric intellectual delight; it was also designed to secure his superiors' patronage and promotion. While it established his intellectual credentials both within the Company and wider public, it also demonstrated his writing abilities, which Martha McLaren notes was 'an increasingly valuable passport to promotion' for Elphinstone and his colleagues such as Munro and Malcolm.[13]

Elphinstone's *Account*, extraordinary in its breadth and ambition, is a relatively common specimen of the type of ubiquitous work produced by scholar administrators at this time.[14] Indeed, his work on the Afghans was only a rehearsal for his later multi-volume *History of India* authored while governor of Bombay. James Mackintosh, one of Elphinstone's contemporaries from Edinburgh University who later sought a career in the administration of the expanding Indian Empire, encouraged Elphinstone in the production of his *Account*.[15] Elphinstone himself cultivated younger protégés in similar intellectual endeavours, writing to the then Governor-General Lord Minto in support of Lt. Francis Irvine who had accompanied Elphinstone on his mission to Peshawar.[16] Moreover, Elphinstone was not the only member of the mission to either keep a journal or publish parts of it. Indeed, he complained that one of the European members of his staff had published extracts in newspapers, although who it was remained difficult to identify as at least 15 of the mission's members kept journals.[17] One of Elphinstone's Indian contemporaries and colleagues, Sir John Malcolm, published his *History of Persia* in 1815, a work similar in scope to Elphinstone's work on the Kingdom of Kabul. Malcolm's work not only intellectually influenced Elphinstone, but also provided him with a practical argument for permission to publish his journals.[18] Together, these two defined British India's Persian-speaking neighbours for at least a generation of administrators, if not longer. Thus Elphinstone's *Account* was produced in an intellectual milieu which encouraged and cultivated such works.[19]

The Company's information order was at least partially constructed by its servants on the scene. The influence these men exerted over that order endowed their personalities with special significance. Many of the early Company servants involved in the northwest, such as Mountstuart Elphinstone and William Moorcroft, were disciples of the Scottish Enlightenment and in a peculiar way, servants of the exotic. Intellectual renaissance men, their explorations were driven by curiosity of the unknown and the desire to draw that unknown into the world of Britons – categorizing, ordering, and by doing so, taming and controlling.[20] Elphinstone epitomized these late-Enlightenment servants of the exotic. He attended the University of Edinburgh between 1791 and 1793, following courses in humanities. His later patron who dispatched him to the Kingdom of Kabul, Gilbert Elliot, Lord Minto, also attended lectures at Edinburgh.[21] Like Elphinstone, Moorcroft was also an archetype of these early Company servants.[22] Although dispatched by the Company on trade missions ostensibly to improve the quality of the Company's stud stock, he was principally compelled by curiosity of the unknown. His reports and journals are filled with pages of descriptions of local conditions and industry.

Moorcroft and Elphinstone represented an older generation of Company servants imbued with the cultural and political values of the late eighteenth century. They embodied the idea of an aristocratic republic of letters driven by enlightened self-interest in public service. These Company officials, including Malcolm, Metcalfe and Munro, understood the business of government as an essentially conservative task, codifying and protecting the traditional village way of life.[23] Their vision of British India, based on the *ryotwari* system of land settlement and general administration, was one of a self-governing 'village republics', autonomous and self-sufficient.[24] Here can be seen not only the influences of the Scottish Enlightenment, but the Romantic Movement as well.[25]

While Elphinstone may have been the first, he was not the only British official to record his observations of Afghanistan. Elphinstone's travels to the Afghan lands were not followed, at least in documented form, until William Moorcroft's journey in the mid-1820s. Moorcroft's journals, published posthumously, married Elphinstone's cataloguing approach with the emerging travelogue form, a union which became more pronounced over time. As copious and keen an observer was Charles Masson, whose real name was John Lewis, a Company deserter who later became its news-writer in Kabul. His 'Notes on the Hazaras of Bisut' was the only comprehensive description in English of any Hazara group until Hassan Poladi's study in 1989.[26] While his observations on Afghanistan remain largely unpublished, and thus less pervasively powerful on the wider public construction of Afghanistan, they form a central corpus of the Company's information about the peoples and politics beyond the Indus during the late 1820s and through the 1830s.[27] Masson thus had a disproportionate, though not always direct effect on the formation of the 'official mind'.

Likewise, Alexander Burnes was a key contemporary of Masson whose writings profoundly influenced both popular and official understandings of the region. In many ways, Burnes' *Travels into Bokhara*, and later *Cabool*, mimicked Elphinstone's earlier work, presenting an anthology of knowledge about these places.[28] At the same time, however, his writings reflect the early Victorian move away from such Enlightenment-styled celebrations of knowledge and into the more popular travelogue form. Yet all these subsequent authors wrote upon a stage already set by Elphinstone. Thus their presentation of observations, and indeed the observations themselves were not simply conditioned on the requirements and tastes of their contemporaries, but more profoundly by the universe Elphinstone first imagined.

Unlike later bodies of colonial knowledge, this knowledge was not designed for the direct political control to the Afghans. Rather, consistent with the Enlightenment ethic of the inherent and self-referential value of knowledge, many of the observations these men recorded aimed at controlling information, not people. Their efforts focused on taming the exotic, not necessarily subjugating the Afghans. With the exception of

William Moorcroft's journals, the published works differed only slightly from the official correspondence on which many were based.[29] Published a mere seven years after the return of his mission, Elphinstone's *Account* is virtually identical to the notes and reports he provided the Company on his return from Peshawar. These published accounts emphasize a key component of taming the exotic – namely making it knowable and accessible to the wider educated public. The manuscripts constructed an image of Afghanistan built upon a Eurocentric intellectual facade, written for the consumption of a European audience.

Yet as time passed, a generational rift appeared between these older Company servants, and more reforming elements within the Company bureaucracy, which David Washbrook has termed 'the Haileybury generation'.[30] This later generation was not interested in documenting the exotic, but rather in controlling it. In the words of Charles Masson, the Afghans needed to be 'Anglicised,' not simply appreciated as old India hands might suggest.[31] With the generational shift, knowledge became more overtly a tool of political control. The cultural valuation of knowledge as a good in and of itself gave way to a more utilitarian understanding of the significance of knowledge in the formation and application of policy. The Company sought to more effectively control Indian society, and thus attempted to more deeply penetrate it and concurrently rationalize its governing structures.

For this later generation of colonial administrators, the Company's penetration of Indian society was not designed to gather knowledge about India, but rather to impose its vision of government and order on Indian society. To accomplish this penetration, the Company institutionalized its intelligence network and increasingly bureaucratized its ranks during this period.[32] This bureaucratization engendered a move away from networks of human knowledge towards statistical knowledge.[33] Company officials, who previously 'cooked their reports with one part scientific discipline, one part military discipline, and eight parts local wisdom, to produce an Anglo-Indian creole form of colonial knowledge', now packaged it in standardized form.[34]

The governing power structures erected during the 1820s and 1830s were fundamentally handicapped by the vision on which they were founded. The new generation of Company servants had to contend with an existing mass of knowledge about Afghanistan. The voluminous intelligence and information about the lands beyond the Indus was in the main a recitation of Elphinstone's original collection up to the First Afghan War (1839–1842). When new information was later added by news-writers and travellers, it was assimilated into the body of colonial knowledge through an Elphinstonian episteme. While there were details which remained to be filled in, Elphinstone definitively delineated the universe of the knowable regarding Afghanistan. All subsequent information, recorded and archived for the colonial state, would have to be fit into this episteme in order to be transformed into knowledge.

The corpus of colonial knowledge which emerged through the mid-nineteenth century was not a homogenized monolith when Elphinstone began its inscription. While he definitively set its limits, its content remained contested and the Company's information order and colonial knowledge about Afghanistan was contoured by multiple, often-competing understandings. Perhaps more importantly, the Elphinstonian episteme originally had very little purchase beyond the Indus. Unlike the Indian plains, where Company power was steadily becoming more deeply entrenched, in the Afghan lands it had yet to be felt. Nor would it be felt, save during the brief occupational interludes punctuating the Anglo-Afghan wars, until the end of the nineteenth century and the British administration of the tribal areas on the Indian side of the Durand Line. Even then, British governance maintained a light touch, as much by necessity as by choice. Its lack of traction meant the colonial conceptualization did little epistemic violence to the Afghans, who remained largely aloof of British understandings of them. Rather, the main victims of any epistemic violence which did occur were the British themselves. Their belief in their own understandings of Afghan society is a testament to the stubbornness of imperial will, surviving three defeats in Anglo-Afghan wars and innumerable 'tribal uprisings' along the frontier.[35]

The British refusal to abandon the idea of Afghanistan first authored by Elphinstone eventually paid off as the reality on the ground came to more closely approximate it. But this was the result of a process which did not take root until the late nineteenth century at the earliest. In place of that later success, the British were faced with the repeated failure of their policies towards the Afghan lands based upon the Elphinstonian episteme. This was first decisively demonstrated to them in their defeat in the First Afghan War, a defeat predicated on their poor understanding of the Afghan political universe they attempted to shape. The importance of the colonial conceptualization of Afghanistan, contested as it was in the official mind, is thus not how it shaped an Afghan reality on the ground. That would come later. Rather, it is how the understandings it produced shaped British actions, and how those actions went awry because of the negligible influence those understandings had beyond the Indus.

Afghan tribesmen and the Scottish highlands

Neither Elphinstone nor Moorcroft, nor subsequent figures important in the conceptualization of Afghanistan, such as Burnes and Alexander Connolly, approached the peoples of region free of preconceptions of how to record and order the inhabitants of this hitherto *terra incognita*. Several of these men were Scotsmen, intimately familiar with the dismantling of Highland society during the eighteenth century, culminating in the Highland clearances.[36] Thus it is unsurprising to encounter more than one comparison between Highland Scots and the rugged Afghan tribesmen.[37] Elphinstone thought 'the situation of the Afghaun [*sic*] country appears to me to bear a strong resemblance to that of Scotland in ancient times.'[38] He compared Khushal Khan Khattak, a famous Pashtun poet and leader, to William Wallace.[39] Colonial observers recognized both Scottish Highlanders and the Afghans organized themselves in clans, based on family relations and generally elevated a tribal *khān* or Highland laird to leadership positions of differing authority.

In encountering the unknown, these observers attempted to rationalize the society they discovered through comparison with those they were familiar with. The mountainous nature of Afghanistan and fiercely independent character of its tribesmen distinguished them from the plainsmen of India. Thus, many of the Scotsmen first recording their encounters with the Afghans found their native countrymen a more appropriate comparison. Further, these Scottish officers' association with the clans of the Highlands offered not only an intellectual analogy, but also a policy blueprint.

The comparison, though superficially satisfactory, was profoundly mistaken. Unlike their Scottish counterparts, the Afghans had no history of central control or a unified political culture. Furthermore, the 'tribal' equivalent in Scotland, the clan, was more a putative connection, with loyalty bestowed to a land-owning family whose wealth and status was hereditary rather than elective.[40] The *Pashtünwâlî*, or Pashtun tribal code, stood firmly against social heirarchization and hereditary status and wealth.[41] More profoundly, the Scottish clans represented a territorially organized society where wealth, loyalty and political power were vested in land. The Scottish *sliochdan*, or family segments which clans subdivided into, depended on the availability of land for both their genesis and continued survival.[42] The Afghans, however, represented a different ordering of political space, in which connections were genealogical as opposed to territorial.

Additionally, British experience largely centred on the southeastern part of Afghanistan, along the frontier created by Sikh successes in the early nineteenth century which became a culturally conservative space for the maintenance and reinforcement of Pashtun culture.[43] Basing their larger generalizations about Afghan society on the limited knowledge of these peripheral tribes, Company servants mediated their understanding of Afghanistan through them. Many in the British policy establishment simply understood the chaotic situation regularly depicted in intelligence reports from beyond the Khyber as endemic of 'wild tribes' similar to those in the Khyber.[44] The narrow experiential base on which much of the British 'official mind' perspective was based severely hampered a more dynamic and penetrating institutional understanding of their northwestern neighbour.

More profoundly problematic than the Scottish comparison is the tribal motif employed by Elphinstone which found favour in the late-Enlightenment intellectual world he inhabited. Rather than conjuring images of the cruel and racially inferior native that predominated the late nineteenth-century world, tribe continued to resonate with Rousseau's image of the noble savage. Elphinstone's juxtaposition of the Afghans' 'rude independence' with Persian decadence emphasized the former's lack of civilization while at the same time invigorating it because of their freedom from its degeneracy.[45] Such a portrayal emulated Gibbon's picture of the Germanic tribes and their role in the fall of the Roman Empire.[46] The Roman motif exerted a pronounced influence on the intellectual universe of this generation, with Elphinstone reading Tacitus as he travelled to his reception with Shah Shuja, a choice which undoubtedly coloured his own writings.[47] Although barbaric and uncivilized, these tribesmen maintained an essential nobility and purity the corrupt members of the empires they destroyed lacked.

Free of the late nineteenth-century racialization of tribe, its use here was not an explicitly negative or pejorative labelling. Indeed, Elphinstone and his contemporaries' comparison of the Afghans to the clans of Highland Scotland drew a direct link with their own past. It provided a connection of familiarity, albeit a distant one, rather than an exclusive and alien othering. In the Afghans, they recognized a distorted and faint image of themselves, although lower on the hierarchies of civilization. Such a presentation, based in contemporary traditions of philosophical history infusing late Scottish Enlightenment thinking, emphasized the universality of human experience and inevitability of common outcome.[48] This contrasts sharply with later nineteenth-century ideas of the essentiality of human difference, built upon the intellectual edifice of social Darwinism.

The positive connotation of tribe latent in Elphinstone's writings has given the concept an acceptable permanence which was taken up not only by subsequent imperial administrators, but also by later academics.[49] Elphinstone tribalized our understanding and vision of Afghan society through his original depiction of it. Yet this tribalization was not simply a *fiat* of some monolithic imperial hegemon, even if solely intellectual in form. Like much colonial knowledge about Afghanistan, it evolved out of a multifaceted intellectual dialogue within colonial discourse, as well an unequal confrontation with indigenous concepts of space and community. This creation of knowledge was, in the words of Eugene Irschick, a 'dialogic and heteroglot' process.[50] Elphinstone himself was highly dependent on native informants for his *Account*. Thus the picture he produced was necessarily mediated through an indigenous conceptual framework.

The Afghans themselves maintained a strong sense of social order based on 'tribal' divisions for a significant period pre-dating Elphinstone's arrival, as evidenced by the widespread dissemination of tribal genealogies such as that in Neamat Ullah Harawi's seventeenth-century *Makhzan-i Afghani*, translated into English between 1829 and 1836.[51] This was a complicated process of intellectual exchange in which indigenous ideas of social order were interposed through the conceptual prism of the colonial administrators who documented them. Over time, as the power of the colonial state became more penetrative in Afghan society, the Afghans began to act in the ways the colonial conceptualization of them warranted.

Elphinstone's tribalization of Afghan society was based on pseudo-ethnographic descriptions of the various Afghan tribes which permeated both his published *Account* and more substantive official correspondence. These descriptions, prevalent throughout India, underpinned later colonial administration in the form of the 'ethnographic state'.[52] While Elphinstone's interest may have sprung from the late-Enlightenment values of his education at Edinburgh, that of later colonial ethnographers slowly evolved to a grounding in more utilitarian concerns. The ordering of information which formed a central part of these ethnographic enquiries, with taxonomies of tribes, rendered that information both understandable as well as usable to the official mind. Rather than facing an alien society of unknown and poorly understood character, Elphinstone and his intellectual progeny rendered Afghan society knowable for later imperial administrators in discrete fragments described in the familiar and accessible idiom of tribe. 'Knowing the tribes' became the objective of the colonial information order in regard to Afghanistan and the frontier, and at the same time the justification for its existence.

Territoriality and the delineation of power

Included in this ambitious project was an attempt to represent the Kingdom of Kabul territorially in the form of a map drawn up by Lt. John Macartney, the Elphinstone mission's surveyor.[53] The map stands as testament for the breadth of its undertaking, its detail and its essential geographical inaccuracy. In constructing the map, Macartney, like Elphinstone in his more textual record, relied heavily on native informants, whom Elphinstone characterized as 'remarkable for [their] observation and veracity'.[54] Macartney used natives' information in the construction of his own image of Afghanistan, divorcing that information from the conceptual framework in which it was embedded. The most striking aspect of the map is not its geographical features, nor its attempts at mathematical precision.[55] Rather it is the labelling of tribal areas or homelands. The map is, simply put, the first and most exhaustive British attempt to fix Afghan tribes to a specific territory. This territorialization served as the foundation of the British understanding of Afghanistan, and as such was a bid at colonial control.[56]

In India, the concept of territory was central to British claims of power, legitimacy and sovereignty; for the Company 'it was crucial that land be transformed into territory' for the assertion of the state's control.[57] Yet Afghanistan lay beyond the physical reach of Company control at this point. Thus it was not land which Macartney's map attempted to territorialize, but people, or rather, information about people. By dictating the way in which information would be categorized, and thus communicated and cognized, the British attempted to monopolize the power of definition, objectifying difference through territorial boundaries. Macartney's map was simply the extension of a way of recording and ordering information the Company employed elsewhere in India.[58] But by mapping Afghanistan, he introduced this informational framework to an environment where these European conceptions of space and order had little traction.

Macartney's application of a form of information ordering which was becoming standardized in British India emphasizes yet another lasting consequence of Elphinstone's episteme. The men who documented the Afghans and their society were not solely influenced by the familiar models of social order from the metropolitan centre, but were also conceptually conditioned by their service in South Asia. For them, the Kingdom of Kabul was simply another Mughal successor state filling the vacuum created by its eighteenth-century decline. As the Company asserted itself over those successor states in South Asia, they gained a knowledge of and fluency in the languages of South Asian politics which not only paved the way for the Company's success, but also fundamentally transformed it into a hybrid South Asian polity itself.[59]

Their familiarity with the South Asian political universe enabled Company servants to subsume the Afghans within it, and by doing so 'Indianize' their political identity. Consequently, the Afghans were understood in reference to the larger South Asian universe they were imagined to be part. This 'Indianization' of Afghan identity ensured British understandings would be coloured by their Indian interests. It continues to resonate today with the Khyber remaining, in the minds of many, the most important access point to Afghanistan. By intellectually fixing Afghanistan into the constellation of the South Asian universe, these early servants laid the foundation for later, more formal attempts at integrating Afghanistan into the imperial system of British India. Their conceptualization of the Kingdom of Kabul as a South Asian successor state thus shaped the expectations of the colonial state when it came to dealing with the Afghans politically.

In addition to their own biases and conceptual predispositions, the British reliance on Indian informants ensured their understandings of the Afghans would be heavily coloured by a South Asian perspective. Like the British themselves, these informants dealt with Afghanistan's south and east most extensively. In addition to enquiries while in the 'Afghan dominions', Elphinstone noted his reliance on the native informants who accompanied the mission after its return to 'Delly [sic]', attendance at the 'fair at Hurdwar (the great rendezvous of the countries north-west of India)' and his visit to the colony of Afghans in 'Rohilcand'.[60] C.A. Bayly notes Elphinstone's reliance on *unani hakims*, Muslim physicians who were also itinerant traders.[61] The intelligence network Elphinstone left in place on his retreat from Peshawar was manned by Indian news-writers. Though it was allowed to lapse, when re-established in the 1830s, the first Company news-writer in Kabul was himself an Indian *munshi*, Karamat Ali. Thus not only did their

South Asian experience colour the British understandings of Afghanistan, but so too did their South Asian personnel and informants who were central to the intellectual construction and definition of Afghanistan.

The focus on the southern and eastern Afghan tribes also narrowed British understandings of Afghan political society to one almost solely constituted by the Pashtun. Elphinstone's *Account* documents an exclusive vision of Pashtun political society, with Afghanistan's other 'ethnic' groups, such as the Uzbeks, Aimaqs, Hazaras and Tajiks relegated to chapters listed under 'Book IV: The Provinces' in the second volume.[62] Similarly, later colonial travellers, administrators and ethnographers perpetuated this focus on the Pashtun, noting other ethnic groups largely for their subservience to Pashtun political authority. Anglophonic scholarship and attentions continue to focus on the Pashtun, with the elision of Pashtun and Afghan a common occurrence in popular depictions.[63] While this privileging of the Pashtun is understandable in historical origin – Elphinstone did visit the court of the Durrani monarch – it has led to an underlying presumption political power ultimately rests with the Pashtun. The British were at pains to stress the tribal and genealogical legitimacy of those they supported, either directly or indirectly. They conceived an Afghan political entity where none but the Pashtun could be the ultimate arbiters, if not exercisers of power. This 'Pashtunization' continues to hold sway over both foreign interventions and popular conceptions of political authority in Afghanistan.[64]

III.   Elphinstone's legacy

Elphinstone's conceptual episteme did not simply frame subsequent understandings of Afghan society as tribal. It also narrowed ideas of what constitutes legitimate political order and community in Afghanistan. This narrowing exerted a formative effect over both colonial policy and colonial knowledge, and it continues to influence international efforts in Afghanistan today. Once the space occupied by the Afghans had been cognized in terms of the Elphinstonian episteme, the colonial state began to contour that space with political expectations. Having construed the Afghan political entity as essentially South Asian in character, the Company, and later the Crown, expected the Afghans to act like other political entities with which they interacted in the subcontinent.

Secure in the intellectual façade of 'Oriental despotism', as well as its experience with strongly centralized states on the subcontinent, the Company looked to the hallmarks of centralized state power with which it could deal. While Elphinstone's own *Account* portrayed the weakening of the Durrani monarchy from its zenith under Ahmad Shah, it did not posit an alternative but simply explained the decline. Thus the British attempted to identify the legitimate structures of the state as the sinews of social and political authority. In doing so, they relegated the alternative social formations, such as tribes and religious brotherhoods filling the vacuum left by the collapse of the Durrani state, into antagonistic and illegitimate opposition.

As the British increasingly monopolized the South Asian political universe, they shaped the form if not content of its inhabitants. European norms of political order became more and more entrenched in this universe as political control led to cultural transformation. Thus the Company steadily moved away from its hybrid character as both a European and South Asian political actor, losing the ability to speak the languages of South Asian politics in the process and endangering its very existence with the Mutiny of 1857.[65] With the suppression of the Mutiny in 1858 and the establishment of Crown government, the transformation of the colonial political order into one of almost wholly European form and content neared completion. This European form demanded of its adherents certain constituent elements in order to be recognized as a state.

To the British, political order was fundamentally territorial in nature, with a supreme sovereign who stood as the exclusive recipient of allegiance, and thus the sole wielder of legitimate authority. This was a far cry from the suzerain political universe of previous epochs in which overlordship was claimed simultaneously by multiple centres of authority, none of whom made such claims exclusive.[66] This move from a suzerain to a sovereign universe marked the ascendance of a political order exemplified by and composed of the Weberian states of Europe and their colonially imposed counterparts. Although the Afghan kingdom was not subject to direct colonial control, Elphinstone's conceptual colonization meant that in dealing with the Afghans, the EIC and later Government of India (GoI) increasingly expected the Afghan political entity they dealt with to conform to their norms of political order.

The colonial state's attentions focused on institutions and individuals, such as the Afghan rulers and larger institution of monarchy, representing a centralization of political authority under the auspices of an Afghan state. The British thus looked to a state of identifiable form, with a central political authority monopolizing legitimate forms of violence and exerting control over a population inhabiting a territorially delimited unit of space. All other forms of political authority were understood to be illegitimate competitors for power rightfully belonging to the Weberian state.

British ideas of political order required the territorialization of authority – namely its association with, or rather limitation to, a discrete physical space. An evolving political concept, in the early nineteenth-century Afghanistan had to be firmly fixed as a physical reality, with its subjects inhabiting a discrete territory. Territorial fixity, ideally defined by borders which were a pre-requisite of good governance for the British, categorized and in many ways created 'states' from less territorialized understandings of political community. The British set about establishing fixity by mapping the

Afghans, through the efforts of Macartney and his successors. By doing so, their imperial conceptualization of space abrogated and replaced previous indigenous understandings. In the popular imagination, this territorialization assumed the form of the image of 'wild Afghan tribesmen' bred of their harsh environment.[67] The Afghans thus became the personification of the land they inhabited. The continued currency of the 'wild Afghan' motif testifies to the dominance of the British, or rather Western conception of space in popular understanding of the region. Yet this territorialization of the Afghan tribesmen was not an uncontested *fait accompli*.

By the late eighteenth century, the Durrani Empire evolved out of a truncated core of territory where the various Afghan tribes lived.[68] This core stretched from west of Kandahar through Ghazni, Kabul and Peshawar into the valleys now forming part of Pakistan's North West Frontier Province. These eastern areas, including the former winter capital Peshawar, were never recovered by the Afghans, but were instead incorporated into the Sikh, then British and finally Pakistani state. Thus, unlike other indigenous states developing during this period, such as Iran, the Afghan state developed from a territorial area which excluded some of its most important cities, agricultural areas and tribal confederacies.[69] This had significant implications for the evolution of the Afghan political community and state. The loss of these areas, and tribes, to the Sikhs, shortly followed by the British invasion in 1839, forced Dost Muhammad Khan, the then nominal Afghan leader, to territorialize ideas of political space and authority precisely at the moment the physical area over which he claimed to rule had severely diminished.

Whereas the Company state required territorial fixity, Afghanistan's alternate social formations thrived on territorial flexibility, defining space relationally. Distance, especially in regards to authority, was judged not in terms of *farsangs*, but in a genealogical idiom. Afghanistan encapsulated a multiplicity of segmentary societies, and consequently segmentary political orders. Political authority was exercised over people rather than land. Yet the fact Afghans were not territorialized in the British sense does not mean land was unimportant to them.[70] They were, however, more powerfully tied to specific kin relationships, mapped by the genealogical connection defining their contours. This kinship conception of space retained flexibility similar to that present in a territorialized one. Just as Afghan tribesmen could, and did physically migrate with their stock, so too could they migrate their kinship relations through the creation of fictive kinship ties such as the *hamsāya* (neighbour).[71]

Genealogy and kinship

British efforts at documenting the Afghan's genealogical system, and their integration of that documentation as a cornerstone of colonial knowledge, irrevocably altered that system. Elphinstone and his contemporaries picked up on the seeming importance of familial lineages in Pashtun society, something subsequently developed and elaborated by anthropologists. Genealogy was depicted by the British not only as the marker of tribal membership, but also as the legitimator of power and authority. But the narrow understanding and construction of genealogical relations by colonial administrators denuded the system of its flexibility by regularizing the channels, and universalizing the genealogical histories. The colonial state thus rigidified categories of social self-understandings through the act of recording.[72]

Genealogy was the idiom through which the EIC understood Afghan society. This was at least partly a consequence of the reliance on the Scottish Highland comparison by Elphinstone and others. When Elphinstone first deployed this understanding, he found himself, to his great surprise, rebuffed. Shortly after his party crossed the Indus on their journey to Peshawar, they encountered a group of mounted Afghans with whom they fell into conversation. Asking one of the Afghans which tribe he belonged to, Elphinstone recorded that '[t]his was an unlucky question'. The Afghan, after initially responding that he had not asked Elphinstone his tribe, admitted 'that [neither] his father nor his grandfather had ever mentioned to him what tribe he was of …'.[73] This did little damage to Elphinstone's episteme however, and he eventually went on to record 392 Pashtun tribes.[74] Charles Masson, writing three decades later, differed with his predecessor by ten, listing 382.[75] The tribal genealogies recorded by colonial observers offer a comprehensive genealogical history of the Pashtun stretching back hundreds of generations and spanning thousands of years. Masson's genealogy traced the lineage of the Sultans of Ghol back forty generations, following the line for 1200 years.[76]

Colonial understandings have carried on until today, with the British structural functionalist school of anthropology dominating studies of this region. These studies have integrated the Elphinstonian episteme, though in modified form. Recognizing that '[t]ribal structure exclusively based on kinship never existed, although tribal people tended to perceive community in these terms', anthropologists have instead emphasized their representational value.[77] Ties of 'fictive kinship', where the reality of blood relations is not as important as the rhetoric, are thus created through genealogical memory. According to such arguments, the perception of common descent, creating kinship solidarities classically termed '*asabiyah*, cements tribal loyalty and community.[78] Genealogical lineages are used to explain social divisions. As tribal membership expanded or contracted, the genealogy demarcating tribal membership adjusted to reflect those changes. The creation and codification of collective memory through accepted genealogical myth served to define group membership and cement tribal loyalty. Thus the discrepancies between Elphinstone's and Masson's tribal lists reflected the malleability of the genealogical idiom and porousness of tribal boundaries.[79]

Colonial administrators and later anthropologists who understood Pashtun society in this way constructed the history of the Afghan political entity as genealogically and thus tribally defined. The Durrani shahs who rose to power following Ahmad Shah Abdali's establishment of the Durrani

Empire in 1747 relied upon their Pashtun, or more narrowly their Durrani kinsmen, for support and limited the channels of power to those who could genealogically identify themselves as Durrani. This fuelled a narrowing of Pashtun self-definition and tribal membership to one of ancestry based on patrilineal descent, including only those who successfully traced Pashtun ancestry. At the same time, though, it broadened membership definition by transcending culture, territory and language. The depth of the Pashtun origin myth enabled its genealogical pliability which allowed for the integration of new tribal members. It also married the Pashtuns' 'Muslimness' with their tribal identity. The Pashtun claimed descent, through marriage, from Khalid bin Walid, a general of the early Islamic expansion. This claim afforded them an early conversion, negating a collective memory of forced conversion. It also instilled a hallowed tradition of martial experience.[80]

Colonial and anthropological understandings of genealogy as the primary *modus operendi* of Pashtun tribal society meant that it not only creates the bounds of tribal society, but also shapes the channels and limits of socially acceptable competition and violence. The *tarbûrwâlî*, the rivalry between paternal cousins or agnates, acted as a restraint and regularized violence in Pashtun society.[81] The *tarbûrwâlî* is encapsulated by the *Pashtünwâlî*, and is thus one of the ideal norms regulating Pashtun society. This structuring of violence profoundly affected the evolution of state power, especially in the succession struggles for the Afghan throne.[82] While in the main European observers failed to grasp the structure of violence, instead understanding the apparently chaotic levels of violence as endemic in Pashtun society, some of the more attuned observers clearly discerned it.[83] Yet the *tarbûrwâlî* offers a glimpse onto another understanding of tribal identity, one not simply genealogically defined, but rather performed.

Performative identity

Rather than thinking of the bounds of group membership delineated by relatively rigid genealogical categories, it is more useful to think about the performance of one's identity within a specific context as endowing it with meaning. The performance of one's identity is central to the actuation of group membership, a social reality echoed by a Pashtun proverb '[t]o be Pashto, one must not only speak Pashto, but *do* Pashto'.[84] According to the Elphinstonian episteme, for the Pashtun, formal acceptance of a tribal membership was expressed through a genealogical idiom, with one subscribing to the group origin myth and consequent lineage system. However, substantive acknowledgement by one's peers as a Pashtun required the visible doing of Pashto, or living one's life according to the precepts of the group's normative order, the *Pashtünwâlî*. This performance was thus a process of signalling and acceptance, by both the group and its individual members.[85] The more narrowly constructed communal grouping of tribe was bounded by acceptance of the *rawaj*, or tribal customary law.

The acceptance of ever-more tightly drawn normative orders was mirrored, for the Pashtun in the language of genealogical proximity. Distant relatives could subscribe to the *Pashtûnwâlî*, but only members of the same tribe accepted the communal *rawaj*. Thus tribal boundaries were marked by personal adherence to a tribal normative order, regulating interactions between individuals within tribal groups as well as between the groups themselves. These normative orders, or shared 'basic value orientations', admitted a collective recognition of a specific normative order within a contested space.[86] But tribal membership was predicated on the performance of such orders, as with the *tarbûrwâlî*.

One key issue was the disjuncture between the performances expected by the Pashtun and the British. The British attempt to territorialize Afghan tribal identity created certain expectations of behaviour, while the Afghan relational concept of space created other, divergent ones. The resilience and pre-eminence of the social categories these expectations constituted rested on the dynamics of power shaping the relationship between the endogenous and the exogenous.[87] The British asserted the authority of intellectual definition with Elphinstone, but this authority was largely unfelt and thus unchallenged amongst the Afghans until it assumed the form of imperial policies. Thus the colonial state constructed multiple understandings, and misunderstandings, of Pashtun society which underlay its actions.

Once the colonial state started to act based on the knowledge conceived and created within the Elphinstonian episteme, the Pashtun at times challenged, at times subverted, and at times accorded that knowledge. Its belief in the paramountcy of royal legitimacy led the Company to support Shah Shuja in his multiple attempts to regain his throne during the 1830s, culminating with the Company invasion of the Kingdom of Kabul in 1839. The Afghans, however, confounded the premises on which such a policy rested, rejecting Saddozai rule and instead rallying around religious and tribal leadership.

As the power of the colonial state steadily penetrated into the Hindu Kush, however, the Pashtun inhabiting the area began to conform to the modes of behaviour in ways which colonial knowledge expected of them.[88] British imperial pressure could encourage tribal homogeneity to safeguard cultural values, while at the same time exacerbating internal agnatic rivalry through subsidies and titles.[89] The key, but contestable example of this, was the tribal subsidy policy initially adopted by the British during the First Afghan War, and subsequently continued during their administration of the frontier. While this policy was at best an ambivalent success in terms of securing cooperation and acquiescence, it profoundly affected the tribes themselves, fundamentally redefining the dispersal of power within the Afghan tribes.[90]

Patterns of leadership

British subsidies and titles attempted to centralize tribal authority, generally in the person of the chief or tribal *khān*, disrupting 'traditional' patterns of leadership where authority was previously dispersed.[91] Much to their dismay, during the First Afghan War the British found the khāns of the Khyber tribes both unable and unwilling to restrain their tribesmen from plundering passing caravans after the subsidies had been paid.[92] This failure was largely a consequence of the state of colonial knowledge about the Afghans based on the pseudo-ethnographic observations of Company servants. Here, the Scottish officers' predilection for the comparison of Afghan tribes to Highland clans manifested its failings. Whereas clan lairds could be held responsible for the behaviour of their clansmen, Afghan tribal khāns could not, nor did they perceive it as their role. Over time, however, the expectations of the colonial state, backed by patronage and punitive force, began to mould a reality in line with its notion of tribal society.

The activities of modernizing state actors exerted a largely conservative influence, preserving and codifying 'tradition' and 'custom'. The subsidies stabilized and preserved a system which otherwise would have succumbed to the pressures of change as they encountered elements of European modernity in the form of the British Empire. The khāns of the Khyber tribes served as the boundary between tribe and empire, attempting to exploit the latter in order to assure their position in the former while at the same time securing the tribes' place within the imperial schema. The individual thus stood as a mediator between tribe and empire.[93] Because the khān's position was not based on lineage, but rather based on ability to distribute wealth within the tribe, his main aim in relations with empires was to ensure a steady flow of subsidies.

The tribal khān normally achieved this by promising good behaviour in return for a reasonable subsidy. However, a state's decision to deal exclusively with the khān as the repository of tribal authority did not necessarily reflect his coercive power over tribal members. The British and subsequent Pakistani policy of subsidies to local khāns institutionalized and entrenched power structures within the tribes which otherwise would have been subject to greater challenge.[94] By elevating a specific individual as the representative of tribal interests when dealing with the state, the subsidy policy embedded new hierarchies of power within Pashtun society. The colonial state thus created a tradition of leadership which the Pashtun frontier tribes found themselves conforming to. However, this 'tradition' and the authority it vested in colonially recognized tribal khāns remained hotly contested, a fact evidenced by the poor record of the Raj's subsidy policies.

The traditions constructed and preserved by the colonial state and acted out by the Khyber tribesmen, as well as the social categories they delimited cannot be viewed as either monolithic or static. Rather, they were malleable and responsive to individual, communal and colonial challenges, constantly being contested and redefined. What constituted 'tradition' for whom and when was always a highly contentious issue. This continual process of redefinition made group boundaries readily permeable, making them little more than 'lines of orientation' of expected social behaviour.[95] Yet their permeability served as a strength, rather than weakness of these boundaries, allowing a fluidity and dynamism which ultimately reinforced their definitional power.[96] Thus while one needed to 'do Pashto' and perform in accordance with the precepts of the *Pashtünwâlî* in order to be considered Pashtun, the contours of what exactly 'doing Pashto' entailed were contextually defined.

Ecology

Elphinstone originally observed an egalitarian ethos as a core value of the *Pashtünwâlî* allowing no man to be the subject of another, something later anthropologists argued as predicated on ecology, with pastoral tribes forced to leave a large space for choice and freedom of political affiliation, engendered by nomadic mobility.[97] The natural ecology in which tribes found themselves embedded was one such contextual element affecting tribal structure which received substantial attention from Elphinstone and subsequent colonial administrators, as well as contemporary anthropologists.[98] Environment is socially dispositional rather than determinative, creating ecological opportunities and limits. These were often complemented by circumstances created by relations with neighbouring political entities, such as states, empires, or even other tribes. In the Afghan case, the closure of the north Indian plains to their plunder raids by the end of the eighteenth century combined with the poor ecology of their lands to throw them into a political crisis. Collectively, these ecological and relational circumstances affected Afghanistan's various social groupings tribal structure and social organization, such as the distribution of wealth and hierarchies of authority, as well as their relations with one another and outside powers.

The low productivity of settled agriculture in Afghanistan militated against permanent sedentarization save in a few important well-watered river valleys, such as the Kabul and Hari Rud, which did support large-scale permanent settled agriculture.[99] The ecological richness of these areas enabled those inhabiting them to develop social structures able to extract surplus and deploy it towards communal ends, not to mention the development of population centres – cities such as Kabul, Herat and Kandahar. These tribes tended to be hierarchally structured, enabling the creation of supra-tribal confederations based on wealth distribution. These confederations were led by a <u>khān</u>, whose position was a political office used for the consolidation and exercise of personal power, rather than the perpetuation of an institutional hierarchy.[100] The Afghan shahs of the Durrani Empire, whom Christine Noelle characterizes as *primus inter pares*, followed this mould of leadership.[101] Their power rested on the ability to distribute wealth to followers. While this wealth could come in the form of taxes collected from agricultural surplus, the relatively small size of the stable, permanent agricultural population meant that Afghan rulers buttressed their rule through other means, especially war booty from raiding.[102] But the establishment of Company power made this option no longer viable.

A tribal society?

Collectively, these elements – genealogy and kinship, performative identity, patterns of leadership and ecology – served as the edifice upon which both colonial and subsequent anthropological understandings of Afghan society have been constructed. While the effect of Elphinstone's conceptualization of Afghan society was most profound on the subsequent construction of the colonial knowledge, it continues to exert a palpable effect over scholarship and policy today. That effect is most visible in the anthropology of the past fifty years documenting Afghan, or more properly Pashtun society. The likes of Fredrik Barth, Charles Lindholm and Akbar Ahmed, all central figures in the development of the anthropology of the region, have been at least partly beholden to Elphinstone's tribalization of Afghan society. Critiques of structural functionalist anthropology over the past twenty years have resulted in challenges to the entire idea of 'tribal society', especially in the African context.[103] While none have directly addressed the characterization of the Pashtun as a tribal society, the efficacy of these critiques at the very least problematizes the application of the concept of tribe to Afghanistan. These critiques thus compel a critical re-examination of the way Pashtun society is conceptualized at present, and an investigation into how that conceptualization has been constructed.

It ultimately benefits one little to assert that Elphinstone's understanding of the Pashtun as a tribal society, buttressed by the works of subsequent colonial administrators and contemporary anthropologists, was 'incorrect'. Such an argument runs a teleological risk, resting as it does on the assumption there is some objective reality the Elphinstonian episteme either ignores or obscures. The servants of the exotic, like Elphinstone, who first documented Afghan society for the colonial state were highly educated and erudite observers. While their vision, much as our own, was limited by the intellectual environment in which they operated, this did not render it fundamentally flawed. Rather, their conceptualization of Afghan society, setting the limits of the knowable about Afghanistan, was the outcome of a dialogic process in which many voices competed, cooperated and affected one another. Shaped as it was by reliance on native informants, privileging certain actors within and without Afghan society, and responding to the intellectual currents of the epoch of its creation, this conceptual framework was no more, nor less 'true' than those from which it was constructed. Rather, the Elphinstonian episteme provided a panoptic gaze over what was then an alien society, making it simultaneously understandable and familiar to a European intellectual world.

IV. Conclusion

As Afghan society was subjected to the scrutiny of that gaze in the form of imperial interventions, it slowly began to act in accordance with it. Elphinstone, Moorcroft, Burnes, Masson and others laid the intellectual foundations on which subsequent colonial policy was constructed. Over time, as the colonial state began to exert itself more powerfully into the Afghan lands, it worked to shape a reality on the ground which fit that contouring the official mind. These efforts were not always successful, nor were the ultimate outcomes commensurate with the original aims or expectations. The tribal society which became entrenched not only in British expectations of, but also operations on the frontier, did not necessarily fit the neat model constructed in *An Account of the Kingdom of Caubul*. But what failed in detail took hold in generalities. Over time, Elphinstone's vision of Afghanistan, grounded in observable reality, began to monopolize the understandings of this space.

As important as the substance of the vision Elphinstone first authored is the context into which that vision was projected. As later chapters argue, the lasting effect of the Elphinstonian episteme during the early nineteenth century was not how it shaped the reality experienced by the Afghan tribesmen, but rather how it served to frame Company actions beyond their frontiers. Those actions took place in a context which though partly moulded by the Company, subsumed the British Indian state within it. This period marked a crucial one for the evolution of the modern global system, predicated on European imperial orders. Thus the British did not act on a blank slate, but rather on one marked by the massive breakdown of the Afghan, and larger regional political economies which were being subjugated and supplanted by connections with a burgeoning system of global exchange. The interaction between the British conceptualization of 'Afghanistan', built as it was upon the intellectual edifice of Elphinstone, and the changing international order constitutes much of the story that follows.

The Elphinstonian episteme worked to narrow contemporary understandings of Afghanistan. The British official mind fundamentally lacked an appreciation of the internal diversity or dynamism of the Afghan body politic, although some of the Company's more sensitive observers were keenly aware of it. Employing pseudo-ethnographic models derived from their native Scotland, Company servants erroneously compared Afghan society to that of the Highland clans, basing their judgments on an extremely narrow experiential base. The British sought to textually fix the Afghan tribesmen to specific territories, making the connection between land and people absolute and explicit. These early efforts, however, differed from their later colonial counterparts in that they were not, nor could they be, bids to directly exert political control. Rather, Elphinstone,

Macartney, Moorcroft and their compatriots wanted to tame the exotic which they served, making it accessible to the educated British public. Yet the territorialization of political space with which these men conceptualized control contrasted sharply with indigenous Afghan ideas of authority and community. Afghan political culture was segmentary, rather than territorial, defined by relations of kinship. The British attempt to force Afghanistan's integration into the emerging imperial system of their construction faltered on their own misperceptions.

Ultimately, Afghanistan remains beholden to the vision of it first laid down in 1808–1809. As the power of the British colonial state became more firmly established in South Asia and it began to more aggressively assert itself outside its frontiers, it began to shape the world beyond those frontiers. British India demanded those that it dealt with conform to its expectations of legitimate authority and action. Having imagined the Afghans in a certain way, the official mind worked hard to process whatever new information and experiences it had of the Afghans within that conceptual framework. That framework arguably did more to constitute Afghanistan for both the British and later the Afghans themselves than the earlier political activities of Ahmad Shah Abdali. The Company's information order and the colonial knowledge it produced were constitutive of the later Afghan state, a fact which in part accounts for its apparent instability. Yet the power of the colonial notion lay not in its conceptualization of Afghanistan, but in the manner it consequently shaped colonial action.

2
The Myth of the 'Great Game'

I. Introduction

Colonial knowledge and the Elphinstonian episteme through which Afghanistan was conceptualized manifested a palpable policy effect in the form of the so-called 'Great Game'. As the East India Company (EIC) solidified its position in the Indian subcontinent in the opening years of the nineteenth century, its gaze turned outwards to pre-empt encroachment on its frontiers and the feared internal loss of prestige. In so doing, it identified the powers it would deal with, how it would deal with them, and the ends to which those dealings would be directed. The Company, unsurprisingly, felt most prepared to counter threats it recognized as most akin to itself in form. The perceived incursions of the Russian Empire into Central Asia, similar to the Company's own expansion in South Asia, provided that familiar form. Yet the Company also had to deal with the local interlocutors inhabiting the more than 2000 kilometres separating its territory from the nearest permanent Tsarist outpost.

In the main, these intervening actors were understood as little more than instruments of the Tsarist menace who exercised limited autonomy. The Company's records detail a story, repeated by subsequent historiography, of Anglo-Russian rivalry skirting the globe, where indigenous agents were pawns in a larger imperial chess game. Yet while this narrative may be the dominant one of the archives, it is far from the only, or indeed the most important one. The Company's archives are full of extremely rich material on the very groups they minimalize as supposed Russian interlocutors. However, the way in which these agents were conceived in the Company's 'official mind' largely denuded them of their autonomy of action, subsequently colouring policy calculations. The information is not lacking, rather the interpretive emphasis has been misplaced, largely because the dominant analytical framework, the Great Game, has so uncritically digested these sources.

The Great Game, premised on Anglo-Russian rivalry for influence in Central Asia, focuses on the effect these European powers exerted in shaping the region.[1] The British wanted to project their influence to protect their imperial prize, India. The Russians, expanding the Tsar's domains, sought to establish themselves as uncontested masters of Central Asia, purposely maintaining ambiguous designs on British India. This story rests on the relatively few Europeans fortunate enough to survive innumerable diseases, hostile peoples and their own incompetence on the Central Asian steppe, making it in the main an addendum to the narrative of European imperialism. Consequently, the history of a people never formally colonized has been misleadingly dominated by the colonial story, severely distorting the historiography of the entire region. A deconstruction of the Game creates historical space for the inclusion and examination of often overlooked considerations affecting British policy, most importantly the place of the Sikhs in calculations regarding the defence of British India.

This chapter discusses the conceptual framework through which the Company understood Afghanistan, the Great Game, and the effect that framework had both on Company policy and Afghan actions. First, in examining the Company's information order, it analyses how the way the Company imagined and understood Afghanistan shaped its policies beyond the Sutlej. Second, the chapter briefly outlines the Company's main policies and activities in the area, setting the background for a longer discussion about the Anglo-Sikh alliance in Chapter 3. The argument emphasizes the dissonance between the perception of the official mind and the facts on the ground, underlining how the Company's understanding was handicapped by the limits of its own imaginative framework. It also questions the assumptions and dominance of the Great Game in shaping our own understanding of the region for this period.

II.   The 'Great Game'

Few countries are as obscured by historical myth as Afghanistan, and few historical myths have gained as much currency in the popular imagination as the Great Game. While Anglo-Russian rivalry was prominent in the minds of British policy-makers and did much to create the modern nation-states of Afghanistan and Central Asia, the Great Game was only part of the story. Yet historians mistakenly consider the Game the defining story of the Eurasian heartland in the nineteenth century, treating indigenous agency as a contributing factor of imperial rivalry rather than a phenomenon separate from it.[2] Best exemplifying the current historiographical approach are Edward Ingram's works, focusing on the high politics of the British Empire.[3] According to Ingram, the Game was ultimately one part of a larger Anglo-Russian rivalry in which the steppes of Central Asia and mountains of Afghanistan provided proxy pressure points. Pressure applied at these proxies won concessions where they were really sought, and mattered, such as in the so-called 'Eastern Question'.[4]

Ingram's work on the grand strategy of Empire is complemented by a second strain of Great Game scholarship characterizing it as an issue of British Indian security. The most erudite and compelling proponent of this understanding of the Game is M.E. Yapp. His tome, *Strategies of British India*, portrays the Game as an internal debate between British policy-makers over competing strategies of British Indian defence.[5] The 'Persian strategy', dominating policy circles up to 1828, endeavoured to cultivate the Qajar state as an ally controlling overland access to British India. The British invested heavily, not only in diplomatic terms, but also in men, monies and material, focusing their efforts on the creation of a Europe-trained contingent within the Persian army. Replacing this strategy after the Russo-Persian peace of Turkmanchai was the Afghan buffer strategy, which envisaged the cultivation of the former Durrani Empire as a friendly buffer state between Company territories and the Russians, as well as their perceived Persian allies. British policy-makers came to see an Afghan buffer as central to Indian security in the 1830s, with Herat being the supposed key to India. According to Yapp, the importance of Herat was a question around which British policy calculations concerning frontier defence centred for the remainder of the nineteenth century.

The difficulty with much of the Great Game scholarship is that in the main it fails to critically digest the official view pervading the Company's archives. The archives' focus on the Russian threat because it provided a familiar threat conceptualization against which it was easier to both initiate and justify action. The British did not fear the actual threat of Russian arms as much as the damage the rumour of those arms might cause the Company's prestige. As George Trevelyan, Secretary to the Government of India, noted,

> ... it was not so much actual invasion by Russia which was dreaded as the moral effect which would be produced amongst our subjects in India and the Princes with whom we are allied, by the continual apprehension of that event. That the Court of Directors looked with dismay upon the financial embarrassment in which we should be involved by the necessity of constant military preparation, not only to meet an European army in the field but to preserve tranquillity in our own provinces and in our tributary states ....[6]

The British establishment was prepared to deal with a Russian army, but ill equipped to counter Indian rumour.

More profoundly, current understandings of the Game fail to recognize that the universe in which it was conceptualized was fundamentally bounded by the limits of colonial knowledge. The Elphinstonian episteme discussed in the previous chapter exerted a profound effect over the form and content of the imperial state's knowledge of what lay beyond the Sutlej. Yet much of the nuance of that knowledge was lost as the Company regularized and bureaucratized its information order. Later colonial administrators, bounded by Elphinstone's universe of what was knowable about the Afghans, largely regurgitated its previously authored content. The edifice of that knowledge constructed expectations the colonial state relied upon when dealing with the Afghans. When they failed to fulfil those expectations, the colonial state looked to those who could be counted upon to, namely the Russians. The Game is thus an outcome of a vision of political order maintained by the colonial state which could not cognize the social ecology of the Afghan political universe.

Yet things changed over time as the colonial state was increasingly able to mould its vision into reality beyond the Hindu Kush. The limited power of the Company state meant that the British conceptualization of Afghanistan was largely limited to its own imagination. As its power became more penetrative, through subsidies, administration, and even direct occupation, the Afghans themselves began to both actively contest and fit into this imaginative universe. This emerging reality, however, is a story of Crown, rather than Company, rule in the latter half of the nineteenth century. During the period examined here, roughly 1800–1850, the only game being played was that of the spectre of the Russian threat on the overactive imagination of British policy circles. The failure of British policies and the later penetration of its authority into the area, combined with elemental shifts in the global and regional economies, as well as more aggressive and successful Russian expansion into Central Asia ultimately led to the Game of the late nineteenth century. To say there was no Great Game before 1842 is not to say there was no Anglo-Russian rivalry, for there most certainly was. This rivalry, however, focused on other theatres of interest and took other forms of competition than it did during the days of Kipling and Kimball O'Hara.

Philosophies of British governance

While the specifics of British actions beyond the Indus were mainly moulded by colonial knowledge, the knowledge conditioning their actions was itself shaped by contemporary ideas and philosophies of governance. These philosophies shaped the systems and institutions the EIC created, as well as set the agenda of British policy towards Afghanistan. By the 1820s and 1830s, one of the central concepts of British political rhetoric was free trade. The British ideology of trade extolled the moral virtues of economy and commerce.[7] Government's role was to facilitate trade by removing barriers impeding it, including its own regulations.[8] The political rhetoric emphasizing the moral value of commerce free of government interference necessarily implicated the Company, seen by many as the symbol of mercantilist corruption and incompetence.[9] To free traders and liberals, the Company of the late eighteenth century was in dire need of reform, if not outright abolition. Increased government control and parliamentary oversight in

London exposed gaping holes in the Company's finances, adding a sense of urgency to the calls for reform. The rhetoric of minimalist government was thus matched by the practical necessity of retrenchment of a near bankrupt Company.

The language of trade served as more than simply a medium of political rhetoric. Instead, trade was the idiom of British governmentality for this generation. British philosophies of governance considered trade, or rather the creation of an environment conducive to free trade, as one of the central areas of sovereign competence. Thus it is unsurprising that Company officials utilized the language of governmental competence in the arena of governmental action. Where possible, Indian administrators adopted the language of trade as the legitimate language of political action. Where necessary, they abandoned it, often exposing themselves to the ire of free traders as well as libertarians. Thus the language of the colonial archives, clothing British strategic interests in the idiom of economic opportunity, cannot be understood simply to disguise strategic actions. Rather it was the code of the political and normative order Company servants found themselves operating within, and it thus shaped their cognitive universe.

In the 1820s, significant cuts in Company spending marked the ascendancy of a new philosophy of government emphasizing both fiscal and political economy.[10] According to proponents of the so-called 'Age of Reform', the conservative philosophy of British Indian governance personified by Warren Hastings and shared by many of the Company's senior servants gave way to Utilitarian and evangelical philosophies.[11] The British no longer simply sought to rule their Indian Empire, but to civilize it as well. Institutionally, the Company became increasingly professionalized and bureaucratized, which in turn meant the official mind became more standardized and less tolerant of pluralism. Belief in the morality of Britain's civilizing mission dovetailed with the economic philosophy of free trade. For this new ethic of governance, commerce was the key to civilization.

Reports from Company servants stationed in Indian kingdoms reflected this marriage of economic liberalism and moral governance, depicting corrupt regimes whose opulence rested upon the labour of the *ryots*. For example, Arthur Conolly denounced the moral decay of Muslim rulers who profited from the abomination of slavery within their territories.[12] Such depictions resonated with long-established tropes of oriental despotism regarding the East. The British framed the 'arbitrary' acts of dispossession perpetrated by indigenous rulers and their apparent discouragement of trade and commerce in terms of legitimacy. The unsettled political state of Afghanistan and the political recalcitrance of the rulers of Sind, and at times the Punjab, prevented exploitation of the Indus trade and limited river traffic.[13] The Indus Scheme, the Company's plan to 'open' the river to commercial traffic in the 1830s, was the key manifestation of the British belief in the moral value of free trade as a civilizing element. As Lord Bentinck, the then Governor-General (1828–1835) wrote, '[t]he opening of the Indus must effect, sooner or later, a vast improvement in all the north-western parts of India, in particular where the effects will necessarily tell likewise upon our foreign commerce'.[14]

Company officers premised the need for the Scheme on the moral decay of the rulers who hampered commerce through onerous taxation, such as Ranjit Singh. Ranjit strangled trade through excessive duty rates.

> Trade, instead of being fostered in the Punjab by the hand of an enlightened prince is subject to repeated exactions from the right which every great proprietor exercises of levying a transit duty which absorbs the fair profits of the trade and deters him from prosecuting a disadvantageous profession.[15]

The Company's opening of the river to commercial traffic would not only relieve merchants from the 'excessive and uncertain duties' levied by Ranjit and the Amirs of Sind, but would also enable the 'conveyance for the manufactures of England and India...'.[16]

Yet economic opportunism and moralism were not the driving forces of policy beyond the Indus. Instead, they provided the language with which the Forward School of Indian defence could clothe its policy prerogatives. By the 1830s, the British decided to attempt to direct what had been a process largely driven by the demands of the market and safety of trade routes. Although the decision was veiled in the language of *laissez-faire* rhetoric, it was a premeditated attempt to project and exercise political power on their territorial frontier. The foothold of British civilization would also signify a foothold of British political interest, making Afghanistan increasingly dependent on the wealth and political stability of British India.[17] The capture of the Afghan market would implant British political influence and create local dependency. Afghanistan offered the opportunity to project British power and prestige through the capture of market share, an exercise in its 'soft power'. The projection of British power would discourage threats before they reached the territorial frontier of British India.[18] Stability would be achieved through economic dependence engendering British political paramountcy.

The Forward School

The key proponents of this strategy towards Afghanistan and the Company's northwest frontier during this epoch were the members of the Forward School of Indian defence. This policy school prescribed an aggressive posture on the frontier, which it bifurcated into a territorial one running along the Sutlej and abutting the lands of Ranjit Singh, and a political one which extended into a nebulous and ill-defined beyond which terminated somewhere in Afghanistan. This bifurcation had profound strategic implications. Afghanistan was no longer seen as a void beyond British control, but the forward base of British power. Unlike the so-called 'Wellesley kindergarten' of Indian militarist who dominated policy through the 1820s and focused on the internal maintenance of order, the Forward School portrayed Russia as the biggest threat to Britain's Indian Empire.[19] The ascendance of this school was secured with the arrival of Ellenborough at the Board of Control and the arrival of Lord Bentinck in as Governor-General in India in 1828.[20] It advocated a provocative, and proactive, course of policy to counter Russia's perceived growing influence in the areas abutting the Company's expanding frontiers. However, the Forward School dressed its strategic objectives in the rhetoric of free trade, as exemplified by its support of the Indus Scheme. Its dominance of Company frontier policy until its eclipse with the disaster of the First Afghan War meant that it heavily coloured the construction of colonial knowledge about these regions.

The 1830s proved an extremely active and crisis-prone decade for Calcutta. The Burmese wars had occupied Company forces from 1824 to 1827, while the tensions in Nepal, as well as Ava (Burma) threatened to erupt into war on the eve of the invasion of Afghanistan. Communications between Nepal and various Afghan *sardārs* (nobles) worried the Company that these two peripheral polities may join forces.[21] After continuing difficulties with China, the Government of India eventually launched the First Opium War in 1838, contemporaneous with the First Afghan War. Most importantly, Sikh ambitions towards Sind emerged as a major concern after 1830. Additionally, the Company faced significant disturbances in the princely states, and its own territories where it carried out campaigns against peasant rebels, 'thugs' and bandits which drained its resources.[22] It was therefore not self-evident to the Governor-General in the 1830s that the northwest frontier was either the most troublesome or important area of concern.

By this time, however, the Forward School of Indian defence was ascendant, and with it the idea of a bifurcated Indian frontier with a territorial one delimiting Company lands along the Sutlej and a political one stretching to the unknown horizon beyond the Hindu Kush. The central aim of this bifurcation was the creation of a zone of stability to protect the frontiers of British India. With their ascendancy, the policy debate shifted from the idea of creating such a zone to its location. Interest in the Afghans was therefore consequential rather than causal. While an Afghan zone of stability would create a barrier to the advancement of Russian influence from Persia, it would also surround the Company's immediate and powerful Sikh neighbour with areas under effective British control. Thus, despite the official rhetoric of Russian threat, this zone of stability essentially aimed at containing the Sikhs rather than keeping out the Russians. It sought to establish British paramountcy in the area intervening between the political and territorial frontiers. By establishing themselves there, the British believed they could neutralize the potential threat of the Afghan tribesmen, stem the perceived tide of Russian expansionism and contain Sikh ambitions.

With the pre-eminence of the Forward School from the late 1820s onwards, an increasingly monolithic interpretation of events can be seen permeating both the intelligence and analysis of the frontier situation. British policy-makers, generally men with little knowledge of, or concern for local conditions, wanted Afghanistan to fit neatly into their larger regional and imperial mental geography. Rather than creating a strategic picture, and consequently policies appropriate to the situation in Afghanistan, they created an Afghanistan to accommodate their policy framework. As those at the top adopted this more aggressive policy orientation, the patronage system ensured this mindset took hold amongst lower political officers wanting to protect their chances of promotion. This engendered a profound case of bureaucratic 'groupthink' in which policy-makers shaped the landscape of the Company's information order.

The lands beyond the Indus came to be viewed through a single analytical prism. Although dissent was tolerated, it was largely ignored, as exemplified by Charles Metcalfe who firmly opposed Company expeditions or expansion beyond the Sutlej. Metcalfe made his opposition clear in his correspondence, writing to Bentinck '[t]o my mind this move on the Indus is the forerunner of perilous wars and ruinous expenditure'.[23] Metcalfe was ignored in favour of those whose estimates of foreign danger were more sanguinary. The content of reports on Afghanistan was not as important as their ultimate message – that of an impending Russian threat and the need to project British power beyond the Indus. Policy-makers in Calcutta were told what they wanted to hear and read into the intelligence what they wanted to see. Information was ordered and understood to reflect their policy priorities. This marked a breakdown of monumental proportions which not only affected the Company's contemporary policy machine, but also continues to pervade the subsequent historiography of the region.

The Company's information order

The archival preoccupation with the supposed Russian threat reflects the intelligence culture of the EIC and its information order. The Company's ideas of what constituted information differed markedly from concepts held by earlier South Asian states such as the Mughals.[24] Yet neither Company nor Mughal concepts of information were static and monolithic. Rather, these ideas were heterogeneous and contestable, changing over time. Consequently, the information gathering systems the EIC created differed considerably from those employed by either the Mughals or contemporary successor states.

For the Company, the most problematic form of information was rumour. India was both an information- and rumour-rich society.[25] The Mughals and their successor states went to great lengths to exploit and integrate rumour into their information order, one of their main tools of governance. The EIC's failure to fully integrate rumour into its information order contrasts sharply with indigenous powers' abilities to exploit rumour. While partially successful in its own domains, rumour originating outside British territories exposed the Company's profound inability to accommodate, understand or manipulate it in a consistent or systematic manner.[26] The inconsistent treatment of rumour mirrored the inconsistent treatment of the objects of rumour. At one extreme, Company officials simply ignored it. While they recorded or reported rumour, they refused to act upon, or even to transform it from information to knowledge in the colonial archives. At the other extreme was a kind of paranoia of the 'dreaded moral effect' of rumour which the Company often demonstrated.[27] That apprehension fed the talk of the bazaars, thus threatening the Company's rule.

Rumour's power lay in its ability to erode British prestige. Company officials recognized the corrosive effects of rumour to be one of the greatest dangers to the authority of the Raj.[28] The British therefore had to control it as best they could. Control of rumour needed to be preventative. Efforts concentrated on combating the initiation of rumour, rather than on containing or refuting one already disseminated. Thus, it was better for the Company to pre-empt a Russian advance on British India via Afghanistan by establishing its power there first. This pre-emptive strategy was combined, in the Afghan case, with a concerted effort to associate rumour with a familiar agent the British could counter. By focusing on the Russians, Company officials sought to engage a 'civilized' threat operating by the recognized norms of European states. It did not require them to either understand or attempt to manipulate the unknown, exotic and uncivilized other. Additionally, because the Russians were distant and little known to the Indian bazaar, the British could control, admittedly imperfectly, information about them. The chimera of the Russians was easier for British policy-makers to grapple than the reality of rumour in the Indian bazaar.[29] Thus the British endowed an agency to the Russians they believed they could control, while simultaneously denying it to the indigenous participants of rumour.

British failures in Afghanistan were largely anticipated by the nature of the Company's information about it. Many of the influential 'intelligence' papers regarding Afghanistan and the Russian threat were little more than propaganda tracts thinly veiled as intelligence assessments, written by men who had never ventured beyond the Indus.[30] The writings of Edward Ravenshaw and George Trevelyan, influential in the early stages of the Indus Scheme, are quintessential examples.[31] Only one of their papers was co-authored by an officer with first-hand knowledge of Afghanistan, Arthur Conolly.[32] The fact Trevelyan consistently referred to the 'Kingdom of Candahar' rather than the 'Kingdom of Caubul' is illustrative of the level of Company knowledge.[33] For the most part, their work, as with so many others, simply recycled Elphinstone's reports, combining them with a distillation of the latest rumours culled from the gossip of the caravan traders.

The large quantity of information the Company gathered about Afghanistan was in part a consequence of the repetitiveness of its intelligence. One would be excused for thinking that Alexander Burnes, reporting on his mission in 1836–1838, not only failed to read Elphinstone's tome, but his own notes from 1831–1833.[34] Although some of the repetitiveness may be excused as accidental bureaucratic reproduction, the Company's investment in the creation and cultivation of a specific image of Afghanistan was by no means unintentional. Officers with first-hand experience beyond the Indus had a vested interest in restricting the knowledge available to the Company independent of them. Their small numbers and knowledge made them essential, increasing the likelihood of promotion. By failing to invest in an intelligence network, the Company placed an enormous amount of power in the hands of a few men.

Considering the demonstrated concern of British policy-makers about the potentially aggressive movements of European competitors in the northwest, the Company under-invested in a skeletal intelligence network in the area. Prior to Elphinstone's mission in 1808–1809, the Company had employed news-writers beyond the Indus in an *ad hoc* manner in all the major cities of Afghanistan, including Kabul, Kandahar and Herat.[35] Although Elphinstone left in place a fairly comprehensive intelligence network on his departure from Peshawar in 1809, it atrophied by 1811.[36] In the years intervening Elphinstone's mission and renewed interest in the area prompted by the Indus Scheme, however, the Company maintained only a few token news-writers beyond the Indus.[37] Instead, it relied on bazaar rumour and reports of European travellers passing through the region.[38] The Company remained without an intelligence network beyond the Indus until 1832, when Governor-General Bentinck approved the employment of one indigenous news-writer in Kabul and one in Kandahar at Rs. 250 per mensem.[39] The first news-writer in Kabul was Karamat Ali, later replaced by Charles Masson, who was expected to communicate with Claude Martin Wade at least once a month, if not bi-weekly.[40]

Even after an intelligence network was re-established, it remained an attenuated system of communication and information gathering based around a few news-writers positioned in central cities. Often these news-writers were indigenous informants without any official EIC position.[41] Their affiliation with the Company, often well known to local potentates, encouraged these potentates to control the flow of information these men both received and reported.[42] They attempted to circumvent this limitation by collecting and digesting the latest bazaar gossip and rumour. The Company, however, had a decidedly mixed record utilizing this information. These news-writers reported to Calcutta through a political agent who collated and edited their reports, usually forwarding what they deemed to be relevant abstracts rather than the reports themselves. This necessarily made the system vulnerable to manipulation. The failure of intelligence was therefore first and foremost structurally based.

The policy priorities and strategic vision of the Forward School were founded upon the intelligence material the Company collected and produced about Afghanistan. The enormous amount of archival material contrasts sharply with the physical absence of men in the area. The sheer volume of the records largely explains the secondary literatures' focus on the Great Game. Much of the intelligence was authored by young, ambitious officers who took liberties when beyond their superiors' control in the hope success would advance their careers. They therefore had an incentive to create opportunities where none existed, becoming the classic 'man on the spot'.[43] Their actions often proved final as lengthy communication made any rescinding or disownment, save in extreme cases, unlikely and ineffectual. Moreover, these officers often wrote to sympathetic superiors, patrons who for reasons of their own, ultimately supported the proactive and often provocative approaches taken by these young subalterns.

The importance of personalities in the formation of Afghan policy was both a cause and reflection of institutional shortcomings within the Company. Of all Company servants, Alexander Burnes combined his own knowledge of Afghanistan and Central Asia with a kind of intellectual sycophancy *par excellence*. After his initial navigation of the Indus and subsequent travels to Bukhara, he travelled to England where he was knighted. On his return to India, he was selected to lead a mission to the court of Dost Muhammad Khan, ruler of Kabul. After the failure of that mission, he was promoted from lieutenant to lieutenant colonel and named deputy political officer to William Macnaghten, envoy to the court of Shah Shuja accompanying the British invasion in 1839.[44] Although at times Burnes disagreed with his superiors, especially concerning their treatment of Dost Muhammad *vis-à-vis* the Sikhs, he never allowed his personal dissent to stand in the way of his professional promotion.[45] He was a loyal Company servant, and was duly rewarded by superiors who valued loyalty above all else.

In contrast to Burnes' success was the failure of Charles Masson. Masson was the most knowledgeable European with years of experience in Afghanistan. Masson travelled extensively throughout Afghanistan in the late 1820s following his desertion from the Bengal artillery.[46] He was recruited by Claude Martin Wade, the Company's resident at Ludiana, who promised a pardon for his services, or imprisonment or exile for his refusal.[47] Compelled into Company service, his ambitions resided in his archaeological interests, rather than in a career serving political masters in Calcutta.[48] His lack of interest in career enhancement, combined with the consummate political skill demonstrated by Burnes, ensured Masson's policy influence was minimal, despite the fact his intelligence reports were foundational to Company activities. Although Masson was vocally ambivalent about Company service, he nonetheless attempted to ingratiate himself with his superiors and was bitterly disappointed when his efforts went unrewarded.[49] The tone of his regular intelligence reports clearly reflects an attempt to frame information within the prevailing policy environment.[50]

Yet not all those charged with the defence of the frontier proved as obsequious as Burnes. As the case of C.M. Wade demonstrates, these men at times abused their position of power in order to forward not their careers, but their preferred policy agenda. Wade, as British resident in Ludiana charged with relations with the Lahore *darbār* (court) of Ranjit Singh, was the channel for all regular intelligence reports from beyond the Indus to higher authorities, including Masson's, with whom he had a rather tempestuous relationship.[51] In forwarding Masson's regular dispatches to the attention of Charles Metcalfe, and later William Macnaghten, Wade selectively quoted, and sometimes misquoted, that correspondence.[52] He laced Masson's extracts with his own political invective. Metcalfe's fear that those whom the Company relied upon for its intelligence 'might suppress most important intelligence if it suited their views to do so' was realized here in full.[53]

Masson was not alone in feeling misrepresented. When the Cabinet published selected correspondence for Parliament in 1839 to justify the Afghan War, Burnes' correspondence with Macnaghten and the Governor-General was severely edited.[54] At one point, Wade declined to forward a letter from Dost Muhammad to Auckland asking for the latter's good offices in negotiating a settlement for Peshawar, fearing the Governor-General was in danger of ignoring or underrating Ranjit's interest in the situation.[55] Wade's ability to interfere with and affect policy formation was in part a consequence of the institutional weakness of the Company's intelligence structure. Yet a structural explanation itself is insufficient, as this same structure worked elsewhere within the subcontinent. The Company's intelligence network, however, was embedded within a different epistemic framework when dealing with the lands beyond the Indus. Unlike areas where the Company's power had at least begun to penetrate in a substantive manner, Afghanistan still lay across the Rubicon of control. Thus the intelligence this structure produced could not be tested against the experience of administration, but instead was contoured by the official mind's imagination.

The Russian threat

Colouring that imagination was the spectre of an ascendant Russian Empire on the Central Asian steppe. Yet despite the obsession with the Russian menace, Company records yield the mention of only a handful of suspected Russians in Afghanistan prior to the British invasion in 1839. With the exception of Captain Ivan Viktoriovich Vitkevich, these Russians remain passing references in a few reports.[56] The archival treatment of 'Stephan', a Russian mercenary in search of employment with Dost Muhammad, presents a particularly interesting example of the official British attitude towards such individuals. The records contain only one mention of him at a time when aggressive policy-makers in London and Calcutta regularly referred to the Russian threat to justify diplomatic and commercial expeditions beyond the Indus.[57] Company officials sceptically received William Moorcroft's reports of a Russian mission to Ranjit Singh via Yarkand. Despite a copy of an intercepted letter from Count Nesselrode to Ranjit which he forwarded, Moorcroft's reports were seen to be the eccentric ravings of an early Russophobe and duly buried in the archives.[58]

Yet not all reports concerning Russian intrigues were treated with such disdain. In contrast to Stephan's barely noted arrival in Kabul, the appearance of an unidentified man of possible Russian origin near Kunduz led to rampant speculation that he was a spy. The supposition, made by the local British agent P.B. Lord, was quickly passed on to London.[59] Even as Stephan was ignored, Calcutta contemplated abolishing the Armenian Orthodox clergy fearing it could be a nesting ground for Russian spies.[60] Likewise, though Government House registered Moorcroft's earlier reports with indifference, by 1830 fears of Russian communications with the Punjab were treated with decided unease.[61] Bentinck's move against Coorg in 1834 was partly predicated on the need to 'flex British muscles' in the face of a rumoured, impending Russo-Sikh alliance.[62] The Company's inconsistent treatment of information about Russians in Afghanistan belies the multiple, competing understandings and misunderstandings of what lay beyond the Indus. Although Elphinstone had set the limits of the knowable, the time elapsed since his mission and changes in the valuation of information in the interval meant the content remained contestable. This was especially when dealing with the Russians, a group over which the Elphinstonian episteme claimed no exclusive authority.

The Russians' physical absence in Afghanistan was nearly matched by that of the British. Beginning with George Forster's transit through Afghanistan in the 1780s, fewer than 150 individuals associated, publicly or privately, with the East India Company visited Afghanistan before the First Afghan War.[63] The paucity of missions to Afghanistan reflects the low importance the British assigned it. No other official Company mission followed Elphinstone's mission in 1808–1809 until 1836. The Company ignored the repeated entreaties of Afghan rulers and *sardārs* to conclude an understanding, if not an alliance after Elphinstone's departure.[64] Few unofficial missions were sanctioned during this twenty-seven year interval. William Moorcroft, visiting in 1824–1825, proceeded against his recall orders.[65] When he and his travelling companion, George Trebeck, died of fever reportedly following maltreatment by Mīr Murad Beg of Kunduz, the Company refused to recover its prestige or avenge the life of a British subject.[66] Not until the launch of the Indus Scheme in 1830 did any but Company deserters intentionally venture into the war-torn Afghan lands.

On the face of it, the Company's correspondence creates the distinct impression that Anglo-Russian rivalry and the need to project British power beyond the Hindu Kush stood as central concerns of the policy establishment by the 1830s. While there was a definite re-prioritization of the defence of British India in the late 1820s, pushing Afghanistan and the northwest frontier nearer the top of the policy agenda, it was by no means the sole, nor even the most pressing concern. There remains a conspicuous incongruity between the archival and secondary literatures' near singular focus with Afghanistan and the lack of concrete policy action. Interest remained informational rather than experiential, just as the Russians remained a potential rather than an actual physical threat.

Furthermore, stark diversity of opinion within the Company has been eclipsed by focus on high-profile individuals. Lord Bentinck was dismissive of indigenous South Asian competitors at the same time he was vocal about a growing Russian threat. Yet his assessment was not shared by many of the senior members of government, such as Metcalfe and Lord Clare, the Governor of Bombay. Bentinck considered Ranjit Singh to be 'a most able man; thoroughly understanding of the superiority of our power; has perfect confidence in our pacific and honourable intention towards him and neglects no opportunity of obtaining our good will', making him the best possible 'intermediate power'.[67] While Lord Clare referred to Ranjit as 'our most excellent friend and ally', he 'distrust[ed] the Sikh chief', fearing that once he controlled Sind 'he will at all times have the power...certainly to annoy us and as certainly to close the navigation of the Indus'.[68] These voices of dissent, however, have been ignored in favour of a Governor-General considered by many of his Anglo-Indian contemporaries with loathing.[69] The tone set by the Governor-General may have framed the language of the policy debate, but that does not mean that other policy-makers did not utilize that language to forward quite substantively different strategic visions or aims.[70]

III. The Indus Scheme

The Forward School's bifurcation of the Indian frontier assumed a practical expression in the form of the Indus Scheme, which came to dominate policy circles in the 1830s and envisaged the establishment of a free trade empire via commercial navigation of the Indus River. Renewed Afghan-Sikh hostilities, Ranjit Singh's aggressive moves towards Sind and the entrenchment of Russian influence in Persia focused the attentions of Forward School policy adherents to this area after years of disinterest. Security became intimately wedded to the rhetoric of free trade and by the late 1820s, powerful sections of the British policy establishment viewed rivers as the commercial highways for British goods and influence.[71] These political imperatives were given further impetus by the newly emergent steam technology which allowed for efficient, and comparatively fast, navigation of rivers.[72] In India, attention focused on the perceived, or rather imagined, potential of the Central Asian market. The gateway to that market was the Indus – the future highway of British commerce into Afghanistan and beyond.

Despite the near total lack of physical knowledge of the river's navigability, by 1830 the Board of Control decided the Indus was key not only to the expansion of British commerce, but also to the projection of British power.[73] The Indus needed to be 'opened' to commercial traffic, which then needed to be both protected and encouraged.[74] In pursuance of this goal, the Company sent Alexander Burnes, under the guise of a diplomatic mission to the court of Ranjit Singh, to investigate the river's potential navigability. Its agents negotiated free passage and customs treaties with both Ranjit Singh and the Amirs of Sind.[75] Much energy was invested to investigate different sites along the river, assessing their feasibility as a location for an annual trade fair sponsored by the Company. In the end, Mithankot was selected as the place where Lohani traders, the key conduit for commerce between British India and the Afghan lands, could exchange their goods with Bombay merchants.[76] Despite all the rhetorical, diplomatic and intelligence efforts, nothing actually came of the Scheme. There is no evidence the trade fair ever actually took place under Company auspices; Indus commercial traffic remained negligible and the tariff scheme negotiated in the Navigation Treaty was never implemented.

The Indus Scheme was designed to establish British economic, and thus political paramountcy in the area, supposedly in order to pre-empt Russian encroachment. Yet British Indian goods were reportedly sold for 200 times their Bombay price in the Kabul bazaar.[77] The heavy taxation merchants were subject to in the Punjab was, in British eyes, responsible for this unreasonable price inflation. Thus the key, as far as the British were concerned, was offering merchants a cheaper, alternative route along the Indus into the Afghan and Central Asian markets. The Company negotiated a Rs. 570 flat tax per boat, divided between the Amirs of Sind and Ranjit, to replace the multiple, variable duties collected along the Indus. Collection was to be overseen by a British officer based at Mithankot, as well as a native British agent at Hari-ki-Pattan.[78] The Indus Scheme promised not only the dominance of British goods in the Kabul bazaar, but also a significant blow to Ranjit's finances. The lucrative taxation revenue garnered from trade was an important addition to the Lahore *darbār*'s coffers, as well as a lucrative perquisite associated with *jāgīr* grants to his nobles.

British hostility towards Ranjit's duty system was aroused as much by suspicion of his growing power as by its effect on the competitiveness of their goods in Kabul. Colonial records from the period progressively assumed a tone of condescension towards perceived excesses of the Sikh *darbār*. Ranjit presented an obstacle to trade, initially unwilling to take part in the Indus Scheme.[79] Trade memos refer to the singularly negative effect of the high tariffs prevalent throughout the Sikh kingdom, not to mention the perpetual instability due to Afghan-Sikh fighting in and around Peshawar.[80] As late as 1837, C.M. Wade, the Company agent charged with relations with the Lahore *darbār* and no friend of the Afghans, continued to decry Ranjit's administration, although he was careful to blame subordinates rather than the Maharaja himself.[81] Russian chintz may have dominated the Kabul bazaar, for what it was worth, but the Company had a more pressing problem closer to home it would shortly have to deal with. By 'opening' the Indus, the Company would inject British manufactures and thus influence into the area. More importantly, however, it would also establish the river as a boundary to Ranjit's expansion.[82]

The Russians, even further removed from Afghanistan and Central Asia than the British, faced similar problems penetrating those markets. Like the British, the Russians had a potential gateway into Central Asian trade via an important river system, the Oxus. Contemporary observers considered it navigable near to Bukhara. British alarmists pointed to the Oxus' navigability as one of the greatest threats to Afghanistan and ultimately British India.[83] The Russians, however, suffered more handicaps than a lack of technological proficiency. Apart from inroads on the Kazakh steppe, they failed to penetrate Central Asia in any substantive way, by either water or overland routes.[84] A combination of geographical ignorance, logistical ineptitude and a healthy dose of local resistance ensured that by the time of Burnes' trade mission to Kabul, the Russians were little nearer Bukhara than they had been 100 years earlier.

The Russian inability to penetrate the Central Asian steppe failed to impress its power and prestige upon the Central Asian *khanates*. Both Bukhara and Khiva openly enslaved Russian serfs taken captive by raiding Turkmen.[85] This treatment did not bode well for Russian merchants. Nor did the heavy-handed reprisals of the Russian authorities against Khivan merchants alleviate the situation.[86] Similar to their British counterparts, Russian traders attempting to penetrate the Central Asian trade faced a host of technical and physical difficulties. These were compounded by the discrimination faced by Christian traders in Muslim trading marts, which meant that much of Russia's trade remained in the hands of Central Asian and Afghan merchants. With the failure, or at least postponement, of the various river schemes of both the British and the Russians, the economic stake European commerce had in the short-range caravan commerce of Central Asia remained minimal. Substantial Anglo-Russian trade interests, representing political influence and prestige in an era of *laissez-faire* governance, were thus largely non-existent.

The Company did not originally envisage the Indus Scheme to involve it directly in affairs beyond the Hindu Kush, although it clearly hoped the Scheme would exert a profound effect there. In the words of William Macnaghten, the then Secretary to the Government in Calcutta, 'it is a matter of indifference...[who holds] paramount sway in Affghanistan [*sic*]'.[87] Over the course of the 1830s, though, this attitude underwent a marked transformation. The EIC eventually committed an army of 10,000 sepoys to place Shah Shuja, a Saddozai and the 'lawful sovereign', on the throne.[88] It was the failure, rather than the success of policies in the earlier part of the decade driving this transformation of official attitudes. The British position in Central Asia and Afghanistan was materially little different in 1839 than in 1830. In spite of the claims of men like John McNeill, Edward Ravenshaw and George Trevelyan, the supposed bonanza of trade awaiting superior British manufactures in the Central Asian hinterlands failed to materialize.[89]

Despite its relative insignificance to British India and the wider empire, Afghan trade assumed a disproportionate political importance as British manufactures and Indian cloths increasingly penetrated the Afghan and Central Asian markets. The Company decided to augment its commercial penetration with commercial intelligence, employing a news-writer in Kabul in 1832, who was replaced by a European in 1835.[90] Alexander Burnes was deputed on a trade mission to Dost Muhammad Khan in 1836 with a brief which scripted political considerations as wholly outside his authority.[91] However, the object of British trade policy – the projection of British prestige and power through its manufactures – paired with the low trade volume between Central Asia, Afghanistan and British India, endowed the mission with a strong political character from the start.[92] Thus when Burnes mission failed in early 1838, the British felt forced to act not because of its economic interests, but because of the potential loss of prestige and concurrent political ramifications.

The EIC's stated policy of 'opening' the Indus was not commensurate with the limited economic benefits British efforts promised. Their policy must therefore be understood not in the economic context of free trade, but rather in the strategic framework of the Forward School clothed in the contemporary idiom of governmentality. Trade was the idiom with which to create political realities, rather than the substance of those realities. Defence of British India required the bifurcation of the Indian frontier to create a zone of stability excluding the Russians, and more importantly containing the Sikhs. These policy priorities were the genesis of Indus Scheme. According to its proponents, the Scheme's success would capture the Central Asian trade, ensuring the penetration of British influence into the area. Furthermore, it would circumvent the increasingly powerful and antagonistic Sikh state. The success of the fair at Mithankot would ensure Bombay merchants' control of the trade, a community whose loyalty was assured by their economic interest in the Company's continuance. Yet the ultimate failure of the Indus Scheme, and the subsequent British defeat in the First Afghan war, severely damaged Company credit, and the entire credit system of north India.[93] The British thus suffered not only a political calamity, but also an economic catastrophe.

IV.   British policy west of the Indus

For all the Company's rhetoric, the Indus Scheme was never about economics. Rather it was about the projection of British power. Although most scholars of the Great Game have associated the Scheme with the strategy of Russian pre-emption, it was fundamentally about Sikh containment.[94] By claiming the right of free navigation of the Indus, the Company effectively checked Ranjit Singh's ambitions on its west bank, especially towards Shikarpur.[95] Ranjit acknowledged this by reportedly complaining to C.M. Wade that the Indus Scheme 'abridged his political power'.[96] By blocking Ranjit Singh's possible avenues of expansion to the west with the Indus Scheme, the British, consciously or not, directed Sikh expansion northwards, away from their territory and towards the Afghan lands. The Scheme was thus an effort to reshape the political geography of the northwest without causing an open break with the Company's supposed ally in the region. As both Sikh and British attentions converged on the same prize, the rich trading cities of Sind, that ally was equally becoming the Company's main competitor. The decision to 'open up' the Indus was to have a major and lasting effect on that alliance and the region as a whole.

Any understanding of British actions along the Indus therefore must be grounded in an understanding of the Company's often-tempestuous relations with the Sikhs. British attitudes towards the Punjab kingdom changed as both the Company's and Ranjit's power expanded and consolidated in the early 1800s. While realizing Ranjit Singh was a man to be allied rather than alienated, by the 1830s the Company was increasingly uncomfortable with his power and success. Company concern with the potential for conflict with the Sikhs on their internal frontier loomed large, a chilling scenario turned reality in the 1840s. While in the main, they decided to deal with Ranjit diplomatically, rather than militarily, it was a diplomacy backed by the latent threat, if not open force of British arms.[97] This was disguised by the Forward School's public focus on the Russians, which also obscured the bifurcation and linkage between India's political and territorial frontiers. The external frontier could not be stabilized without the concurrent stabilization of the internal frontier. Only after British attempts to stabilize the latter, through a carefully crafted policy designed to direct Sikh ambitions against the Afghans, foundered did the Forward School's strategy collapse.

The spectre of the Sikhs, though unacknowledged explicitly, drove British Afghan policy in the 1830s more than the threat of the Russians. While the Russians provided the public justification for Britain's expansionary commercial, political and military policies of the 1830s, Ranjit's Punjab kingdom remained the focus of their strategic calculations. The Russian army simply lacked the immediacy of Ranjit Singh's *Khalsa Dal*, which numbered 85,000 at his death in 1838.[98] In his final year, Ranjit spend more than eight million rupees on his European military and cavalry establishments, an amount soon dwarfed by his successors.[99] By 1835, the Company stationed half of the Bengal army, totalling more than 39,000 troops, along the Punjab frontier.[100] Although scholars such as Douglas Peers have interpreted this as a result of Bentinck's strategic assessment of a growing Russian threat, this was the year in which Anglo-Sikh tensions sharply increased with competition over Shikarpur. The foundation of the alliance was the person of Ranjit Singh, whose strategic calculation to ally himself with the Company as early as 1809, brought about what is perhaps best termed an *entente cordiale*. The personal basis of the alliance rendered it institutionally fragile, a fact Ranjit's deteriorating health during the 1830s made increasingly apparent and disquieting.[101]

The institutional weakness of Anglo-Sikh relations was compounded by the abutment of the territories of two expansionary powers in a relatively rich agricultural region.[102] The Company's policies towards Ranjit reflected his position on its territorial frontier. The Punjab intervened between the Gangetic heartland of EIC domains and the lands beyond the Indus, from whence all the successful invaders of India, the Company excepted, originated. As the Sikh kingdom grew in power, it absorbed large tracts of former Durrani territory, including Lahore, Kashmir and Peshawar, the richest provinces of the former Afghan empire. Sikh successes continually redrew the northwestern frontiers at the same time the concept of well-administered, clearly identifiable boundaries was becoming a pervasive, Company-inspired norm of good governance. The Sikhs' physical mediation between the Afghans and the EIC, as well as their strategic and tactical choices driven in part by their alliance with the Company, profoundly affected the emerging Afghan state. To better understand its influence on events, it is necessary therefore to look at Ranjit's state.

A unique set of circumstances coalesced in the Punjab at the beginning of the nineteenth century to create one of the most powerful indigenous successor states on the subcontinent. Although it ultimately proved fleeting, the Company policy-makers facing the growing power of Ranjit Singh had no way of knowing his kingdom would be dismembered and absorbed into British India by 1850. With the Treaty of Amritsar (1809), Ranjit, recognized the power of the EIC and his own relative weakness.[103] Yet by aligning himself with the dictates of the British at the cost of his own ambitions, he avoided the imposition of a subsidiary alliance, which proved so debilitating for the independence of other South Asian states.[104] The initially tepid relationship between the two allies matured into the 1820s, largely because Ranjit focused on internal reform and expansion to the north and west. By the late 1820s, he had successfully accomplished both these aims to a degree of which startled Company policy-makers. Ranjit had absorbed nearly all the former Durrani vassals east of the Indus and east of the Khyber, as well as created a large European-trained army supported by a nascent military fiscal state, largely bureaucratized according to European substance while retaining Mughal form.[105] In short, Ranjit had established a European proto-state in the heart of agriculturally rich north India, abutting EIC territory.[106]

Ranjit's transformation of the Punjab from a fractured and peripheralized region of decline following the disintegration of Mughal authority into the most successful Indian successor state was extraordinary.[107] Yet it rested fundamentally on the Punjab's agricultural productivity, expanded through the reclamation of land and irrigation works, which garnered up to three crore annually for the state's coffers by 1838.[108] The Punjab's agricultural wealth was protected and cultivated by a sophisticated state bureaucracy whose sole purpose was the extraction of a sustainable surplus for state-building purposes. These not only included the European-trained troops forming the core of Ranjit's *Fauj-i Ain*, but also paid for the supporting structures, such as foundries, which made the Punjab particularly dangerous to the Company.[109]

The Punjab economy was largely monetized, despite the supposed silver famine and economic downturn of British India. This in turn enabled Ranjit to centralize authority in the Punjab to a much greater degree than was possible for other native powers. He paid seventy per cent of his forces, excluding those on garrison duty, in cash.[110] At the time of his death, he directly controlled seventy-four per cent of the *Khalsa Dal's* manpower, relegating vassals' forces to subsidiary duties.[111] The centralization of political authority in the institutions of the Punjab state additionally expressed itself in the demarcation of territorial frontiers. The establishment of a line of fortifications along the Indus was one such exercise in the territorial projection of power.[112] Yet Ranjit's state remained Janus-like, with its eastern face territorially delimited along the Sutlej, while its western and northern faces remained segmentarily defined.[113]

Ranjit's centralization of authority and preponderance of force, aspects Company servants were accustomed to seeing in European rather than South Asian states, proved the siren's call for British policy-makers. By establishing a fundamentally personal alliance with Ranjit, they maintained a direct link to the centre of power. Yet, by centring their cordial relations on Ranjit, the British concurrently ensured that his death would herald untold difficulties in maintaining the alliance so much of their strategic vision had come to rest upon.[114] At least some servants of the Company recognized that his death would likely require British intervention in the Punjab in order to safeguard Company interests. William Macnaghten wrote Lord Bentinck as early as 1831 that '[s]ooner or later after his death I look upon it as certain that his supremacy will devolve upon us by the national consent if we do not inspire the people with hatred towards us by hostility to him whom they now universally acknowledge as their legitimate sovereign'.[115] Not all shared Macnaghten's view that the transition to Company rule would come about peacefully. Indeed, Bentinck himself wrote, '[t]roubles upon his decease will certainly arise and it is impossible to foresee the result as relates to the line of conduct which we may be called upon to pursue'.[116]

After 1823, while Ranjit's expenditures continued to rise, driven mainly by the Europeanization of his army, his income largely flattened.[117] With his military establishment consuming up to eighty per cent of the Lahore *darbār*'s annual budget, Ranjit found his successful modernization of the Punjab came at a cost he was increasingly unable to afford.[118] The areas conquered after the mid-1820s, generally both poorer and more rebellious than earlier conquests, as well as further removed from the Punjab heartland, barely financed themselves. Included in these conquests were territories on the right bank of the Indus, where Ranjit had established his authority by taking Attock and rebuking a concerted Afghan offensive in 1824. Facing the financial weight of growing expenditure, by 1830 Ranjit looked to more profitable opportunities of conquest in the rich trading cities of Sind, premised on the strategic calculation of an outlet to the sea.

As Ranjit cast his gaze upon the trading cities of the Indus, his ambitions came to be viewed as a threat on the other side of the Sutlej. While the Sikhs saw this as a natural area of expansion, the Company wanted to reserve Sind for its interests. More importantly, the Company understood the establishment of its paramountcy along the Indus line as a way of containing and directing Sikh expansion away from its own territory.[119] By blocking the Sikhs to the west, Calcutta calculated the Sikhs would look north towards the domains of the troublesome Afghans.[120] British efforts to 'open' the Indus thus gained a sense of urgency. Governor-General Bentinck clearly indicated his intention to firmly establish British influence on the Indus' left bank by dispatching Alexander Burnes to survey the river in 1831. Burnes' survey was followed by negotiations with the Amirs of Sind for commercial treaties and the dispatch of officers to investigate potential trade marts. Ranjit Singh understood the subdued language of British diplomacy and refrained from pressing the point until 1834–1835, when the chaos following Shah Shuja's defeat opened Shikarpur and the Upper Indus to Sikh influence.

Ranjit's occupation of Shikarpur in 1835 coincided with Charles Metcalfe's temporary assumption of the Governor-Generalship. Metcalfe's views of Forward School policies were decidedly ambivalent, if not outright hostile.[121] In a Minute authored in 1833, he wrote, '[t]o the extension of our political relations beyond the Indus, there appear to me to be great objections. From such a course I should expect the probable occurrence of embarrassments and wars, expensive and unprofitable, at the least, without any equivalent benefit, if not ruinous and destructive.'[122] Metcalfe firmly disagreed with the idea of dispatching a mission to Afghanistan when it was first aired in 1830, calling it commercially unnecessary and politically objectionable. Instead, he favoured a retrenchment of British frontier policy, focusing efforts on cultivating a powerful ally and buffer state in the Punjab kingdom.[123] But Metcalfe's confirmation as Bentinck's successor failed to materialize, and he handed the reigns of power to Lord Auckland, a supporter of the Forward School's strategic vision.[124] Writing to Auckland, he criticized the policy prescriptions of the Forward School not only for involving the EIC in detrimental 'political entanglements', but also for unnecessarily antagonizing

Ranjit. In Metcalfe's views, these policies 'shall hem him in like a tiger in a bush, and he can hardly avoid making a spring which will bring our fire upon him...'.[125]

Auckland firmly rejected Metcalfe's advice, and instead renewed the assertion of Company paramountcy west of the Indus. When he perceived Sikh moves towards Shikarpur, Auckland lost no time in making his displeasure known, albeit diplomatically. He ordered C.M. Wade to dissuade Ranjit from pursuing his ambitions by any 'means in his power, short of actual menace...'. He also directed Col. Henry Pottinger, the agent in Sind, to be prepared, if circumstances warranted, to conclude an alliance with the Amirs of Sind in which the Company would undertake to guarantee their independence from the Sikhs.[126] Reviewing these orders, Auckland, in astonishingly frank language, went on to write,

> On the one hand I shrink from the responsibility, the hazard and the expence attendant upon any thing of military movement and I could have wished to have extended the British influence in that direction by the pursuit alone of commercial and peaceful objects; but on the other I feel that a tone of firmness and a steadfast purpose may best lead to be to the preservation of peace, and *it is impossible that we should tamely suffer the extension of the Sikh power throughout the whole course of the Indus to the borders of our Bombay Government [emphasis added]*...But looking to the position of Sinde, to the shore which it has with the command of the Indus, and to its bearing in regard to Afghanistan, and to the Punjab, it would not be to be regretted, if, without any measures of violence, the permanent establishment of British influence in the country should be the result of these measures.[127]

Auckland referred to the 'restlessness of the old man of Lahore' who had a 'growing appetite for the jungles and treasure of Sinde [sic]'. Yet rather than being satiated by the Company, that appetite needed to be firmly checked.[128] Indeed, far from fearing the tiger Metcalfe referred to in his correspondence, Auckland responded that he did not fear Ranjit would bear his teeth, 'in as much as he will not have any till we supply him with some'.[129]

Auckland's Minute is central to understanding not only the evolution of British policy, but also the role Afghanistan was to play in it. With the British threat of force bolstering their claims, the Sikhs found their field of action circumscribed. Expansion both eastwards and westwards was closed to Ranjit by British presence and paramountcy. There remained only one direction for the Sikh ruler to target his ambitions – north, towards the Peshawar plain and onwards through the Khyber into Afghanistan. The British knew this. Equally, they knew the problems the Sikhs continually faced in their occupation of the vale of Peshawar.[130] After originally conquering the city in 1819, local resistance made occupation unrealistic, and Ranjit thus settled on indirect rule through Afghan vassals who were supposed to annually send tribute to Lahore, though this rarely happened without the dispatch of Sikh troops.[131] The Sikhs re-established their presence in 1830 with Sayyid Ahmad Barelwi's revolt, but did not attempt to re-occupy Peshawar until 1834 and the distractions caused by Shah Shuja's attempt to regain his throne.[132] Even this apparent demonstration of Sikh power appeared tenuous with Shuja's defeat by Dost Muhammad Khan.[133] Ranjit's difficulties in Peshawar hinted, both to himself and the British, at the difficulties awaiting him beyond the Khyber.[134]

By barring Sikh ambitions towards Sind, the Company knowingly encouraged Sikh expansion northwards, which inevitably meant resumed hostilities with the Afghans. Ranjit's French officers were especially enthused by the prospect of hostilities with the Afghans, promising the conquest of Kabul with ten battalions of infantry, two or three regiments of cavalry and five pieces of artillery.[135] The prospect of resumed hostilities reinvigorated the Company's interest in events beyond the Khyber, to which it had been markedly indifferent as late as the early 1830s.[136] Although Dost Muhammad's approaches to the Company for an alliance and Shah Shuja's requests for aid in regaining his throne were treated in the main with indifference during Bentinck's tenure, under Auckland's Governor-Generalship the Company decisively re-engaged with the Afghan kingdom.[137] Burnes was dispatched on a commercial cum diplomatic mission to Kabul in 1836. The Company's renewed interest in the Afghan kingdom, concurrent with their encouragement of Sikh expansion into it, was not accidental.

While it was in the Company's interests to deflect Ranjit's ambitions from the Indus, it would clearly serve the Company little to have either the Afghans or the Sikhs embroiled in an exhaustive war. Although the British sought to direct Ranjit's ambitions northwards, they did not seek to leave those ambitions unchecked. The Company, while relieved to see Ranjit's *Khalsa* tied on the Peshawar plain, had no interest in seeing the Sikhs involved in a struggle totally draining of their strength and resources. Yet nor could they afford to allow Ranjit to be wholly successful in his Afghan ambitions. It would simply create a more powerful, and thus potentially dangerous ally. Thus, the British developed a strategy of conflict management to contain and control Afghan-Sikh hostilities. This management strategy neatly fit the contours of the Forward School's vision of an Afghan buffer state in which Kabul was seen as the gatekeeper against the Russians, and their Persian proxies. By establishing a friendly Afghan regime over which the Company exercised paramount, rather than sovereign, dominion through trade, Forward School strategists saw the possibility of excluding the Russians at the same time they contained the Sikhs.

The Company's first attempt to realize this strategy of conflict management proved lacklustre. Attempting a version of 'empire lite', the Company effectively gave its blessing to Shuja's attempt to regain his throne from Dost Muhammad Khan in 1834.[138] Shuja's attempt shortly followed the first Persian expedition against Herat. Despite claims of strict neutrality, it allowed the Shah to purchase weapons, tax-free, for the expedition in Delhi and even advanced him Rs. 16,000, four months worth of his annual Rs. 50,000 stipend.[139] Given the Company's efforts at actively dissuading Shuja's previous intrigues, this assistance convinced many that it supported Shuja's aspirations to the throne.[140] Indeed, it is difficult to understand the Company's decision to provide Shuja with money, weapons, and on his defeat, the resumption of his sanctuary and stipend in Ludiana, as anything but an endorsement of his actions.

In effect, the Company hoped Shuja's success would create a kind of subsidiary alliance with a friendly Afghan ruler whose territory would intervene between the Russian and Sikh threats. Sensitive of the friendship they had shown Shuja during his exile in Ludiana, some Company servants hoped he returned with a sense of obligation towards the Company, as well as lessons of good governance.[141] In order to recruit Ranjit Singh's aid, or at least acquiescence, Shuja vowed to recognize the Sikh possession of Peshawar and surrounding territories.[142] This attempt seemed destined for success, but for the combination of Dost Muhammad's courage and Shuja's cowardice on the field outside Kandahar.[143] Shuja's invasion drove the Dil brothers of Kandahar, half brothers of Dost Muhammad, into an alliance of convenience under the Dost's leadership.[144] His defeat secured the Barakzai's position within Afghanistan. Ranjit's moves on Peshawar during Shuja's advance provided a rallying point of resistance for the Afghans, and a leadership opportunity for Dost Muhammad Khan. The Company suddenly found itself faced with a situation it had not originally countenanced, but which it did not yet think beyond turning to its advantage.

Shuja's defeat shattered the fragile equilibrium which had marked Afghanistan and Afghan-Sikh relations since the mid-1820s. Dost Muhammad's victory over his uncle not only secured his leadership of the Barakzai *sardārs* within Afghanistan, but also secured him a new legitimacy in the eyes of his fellow Durrani which he took little time to exploit. Almost immediately following Shuja's retreat, Dost Muhammad turned his eyes towards Peshawar and the strengthening Sikh position there. He followed a dual strategy – directly confronting the Sikhs, while simultaneously pursuing the time-honoured tradition of quiet negotiation.[145] With regular intelligence of his battle preparations, local Company agents increased pressure for direct British involvement in the conflict.[146]

Wade suggested deputing Lt. M. Mackeson on a mission to Kabul shortly after Shuja's defeat.[147] His suggestion fit with the belief held by many in the Company that British involvement beyond the Khyber was necessary to shape events there, and consequently British security along the Sutlej. He argued,

I have before stated that it is only by becoming a party to a confederation of the state lying on the Indus that the British Government can hope to exercise a well found influence on that important frontier. The object of such a confederation should be the organization of Afghanistan under a government of its own, and each party to it be bound not to take any measure affecting the state of that country which were not concurred by the rest.[148]

With a stalemate forming at the mouth of the Khyber Pass, Company intercession would not have been considered contrary to the interests of either party. Both Ranjit Singh and Dost Muhammad Khan previously made overtures inviting British mediation of their conflict, arguably aware of the limitations of their power.[149] Perhaps both thought they could benefit from the double game the Company was playing with them.

Auckland's arrival in 1836 saw talk of a British mission to Kabul turned into action. Alexander Burnes was dispatched to Dost Muhammad's court with a brief limited to trade issues. Its ostensible aim was to encourage the Indus Scheme and reception of British and Indian goods.[150] The Burnes' mission figured centrally in the evolving British management strategy of Afghan-Sikh hostilities the Company encouraged to protect its interests. Those hostilities increasingly centred on the question of control of Peshawar. While this had been contested for years, the circumstances of 1837–1838 fundamentally altered British strategic calculations. The Russian-sponsored, Persian siege of Herat appeared bound for success, opening eastern Afghanistan to Russian influence. The spectre with which the British had justified a policy directed against the Sikhs and Afghans was turning into a reality, and needed to be countered. The Company required a solution to Peshawar so that both Afghan and Sikh energies could be turned from one another and focused against the Persians, and their Russian overlords. British policy-makers envisaged Sikh annexation of Peshawar, with Afghan consent.[151] In their eyes, this was simply a recognition of the *status quo*. In turn, Sikh territorial ambitions would have to be satisfied east of the Khyber.

Much to their annoyance, Dost Muhammad refused to renounce his claims over Peshawar or to recognize Sikh sovereignty over the former Durrani winter capital. The Company, understanding this as sheer obstructionism, failed to appreciate the importance of Peshawar, or more precisely contesting Sikh control of it, to Dost Muhammad's security on the throne.[152] Dost Muhammad Khan increasingly employed Islamic norms and rhetoric in order to legitimize his leadership. Sikh occupation of Peshawar provided the necessary justification for a *jihād* which secured Dost Muhammad's tenuous position amongst his tribesmen. The Company, however, viewed Dost Muhammad with increasing alienation and distrust. Consequently, Auckland, with the encouragement of men such as Wade and Macnaghten, decided the Dost was not a man who could be dealt with.[153] The British needed to replace him with a more pliant partner, willing to make terms with the Sikhs over Peshawar. Fortunately for them, they had a former Afghan king in their own territories, Shuja in Ludiana, who consistently demonstrated his desire to regain his throne.

The British could have decisively intervened on the Afghans behalf, but it was not in their interests to do so.[154] By refusing to mediate over Peshawar on any terms save those favourable to Ranjit Singh, the Company bought itself some time.[155] But their failure to diplomatically establish their influence on the west side of the Khyber made the British position increasingly untenable. Dost Muhammad's flirtation with the Russian agent Vitkevich was a measure of his desperation.[156] Everyone, including Ranjit Singh, knew this. As long as the Sikhs and Afghans willingly participated in British designs, the Company's strategy held. As soon as the Afghans abandoned the conflict management offered by the British, however, their grand strategy managing Sikh expansionism collapsed. It was in the vacuum of this collapse the Company decided to intervene more directly beyond the Khyber. Under the pretext of countering an ambiguous Russian threat, the Company decided to act to establish its paramount influence beyond the Khyber by force of arms and ensure its position against a potentially dangerous ally. The trick would be getting the Sikhs to agree to it.

V. Conclusion

The consequences of the narrow approach and interpretation of the Great Game have been persistently unrewarding. This chapter has argued that Forward School policy-makers information coup ultimately proved fleeting. Their information order entered the First Afghan War fighting the Russians, not the Afghans. Yet the irony is that the Russian threat was always rather minimal and acknowledged to be so. The real nightmare was the loss of British prestige which would encourage internal dissent within India. The enemy within lurked in the darker corners of the Company servants' imaginations. Unable to cope with the insidious power of Indian rumour, the British personified the threat to their power in the Russians, a familiar enemy. This decision forced their intelligence and policy attentions away from indigenous agents. The issues raised by this faulty threat assessment, viewed through the corrective lens of hindsight, implicate the fundamental nature of Company government and British philosophies of governance.

The monumental intelligence failure was both an analytical and a structural one, grounded in the EIC's information order. To understand this failure, one needs to appreciate the conceptual framework through which the Company constructed its colonial knowledge of Afghanistan. This knowledge was based upon information gathered by an intelligence network the British erected and later relied upon. The nature of that network needs to be examined, as well as the internal incentive structure pervasive throughout the Company's emergent bureaucracy. The Company's bureaucracy, and consequently its intelligence system, reflected, admittedly imperfectly, the values ascendant within British governing circles during this period. Colonial administrators were forced to rectify those values with strategic necessities. How administrators in both London and Calcutta squared the circle of free trade with the strategic imperatives of the Forward School of Indian defence is thus a central line of enquiry.

Deflating the imaginative power of the Great Game lessens neither the importance of Afghanistan in the eyes of British policy-makers nor its larger importance in the region's history. On the contrary, it frees our understanding of the momentous events taking place from the monolithic and totalizing narrative of a bi-polar imperial rivalry. Instead, historians must look to both local circumstances and local agents, re-assessing their importance within a broader imperial framework. The Great Game has consistently relegated Anglo-Sikh rivalry to secondary importance in this history of the British Empire. Yet this rivalry largely compelled British action in the 1830s. It shaped British responses to the frontier and Afghanistan, with substantial long-term implications for South and Central Asia. Only once the Game has been properly contextualized, can the full implications of the Company's relationship with Ranjit's kingdom be understood. It is to that relationship the next chapter turns.

3
Anglo-Sikh Relations and South Asian Warfare

I. Introduction

While British activities on the Indus and beyond during the 1830s were ostensibly designed to counter a perceived Russian threat, and have been understood in these terms since then, many of their actions directly affected Ranjit Singh's Punjab kingdom. By establishing British paramountcy in Afghanistan through the penetration and capture of the region's trade, the British sought to create a buffer against both the Russians and the Sikhs. Although the Russians encouraged Persian expansionism in the 1830s and the friendly reception of a Russian agent in Kabul created a sense of near panic in Calcutta, Sikh successes around Peshawar catalyzed Government House's swift and firm action. A Sikh triumph over the Afghans would severely retard the establishment of British political paramountcy in this sensitive buffer region. It would also destroy one of the main counterweights to Sikh power, leaving the Company's own forces as the only power strong enough to resist Ranjit's *Khalsa Dal*. Although little chance of an open breach existed during Ranjit's tenure, the Company could not take his successors' good faith for granted.

The argument here is that Anglo-Sikh relations were central to the political evolution of the Punjab, Afghanistan and Central Asia during this period, with Ranjit Singh's success profoundly influencing British strategic calculations.[1] Yet the British policy establishment maintained an insular vision of Indian defence which purposely over-emphasized the nascent Russian threat in order to disguise the Company's belligerence towards the Sikhs and its strategy of containment. Afghanistan and the Punjab presented the most pressing potential threats to Company territories. Consequently, the Company played a double game west of the Indus. While promoting an Afghan buffer state and an Anglo-Sikh alliance, the Company simultaneously encouraged conflict between the Afghans and the Sikhs which it could manage in order to negate both as latent dangers to British India. The British strategy ultimately failed, forcing their direct intervention in Afghanistan and as well as later in the Punjab. These interventions left their imperial reputation permanently sullied with the memory of inglorious defeat at the hands of uncivilized natives.

What made the Sikhs and, to a lesser extent, the Afghans such a potential danger in the Company's eyes was their role and involvement in South Asia's burgeoning military labour market. Although the Company's success on the north Indian plains had led to the collapse of the cavalry mercenary market prevalent throughout much of eighteenth-century South Asia, it also introduced new modalities of warfare which successor states such as Ranjit's Punjab were quick to emulate. That successful emulation took place in an area with long-standing military traditions that had formerly been locations of *fitna* (rebellion) against central authorities. The confluence of new technologies – mechanical, administrative and organizational – with martial traditions was unsettling. This was doubly so when those areas also were the ones intervening between East India Company (EIC) territories and the Tsar's Empire, with its ambitions in Central Asia.

This chapter presents an argument partly based on the limitations of the Elphinstonian episteme previously discussed, but also challenging long-held assumptions about British strategic calculations beyond the Sutlej. It continues the argument, outlined in Chapter 2, that Ranjit Singh's ambitions for the trading cities of Sind put him on a collision course with the British, who shared those ambitions. Rather than provoking a military confrontation, however, the EIC developed a strategy with which to manage Ranjit's power and ambitions. While warning him off expansion into Sind, it encouraged his appetite for expansion into the Afghan lands. It was hoped this would both satiate his ambition and tie down his forces on the frontier opposite the Company's. Ranjit was perceived as a growing threat to the Company's order because of his military power, based on both his successful mimicry of the EIC's own military fiscalism as well as his recruitment of European mercenaries from South Asia's military labour market. Yet the Company's calculations in managing the conflict it encouraged between Ranjit and his Afghan counterpart, Dost Muhammad Khan, were conceived in a conceptual framework which no longer fit the Afghan reality. British efforts therefore failed, and they were forced to intervene more directly, to their great cost and embarrassment.

II.   The failure of British strategy

Although Afghanistan's position within the Company's strategic framework altered significantly in the thirty years since Elphinstone's mission in 1809, one thing had not. The Company remained reluctant to commit significant resources to its Afghan strategy, a fact demonstrated by its refusal to cover the expenses of Dr James Gerard, Burnes' travelling companion to Bukhara in 1831, leaving Gerard financially insolvent.[2] Yet this recalcitrance radically changed in 1838–1839 with the decision to place Shah Shuja on the Afghan throne at the head of a Company army. What happened in the intervening period, moving British policy opinion from indifference to direct intervention in Afghanistan on the side of forces it deemed legitimate? While much of the explanation lay in Ranjit's growing power and ambition, this in itself remained insufficient. Compounding Sikh activities were Persian ambitions for the lands of Afghan Khorasan, most especially Herat which they twice sent expeditions against between 1832–1833 and 1837. While both attempts ended in unmitigated failure, the Russian intrigues supposedly behind these expeditions played into the hands of British Russophobes who painted the Russian threat to India as imminent.[3] To them, the Persians' failure to subdue Herat, not to mention the sheer distance intervening between the Company's frontier and Persian, or rather Russian forces, counted for little.[4]

While Herat had long been a point of contention between the Afghans and Qajar dynasty, Persian attempts to conquer the city in the 1830s were profoundly different in character from previous ones. The central difference was the involvement, both moral and material, of the Russians. While Abbas Mirza's attempt to take Herat in 1832–1833 was largely a Persian affair, the Russian ambassador in Tehran firmly advocated the undertaking.[5] The Russians supported the Persian's return in 1837–1838 even more forcefully than in 1832–1833. Although it remains open to question the amount of influence the Russians actually exerted over Persian actions, to Forward School policy-makers the guiding hand of Russian expansionism was clear. While Russian involvement concerned both the British mission to Persia and the Home Government, the Government of India remained aloof of direct involvement.[6] Instead, they encouraged and sponsored Shuja's attempts to regain his throne. Yet their proxy activities ultimately transformed into direct involvement, spurred by a more immediately pressing concern than Persians or Russians around Herat. Renewed Afghan-Sikh hostilities over Peshawar combined with Perso-Russian activities to present a clear and present danger to India's security.

The turning point for direct Company involvement was the battle of Jamrud in April 1837. Located near the eastern end of the Khyber Pass, Jamrud was the site of a Sikh fort. During its construction, Afghan tribesmen dammed the stream providing the fort's only water supply, provoking a number of skirmishes. Fearing the permanent garrisoning of the fort, the Afghans decided to move against it.[7] A large party, led by Muhammad Akbar Khan, Dost Muhammad's son, engaged a strengthened Sikh garrison under the leadership of Hari Singh, considered by contemporaries as Ranjit's best general. After a long and bloody battle, the Sikhs eventually broke, due to the timely arrival of Afghan cavalry reinforcements and the mortal wounding of Hari Singh, which demoralized the Sikh ranks. Yet the Afghans proved neither willing nor able to press their advantage, allowing the Sikhs to retreat to Peshawar. Both sides had been badly mauled.[8]

Jamrud was the Afghans' last quasi-victory against the Sikhs in the battle for Peshawar. It failed to advance their position towards Peshawar, but instead stemmed the flow of Sikhs into the Khyber. The Sikh defeat and death of Hari Singh angered Ranjit, who dispatched Paolo Avitabile to Peshawar with reinforcements, ending the short-lived autonomy of its Saddozai *sardārs*. Yet Ranjit's ability to chastize the Afghans was dependent on the Company's acquiescence, if not support.[9] Well-informed of the action and its potential consequences, Calcutta realized their management of Afghan-Sikh hostilities needed to be more forceful and direct lest their ability to exert their influence beyond the Khyber be permanently impaired. The British, wanting to stabilize their external frontier at Herat, were coming to understand the need for action to secure their internal frontier at Peshawar.

With the action at Jamrud preceding his approach, the news received by Alexander Burnes as he neared Kabul on his mission to the court of Dost Muhammad decidedly mixed. Passing through the Khyber, Burnes was escorted by Khyber tribesmen before being received on the west side by the officers of Dost Muhammad dispatched from Jalalabad. He reported the pass could easily be reopened to commercial traffic in the near future, citing the reasonable toll expectations of the Khyber chiefs – a mere two and a half per cent *ad valorem*, the *sharīa*-sanctioned rate.[10] Burnes' enthusiasm was tempered by C. M. Wade's political realism. He forwarded Burnes' report with cover letters arguing the recent hostilities precluded the re-opening of the Khyber in the foreseeable future.[11] Burnes' political naivety unfortunately remained with him through the rest of his short career.

On his arrival at Kabul, it immediately became apparent that Burnes would be required to exceed the unrealistically restrictive limits of his brief. Dost Muhammad's paramount concern was British mediation with the Sikhs over Peshawar, rather than the establishment of Company paramountcy in his kingdom through trade. To him, Burnes' arrival signalled the powerful favour of the British Government, which alone could accomplish the victory over the Sikhs his forces had thus far failed to gain. In this presumption, Dost Muhammad found himself wholly misguided. The Company did not want Burnes' mission to be construed as an acknowledgment of Dost Muhammad's supremacy within Afghanistan.[12] Yet he was not alone in thinking Burnes' arrival did precisely that, as well as marking a shift in British willingness to intervene in the conflict. Ranjit Singh watched with unease the progress of Burnes, alternately seeking Wade's assurance of British neutrality and threatening against British intervention.[13] The Sikh's reservations are understandable, for British intervention could only come at his cost. It quickly became obvious, however, that Ranjit's apprehensions were as misplaced as Dost Muhammad's confidences.

Burnes spent the next several months at the Kabul court, cultivating a friendship partly founded on his sympathetic ear for Dost Muhammad's predicament. Hoping to engender British favour, Dost Muhammad sought

Burnes' advice on a number of matters, including the fateful reception of the Russian envoy Vitkevich which later led to his downfall.[14] Burnes encouraged Dost Muhammad's hopes with inflated assurances of the Company's favour, even implying the Company's willingness to mediate on his behalf. These assurances, however, were definitively laid to rest with a curt reply from Governor-General Auckland.[15] He was perfunctory and direct – Calcutta valued its Sikh alliance much more than any potential Afghan one. The British would not abandon Ranjit Singh, with whom their interests were by now too closely intertwined. Auckland advised the Dost to negotiate a settlement of Peshawar with Ranjit on the latter's terms. Disgraced and firmly reprimanded, Burnes returned to Company territory, leaving a bitter taste in Dost Muhammad's mouth.[16]

But Auckland had overplayed his hand. Disappointed with an emissary offering only platitudes, Dost Muhammad reluctantly turned to other potential allies against the Sikhs. After initially denying a Persian envoy permission to proceed to Kabul, he received approaches from their political masters, the Russians, in the person of Captain Ivan Vitkevich.[17] Despite the attention and speculation Vitkevich's mission generated, it was an abject failure. Dost Muhammad accepted offers of Russian assistance, alienating the British in so doing, only to find Vitkevich had been publicly disowned and his mission disavowed.[18] This action, prompted by Auckland's categorical rejection of Afghan claims, created the maelstrom requiring direct British intervention. With a Russian-sponsored siege of Herat on the brink of success, the reception of a Russian agent at the court of Kabul, and rumours that Vitkevich intended to approach to Ranjit, the Company had to act decisively. It did so by invading Afghanistan in order to place Shah Shuja firmly on the throne.

British invasion

By the time the Army of the Indus reached Kabul in the summer of 1839, the Persians had retreated from Herat and Ranjit Singh had died, leaving an unclear succession. In spite of logistical problems, near-constant harassment by Baluch tribesmen, and the silent reception of Shah Shuja in both Kandahar and Kabul, Auckland's upbeat tone was largely justified.[19] The only major action, the storming of Ghazni, proved a textbook victory for the British with relatively scant loss of life. Organized resistance largely collapsed with its surrender. After mounting some resistance in the Bamian valley, Dost Muhammad was forced to flee to Bukhara. He later surrendered to British forces and was exiled to Ludiana, where both Shah Shuja and his brother Shah Zeman had spent their years in British territory.

The speed of the British victory allowed a quick rotation out of the country for most of the army, leaving a smaller occupying force to buttress Shuja's untested power. But the triumphalist tone of official correspondence disguised the fact the invasion was itself testament to the failure of Forward School policies. The Company's inability to establish its paramountcy on the far side of the Khyber peacefully placed it in an untenable position. With the Russians besieging Herat and a resumption of Afghan-Sikh hostilities leaving little room for compromise, the Company scrambled to protect its prerogatives in the area. Shuja, indebted to the Company for the magnanimity it showed him in exile, had to be placed on the throne, securing with him unquestioned Company paramountcy in Afghanistan. The time had come to create its Afghan subsidiary alliance by force.

With the success of their arms, the British expected to quickly abdicate control to Shuja. Auckland, facing a situation of imperial overstretch with forces committed to fighting the First Opium War, was anxious to return the sepoys to India. Yet contrary to expectations inspired by misleading reports authored by William Macnaghten, Company forces were required to support an increasingly unpopular sovereign viewed as little more than a British lackey. Macnaghten, however, had Auckland's ear. Into it, he poured a stream of delusionary estimates of Shuja's popularity and ability, often directly contradicting the recorded opinions of other Company servants.[20] Calcutta felt assured the situation was well in hand. By the time of Dost Muhammad's capture, though, the British found themselves increasingly alienated from Shah Shuja and his apparently incompetent stewardship of the Afghan kingdom. More than one British officer, witnessing the dignity with which Dost Muhammad bore himself in defeat, questioned whether the Company supported the wrong man.[21]

Shuja's failure to assume the role so carefully cultivated for him endangered the success of the British mission. His reliance on political and financial support drained the Company's resources and endangered its financial solvency.[22] By 1841 the British had become so disillusioned with the 'perfidy' of Shuja's governance that they assumed direct control of revenue collection.[23] Shuja's increasing reliance on the British for his security proportionately decreased his popularity amongst his subjects.[24] The Company discovered to its dismay the security of its paramountcy more and more required the responsibilities and costs of sovereignty, something it had neither anticipated nor wanted.

The Afghans presented only part of the Company's political difficulties. The death of Ranjit Singh in the summer of 1839 could not have come at a worse time for the British. Suddenly, between Company territory and their main expeditionary force lay a headless military giant whose disposition was unclear. The Punjab kingdom remained calm following the Maharaja's death. Although no successor of his ability stepped forward, the Sikh government decided for the moment to keep faith with Ranjit's policies. This included treating the British expedition to Afghanistan with studied ambivalence, an attitude maintained until the outbreak of the First Sikh War (1845). The Lahore *darbār*'s evasiveness was inspired by recognition of what the expedition meant for future Sikh expansion. The Tri-Partite Treaty of 1838 recognized Sikh suzerainty over Peshawar while simultaneously placing a British protégé on the Afghan throne.[25]

The British expected Lahore to abide by Ranjit's commitments. With the Afghan shah enthroned by British arms, the Company obviously would not countenance continued Sikh aggression into Afghan territories. Yet distrust of their Sikh ally grew as time passed and the Lahore *darbār* remained lukewarm in honouring its commitments to the Company and Shuja. By 1841, Auckland had concluded that Sikh power was an undesirable danger for the EIC, writing,

> It is not clear to me that we should hastily declare that whatever we hold we hold strictly in trust for the Maharaja Sher Singh and more particularly on the side of Peshawar. I am of opinion that if the Sikh authority should be dissolved and expelled, its restoration is not to be regarded, as a thing practicable, even if to be desired. That what we take we must take neither for Maharaja nor Shah, but in the name of peace and good order. Yet we shall not be able to hold long in such a name, there must, I presume be Sikh or their must be Mahomedan[*sic*] supremacy and the latter I conceive must prevail. But it should do so under our care and management, and if the Shah's name should ultimately be restored, that care and management should on no account be withdrawn. ... When the Sikhs can no longer protect their frontiers or their provinces or even their capital, they may surely be told that they have no longer a government and that the taks[*sic*] of maintain order has passed into other hands. Things have not yet reached this crisis, but they appear to be fast approaching to it.[26]

The British had previously checked the Sikhs to the south, east and west. Now they blocked Sikh ambitions to the north. But that which kept the alliance's rivalry muted, Ranjit's political acumen, was no more.

British defeat

The delicate equilibrium on which the British occupation of Afghanistan rested was shattered in the autumn of 1841 with the outbreak of the Afghan revolt in Kabul.[27] Eventually claiming a British garrison of 5000 soldiers and almost twice as many camp followers, the revolt began somewhat appropriately on the doorstep of Alexander Burnes. Burnes and his younger brother James perished at the hands of a mob incited by rumours, partly true, of liaisons between British troops and Afghan women.[28] The month following the revolt's outbreak witnessed a parade of incompetence and negligence rarely equalled by the British military or political command. Their failure to react firmly to Burnes' death demonstrated weakness and a lack of resolve at a critical juncture, providing the burgeoning Afghan resistance time to organize itself and confidence to face an apparently paralysed foe.

By December, the Afghans besieged the British cantonment in earnest. By January, the British command accepted what they thought to be an ignominious, but recoverable defeat, negotiating an immediate withdrawal from Kabul to Jalalabad in the middle of winter. The courage, or stupidity, of the Company ranks as they entered the passes between Kabul and Jalalabad is well known. The emergence of Dr Brydon onto the Jalalabad plain, immortalized by Lady Butler's *The Remnants of an Army*, signalled a highly sophisticated propaganda coup by the Afghans.[29] Others would later emerge, be ransomed or rescued, but in the collective memory of empire, only one man survived the Kabul fiasco.[30]

At the centre of the British defeat lay misconceptions of the indigenous actors they were dealing with. Thirty years of discussion of Afghanistan in the Company's information order had led to a conceptualization of Afghan society which proved impermeable to observed reality during the occupation of 1839–1842. The Company believed it could establish its paramountcy by installing Shuja as the king of Afghanistan. Forward School adherents justified the move in terms of the royal legitimacy of Shuja and Dost Muhammad's illegitimacy as a usurper.[31] Yet such claims only highlighted the dissonance between the official mind's understanding of the Afghan political community and the fractured reality of Afghanistan's social ecology. Their association with one another fatally tainted the British and Shuja. Both Shuja and the British failed to learn or engage in the new language of Afghan politics which had developed since his overthrow in 1809. Neither recognized that the authority Shuja claimed was simply not that of the Afghan monarchy, but the leadership of the nascent Afghan state, effectively destroyed by British intervention. Consequently, both fundamentally compromised their claims to authority. As the Company lauded Shuja's royal credentials as a Saddozai monarch, resistance congealed under new idioms of legitimate political authority – Islam and tribe.[32]

The failure of British arms beyond the Hindu Kush reveals more about the Company's nature than simply its under-investment in an intelligence structure for the region. For the Company possessed a wealth of information about Afghanistan and its inhabitants. Yet like so much of Company governance during this period, it lacked an institutional memory with which to process this information. Information remained precisely that, untransformed into knowledge which could then be deployed for the purposes of control. But why? In other areas the Company faced similar knowledge gaps, or as C.A. Bayly has termed them 'information panics', which it eventually overcame.[33] Within India itself, the Company absorbed the local information systems proliferating in the successor states of the eighteenth and early nineteenth century. It even demonstrated some early success dealing with Afghan information, recruiting indigenous sources upon which it could construct an image and understanding of the Afghan polity. Elphinstone's mission stands as the apogee of that success. Yet there was a limit to both Company ambitions and abilities. The Company's ability to insert itself decisively into indigenous political environments which it could then fashion to its liking lessened the further removed these areas were from its presidencies.

Yet the Company's weakness was in part self-imposed, especially its decision to disengage with the Afghans following the Elphinstone mission. This disengagement grew out of a need for retrenchment, itself a consequence of the Company's changed aims and turnover of its personnel. Elphinstone wanted to document tradition, and by doing so, invent it to a certain extent. Burnes, Conolly, Wade and Masson wanted to bask in the glory of empire, shaping alien societies rather than simply documenting them. This attitude arguably contributed to the revolt of 1857, and undoubtedly led to recriminations about the purposes of Company rule. But the change in attitude only became dangerous with the degradation of the Company's ability to counteract indigenous resistance to it. The true Achilles heel of the Company's imperial overstretch was its informational overstretch. Part of the Company's intelligence failure lay in the absence of its ability to usurp indigenous information systems beyond the Indus as it had done on the Indian subcontinent.

The avenues of collaboration the Company exploited in South Asia took unfamiliar and uncertain turns in the Kingdom of Kabul. With the recession of the perceived European threat to its northwest frontier, the Company consciously decided not to explore those turns because of its disinterest in events beyond the Khyber and need for economy. By the time the Company decided to re-engage with Afghanistan in the 1830s after a nearly twenty-year hiatus, the information networks Elphinstone previously exploited and usurped had frayed. More importantly though, in the Company's eyes, the period of its political tutorial had passed. No longer was it a student of the South Asian political universe, but its master.[34] This generation of Company policy-makers decided to engage with the Afghanistan they 'knew' rather than learn the one they did not know. Unlike in India, however, the structures of persuasion and coercion enabling them to successfully shape the Afghan political universe in their image were wholly absent. The Company thus failed, and did so magnificently in its ignorance.

Such is the capricious nature of popular memory that disasters are remembered with more clarity and passion than successes. In the spring of 1842, the British dispatched an Army of Retribution to relieve British garrisons in Jalalabad and Kandahar, rescue British hostages and chastise the Afghans. After forcing the Khyber, the Army lived up to its name. The Afghan uprising, while expelling the British and ending the reign of their perceived puppet, Shah Shuja, cost the Afghans dearly. Upon reaching Kabul, the British burned the bazaar, the largest in Afghanistan. The irony should not be lost. British involvement with Afghanistan ostensibly began in order to expand British trade. It ended with the premeditated destruction of the main commercial mart. On withdrawing from Afghanistan, after negotiating the release of British hostages held by Muhammad Akbar Khan, the British released his father from his exile in Ludiana. Dost Muhammad left an empire whose prestige beyond the Khyber was in a state of destitution matched only by the destruction awaiting him in Kabul. The Company's failure in Afghanistan did more to feed bazaar rumour and damage British prestige than any Russian army could have. In combating the Russian phantom, they created the very situation of internal disgrace they sought to prevent.

The strategy with which the British attempted to peacefully manage the growing ambitions and power of Ranjit Singh's Punjab failed largely because of the insularity of its vision. As the previous chapter demonstrated, the ways in which the British official mind were coming to understand the Afghan lands by the 1830s were handicapped by its narrowing, a consequence of contemporary political, intellectual and administrative values. The British felt more comfortable regarding the Afghans as a surrogate for European power, either their own or more ominously the Russians'. But this stunted their ability to deal with the emerging Afghan polity. Further, it became doubly dangerous as the Company deployed these understandings in order to peacefully play off Ranjit Singh; by encouraging his ambitions towards Afghan lands, it hoped to contain the power of the Lion of Lahore. But the disruptive potential of both the Afghan kingdom and the Sikh state had deeper roots than fleeting strategic concerns.

III.   The Punjab and the 'military labour market'

Ranjit's *Khalsa Raj* constituted a potential threat to the Company not only because of its location, but also because of its participation in South Asia's new 'military labour market'.[35] Both the Punjab and Afghanistan, historically on the periphery of central control, had been key suppliers to the Indian military labour market during the reign of the Mughals and their successor states. During the eighteenth century, Afghan cavalry mercenaries provided the backbone of a number of local potentates' military power and thus political authority.[36] The arrival of the Company heralded a new mode of warfare.[37] More importantly, however, it also brought with it a new model of statehood, articulated through its various revenue settlements, underpinning this aggressive military machine.[38]

South Asian states and the South Asian military labour market responded to the EIC successes. Local potentates attempted to mimic the Company's triumph through the importation of European military skills and the men to teach them. The confluence of the military labour market with the fragments of peripheralized political entities in Afghanistan and the Punjab provided a source of great concern for the British. For example, the Company was particularly sensitive to the possibility the Afghans would join some of their other Indian foes, such as Tipu Sultan, who sent an emissary to Zeman Shah.[39] This confluence, between the new military labour market and the political peripheries beyond the scope of Company control, made these areas particularly threatening, overshadowing the perceived menace of Tsarist armies 2000 kilometers removed.

In order to understand the concern with which the Company watched the successes of Ranjit's *Khalsa Dal*, and to a lesser extent European-trained Afghan contingents, it is necessary to understand the military changes transforming South and Central Asia in this period. Military superiority played a central role in the European expansion and conquest much of Asia. The combination of new technologies, tactics and supporting social structures known in the European context as the 'military revolution' took hold in South Asia during the second half of the eighteenth century.[40] The collapse of the Mughal Empire created an environment which incubated a number of important changes in Indian states and the ways they waged war. But the success of the East India Company in the mid-eighteenth century accelerated these changes, most profoundly transforming structures of state military fiscalism.[41]

States had to more efficiently extract revenues because the discipline and tactics of Company sepoys, superior to the marauding cavalry units widespread throughout India, forced the Company's South Asian contemporaries to emulate its success. This was expensive, however, as the Company's military establishment rested on a professional, standing army which was regularly paid. More importantly, the eclipse of cavalry as the mainstay of military power meant the fiscal structures which underpinned it and which state finances were based upon, such as the *tiyūls* and *jāgīrs* (landed estates given to elites in return for military service), collapsed.[42]

Instead of tax-farming and the provision of military men by landed elites, the successor states of the Safavid and Mughal Empires required cash to pay for weapons and troops. Rulers therefore moved to centralize revenue collection, as well as their military resources and establishment, thus challenging the privileges of landed aristocrats. For the Afghans, this was particularly problematic as *tiyūl* holders were often also tribal chiefs. The attempts to break the power of these chiefs over the state's coercive resources thus implicated the Afghan shahs' position as paramount chiefs leading a tribal confederacy.[43] In order to break free from the influence of these chiefs, Timur Shah moved his capital from Kandahar, in the Durrani tribal heartland, to Kabul in 1773.[44] These efforts increased in the early nineteenth century as contenders for the Afghan throne tried to assert their independence and authority. Dost Muhammad's employment of a regular military contingent under the command of William Campbell, loyal only to his court and paid in cash, is a prime example of such efforts.[45]

Additionally, the EIC's success made it more and more willing to abandon the norms of South Asian warfare, most notably the resolution of conflict through negotiation and financial inducement.[46] After Lord Hastings' declaration of paramountcy in 1818, the latter ceased to be a central tenet of British Indian diplomacy.[47] Thus warfare became exponentially more expensive, doubly so for native states which need not only European war materials, but also European knowledge and skill. Thus the military revolution catalysed by the Company generated a demand for both men and material in the Indian military market.

While the European military revolution arrived comparatively late to the Punjab and Afghanistan, as elsewhere its arrival heralded enormous changes. The employment of European mercenaries in these lands represented a historical reversal of flow of military labour, especially for Afghanistan. While India had a massive indigenous military labour market of peasant mercenaries, estimated to be as large as two million men by the end of the eighteenth century, the most sought after troops were Afghan cavalry mercenaries.[48] But the Company, which little valued cavalry, focused its recruitment instead on western Bengal and eastern Bihar where it cultivated the traditions of the peasant foot soldier.[49] With the success of the EIC and its preference for massed infantry formations of professional soldiers as opposed to unruly cavalry contingents of mercenaries, the old Indian military labour market slowly crumbled as the European military revolution set in. What little demand there was for cavalry the Company filled from its own territories, transforming Afghanistan from a net exporter of men into a net importer of military knowledge personified by a few European-trained soldiers.

The rise of a European military labour market proved a source of considerable unease for the Company, which attempted to control the flow of military knowledge towards indigenous states. This was especially true of Ranjit Singh's Punjab. The Company, with Ranjit's agreement, closed the frontier to European military interlopers and entrepreneurs.[50] Surprisingly, the Sikhs often detained and returned those who ignored the Company's closure of the Sutlej, especially if they were Company deserters.[51] While the Punjab was the Company's more immediate concern, Afghanistan caused no less disquiet when it came to the export of military knowledge and skills. The Company's discomfiture stemmed from the Punjab's and Afghanistan's character as areas of *fitna*, or rebellion.[52] These areas, with generally low agricultural productivity and an over-abundance of labour, were at the crossroads of considerable international trade, including weapons, and incubated highly militarized societies. They represented the conjunction of the military labour market with societies accustomed to warfare and the sale of excess military labour.

When the military traditions of Afghanistan and the Punjab combined with the large number of European military professionals demobilized at the end of the Napoleonic wars, Company anxiety mounted. Many of these Europeans sought service with indigenous powers in India. Joining them were the ever-present deserters from Company forces.[53] Together, they made an explosive combination on the Company's northwest frontier. Ranjit Singh exemplified indigenous rulers who exploited the international flow of military labour with the traditions of his own militarized society to create one of the most powerful states in South Asia. He regularly employed European and Anglo-Indian mercenaries, with the earliest report of their recruitment, a certain 'Jackson who is styled general of artillery', dating from 1812.[54] Indeed, Ranjit's reputation for employing European mercenaries was so prolific that he had an over-abundance of job seekers, many of whom he turned away.[55] Under no circumstances would the Company countenance a repetition of his success west of the Khyber.

Many of Ranjit's officers were French, and virtually all had served in Napoleon's armies, a fact the EIC was well aware of. Messrs Court, Avitabile, Ventura and Allard were essential to the success of Ranjit's army, and thus the Sikh kingdom.[56] They commanded an army of fifty infantry battalions and over 250 pieces of artillery, which was built upon Ranjit's successful embrace of the military revolution.[57] During his first visit to the Lahore *darbār*, Wade was subjected to an almost daily spectacle of the *Khalsa Dal*'s manoeuvres which duly impressed him.[58] Sir Henry Fane, the Commander-in-Chief, and his staff later shared Wade's positive impressions during their visit in 1837. The precision with which the Sikh ranks executed their drill reportedly unsettled the officers, some of whom even voiced the opinion the *Khalsa Dal* looked better than the Company's own forces.[59] The presence of these officers could be advantageous to the Company though. Most entered the Punjab overland through Afghanistan, providing Ranjit and occasionally the British with valuable information of the lands beyond the Khyber. The Company paid Messr Court, who arrived at Lahore in 1827, Rs. 5000 for his geographic memoir of Afghanistan.[60]

The training and organization these European officers offered local potentates constituted an immediate potential threat to Company power and the stability of its rule in South Asia. Ranjit's French-trained corps, the *Fauj-i Khas*, was unquestionably the most effective body of Sikh troops. For the British, however, the danger presented by these officers stemmed not only from their technical and organizational knowledge, but also from the personal relationships many of them had formed with contemporary officers of the Tsar with whom they had served under Napoleon.[61] Such personal connections undoubtedly amplified the abstracted threat of Russian power projection. Yet these officer's positions could be tenuous, a fact they were conscious of. Consequently, they kept their lines of communication with the Company open. Fast, Harlan, Court and even Ventura, provided valuable political intelligence to the Company about Afghanistan and Dost Muhammad Khan at least once in their mercenary careers.[62] The EIC, however, remained wary not only of these men's different national allegiances, but also their character as mercenaries.[63]

Dost Muhammad's employment of European, and in at least one case American, mercenaries largely grew out of his encounters with the *Khalsa Dal*. William Moorcroft's report of the Sikh victory at the Battle of Nowshera in 1823 offers a detailed account of one of the most important encounters between Sikh and Afghan forces.[64] Despite the courage of the Afghan *ghāzīs* (religious warriors), led by mullahs who 'rushed into battle with their sword in one hand, and the Koran in the other', the discipline of the Sikhs ultimately overcame the religious fervour of the Afghans.[65] Yet the latter's repeated onslaughts at one point captured four Sikh batteries and forced the main body of Sikh troops to retreat in disorder. While the discipline and concentrated firepower of the European-trained troops eventually broke the Afghan assaults, it was the failure of the Afghan leadership to reinforce the *ghāzīs* which ultimately gave the Sikhs the field.

While questions remained about the superiority of European-trained troops and tactics, later experiences convinced Dost Muhammad of the need to employ European mercenaries. After defeating Shuja in 1834, Dost Muhammad employed the survivors of two battalions of 'Hindustanis' commanded by Mr Campbell, a Company deserter, who had fought for Shah Shuja and borne the brunt of the action. So impressed by their skill and courage, he reportedly employed the survivors on the field of battle.[66] The juncture of European-trained militaries with peripheral political entities, or *fitna* areas, which could potentially challenge or disrupt the Company's tenuous authority made many officers uncomfortable. But it also had adverse effects on the political stability of these native kingdoms. Such European-trained militaries, loyal to the ruler alone, represented a centralization of political authority, and likewise necessitated a centralization of revenue structures. They therefore presented a very real threat to the land grant structures of military-fiscalism which underlay the old order of warfare.[67]

The European mercenaries who brought with them technical skills and training in great demand were key drivers of the military revolution in South and Central Asia. Artillerymen were a particularly valuable breed of European soldier, and few local rulers entrusted their artillery to the command of local soldiers.[68] Many of these Europeans were deserters from the Company's forces. Josiah Harlan, an American, was formerly a surgeon in the Bengal artillery.[69] Mr Fast, Robert Dicks and Mr Campbell, all later employed by Afghan chiefs, originally gained their much sought after expertise in the Company's forces.[70] Apart from deserters, a substantial proportion of the European mercenaries were so-called 'adventurers', military men who for a variety of reasons had been denied a military career in their native countries. This was particularly true of the French officers serving Ranjit Singh.[71]

The ex-Napoleonic officers, Anglo-Indians and deserters forming the bulk of these military adventurers faced discrimination serving in the ranks of European armies with at best limited opportunities for career advancement. The only major exception was the Tsar's army, which absorbed a significant number of Napoleonic officers following French defeat. Yet the Russian army not only gained men from the global military labour market, but also lost some to it. Wade reported Russians in the service of the *sardārs* of Peshawar and *darbār* of Lahore.[72] Few Russians, however, penetrated so far south. Most of their activities centred in Persia, where at least one battalion of Russian deserters served *Shahzadeh* Muhammad Shah, commander of the expeditionary force sent against Herat in 1832–1833.[73] In the 1837–1838 siege, this battalion was joined by a number of Russians seconded by the Russian ambassador to assist the Shah in his conquest. At least three ranking Russian officers died during this siege in a massive final assault.[74] These European mercenaries personified the 'new' military labour market penetrating South and Central Asia.

IV. The Afghan-Sikh conflict

Although Ranjit Singh had once been a vassal of Zeman Shah (r. 1793–1800), the Afghan monarch, the collapse of the Durrani Empire and his concurrent rise ensured his subservience was never more than a literary formality.[75] In the first decade of the nineteenth century, Ranjit assumed paramountcy over the former Durrani lands on the Punjab plain. The Durrani's were not in a position to challenge his assumption of authority and it was only with his attacks on, and eventual conquest of Kashmir in the second decade of the 1800s which brought the Afghans and Sikhs onto a collision course. Following his successful defence of this prize, Ranjit decided to attack Afghan lands directly, aiming his ambitions at the vale of Peshawar which he first gained in 1819. From then until his death in 1839, the Afghan rulers of Kabul continually contested Sikh paramountcy over Peshawar. This contest was marked by shifting alliances of convenience which saw the Peshawar Durrani *sardārs* embrace Ranjit's rule. It also witnessed Ranjit's encouragement and tepid support of attempts by Shah Shuja to regain his lost throne.

Sikh control of Peshawar largely rested on the collaboration of the city's leading *sardārs*. By skilfully exploiting divisions between the Barakzai brothers, Ranjit was able to play them off against one another and secure his rule. Sultan Muhammad Khan's, senior *sardār* of Peshawar, demonstrated antipathy towards his half-brother Dost Muhammad Khan proved crucial to Sikh success, with his desertion to Ranjit's camp in 1834.[76] In return for their loyalty, Ranjit promised the Peshawar *sardārs* virtual autonomy, requiring only a minimal tribute, including horses and rice.[77] With Sultan Muhammad's acceptance of Sikh overlordship came the permanent alienation of Peshawar from the Afghan heartland. Annexation soon followed, as Ranjit dispatched a sizeable force, estimated to be as large as 80,000, to occupy Peshawar.[78] His efforts to secure Peshawar left him exposed elsewhere, with Lahore and Amritsar, Ranjit's political and spiritual capitals, retaining only enough soldiers to man the gates.[79] Despite the size of the occupation force, the security of Sikh tenure in Peshawar continued to rest on the acquiescence of powerful sections of the city's ruling elite.

Sultan Muhammad's dealings with the Sikhs highlight the older norms of South Asian warfare and their decided rejection, driven by imperatives of the new language of political legitimacy. The continued importance of negotiation in South Asian warfare, often proving decisive, was underlined by the Afghans negotiating with and intriguing against their enemies either for defections or indemnities.[80] But the failure of negotiations between Dost Muhammad and Ranjit Singh over Peshawar signified a decisive break with the past. The emerging religious language and character of Afghan kingship made negotiation and compromise with the Sikhs increasingly difficult.[81] While Ranjit's intrigues with Sultan Muhammad Khan and Shah Shuja demonstrated his faithfulness to Asian modalities of warfare, his unwillingness to negotiate with Dost Muhammad after 1835 marked his adoption of Company norms of warfare in which negotiation played a minimal role. Emboldened by the military revolution which transformed his *Khalsa Dal*, Ranjit was confident in his ability to decisively defeat the Afghans. His struggle with Dost Muhammad thus transformed from one of advantage to one of survival. Ranjit faced a looming external crisis in the form of the EIC, while Dost Muhammad attempted to recreate the foundations of the crumbling Afghan proto-state. These difficulties drove both to innovate the language of politics in their respective realms, abandoning older norms of political discourse while adopting those of the subcontinent's emergent hegemon, the Company.

Sayyid Ahmad Barelwi

Since their initial conquest of Peshawar in 1819, the Sikhs experienced difficulty establishing a permanent footing in the valley. Their presence in the old winter capital of the Durrani Empire was unwelcome by its inhabitants and the surrounding Afghan tribesmen. Even with the power of the *Khalsa Dal* behind him, Ranjit knew the limits of his authority in the vale of Peshawar, generally requiring only token tribute from the Afghan *sardārs*. Resistance to the Sikh regime most powerfully assumed the guise of religious rhetoric. Afghan attempts at recapturing Peshawar in 1823, culminating in the battle of Nowshera, heavily replied upon the numbers and courage of *ghāzīs* heeding the call of *jihād* against the infidel Sikhs. After the Afghan *sardārs* had abandoned this course with their defeat, Sayyid Ahmad Barelwi, a so-called 'Mohammedan fanatic', resumed the *jihād* against the Sikhs in the late 1820s.[82] His revivalist message of Islam, later earning him the derisive title of 'Wahabi' from British authorities, found fertile ground amongst the *Yusufzai* Pashtun of the Swat valley.[83] By skilfully cultivating the tribesmen's resentment into religious fervour, Sayyid Ahmad wreaked havoc on both the Sikhs and the ruling Peshawar *sardārs*, occupying the city in 1830.[84] Yet, he later found to his cost the capricious nature of Afghan religious loyalties as his *Yusufzai* hosts eventually turned on him once their narrower tribal objectives had been served.

The attempt by later British authorities to vilify Sayyid Ahmad as a Wahabi was a rhetorical ploy to cover the double game played by the Company in the northwest. British relations with Ranjit and Sind shaped their attitudes towards Sayyid Ahmad, as well as other 'fanatics' active in the area.[85] Those who threatened British interests, such as the Mazaris who inhabited an ill-defined area between the Punjab and Sind around Multan and Shikarpur, were derisively labelled 'Mohammedan fanatics'.[86] Such labelling was not simply self-indulgent simplification and Orientalizing by experienced Company servants. Rather, it reflected conscious efforts aimed at reshaping the region's political geography through the normative categorization of local actors. 'Fanatics' stood outside the pale of normal political intercourse, occupying a realm beyond the force of reason and penetrated only by force of arms. These efforts were part of the process of the construction of colonial knowledge and the monopolistic power such knowledge entailed over definition. Yet as with Elphinstone's use of the idiom of tribe, the religious language used by later colonial administrators resonated with indigenous traditions of political legitimacy framed in terms of moral efficacy.[87]

The Company's verbal demonization of 'Mohammedan fanatics', however, disguised their practical indifference, if not endorsement of the activities of such people. Sayyid Ahmad, who had fought in the army of the Nawab of Tonk, was reportedly expelled from Company territory in 1825.[88] Yet the Company did nothing to restrict his movements, nor those of his supporters, to the areas of the Afghan-Sikh frontier. The Company 'was not inclined to suppress a movement which was sure to add to Ranjit Singh's difficulties with the tribes in the north-west and also restrain his ambition to swallow Sind'.[89] By distracting Ranjit and draining his resources, the movement provided the British with an opportunity to shape the situation in the northwest and Sind to their advantage.

Sayyid Ahmad was a militant disciple of emerging consensus of Islamic dissent inspired by Shah Wali Allah's *fatwā* declaring India part of the *dār al-ḥarb*, and the threat such a consensus potentially engendered to Company rule, of which it was well informed.[90] It was also aware of the movement of the proponents of this consensus, noting the arrival in Kabul of a Delhi *sayyid* who encouraged Dost Muhammad Khan to attack the Sikhs as part of his religious duty.[91] Sayyid Ahmad's expulsion from British territories meant the immediacy of any threat he represented to Company order receded. Instead, his fomentation of a rebellion against the Sikhs served to distract the growing Sikh threat.

Although Sayyid Ahmad's revolt had relatively limited practical impact, the ideas he represented and propagated did have a significant one. Sayyid Ahmad had attempted to assume an office of religious leadership with the classical trappings of the caliph. He claimed the title *amīr al-mu'minīn* (leader of the faithful), had his name mentioned in the *khutba* (Friday prayers), and had coins struck in his name.[92] Sayyid Ahmad's actions must have inspired Dost Muhammad Khan, who assumed the mantle of leadership of religiously inspired resistance against the Sikhs in order to buttress his claims to the Afghan throne. Declaring a *jihād* against the Sikhs in Peshawar, Dost Muhammad rallied *ghāzīs* to march through the Khyber on Peshawar.[93]

Despite Charles Masson's prediction that any action between the Sikhs and *ghāzīs* would be 'sanguinary', little initially came of the Dost's efforts.[94] He failed to decisively engage the Sikhs, and the cost of fielding so large an army soon exhausted his meagre resources.[95] The desertion of Sultan Muhammad Barakzai, *sardār* of Peshawar and the Dost's half-brother, to Ranjit Singh did little to further his cause.[96] Forced to beat a hasty retreat, Dost Muhammad retrenched his strategy to contain the Sikhs on the east side of the Khyber rather than retake Peshawar. Despite his best efforts, this retrenchment gained a permanent footing as the cost of conflict with a militarily superior enemy wore away limited resources. Surprisingly, however, Dost Muhammad's reputation amongst the Afghans suffered little as he continued to employ the language of religious confrontation.[97]

The prominence of religious idiom in resistance to the Sikh occupation of Peshawar raises broader questions about the role of Islam in state formation on the periphery of British India. In the Afghan context, Islam provided a powerful and universal rallying point of dissent for Afghanistan's diverse social groupings against virtually all of its encroaching neighbours – the infidel Sikhs, the heretical Persians, and further afield the *firengi* British and Russians. Islam has remained the foundation of Afghan nationalism since its politicization in the Afghan-Sikh confrontation, serving as the rhetorical basis of the *mujahadeen*'s resistance to the Soviets in the 1980s.[98] Dost Muhammad's rhetorical turn towards a religious idiom of political legitimization explicitly introduced ideas of Islamic state formation into the developing Afghan political community.[99]

The violence of Sayyid Ahmad's religious revival, 'Wahabism' as the British contemptuously termed it, exerted a powerful effect on the 'official mind' of the Company. The Company's sensitivity towards calls for religiously inspired rebellion was founded on its suspicion of rumour, a sensitivity heightened by the role played by peripheral areas in state formation. Sayyid Ahmad, though ultimately ineffectual, injected a new language of legitimacy Dost Muhammad would later avail himself to, and presented an opportunity to the Company to advance its *realpolitik* agenda of containment against Ranjit. Yet while his use of religiously inflamed language and revitalization of the concept of *jihād* represented a pressing threat to the Sikhs, it also threatened the Company as a legitimate target for religiously sanctioned rebellion.

V.   Conclusion

The British failure in the First Afghan War was predicated on an intelligence failure of massive proportions. This was not simply a failure of information, for the British were undeniably aware of the happenings in the Afghan kingdom. Rather, this was a failure of knowledge constructed through their information order. That order reflected the priorities and values of the Company's governmentality, as well as the institutional weakness of the system it put in place to tap into the larger South Asian information order. The British conceptualized the Afghan kingdom through a lens which constricted their view as the early nineteenth century wore on. The nuance of the Elphinstonian episteme was lost as its author receded from the scene, the valuation of information changed, and the need for economy became a paramount concern for the Company. While still employing its conceptual framework, a new generation of Company servants used the episteme to justify their own policy priorities and the expansion of Company paramountcy. They conceptualized an Afghan state fitting with their expectations and experiences of South Asian successor states. They then sought to use that state to establish security on their frontiers by limiting both the Russians and the Sikhs.

The projection of British power into Afghanistan and Central Asia was motivated by the perceived need to secure the Company's frontiers. According to proponents of the Forward School, the political, or external frontier required strengthening to meet a potential Russian threat. More importantly, the territorial, or internal frontier faced the more pressing threat of Ranjit Singh's *Khalsa Dal*. Although the first was an avowed enemy, fighting the British through its Persian proxy, the second was a supposedly trusted and long-standing ally. Both threats could be neutralized with the establishment of British paramountcy in Afghanistan. A stable subsidiary alliance with a friendly Afghan regime would hold the line at Herat and the Khyber, limiting Russian influence and Sikh expansionism.

Yet this calculation ran counter to Company efforts to direct Sikh expansion northwards. Just as the Russians encouraged the Persians to make up the lands lost in the Treaty of Turkmanchai (1828) by looking to the east, so the British channelled Ranjit's ambitions towards Afghanistan by methodically denying him any other avenue of expansion. The Company bought itself some time by developing a management strategy for Afghan-Sikh hostilities. But when their bid to establish their paramount influence foundered on the rocks of Dost Muhammad's perceived obstinacy over Herat, their ship ran aground. Massive and decisive action by the Company was the only hope of salvaging the Forward School's strategic blueprint of Indian security.

British policy in Afghanistan suffered from an inherent contradiction born of the two purposes it was designed to serve. To secure its political frontier against Russian incursion, the British need to support the establishment of a stable and prosperous Afghan state, preferably under central leadership. By doing so, they endangered their internal frontier by depriving the Sikhs of the one area of expansion where their ambition and opportunity converged. The recognition by the Governor-General of the need to assuage Sikh demands for Peshawar complicated his attempts to place Shuja on the throne and establish a stable Afghanistan.[100] From the outset, the terms of the Tri-Partite Treaty branded Shuja not only a British puppet, but also demonstrated his willingness to mortgage part of his realm to the infidel Sikhs. The tension between the demands of the internal and external frontier, latent in British policy, ultimately led to its failure. In the long term, the bifurcation of the political and territorial frontiers and the attempt to simultaneously exert political control over both led to the collapse of the two into one with the conquest of Sind and Punjab. The British, too clever by half, had only themselves to blame for the disaster in Kabul and the collapse of their grand strategy.

This grand strategy was only one part of a larger story unfolding throughout the region. Affecting Central and South Asian societies more deeply were fundamental economic shifts in both patterns of trade and consumption. These shifts affected indigenous powers' revenue bases. Central Asian and Afghan trade patterns were forced to adjust to the collapse of the neighbouring Muslim empires, the rise and fall of their successor states, and the metamorphosis of European maritime commerce into the territorial empires of British India and Russian Central Asia. Compounding these changes were the transformations wrought by the military revolution. As indigenous rulers adopted the European model of warfare, they required technical knowledge and personnel. This change in the ways of war brought with it changes in the movement of people associated with warfare. The presence of European mercenaries in Afghanistan represented the reversal of a long-standing flow of military labour out of Central Asia into the Indian military labour market. Equally important was the change in the norms of warfare this military revolution heralded.

Any understanding of the Afghan situation during this period is intimately tied with the fortunes of the Sikh state under the leadership of Ranjit Singh. Because of his physical location between the British and the Afghans, as well as his growing power and ambition, Ranjit mediated and influenced the interactions of the Afghans and the Company. Emboldened by European-trained armies, while simultaneously pressured by an expanding Company, Afghan-Sikh hostilities transformed into an unlimited struggle for control of northwest India. This represented an unacceptable risk to the Company's interests. The Company acted, at least in part, to pre-empt the growth of Ranjit's power west of the Indus and the incumbent threat such growth would present to their paramountcy.

The Great Game was as much a consequence of the 'failure' of the colonial encounter in the early part of the century as it was of the 'success' of that encounter in the latter half. The limited British political engagement seen before the First Afghan War was primarily driven by British weakness, and an acute sense of that weakness within the policy-establishment. Such self-critical understanding ultimately gave way to hubris, largely driven by ambitious men on the spot. More than anything, it was encouraged by an overriding sense of vulnerability in the area. The British cast a wary eye over the powers on their periphery, the Punjab and Afghanistan. They were keenly aware the location of these two placed them at the confluence of the 'new' military labour market with the fragments of peripheralized political entities. These *fitna* areas had historically raided the Gangetic Plain to devastating effect. Attempts at engagement turned into occupation based on a poorly calculated gamble – not to stem the tide of Russian expansionism, but to draw Afghanistan into the orbit of the imperial influence. The tools which gave the British advantage elsewhere were wholly absent in Afghanistan. This forced the British to over-extend themselves in a war they lost. Their defeat drastically altered the course of the colonial encounter in Afghanistan and Central Asia with profound ramifications for the region, as well as the British Empire in India. Yet those ramifications continue to be obscured by the myth of the Great Game.

4
Ontology of the Afghan Political Community

> ... [T]here is reason to fear that the societies into which the nation is divided, possess within themselves a principle of repulsion and disunion, too strong to be overcome, except by such a force as, while it united the whole into one solid body, would crush and obliterate the features of every one of its parts.[1]

I. Introduction

When the Company decided to withdraw from Afghanistan following the destructive rampage of the Army of Retribution, it temporarily abandoned its efforts at integrating Afghanistan into the British imperial system. With that abandonment, it likewise abstained from conscious attempts to affect the character or development of Afghan political authority, concentrating instead on isolating the Afghans from Company territories. The East India Company (EIC) released Dost Muhammad Khan from his detention in Ludiana. On his return to Afghanistan, he immediately faced challenges to his authority which occupied the remainder of his reign. These challenges were the manifestations of what David Edwards has termed the 'moral fault lines' of the Afghan political community which all claimants of Afghan leadership have had to contend with, in varying guises, since Ahmad Shah Abdali.[2] As the quotation above demonstrates, Elphinstone recognized the centrifugal forces in Afghan society which kept central power at bay.

The British invasion had marked not only the culmination of Company policy towards the Kingdom of Kabul over the course of the 1830s, but more importantly put a definitive end to attempts to resuscitate the moribund Durrani Empire. Although Ahmad Shah Durrani had established the Empire on Nadir Shah's death in 1747, by the end of the eighteenth century it had entered the throws of its final collapse. Ahmad Shah's progeny continued to rule the Empire's remnants from Kabul, but its contraction put subsequent rulers' authority under severe strain, and eventual challenge. The challenges first emanated from within the royal household, as Durrani Saddozai heirs vied for the throne. Zeman Shah, Shah Mahmud and Shah Shuja contested one another for the throne in the first decade of the nineteenth century. This family feuding, however, gave way to a challenge to the Saddozai's mandate. In 1818, a civil war broke out between Ahmad Shah's Saddozai heirs and their Barakzai cousins who had served the royal house as *viziers*. The Barakzais triumphed, although authority splintered with their victory. Dost Muhammad Khan assumed control of Kabul in 1826, and with it pretensions to the Afghan throne. However, his brothers ruling Peshawar and Kandahar refused to demur and with their refusal the political unity of the Durrani Empire finally fractured.

Like his predecessors and successors, Dost Muhammad Khan confronted the 'moral incoherence' of the Afghan political community, a community founded upon 'profound moral contradictions that have inhibited the country from forging a coherent civil society', or sense of nationhood.[3] And like his predecessors and successors, he proved unable to construct a 'morally coherent' model of political authority with which to rule the Afghan political community. The failure to create a coherent model of political leadership or community remains the central story of Afghanistan. The political problems of its present lay in the unresolved contradictions of its past, originating with the establishment of a separate Afghan political entity. In order to understand the challenges faced by Dost Muhammad, one must look to the political universe in which Afghan leaders operated and the strategies they employed to both navigate and shape it.

The 'incoherence' of the Afghan political community, however, is fundamentally situational in nature, relating to the 'failure' of the diverse groups inhabiting Afghanistan's social ecology to create the necessary environment for the construction of a Weberian state-project. While the motif of Afghanistan's 'moral incoherence', discussed here, provides a useful analytical framework with which to understand the difficulties facing Afghan state formation, it runs the risk of teleological determinism. Like Elphinstone's thesis which recognized these breaches in Afghan society 200 years before, such an argument is, in its own way, a philosophical history of Afghan political society, accounting for its 'failure'. Such a 'failure' and 'incoherence' narrative obscures the deep linkages intertwining different Afghan constructs of authority, or normative orders. Further, it ignores that the Afghan 'failure' to construct a viable state structure or national community has less to do with their lack of ability than with the model's inappropriateness to their circumstances.

To understand the complicated processes shaping the Afghan political order, this chapter inverts the perspective presented in the first three chapters, looking at the land of the Afghans from the inside, rather than the outside. British fears of a 'tribal breakout', although overstated, were not without historical foundation.[4] Yet the Afghan plundering raids of the eighteenth century which terrorized the imagination of some Company officials had their own logic and causes. By analysing the character and problems of the Afghan political community during this period, one may better understand its regional role, as well as account for, in part, the failure of British designs. While this analysis is based upon British colonial records, it was the British who through the Elphinstonian episteme both documented and helped rigidify the contours of this political community. The failure of these designs led to Afghanistan's effective exclusion from the global order, based in a very different socio-political universe, being constructed by the British at this time. The Afghan's would not be brought into this order until the end of the nineteenth century, and then only partially as a fiscal colony of British India.[5] Understanding the nature of the Afghan political community is thus fundamental to understanding its subsequent marginalization.

II.　The contours of Afghanistan's social ecology

Afghanistan is a state whose boundaries were delimited by neighbouring colonial powers in their totality. Like many other societies faced with the juggernaut of imperialism, the Afghans were given little choice but to adopt the forms dictated by European political theory and practice. But unlike societies with direct experience of colonial governance, the Afghans were expected to construct a European-like state without such familiarity. To discuss the failure of the Afghan state is to address the issue of why its constituent communities have not adopted these largely alien concepts of political order. The 'incoherence' of the Afghan moral universe is not due to the Afghan inability to construct a viable civil society. Rather, the dissonances between the normative orders – the values on which the Afghan political society is founded and legitimized – shaping the Afghan socio-political universe have continually frustrated attempts to erect a larger unit of political community expressed through state structures. The 'failure' of the Afghan state is premised on the successes and coherence of groupings within the Afghan socio-political universe, and must be understood as a relative rather than absolute phenomenon. In Elphinstone's words, the 'separate societies into which the nation is divided' retained their individual features, rather than being crushed and obliterated by the centralising state.

The Weberian idea of the modern state, controlling a delineated territory over which it maintains a monopoly of organized violence exercised through bureaucratic means, was ill-defined at best in the early nineteenth century in general, and in Asia in particular.[6] Indeed, in the case of Afghanistan one may call it nebulous, if not non-existent, at least until the end of the nineteenth century.[7] Social order was maintained and political power exercised over subjects through the tribal and religious institutions. These institutions, or alternative social formations, formed the basis of an attenuated political structure pervasive throughout Afghan society and contoured Afghanistan's social ecology. The weak institutional character of tribal governance, the individualist norms of the *Pashtünwâlî*, and lack of centralized authority made it a largely self-policing system.

The absence of discrete state structures penetrating Afghan societies meant that alternative social formations continued to exist, and fulfil the functions normally performed by state institutions. These formations survived not only attempts by a weak Afghan state to supplant them, but the more forceful challenge of their exclusion along with the rest of the Afghan political community by the British in the wake of the First Afghan War. Despite this exclusion, alternative social formations separate from the Afghan state or 'nation' remained the centre of both political and communal consciousness. Many of these formations, including cities, tribes and tribal confederacies, not only survived, but flourished on the outlands of the emerging global order. They created their own political and economic niches, mediating between the new global order and marginalized communities of the periphery less able to adjust. The persistence of these alternative social formations in the face of the assimilative pressures of European imperialism underlines the resilience of indigenous identities during this period.

Afghanistan's normative ordering

Nearly all the conflicts Afghanistan faced, both internally and externally, during the early nineteenth century centred on schisms within the Afghan political community. These schisms were not simply dynastic competitions, as some authors have argued, but represented deeper clashes of alternative visions of Afghan society, visions based on the different normative orders simultaneously held by the Afghans themselves.[8] The central normative orders shaping the Afghan socio-political universe were tribe, Islam and royalism.[9] The Afghan political community suffered from a lack of consensus regarding the prioritization of these normative orders in shaping the Afghan socio-political universe. These three orders rested in a tenuous balance increasingly upset by the changing world around them. This balance turned to competition as leaders attempted to legitimate themselves according to the precepts of these orders. The failure to integrate these elements into a complementary template for political authority ensured the fragmentary nature of the Afghan political community driven by the centrifugal forces of an unresolved moral landscape.

The Afghan political order at this time represented a 'tribal kingdom' – a political entity founded upon personal, rather than territorial boundaries of political authority and defined by the putative relations created by membership to tribal bodies. From its inception under Ahmad Shah Abdali, this kingdom was founded both upon the Durrani confederacy, an alliance of Pashtun tribes, and the force of mercenary arms ensured by plunder. The kingdom's political coherence rested on the opportunities for plunder afforded the Durrani at the time of its establishment. As those opportunities receded and the economy of plunder became increasingly untenable, so too did the original foundations of the proto-state. Subsequent rulers were forced to look elsewhere to legitimize their authority. Abandoning the tribal normative order, they looked to the other two shaping the Afghan socio-political universe – Islam and royalism. While each offered Afghan rulers opportunities to better secure their rule, they also contained within them profoundly contradictory elements limiting their utility.

The construction of political authority needed to keep faith with the political precedents familiar to their Pashtun tribesmen, as well as fit within the Afghan socio-political universe. Consequently, Afghan leaders adapted past experiences to fit present circumstances, while at the same time introducing, or rather reinterpreting aspects of the Afghans' different normative orders to better secure their authority. By combining and emphasizing the various elements of tribe, Islam and royalism, Afghan rulers sought to produce a legitimizing formula guaranteeing their position and the stability of the Afghan political community. They sought, like other pre-colonial states in South Asia, to live in a universe where 'conflicting principles of political association [existed] in the same time and place, and among the same people, and that these different principles [could] also be understood as appropriate, or "legitimate"'.[10] The differences, however, between tribal, Islamic and royal conceptions of political order represented the fault lines between different visions of authority. None of these visions necessarily sought to monopolize Afghanistan's political space. Yet when the demands of one order contradicted those of another, their exclusivist proclivities became clear.

The particular difficulty facing the Afghan leaders was the essential weakness of the state in the face of these competing pressures. Unable to compel, leaders were thus forced to attempt to co-opt these normative orders into the constructions of the state, so that the state would be powerful enough to later subvert them to its own ends. This chapter examines that attempted co-optation, outlining the political universe the Afghans occupied with the establishment of the Durrani Empire in 1747. By outlining the past precedents on which Afghan leaders sought to construct their state, one can then understand the failure of later innovations. Chief amongst these was the attempt by Dost Muhammad Khan to move the language of legitimacy away from tribal justification and royal charisma, to a political lexicon defined by Islam. While there had been previous attempts to construct alternative social formations on the precepts of Islam, not until Abdur Rahman Khan did the state so consciously attempt to legitimate itself on a religious footing.[11]

The attempt to construct or coerce a legitimatory consensus for the central state largely failed during this epoch, devolving the powers and responsibilities it attempted to usurp to alternative social formations. The failure of the Afghan state, however, was not the failure of Afghan politics. Instead, the Afghan political community expressed its aspirations, and fulfilled its needs though other institutional frameworks. The difficulty Afghan leaders faced in legitimizing and maintaining their authority internally offers insight into the challenges the Afghan body politic faced externally, especially its exclusion from the emerging British global order. Faced with political formations which refused to assume the form of a modern state, the British initially attempted to co-opt them into their imperial schema. However, as with their Afghan predecessors, they failed. Their failure led to the abandonment of external attempts at state imposition until the late nineteenth century, while fundamentally undermining the internal foundations for attempts at state construction. Afghanistan's peripheralization was therefore due to its retention of forms of political community which did not fit the world order emerging during the mid-nineteenth century.

III.   A tribal kingdom: The evolution of the Afghan proto-state

The Durrani Empire of the late eighteenth century had been little more than a supra-tribal confederation, constructed on the waning norms of Central Asian plundering polities.[12] Its collapse at the beginning of the nineteenth century meant much of the authority previously invested in the monarchy dissipated to other social formations populating Afghanistan's social ecology. Afghan leaders of the nineteenth century, whose own bases of authority were at least initially founded in these alternative social formations, especially tribes, had to counter the centrifugal tendencies of tribal interests if they were to construct a centralized political authority. The fall of the Durrani Empire, and the circumstances responsible for its dissolution, closed the possibility of erecting stable political authority on a supra-tribal confederacy to these leaders.[13] Moreover, interactions with the newly arrived British and newly ascendant Sikhs injected foreign concepts of political authority and order increasingly being forced upon the Afghans. These concepts took definite form with Sikh and British incursions into Afghanistan, including the subsidy policies of the latter which Shah Mahmoud Hanifi has argued were central to the later construction of the Afghan state.[14]

In conceptualising their kingdom, the Afghan shahs attempted to fit the universal norms of Islamic empire inherited from their Persian antecedents, the Safavids, within the narrower precepts of Pashtun tribal identity. The difficulty they faced was the transformation of this hitherto peripheral, and largely autonomous tribal group, subjects of larger Muslim 'gunpowder empires', into the central pillar of a newfound political order. Apart from the practical difficulties, from its inception, the Durrani Empire faced profound ideological shortcomings militating against a more expansive vision of political community. By aligning their power with the Durrani Pashtun tribes, Afghan shahs restricted the channels of power in the Afghan successor proto-state in a genealogically defined way.

In order to be Pashtun, the tribesmen to whom state authority was genealogically limited to had to do Pashto, acting in accordance with the individualist ethos ideally stated in the *Pashtūnwâlî*. Ahmad Shah thus circumscribed his imperial aspirations in the long term by centring his power on his Durrani Pashtun tribesmen. The Durrani Empire was thus of limited duration. Less charismatic Afghan leaders retrenched their political ambitions from empire to kingdom, and eventually to city-state as the practical realities of imperial expansion collapsed into the legitimatory void on which it was constructed. By 1809, the facade of a multi-ethnic empire had given way to the reality of a fractious tribal kingdom.

The weak normative edifice on which the Afghan tribal kingdom was constructed was amplified by its even weaker institutional structure. Nadir Shah's eventual destruction of the institutions of the Safavid state in the mid- eighteenth century, paired with his failure to erect coherent structures in its place, left the Afghans with virtually no institutions of governance on their ascendance to power. This was particularly true in terms of state-sanctioned, or state-supported, religious office. As Sunnis, the Afghans had no similar office to the Shi'a Imamate in which to invest religious authority, the idea of the Caliphate notwithstanding. Further, they lacked not only a learned class of Islamic scholars, but also the kind of urban centres which could cultivate such a class, Sunni or Shi'a. Ruling over a tribal society, the Afghan rulers faced the need to create a separate foundation of authority from their narrow tribal allegiances in which they could institutionalize super-tribal cooperation and confederacies. This separate foundation would serve as an independent base of power with which they could exert cooperative and coercive authority over recalcitrant tribes.

Afghan rulers initially looked to usurp the institutions of tribal governance to strengthen their positions of power. All tribal leaders were subject to the authority of the *jirga*, or assembly of elders, the key institution of the *Pashtūnwâlî*. In the absence of a codified law, the *jirga* was fundamental to social order, regulating all facets of social life. Membership was issue-dependant and changed often, at times even including all male members of the tribe.[15] The *jirga* played a decisive role, even if only formally, in the ascension of both Ahmad Shah and Dost Muhammad Khan. In his assumption of the title of *amīr al-mu'minīn* (leader of the faithful), Dost Muhammad intentionally recreated Ahmad Shah's election ceremony, including a *jirga* assembly of tribal chiefs and his nomination by a religious leader, in order to legitimize himself in terms of past precedent.[16] His assumption of a religious title, previously unused by Afghan shahs, and nomination by a person of established religious charisma and credentials, underlined the shifting grounds of legitimacy upon which he based his claim to authority.

The *jirgas'* decisions were based on a combination of *sharīa* and Pashtun custom.[17] The institutions of tribal governance, such as the *jirga*, were institutions of collective action adjudicating dispute resolutions through self-help. They had little authority to compel. Because of this weakness, the intrusive power of any kind of centralized authority, much less a state, was rather limited. It simply lacked the coercive force, or reputation of such, to enforce its will on subjects. The state could not compel individuals or groups acting contrary to its will, but instead had to rely on the collective institutions to do so. This, however, necessarily required the individual members of the *jirga* to themselves consent to and actively participate in collective action. It is little wonder Elphinstone characterized Pashtun tribal society as composed of 'high-spirited republics'.[18]

In addition to the tribal institutions of secular government, Afghans had recourse to other accepted institutions of governance, most notably Islamic courts headed by *qazīs*. These were largely controlled by the Afghan ruler who appointed a number of officers charged with enforcing his will over the local community. Virtually all appointments to state offices required some religious learning.[19] These appointments, however, were generally limited to urban areas where monarchs could exert their authority with a modicum of success. That authority was, however, potentially compromised by officers' dependence on the community for their salary and livelihood.[20] Petitioners could, theoretically, take their case to the ruler for adjudication. Dost Muhammad is described by numerous sources as conscientious and fair in hearing petitions, more so than any former Afghan monarchs.[21]

Rather than resorting to state religious authorities though, many looked to religious leaders, especially *sayyids* and *mians* to settle their disputes when tribal institutions failed. These individuals' revered status and their independence from the state often granted them a unique authority to resolve civil and family disputes.[22] The weakness of official, state-appointed *'ulamā'* was made painfully clear during the British experience of occupation.[23] Although the Company lavished substantial subsidies on the official *'ulamā'*, these individuals exerted little influence over public opinion and the British instead attempted to bribe the *sayyids*.[24] The continued viability of these extra-statal institutions of governance underlines the difficulties faced by Durrani shahs attempting to monopolize the space of government.

The state's weakness was a consequence of the political circumstances out of which it was born. From the inception of an independent Afghan political entity, the Durrani tribes who served as the basis of the rulers' authority contested the independence and autonomy of the state. Because of the tribesmen's antipathy towards central state control, Afghan monarchs were forced to look to other communities to provide the personnel for a nascent state bureaucracy. But there was a more profound change afoot than simply a new, relatively insecure monarchy attempting to solidify its position by establishing an independent powerbase in the institutions of the state. Rather, the military-fiscal model on which the previous Mughal and Safavid Empires were based were being eclipsed by the innovations in warfare discussed in the previous chapter.

Just as Ahmad Shah adopted the norms of political legitimacy from earlier Persian precedent, his successors adopted a model of state and its bureaucracy.

The Qizilbash, left in Kabul by Nadir during his invasion of India and previously servants of his bureaucracy, became the basis of the Afghan bureaucracy.[25] This had important consequences for the distribution and competition for power in Afghanistan, as well as for the character of state-based political authority. Although numerically small, the Qizilbash wielded a disproportionately large amount of political power in Afghanistan. They served as the Persian secretaries of rulers and chiefs, constituting the nascent bureaucracy of the Afghan tribal state.[26] This made them the object of much animosity, especially from the Pashtun tribal nobility who viewed them with disdain, as *Darî*-speaking, non-Pashtun urban dwellers and Shi'as.[27]

The Qizilbash employed Persian as the language of state business. While in ways the obvious language of government, with a wealth of bureaucratic language developed over time, the choice made the language of state for the Pashtun tribal kingdom a foreign one. The choice of Persian over Pashto reflected deeper cleavages and antagonisms in the Afghan political landscape. Pashto represented a rural tribal tradition which viewed the state, and monarchy, as justified only so long as they satisfied the demands of wealth distribution. In contrast, Persian represented a bureaucratic tradition which simultaneously sought to serve as an independent power-base for the monarchy as well as an autonomous and sovereign power itself. It also represented an urban culture seeking to identify itself with the larger Persianized cultural ecumene of which Afghanistan was a part.

The tensions embodied in this linguistic division – between the tribes, the monarchy and the state – where each existed at the same time autonomously and in alliance with one another, remained one of the central and most volatile fault lines of the Afghan political community. This fault line was additionally compounded by the attempts of Dost Muhammad Khan to Islamicize the norms of political legitimacy. In so doing, he also attempted to extend state control of official belief through the appointment of religious officials. This strategy was fatally handicapped by the absence of urban '*ulamā*' who could cooperate with and enforce the Islamicization of the state. Political authority and the state thus remained both contentious and largely absent in the lives of most Afghans. Instead, tribal institutions and independent religious leaders personified communal authority and provided an attenuated political structure of social order.

IV.   Afghanistan's plundering polity model

In their attempt to construct a state, Afghan leaders deployed resources of suasion and coercion with which to gain acceptance of the state. Those resources assumed specific theoretical form which underlay later action. The presence or conversely the absence of three elements – political theory, symbolic legitimization and religious sanctioners – defined the viability and success of the Durrani regime.[28] The volatility of Afghan political theory required more frequent rituals of symbolic legitimization. These rituals, however, were undermined by the lack of a religious cadre which could continuously expound the justificatory value of these rituals, much less the underlying efficacy of the political theory. Yet the theories, rituals and people the Afghan rulers employed to justify their rule were not without historical foundation. Rather, the Afghans relied on the theories and practices they knew best – those of the Safavids as mediated by Nadir Shah. This reliance, however, only served to compound the Afghans' difficulties as Persian legacies proved themselves problematic, especially when applied to the Pashtun political community.

Afghanistan's position as an important conduit between South, Central and West Asia meant that it was an area which competing empires loosely controlled politically, but where their cultural penetration and paramountcy was profound. The Afghans were both subjects and heirs to the political traditions of Safavid, Mughal India and Timurid Central Asia, a legacy which proved problematic when independence came. By the founding of the Durrani Empire in 1747, all three of these empires had collapsed, leaving a patrimony of political culture rather than palpable tradition of political authority. Of these, the Safavid heritage exerted the most immediate influence on the character of the Afghan successor kingdom. Yet, a strong undercurrent affecting Afghan political culture was the Timurid political legacy reinvigorated by Nadir Shah in the mid-eighteenth century.[29] Nadir Shah's success in Afghanistan, and his recruitment of formerly recalcitrant Afghan tribes into his army, especially the Abdali confederacy, profoundly affected the course of Afghanistan's future.

Both the Mughals and Safavids were originally conquering tribal groups propelled into paramount positions of political authority. The requirements of government forced the Safavids and Mughals to abandon many of their tribal traditions and adopt, or develop, state-centric norms of governance. Like the later Durrani, the newly established dynasties needed to create power bases independent of tribal foundations from which they could challenge tribal dominance. The non-tribal modalities of power they turned to were both historically and culturally grounded. Persia had a long and developed discourse of kingship, predating the Islamic conquests. The Afghans, part of this larger Persian cultural ecumene, could relate to the norms and institutions of governance these empires had developed. Thus when time came for them to legitimate their own rule, they naturally turned to the norms they had hitherto subscribed to as vassals of empire.

The model of governance adopted by the Afghans, however, was not that of the strong centralized state forming the Safavid and Mughal experiences at the height of their power. Rather, the plundering polity model, based as it was on the political values of the nomadic societies of Central and Inner Asia, which constructed authority on the ability of leaders to collect and distribute wealth gained through booty raids of neighbouring territory found favour. It was fundamentally a parasitic model of political order, premised on proximity and access to wealthier, sedentary societies. The booty raids not only garnered wealth with which to buy tribal loyalties, but also provided an important outlet for competition and violence which might otherwise be directed inwards. Both the Mughals and Safavids originally relied on this model of imperial genesis before abandoning it for more indigenously framed and appropriate templates of state construction. But the disintegration of these empires at the beginning of the eighteenth century created the opportunity to resurrect the plundering polity paradigm. Nadir Shah quickly adopted it as the former shell of the Safavid state collapsed around him, and it was this model which was passed directly to his lieutenant and heir in Afghanistan, Ahmad Shah Durrani.

The political traditions the Afghans found themselves heirs to in 1747 were shaped as much by the failures as the successes of the Safavid state. The Safavids secularized kingship, embracing the bifurcation of political and religious authority which began with the fall of the Caliphate in the thirteenth century and returned to earlier Sassanian ideas of kingship.[30] Authority divided between political authority residing in the shah and religious authority residing in the Imam. The shah's primary responsibility was to cast God's Shadow over his own temporal realm.[31] Thus while Safavid shahs did not legitimize their rule through religious authority, they were nonetheless beholden to it.

With the disappearance of the twelfth Imam, the Shīʻa 'ulamā' claimed stewardship of the Imamate pending his return. This division of authority could potentially prove destabilizing, engendering a power struggle between the shah and 'ulamā' as it later did under the Qajars.[32] The Safavids avoided this outcome through their claimed descent from the seventh Imam. In addition to endowing the Safavid shah with an independent religious authority rivalling that of the 'ulamā', it echoed the norms of genealogically defined leadership prevalent amongst the Sufi orders and Turkic tribes central to the founding of the state. By employing a political language familiar to both the tribes and 'ulamā', Safavid shahs pre-empted both groups' claim to political authority by creating an independent and largely unassailable rhetorical basis of legitimacy.

Nadir Shah

The fall of the Safavid Empire in 1722 meant the Safavid political paradigm lost much of its currency and power. Yet it was not totally rejected. Successors claimed to be heirs and restorers of Safavid power and authority. The presence of Safavid pretenders throughout the eighteenth century demonstrates the dynasty's continued hold over the Persian political imagination.[33] Although Nadir Shah initially claimed to be a Safavid restorer, his assumption of the throne in 1736 forced him to abandon such pretence in favour of his own claims to legitimacy. Nadir abandoned the traditional Safavid ceremony of coronation, instead convening a tribal council on the plain of Mughan to elect him as king.[34] His reliance on tribal election, exclusion of religious authorities and decision to locate his coronation away from Ishfahan, the former Safavid capital, all underscored his efforts to distance himself from the Safavid past. Instead of resuscitating the Safavid genealogical link to the Imams, Nadir turned to Timurid norms of legitimacy, laying claim to Chingizid ancestry and descent from Chingis Khan.[35] He further assaulted the former institutions of the Safavid state by attempting to have Shi'ism recognized as a fifth school of Islamic jurisprudence, the Ja'fari *mezhab*, by the Ottomans.[36]

Nadir's legitimacy derived not from his character as God's Shadow on Earth, but from the tacit, albeit forced consent of the tribal chiefs.[37] This reflected a new form of political legitimacy, or more properly, the restoration of an old tribal one superimposed on the ruins of the Safavid order. By discarding the ceremonial forms of political legitimization, Nadir cut himself loose from the moorings of religious responsibility. He instead signalled his rule would not be legitimated by its justice, the Shi'a standard, but rather by one more appropriate to the Turko-Mongolian mantle of legitimacy he laid claim to – the distribution of plunder.[38] Here again, Nadir borrowed the norms of Timurid leadership to legitimate his rule, while assiduously avoiding claim to that legacy. Nadir's reintroduction of the plundering polity paradigm carried his armies to Delhi, and the Peacock throne back to Iran.

Yet his rejection of Safavid norms was not total. Indeed, many of his actions were justified to the outside world as an abrogation of the Safavid legacy while internally they were depicted as protecting its essence in a changed world.[39] The Nadirite paradigm was in many ways a merger of the Safavid and Timurid legacies which historically shaped the political landscape of Persia.[40] Because the Safavid legacy was too politically potent to reject outright, Nadir sought to initially modify, and ultimately subvert it with a return to the plundering polity paradigm of Timurid Central Asia.

Nadir's iconoclasm was not so much a revolution as a reinterpretation of long-established norms of political authority done to meet the demands and exigencies of their respective presents. The Safavids themselves adopted a language of legitimacy long used on the Central Asian steppe, a Chingizid idiom which gave political coherence to the norms of nomadic conquests and plunder practised by Central and Inner Asian Turkic tribes. The support of the Qizilbash enabled the Safavids to forcefully translate these norms into the Persian context. Just as the Afghan rulers later employed an amalgamated language of the different normative orders shaping their socio-political universe to justify their rule, so too did their Persian predecessors.

The relative weakness of Nadir *vis-à-vis* the great Safavid monarchs such as Shah Abbas was underlined by his lack of an independent state source of authority, backed by a community of religious learning, helping impose his authority upon his subjects.[41] By the eighteenth century, the few remnant institutions of the Safavid state lay moribund, and the Shi'a clergy as a community were divided and weak. Without the buttress of a state, he invested his power in the tribes forming the core of his confederation and thus the foundation of his rule. Yet he maintained his position as a 'dispensary monarch' and was able, with some success, to replace tribal leaders with royal governors.[42]

Nadir's effective dismantling and tribalization of the Safavid state, combined with his rejection of Safavid political theory and its legitimizing ritual, bequeathed the Afghans a bastardized and largely incoherent tradition. His failure to establish an Afsharid dynasty in Persia, much like Timur's earlier failure in Central Asia, contributed to Persia's continued instability and political volatility.[43] Nadir's murder forced the Persians and Afghans to engage with the distorted Safavid legacy he failed to either eliminate or successfully negotiate.

The success of Nadir's reign was built upon the confluence of a waning opportunity for a plundering polity type of parasitic political order constructed on the foundations of a tribalized state. His failure to establish stability or dynastic permanence demonstrated the fleeting potency of a plundering polity, predicated on the parasitic destruction of its neighbours. The initial success, and subsequent failure of his, and other plundering polities, was fundamentally founded on the weakness of richer neighbouring states. Such weakness represented a window of opportunity for raiding nomadic tribesmen to sweep into wealthy societies constructed around sedentarized agriculture. The weaker the state, the more successful the tribesmen's incursion.

Yet the more efficiently they stripped their parasitic prize, the less able it would be to provide, in future, the necessary plundered wealth. Nadir's success was at least in part a consequence of his timing, with the disintegration of Mughal authority in north India in the first half of the eighteenth century allowing the Nadirite hordes virtually unhindered access to the riches of north India.[44] The £30 million of plunder he absconded with from Delhi financed Persian trade with India until the end of the eighteenth century.[45] Yet the window of opportunity which Nadir took advantage of was closing fast.

Ahmad Shah

Ahmad Shah Abdali, founder of the Durrani Empire, based his authority on the same plundering polity model he had once benefited from while in the service of Nadir Shah.[46] Weakened by the latter's incursions, '[t]he state of foreign powers was equally favourable [for the Afghans]'.[47] They initially repeated Nadir's success, defeating the Marathas at Panipat in 1761 and subsequently sacking of Delhi. According to Elphinstone,

> For the consolidation of his power at home he [Ahmad Shah] relied, in a
> great measure, on the effects of his foreign wars. If these were successful, his

victories would raise his reputation, and his conquests would supply him with the means of maintaining an army, and of attaching the Afghan chiefs by favours and rewards: the hopes of plunder would induce many tribes to join him, whom he could not easily have compelled to submit....[48]

Ahmad Shah, however, was eventually forced to confront the legacy of Nadir's previous success. North India was no longer the rich jewel of years past. This meant the Afghans had to return more frequently in search of plunder, a task made increasingly difficult by the rise of powerful successor states to the Mughals, such as the Marathas and the Sikhs. In the end, Ahmad Shah's victory over the former enabled more formidable powers to dominate the north Indian plain. The establishment of Ranjit Singh's Punjab kingdom and the power of the EIC effectively closed the window of opportunity for plunder by the beginning of the nineteenth century.

Ahmad Shah Durrani not only subscribed to the Nadirite paradigm of a plundering polity, but also continued to employ Safavid ideas of kingship and political authority. By assuming the Persian title *pādshāh*, rather than the Arabic *amīr* or Pashtun *khān*, he turned to language, literal and figurative, familiar to him and his people, long culturally Persian, when he embarked upon the ceremonial legitimization of his newfound empire. The innovations forced on that language by Nadir Shah, with the concurrent weakening of Shi'ism as a political force, made the adoption of that language tolerable to the Sunni Afghans. Their tribal background, combined with their service to Nadir, made the Durranis at least susceptible to the legitimization of power as practised by the Nadirite, and earlier Safavid state. As Elphinstone noted,

> In framing his government he appears to have had the model of that of Persia before his eyes. The forms of his court, the great officers of state, the arrangement of the army, and the pretensions of the crown, were exactly the same as those of Naudir Shauh; but the difference in the situations of the two monarchs was apparent in the manner in which Ahmad Shauh was obliged to modify Naudir's plan, both in the administration of his internal government and in the order of his measure for advancing his power at home and abroad.[49]

But the adoption of this legitimizing language failed to address the contradictions created by the Nadirite legacy, forcing Ahmad Shah to 'modify Naudir's plan'. Nor did it comport with the political weakness of Afghan shahs. Whereas in Persia, charismatic individuals like Nadir or Shah Isma'il could thrust themselves into positions of supreme authority secured on previous institutional structures and a societal memory of hierarchal authority, Afghan aspirants for power could not. At best, an Afghan shah could become a *primus inter pares* of Afghan tribal chiefs, a paramount suzerain rather than regal sovereign.[50]

By claiming the mantle of Safavid authority in an area never a centre of Safavid power, Ahmad Shah Durrani established his rule on a political morass. As subjects long on the periphery of empire, and thus removed from the moral and coercive force of the centre, the Afghans' social and political structures were highly contested. Ahmad Shah's claim to the Safavid legacy, mediated by Nadir's reign, was extremely problematic. Nadir's innovations from Safavid ceremonial forms were designed to fit the circumstances of his rule in Persia. His council coronation appeased the powerful tribes of Turkic origin by communicating the passage of legitimate authority in a political language culturally appropriate to the clan-based tribes of the Central Asian steppe.

The tribes Ahmad Shah and his successors claimed authority over were neither Shi'a nor Turkic, making the languages of legitimacy of their Persian predecessors inappropriate to the circumstances they faced. As the Afghans' collective memory of Safavid writ over their lands and political institutions faded, so too did their Safavid-enforced, Persianized collective character, eroded by a growing sense of tribally defined consciousness. They were Pashtun. Political authority within their kingdom increasingly needed to reflect this growing sense of distinct identity. Ahmad Shah Durrani was a charismatic leader, able to rule through his skilful manipulation of factional rivalry and his ability to co-opt loyalty through the distribution of subsidies acquired by his perennial invasions of Hindustan.[51] His successors, however, shared neither his political acumen nor his financial success. Timur Shah lost much of his father's empire through attrition and mismanagement.[52]

The shah's authority depended on his ability to subsidize, not centralize, meaning the alienation of north India as a regular source of plunder weakened the Afghan monarchy and made the shah's position increasingly tenuous. This was compounded by the frailty of the Afghan state. By borrowing the Safavid concepts of political authority and imposing them on a society lacking the underpinning institutional structure, Ahmad Shah created an inherently unstable political order. His successors found themselves legitimizing their rule through the slow accretion of invented tradition, constantly shifting their rhetoric of legitimacy while continually trying to secure their precarious paramountcy through the disbursement of plunder.

The internalization of plunder

The Afghans' inability to mount large-scale plunder raids into the rich north Indian plains, combined with Persian bankruptcy, ultimately undermined the authority of Afghan shahs no longer able to distribute loyalty-ensuring plunder. Lack of external booty meant contestants for the Afghan throne were forced to rely on indigenous sources, internalizing their plunder raids. They had two main revenue sources: (1) land taxes and (2) caravan duties. Collecting the first proved extremely precarious because of the system of land tenure developed by earlier Durrani shahs, adopted from the Mughals and Safavids.[53] Apart from the royal lands providing income to state coffers, much of the land had been alienated from the state through the granting of *tiyūls*, tax-free land grants requiring military service to the court. These *tiyūls*, distributed in the main to Durrani *sardārs*, provided no income to the Afghan state.[54]

While subject to re-affirmation by the new monarch, a new incumbent insecure on the throne could ill-afford to alienate many *sardārs* through the termination of their *tiyūl*.[55] As land vested through re-affirmation by increasingly weaker Afghan shahs, the ability of the monarch to reintegrate these lands back into the state revenue structure became more and more unrealistic. *Sardārs* with *tiyūls* estranged from state coffers understood the precarious situation of the shah's centralized authority and seized the opportunity to discontinue the levies their *tiyūls* rested upon, secure in the knowledge the shah could neither force nor displace them.[56]

The abrogation of *tiyūls* was not simply a consequence of economic necessity, but more importantly it represented an attempt by Afghan rulers to establish their political authority independent of the tribal chiefs holding these rights. The rulers were trying to centralize both revenue collection and coercive authority, in the form of armed retainers, in the state. This necessarily challenged the mediatory role played by *tiyūl* holders in access to both these resources. Shah Shuja and Shah Mahmud both abrogated *tiyūls* to recover revenue, as well as undermine potential political threats.[57] Dost Muhammad's abrogation of *tiyūls* previously granted alienated many *sardārs*, as did his attempts to independently employ soldiers loyal to his court and paid for in cash.[58] Thus, while Shah Shuja later attempted to shore up his crumbling legitimacy under British tutelage by affirming *tiyūls* granted by the Barakzai, the damage had already been done.[59] The old consensus which underlay political authority, based on the provision of soldiers by chiefs in return for land grants, thus broke down as shahs asserted the sovereignty, as opposed to paramountcy, of the central state. In doing so, the shahs were forced to rely more heavily on the royal lands they tax-farmed, aggravating an already over-taxed peasantry.[60]

The abrogation of *tiyūls*, combined with the return of royal lands previously exempted into service of the treasuries, meant Afghans themselves carried a greater part of the plunder burden. Yet these measures proved insufficient. Trade duties thus became a staple source of revenue, even for agriculturally rich and political stable kingdoms like the *amirate* of Bukhara. Visiting the city in 1812, Mir Izzat Ullah reported customs receipts as the second most important source of revenue for the Bukharan *amīr*.[61] When William Moorcroft arrived thirteen years later, a Bukharan minister testified to him that one *kâfila* (caravan) alone had yielded twelve lakhs of rupees in duties.[62] For the rulers of Kandahar, Kabul and Herat, these duties were even more important and they all increased trade duties well above the *sharīa* sanctioned two and a half per cent. When this failed to garner adequate tax receipts, they resorted to plundering caravans and extorting money from merchants. These traders represented an important source of wealth little able to resist rulers' demands.

The alienation of land revenues transformed caravan duties into important sources of taxation. Trade duties thus became the foundation of the Afghan political economy, and the cornerstone of the rulers authority. Increasing receipts from these duties strengthened the rulers position *vis-à-vis* tribal *sardārs*. Falling receipts had the opposite effect. Royal authority increasingly centred in places of the collection of that wealth – cities. Cities additionally offered the advantages of bazaars, so that not only could the transport of commerce be taxed, but so too could its sale and exchange.[63] Yet while cities offered legitimacy by regularising plunder in the form of tax receipts, they also bred an undermining cycle. The more wealth the ruler could distribute, the more secure his place on the throne. This in turn encouraged greater taxation, systematically discouraging trade and ensuring smaller tax receipts. Such a self-defeating cycle might have been offset by control of all cities in Afghanistan, denying merchants the option of redirecting trade to cities with lower duties. But the paramount character and weakness of Afghan rulers prevented such centralization and their authority often extended little distance beyond their metropolitan centres.

The urbanization of political authority profoundly affected the character of Afghan kingship. The essentially un-tribal nature of cities made them a space where centralized authority could pre-empt the *Pashtūnwâlî* with its own code of conduct.[64] While the demands of tribally dependent, plunder-based political authority created the conditions for the urbanization of Afghan political authority, by concentrating authority where they could practically guarantee plunder, Afghan rulers transgressed the values of rural-based tribal society. The Afghan moral economy ultimately suffered from the peril of plunder and proved unable to support its internalization. Despite the efforts of Dost Muhammad Khan to create a new legitimizing language of political power, his inability to redefine the parameters of the political and moral economy stood at the heart of the crisis of kingship, and Afghan political authority.

To compensate for the loss of prestige in the eyes of rural tribesmen, Afghan leaders attempted to shift the criteria of authority away from tribal notions of authority, towards Islamic and royal concepts. Yet Afghan cities offered little in the way of legitimizing religious resources or discourse and the Barakzai *sardārs* could not effectively challenge the Saddozai monopoly of royal charisma. A chaotic spiral therefore engulfed Afghan internal politics as political legitimacy became increasingly fragile and control progressively tenuous. As the window of opportunity closed, the plundering polity model failed the Afghan rulers, who were left scrambling to forge an alternate basis on which to construct their authority.

V.   Afghanistan's Islamic moral landscape

The urbanization of Afghan political authority ultimately alienated Afghan rulers not only from the tribal normative order of the Afghan socio-political universe, but also from the Islamic one. Few Afghan cities could claim to be centres of religious learning. Poorly endowed in terms of Islamic resources, with few urban *'ulamā'* or religious institutions, the importance of Afghan cities derived not from their role as models of Muslim community, but from economic exchange and political authority. This made them almost as un-Islamic as they were un-tribal, a fact greatly affecting the character of the Afghan polity. The location of these cities bounded their influence on the kingdom, as well as their own development and evolution. With the exception of Kandahar and Kabul, the largest and most important cities sat precariously on the Kingdom's periphery.

Afghan cities were home to an extremely diverse population, a fact which set them outside the normative universe of rural Pashtun tribesmen. Minorities, such as the Shi'a Qizilbash and Hindu bankers, tended to congregate in cities for protection. The economic and bureaucratic power of these minorities, and the resentment it engendered, was only amplified by their geographic concentration. These minorities' precarious existence outside the tribal normative order was underlined by their physical exclusion from tribal space. Additionally, their religious heterodoxy put Afghan cities at odds with the Islamic normative order in which they should serve as models of right community, further aggravating Pashtun tribal resentment towards them. Kabul became the proverbial Babylon of Afghanistan, and those residing there, including its ruler, fundamentally lay outside the normative order of the *Pashtūnwâlî*, as well as tribal understandings of Islam.[65]

As the tribal idiom increasingly failed to legitimize the authority of Afghan rulers, they turned to Islam to sanction their rule, colouring the norms of Afghan leadership. Yet the tribal values dominating Afghan society, and the weak relatively Islamic infrastructure made the use of religion in public life and political discourse problematic. For the Pashtun, Islam was subsumed within their own tribal identity, yet one in which the contours of the socio-political universe were shaped as much by the *Pashtūnwâlî* as by the *sharīa*. Pashtun society was thus fundamentally Muslim, although not necessarily Islamic.[66] Tribal religion accommodated theological complexity by interpreting it through its own normative lens, as demonstrated by the *Rawshani* movement.[67] Whereas the *Pashtūnwâlî* espoused an individualist ethic reflective a tribal normative order based on honour and equality, the *sharīa* offered a design for the communal life of believers. By compartmentalizing moral authority in such a way, tribesmen transformed seeming contradictions into paradoxes of behaviour. Tribal norms maintained a paramountcy of moral suasion in regard to a particularized code of conduct for a local community, while Islam claimed a universal moral currency.[68]

The strength of that currency was buttressed, at least in part, by the religious learning it was founded upon. There was a great disparity of the level of formal learning between urban and rural areas. Cities such as Bukhara, Peshawar and Herat were considered centres of Islamic learning.[69]

The opinions of European observers on the abilities of Afghan *mullahs* varied considerably. Elphinstone, referring to the *mullahs* of Peshawar, characterized them as 'comparatively able men...in possession of the greatest part of the learning of the country'.[70] But Burnes, writing of the inhabitants of Bukhara's 366 *madrasas*, insisted, '[a] more perfect set of drones were never assembled together'.[71] Masson, echoing Burnes' sentiment, considered the rural *mullahs* in particular to be largely ignorant with their learning limited to 'the ability of repeating prayers, and relating legends and traditions of the most extravagant character'.[72]

The learning and ability of religious functionaries was dependent on their location, with a heavy concentration of the better educated in urban spaces. Rural *mullahs* were often poor tribesmen with only limited religious education. Their tribal origins placed them firmly within the tribal normative order, but by doing so deprived them of an independent authority outside the tribe's agnatic lineage. As they were dependent on other tribesmen for their livelihood, they were viewed as dependants, similar to *humsaya* ('neighbours').[73] Tribesmen often viewed state-appointed *mullahs* as outsiders and consequently disliked and distrusted them. C.M. Wade reported, '[i]t is a common expression among the Afghans, when any one wishes to take a thing from them against their will "Our village does not require a mullah nor does our tribe like him."'[74]

Yet *mullahs* were not the only religious functionaries present in Afghan society, nor were they necessarily limited to fulfilling only one Islamic office.[75] Indeed, there was wealth of religious offices found throughout Afghanistan, some associated with the state and some independent of it.[76] The conflation of spiritual and textual religious authority meant *mians*, *mullahs* and *sayyids* were often the same person.[77] While *mullah's* authority was based on claims of learning, those of *sayyids* and *mians* derived from their claimed descent from the Prophet. *Sayyids* and *mians* maintained their own spiritual genealogies of descent and discipleship, often tied to the veneration of *zîâratgah* (shrines), some of which imbued political authority, such as the Hazrat Ali shrine in Mazar-i Sharif.[78] Prophetic descent could be created through learning, granting a certain amount of mobility into the saintly class.[79] Furthermore, unlike their tribal counterparts, spiritual genealogies were not as exclusive as tribal ones; a person could belong to more than one simultaneously.[80] The use of the genealogical idiom, the 'sine qua non of identity upon which all other claims to social respect and influence were inevitably based', translated the norms of Islam, personified by *sayyids* and *mians*, into the tribal normative order.[81]

Numerous contemporaries, including Elphinstone and Moorcroft, remarked on the great sway *sayyids* held over the local populace.[82] Masson, writing of the Hazaras of Bisut, commented,

> In religion...they limit their pious offices to an excessive veneration for Saiyads and the shrines at Azaret Ali, for excepting some of their chiefs,

few of them ever say prayers or are acquainted therewith, and it is very rare to find a *majit* or place of worship, even in the castles of their Mirs.[83]

Certain areas within Afghanistan, notably the Pashtun crescent in the south and the northeast under the rule of Mir Murad Beg, were particularly *sayyid* rich.[84] Their respected status gave them not only opportunities for religious leadership, but also economic advantage. For example, the *sayyids* of Pishin, from Quetta, became an extremely powerful trading community.[85] *Kâfilas* often attempted to travel with *sayyids* as their status offered protection, and benefiting the *sayyids* through economic activity and trading.

The relative paucity of urban centres, and under-development of an urban religious class of *'ulamā'* reinforced the tribal predisposition towards a non-theologically literate form of Islam. But tribal illiteracy, while barring the textual religious understanding of the urban *'ulamā'*, succumbed to the penetration of religious education through oral dissemination. *Sayyids*, *mians* and rural *mullahs* disseminated learned and literate traditions through oral narratives, public readings and performances such as recitations of the *Panj Kitab* (five books) and the Koran.[86] The widespread use of the *Panj Ganj* (five treasures) and *Kulliyat-i chahar Kitab* (complete four books), traditional primary readings in the *mektab* and *madrasas* presenting the central corpus of Islamic knowledge through the use of mnemonic devices and narrative, was common.[87]

Deprived of the literate resources and urban centres of learning available to other Islamic societies, rural Afghan Muslims were forced to cope with the resources at their disposal.[88] This meant that Sufism, especially its Persianate traditions, was extremely widespread and important in Afghan religious discourse and practice.[89] The strength of tribal custom combined with the syncretic character of Sufism to create a form of Islam in Afghanistan which the conservative class of urban *'ulamā'* agitating for a return to a stricter religious orthodoxy likely would have deemed heterodoxy. Yet neither Sufism nor the Islamic beliefs or practices of Afghan tribesmen were insulated from the trends of the wider *umma*. The political and religious environment of the early nineteenth century created an intellectual milieu in which movements of Islamic revival took root.[90] Yet many of these movements were more reformist integrations seeking to annex the Sufi tradition to proper Islamic orthodoxy. Adherents, such as the *Naqshbandiyah*, did not reject the accommodating practice of Sufi syncretism with local practice, despite emphasis on strict adherence to the *sharīa*.[91]

In the Afghan case, this revivalism took a violent turn with Sayyid Ahmad Barelwi's revolt in 1826.[92] Sayyid Ahmad's status as a Sufi leader with his own brotherhood, or *tariqa-i Muhammadiyah*, provided him with religious authority, communicated in a genealogical idiom at a time the *Yusufzai* tribesmen faced an external challenge. While that challenge provided Sayyid Ahmad with the leadership opportunity, his ability to partially integrate himself into tribal society through his Sufi *ṭarīqat* provided him the practical support network on which to base his leadership.[93] Yet while the *ṭarīqat* enabled Sayyid Ahmad to speak to the tribesmen in a genealogical idiom they understood, he remained outside the tribal genealogical structure, and thus normative order.[94] His lack of standing within the Pashtun agnatic lineage, due to his claimed Prophetic descent, limited his opportunities for leadership to instances of outside interference. This explains the short tenure of the *Yusufzai's* adherence to Sayyid Ahmad Barelwi's leadership.[95]

Islam provided the Afghan socio-political universe the conceptual language with which to describe its non-tribal neighbours who stood outside the agnatic normative order. It therefore served as the medium of communication, and at times an idiom of confrontation, for interacting with those people.[96] As Afghans increasingly found themselves faced with hostile and powerful non-Muslim foreign powers, leaders employed the language of Islam to rally tribesmen as well as de-legitimize first Sikh and later British encroachment.[97] Yet while it provided tribesmen with a language with which to conceptualize and understand the non-Pashtun alien world they regularly interacted with, it did not fulfil that same role within Afghan society. This function was instead performed by the tribal idiom of genealogy and the *Pashtūnwâlî*. This dissonance of dialect proved insurmountable to Afghan rulers as they attempted to legitimate their rule through Islamic language and ceremony. These efforts were successful only so long as the threat necessitating the use of that idiom persisted.

Afghan rulers were severely handicapped by the lack of a body of religious scholars, independent of their patronage, who could theologically legitimate and endorse their rule. Their reliance on a literate, royally patronized Islamic clergy, often of foreign origin, did little to ingratiate the Afghan shahs with their increasingly alienated tribesmen.[98] Consequently, Afghan shahs were in the main denied meaningful spiritual sanction or charisma. The loss of Peshawar, the most learned city of the Afghan kingdom, to the Sikhs in 1819 denied the Afghan state an important religious resource. As rulers centred their authority in cities, they employed Islamic rhetoric and ceremony to bolster their claims to authority in the face of their failure to 'do Pashto'. Without the structure and authority provided by an institutionalized class of religious scholars, these ceremonies provided fleeting revitalizations of legitimacy. Rulers thus had to more frequently renew their claims of religious legitimacy with other ceremonies successfully tapping the religious sentiment of their followers. The need for constant renewal lent neither stability nor depth to this ceremonial legitimization, leaving rulers of the shifting ground of public sentiment animated by religious fervour.

VI.   'Royalism' in an egalitarian society

With neither the tribal nor Islamic normative orders sufficiently justifying their rule, Afghan shahs attempted to bolster their legitimacy with a third legitimatory language – royalism. They sought to imbue originally the Saddozai and later the Barakzai clans of the Durrani confederacy with exclusive royal charisma, privileging members of those clans as claimants to the mantle of Afghan leadership. Such exclusive prerogatives to power, however, contradicted the inclusivist egalitarianism of the *Pashtünwâlî*. Claimants to the Afghan throne were thus forced to construct an ideological legitimation of their rule which appeared adverse to tribal norms of authority. Afghan shahs sought to fulfil the requirements of those norms by employing the political language, imagery and institutions of the *Pashtünwâlî*, while at the same time doing something substantively quite different. As political expediency forced Afghan shahs to centre themselves in cities, they strove to offset the perceived compromise of their ability to 'do Pashto' with the elevation of the royal person. They attempted to reshape the Afghan socio-political universe, placing the monarch above reproach from either tribal or Islamic normative orders. Royalism thus sought to fill the legitimatory void created by urbanization.

In becoming the ruler of the Afghans, aspirants needed to be more than simply paramount Durrani tribal chiefs. It was essential for them to create an independent, institutional repository of power rather than be subject to the ephemeral nature of super-tribal confederacies. The paradox aspirants faced was that while they could only attain their status with tribal support, they could only maintain it by subjugating tribal independence to their own authority. That authority needed to reside in the state, which became inseparably associated with the person of the monarch. Yet to be successful, the state had to be erected through the tribal idiom – genealogy. Thus Afghan rulers were required to endow their position with an exclusive association to their Durrani tribesmen. Herein lay the origins of Pashtun, or more narrowly Durrani chauvinism.

When Ahmad Shah Abdali was selected as leader of the Afghan tribes, he asserted himself over a political legacy imparted to him by Nadir Shah and largely based upon the foundations of former Safavid rule. While professing to rule in the name of the defunct Safavid shah *de jure*, his assumption of the Persian title *shâh* meant that in reality he assumed the mantle of kingship *de facto*. In doing so, he elevated not only himself but also his tribe to regal status, assuming the name *Durrani* ('pearl of pearls') and bestowing it on his Abdali tribesmen as well. The Durrani, in general, and the Saddozai, in particular, became the royal tribe of the Afghans. Royalism was thus a strategy of state creation wherein tribal identity was usurped by the state.

By exclusively associating the Saddozai clan with the monarchy, and thus the state, Ahmad Shah created a relationship in which the fortunes of the tribe depended on those of the state. Yet his pretensions to regal authority imbued not only his person, but his clan, the Saddozai, and tribal confederacy, the Durrani, with an aura of royal mystic which over time would in itself became a self-justificatory entitlement to power. Elphinstone characterized his efforts with the tribesmen in the following terms:

the troops also, having the king continuously before their eyes, and witnessing the submission of their hereditary chiefs, would learn to regard him as the head of the nation; and he might hope, as the event proved, that his popular manners, and the courage, activity, vigilance, and other military virtues which he possessed, would impress all ranks with respect, and strongly attach his soldiers to his person....[99]

Ahmad Shah's heirs continued this cultivation of royal mystique, both with regards to the Afghan tribesmen as well as foreign powers such as the EIC. The use of titles when relating to foreign powers was an especially important performative assertion of the Saddozai's royal status.[100] Ahmad Shah's successors continued to employ the Persian epithet of the 'Shadow of God on Earth' as one of their titles.[101] The Durrani Empire's success under his leadership largely achieved the exclusive assertion of Saddozai regality, so much so that Elphinstone commented, '[n]o other family but that of Saddozai could pretend to the crown with the smallest chance of success as long as the Doorraunees[sic] maintain the ascendancy, and no other Suddozye [*sic*] could contend with a descendant of Ahmad Shah'.[102] This royal prerogative was recognized externally as well as internally, with Ranjit Singh referring to Dost Muhammad Khan simply as *sardār* in correspondence rather than *amīr*.[103] When the Barakzai, a numerically superior clan, began to compete with the Saddozai rulers for power by the turn of the nineteenth century, they did not do so openly.

The Barakzai, whom the British later characterized as 'royal usurpers,[104] began to wrest power away from the Saddozai monarchs under Payinda Khan, vizier to both Timur Shah and Zeman Shah.[105] This competition climaxed with Fath Khan, Payinda Khan's son, who positioned himself as Afghanistan's power broker as Shah Mahmud's vizier. His execution in 1818 by *Shahzadeh* Kamran, Mahmud's son, turned the hitherto internecine rivalry for the throne into a civil war between the Saddozai and Barakzai clans.[106] When the Barakzai *sardārs* emerged victorious, they refrained from forwarding themselves as royal aspirants.[107] The deeply ingrained respect for royal status and its association with the Saddozai monarchy amongst the Durrani, and wider Pashtun population, prevented the Barakzai *sardārs* from claiming the mantle of royal legitimacy outright. Despite their defeat and exile to Herat, Shah Mahmud and Kamran maintained their claims to royal legitimacy through their use of titles.[108] Just as Ahmad Shah Durrani found himself constrained by the legacy of the Safavid shahs, so too were the victorious Barakzai prisoners of the past.

By associating royal authority with one tribe, the Afghan shahs limited access to that authority in the same way the Pashtun limited tribal membership – through the idiom of genealogy. It therefore became incumbent on any claimant of that authority to either justify his authority through descent or overturn this theory of legitimization altogether. In this way, the latent tension between the egalitarian ethic of the *Pashtūnwâlî* and the Saddozai royalism was reconciled through the genealogical idiom central to Pashtun identity. The victorious Barakzai *sardārs*, though members of the Durrani tribal confederacy, could not fit themselves into the genealogical idiom of Saddozai descent. Unable to claim royal legitimacy, they were forced to abandon it in favour of other sources of legitimacy. The Barakzai sought to supplant Afghanistan's other normative orders with one they could employ for their own legitimization. They thus turned to the religious idiom.

Dost Muhammad Khan

Dost Muhammad Khan asserted his claims to political and moral authority of the offices of Afghan leadership at the moment of their collapse. A younger half-brother of Fath Khan, Dost Muhammad found himself in control of Kabul by 1826, and Ghazni and Jalalabad by 1834. His singular control of the former royal capital stood in stark contrast to his Barakzai competitors who shared control of Kandahar and Peshawar. It also made him the most powerful ruler emerging from the Afghan civil war (*c.* 1818–1826). Yet he, more than any of his predecessors, faced the full weight of the competing and increasingly contradictory norms of kingship.

By the mid-1820s when the external opportunities for plunder had ceased, the fractured nature of the Afghan body politic and derelict state of Afghan cities made the manageable tensions within the adopted Safavid political theory unbearable. His inability to distribute plunder, as well as the fact his mother was a Shi'a Qizilbash, made Dost Muhammad's tribal legitimacy suspect.[109] Additionally, his Barakzai descent alienated him from the legitimizing language of Saddozai genealogy and associated royal charisma. Dost Muhammad therefore attempted to create a new basis of legitimacy, primarily Islamic in nature. But Dost Muhammad's efforts to construct a facade of Islamic legitimacy relied on his weaknesses rather than his strengths.

With Afghan realms under threat from within and without, Dost Muhammad attempted to capitalize on these threats by casting them in religious terms. The war against the Sikhs over Peshawar was thus transformed from a dynastic struggle to a *jihād* against the infidels. Although past rulers had attempted to gain support in their contests against Ranjit, nobody was as successful at religiously sanctifying this fight as Dost Muhammad. He proved himself religiously committed at the Battle of Nowshera in 1823, commanding *ghāzīs* against Ranjit's French-trained *Fauj-i Khaus*. Sayyid Ahmad Barelwi's efforts at *jihād* maintained the tone of religious fervour at a time when direct confrontation between Dost Muhammad and Ranjit Singh had subsided.[110] But Barelwi's use of Islamic idiom expanded Dost Muhammad's lexicon of legitimacy. Dost Muhammad returned with renewed energy to the struggle against the Sikhs following his narrow defeat of Shah Shuja's attempt to regain the throne in 1834.

Unsettled by the re-appearance of a former Saddozai monarch directly challenging his legitimacy, Dost Muhammad's resumption of hostilities against Ranjit Singh must be understood as an attempt to strengthen his legitimacy in the eyes of his tribal subjects. He adopted the title of *amīr al-mu'minīn* and formally declared a *jihād* against the Sikhs.[111] His adoption of the Arabic title *amīr*, in lieu of the more traditional Persian title *shâh*, marked a definitive rejection of the Persianized, or more specifically, Safavid, norms of kingship employed by his predecessors. Charles Masson, the Company news-writer in Kabul, related his coronation ceremony:

> Dost Mahomed Khan, in the 4th of this month, repaired to a spot called siah sung, where amid a concourse of his troops and inhabitants of Kabul, a son of Meer Weiss [head religious authority of Kabul] repeated prayers and read the Kotbah, conferring on him the title of Ameer ul Momundeen Dost Mahomed Ghazie.[112]

To powerfully visualize the Islamic legitimacy the ceremony enveloped him in, Dost Muhammad donned the *khirqa-i mubaraka*, a piece of the Prophet's cloak given to Ahmad Shah by the Tuqay-Timurid rulers of Bukhara.[113] Their previous use of the *khirqa* in ceremonial legitimization endowed Dost Muhammad's coronation with Timurid resonances.[114] In addition to the customary reading of the *khutba* in his name, Dost Muhammad also had coins struck with an inscription about his newly declared *jihād*.[115] Masson reported that over 100,000 *ghāzīs* flocked to his call.[116] His ability to rally such numbers independent of the obligations of *sardārs* freed him of reliance on their troop contributions and gave him an important source of authority.[117] Yet his success at mobilizing his tribesmen also proved his demise. His meagre resources could not support such a massive number of men and Dost Muhammad was forced to abandon his *jihād* before definitively engaging the Sikhs.[118]

Dost Muhammad Khan's turn towards a religiously defined ideal of leadership, epitomized through this adoption of the title *amīr*, opened a Pandora's box. It challenged established ideas of political authority with new Islamic norms. By adopting the religious idiom of legitimization, Dost Muhammad hoped to escape the more restrictive language of Saddozai genealogical descent, thus broadening the field to claimants of royal authority. Aspirants no longer needed to be Saddozai, or at least proclaimed servants of the Saddozai cause, but rather they simply needed to be Muslims. While in the short term it rallied support amongst tribesmen, it also created leadership opportunities for others. Through his political skill, Dost Muhammad maintained an effective monopoly on the invocation of Islamic rhetoric in resisting initially Sikh, and later, British, aggression. With his defeat by and eventual surrender to the British, however, royal leadership of resistance lay disgraced.

In its stead, tribal and religious leaders led the fight against the Company and its Saddozai puppet Shah Shuja, weakening the independence of Afghan kingship.[119] The British invasion thus proved a severe reversal for the independence and authority of the monarchy.[120] Dost Muhammad's defeat reinforced the moral fault lines of the Afghan political community and its leadership. Tribalism, royalism and Islam failed to individually or collectively establish a firm foundation on which Afghan authority could rest. Instead, their exclusivist tendencies and mutual contradictions encouraged the dispersal of authority to the cost of the emerging Afghan state. Despite Dost Muhammad's best efforts, the circle of Afghan kingship remained to be squared. The attempts of Afghan shahs to construct an independent foundation for their authority collapsed like a house of cards, and its re-assertion remained precarious until the reign of Abdur Rahman Khan in the late nineteenth century.

VII. Conclusion

The three normative orders shaping Afghanistan's socio-political universe – tribalism, Islam and royalism – served as the bases for the legitimation of political authority. Yet when combined with the political legacy bequeathed them by the Safavids, they proved a combustible and unstable mix. Claimants to the mantle of Afghan rule found themselves as heirs to a foreign political tradition they adapted to meet their own legitimizing needs. Durrani shahs, starting with Ahmad Shah, cultivated a regal aura not only about his person, but also about his clan, the Saddozai, as an alternative pillar of institutional stability. The alienation of plunderable wealth through the contraction of the Durrani Empire forced the Saddozai monarchy into an economic crisis which served to accentuate the tensions within its legitimizing political theory. The Saddozai loss to the Barakzai *sardārs* made this position untenable and Dost Muhammad was forced to turn to other sources of political legitimacy, especially Islam. Thus by the time the British invaded Afghanistan in the spring of 1839, Afghan political authority and the ideas sustaining it suffered from a severe crisis.

The urbanization of Afghan political authority further upset the equilibrium of the Afghan socio-political universe. Cities' economic importance was offset by their un-tribal and un-Islamic character. While funding political authority, they failed to provide a coherent religious sanction and in fact undermined shahs' tribal legitimacy. This conundrum was further compounded by the royal aura and self-begetting legitimacy held by the Saddozai clan. While Afghan rulers could and did turn to religious ceremony to bestow legitimacy, the lack of institutionalized religious authority underpinning such ceremony made their effect capricious and their value short-lived. Afghan kings were severely handicapped not only by their inability to legitimize their political authority, but also more pointedly by the lack of a coherent and universally accepted theory of kingship. Their tenure in office was thus rendered as transitory as their source of legitimacy was ambivalent.

The urbanization of the political authority of the Afghan state, a consequence of the political economy, was a truly extraordinary phenomenon. It created a legacy which continues to be felt in Afghanistan today. With this urbanization, the central Afghan state became little more than a Persianized governmental sphere restricted to its cities and connected by the trade routes between them. The areas outside this restricted sphere were largely left to their own devices as the state rarely had the resources to counter the hostility its incursions to these areas inevitably provoked. Thus the state model constructed by Durrani elites was extremely narrow in both focus and competence. It was and largely remains an urban phenomenon claiming at most suzerainty over Afghanistan's social ecology.

The instability of Afghan leadership created a seemingly anarchic environment the British perceived to require external intervention to mediate. This intervention became imperative as British strategic calculations sought to mould Afghanistan as a buffer state central to the defence of Company territory in the northwest. As for many societies, the Afghan's colonial encounter proved extremely disruptive. Much of that encounter, however, was felt indirectly, save the three years of occupation during the First Afghan War. Despite the Company's physical distance, the influence it exerted over the region nonetheless had a formative effect. The British, viewing the Afghans through their own strategic calculations and with an intellectual horizon bounded by the Elphinstonian episteme, considered Afghanistan a monolithic tribal kingdom similar to those they had dealt with before.

This, the Afghans patently were not. Their unique location, linking South, Central, East and West Asia exposed them to a wide array of pressures, political and cultural, from virtually every direction. Equally, the British were not a monolithic entity suffering simply from a fundamental misunderstanding of the Afghans. Rather, as the preceding chapters demonstrated, within the ranks of the Company, there were variable understandings and misunderstandings of the Afghans changing over time. These perceptions were driven not only by knowledge gaps and prejudices, but also by occasionally incisive and voluminous intelligence. By the 1830s, however, the British official mind had constructed a version of reality it proved unwilling to depart from, despite evidence to the contrary. In this reality, the Afghans were little more than pawns in the larger Anglo-Russian rivalry evolving on the Central Asian plateau.

The failure of the British policy establishment to navigate the changing contours of the Afghan polity, a dynamic entity in the midst of fundamental change, ensured their inability to co-opt the Afghans into their imperial system. By focusing their energies on a slim segment of the Durrani elite, they ignored Afghan agency and relegated it to an antagonistic position where the only way it could assert itself was through resistance. Thus by marginalizing Afghanistan, the Company empowered it, but in a wholly negative way. Afghanistan continued to exert a powerful, yet largely ignored, effect over British India, requiring the Company to invest resources to bolster its containment from their imperial order. As the previous two chapters have demonstrated, the British saw Afghanistan as a buffer state not only against a phantom Russian threat, but against the more pressing reality of an expansionary Sikh state. Such calculations, however, failed to account for the dynamic socio-political environment of the Afghan kingdom.

The Afghans, having been propelled from the position of subjects to that of sovereigns, attempted to define the norms of legitimate political authority, and with it the nature of the emerging Afghan political community. British intervention in the perceived chaos of Afghan political order proved disastrous not only for their own imperial concerns, but retardant to the growth of an independent Afghan state. Afghanistan was not integrated into the British imperial system, but instead excluded from it. So it would remain until at least the end of the nineteenth century when it was transformed into a British fiscal colony. But the political exclusion of Afghanistan was based upon more than simply the Company's decision to disengage. As importantly, the Afghan economy was subject to massive changes which were economically isolating it from the emerging global order. Collectively, these elements transformed Afghanistan from an imperial buffer state to a contained barbarian beyond.

5

Camels, Caravans and Corridor Cities

The Afghan Economy

I. Introduction

The political crisis faced by contestants for the leadership of the Afghan political community was not simply a consequence of the interventions, or rather inventions of British colonial knowledge. Rather, it was driven as much by changes reshaping the Afghan, as well as global economic landscape at the time. By the end of the eighteenth century, the once great Muslim land empires of Central and South Asia had fallen and the caravan trade connecting them had largely collapsed. In their place, formerly marginal European traders stepped into the breach, establishing the economic foundations of colonial rule. This dynamic and massive shift in the channels of international trade, and the concurrent rise and fall of imperial fortunes, has long attracted scholarly attention. While most of that attention has focused on the better-documented rise of the European maritime empires, their later successes cannot be understood apart from the earlier fall of the Muslim 'gunpowder empires' and the marginalization of their successors.[1] The processes were intimately linked.[2]

To understand the growth and expansion of the East India Company (EIC), one must look to the degeneration and decay of the Mughal Empire and its successor states, as well as analyse the political and economic upheavals affecting Central Asia. Placing the rise of the heirs of South Asian political hegemony in the context of the decline of the powers they supplanted adds a unique perspective on the order these political entities created. While the Company's economic ascendancy has been thoroughly studied, the effect of that ascendancy on the inland economies linked to South Asia's has received less attention.[3] The Company's focus on maritime trade, integrating South Asia into a globalising economy dominated by the British, its vastly different cultures of governance and consumption, and its revenue demands all contributed to the eclipse of the formerly thriving caravan trade linking South Asia with its Asian neighbours through Afghanistan. Changing flows of international finance and Indian consumption largely

110

drove this latter process. At the juncture of these two trends lay, in large part, the explanation for British ascendancy and the concurrent collapse of the post-Mughal successor state system.

Not until the last quarter of the eighteenth century did the short-distance caravan trade patterns surviving the earlier breakdown of regional trade patterns succumb to the pressures of political instability, changing consumer tastes, and competition from European colonial powers.[4] This final collapse marked the beginning of Afghanistan's exclusion from the emerging modern global order of the nineteenth century. The crisis faced by the Afghan economy at the beginning of the nineteenth century was different both in origin and kind than that faced by its Muslim imperial predecessors at the beginning of the eighteenth century. An examination of Afghanistan's economic exclusion is necessary because of its continued influence on the British imperial and larger modern global order solidifying at this time. Afghanistan's net contribution to these larger economic systems may have been negligible, but the cost of its containment was not. Although peripheralized, it retained the potential to disrupt the global economic order.

Afghanistan stood as a corridor of trade and culture, rather than a coherent and unified political entity during the early nineteenth century, supporting a flexible and easily identifiable network of economic interchange channelled through well-established routes. Physically linking China, Central Asia, Persia and India, virtually all the trade of this commercial region was forced to pass through it. Consequently, an active short-distance trade continued in the face of the collapse of the long-distance caravan trade, acting as the life-blood of a contracted, yet still vibrant regional economy. The routes of this trade were multiple, sharing only their passage through Afghanistan. This multiplicity of channels ultimately worked to the advantage of merchants in a politically unstable environment, offering them alternate commercial avenues. Likewise, this diversity reinforced the localized character of political control in Afghanistan.

The breakdown of central authority with the dissolution of the Durrani Empire was largely based on the closure of the window of economic opportunity formerly supporting the Durrani court. The political economy of plunder no longer provided the necessary resources to rule as external opportunities for plunder steadily constricted. As Afghan rulers were forced to look internally for sources of plunder with which to buttress their rule, they found their ability to tap into indigenous sources of wealth limited. Unless a ruler could establish hegemony over all the potential trade routes, a task beyond the meager resources of any early nineteenth-century Afghan ruler, one of their most important revenue sources, trade duties, remained subject to a redirection of trade, undermining their power by starving their treasuries. These trade duties formed the basis of the Afghan political economy and are crucial to any understanding of the contemporary landscape of control.

The Afghan economy was extremely sensitive to external shocks and changes in the economies it transited to. The massive convulsions experienced by the north Indian economy, including the deep depression it entered in the late 1820s overwhelmed its northern feeder economy. The Afghan economy's poor ability to retain trade wealth, previously offset through plunder raids into north India, propelled its political institutions towards a near-continuous crisis in the early part of the nineteenth century. The subsequent breakdown of the Afghan political economy and authority encouraged British policy-makers, who perceived such instability as a threat to their own security, to intervene. When their attempts to exert political influence through economic paramountcy failed, the British were forced to either take more drastic measures or abandon the game altogether. The exogenous shocks precipitated by changes in the global economy combined with the internalization of plunder to undermine the Afghan transit economy.

Afghanistan's economic and subsequent political collapse had important repercussions for the EIC, and consequently for the larger global order. To the British, Afghanistan was, in modern jargon, a failed state. This failure, however, was in a relative sense for Afghanistan continued to be a viable social, economic and political formation despite its lack of European state structures. Examining failed states such as Afghanistan is important because although largely excluded from the modern global order, they continued to effect it. The Company strategy of marginalizing Afghanistan aimed at minimizing and containing those effects. To maintain that containment, the British were forced to act. In order to understand how they arrived at such a position, it is first necessary to look at the convulsions transforming both the global and Afghan economies.

Fundamentally, Afghanistan's exclusion from the modern global order was driven by changes in the patterns of global and regional economic intercourse. Afghanistan was representative of contemporary societies on the fringe of incipient European colonial empires, and thus provides a case study with analytical lessons for similarly situated areas. This chapter discusses the specific factors shaping the Afghan economic model, including considerations of ecology, political community and institutions, and economic resources. Pre-eminent amongst these factors were the networks of merchant-traders who participated in the Afghan transit economy. These networks linked Afghanistan to the shrinking commercial world of which it was once a centre. They enabled its continuing participation in a changing global economic order for a time, and thus assured a modicum of stability in its political economy. The chapter's conclusion examines the Afghan model at the end of the period, as transformed by the factors detailed earlier. It also places Afghanistan's economic fortunes in a broader argument, linking its descent towards economic obscurity with its fall from political grace.

II.   The Afghan transit economy

The Afghan economy of the early nineteenth century represents a type of transit economy common throughout much of the early modern global order. Trade based, with merchant networks providing credit services to a cash-starved economy, the wealth of these transit economies was largely derived from their location between larger political economies. As through trade in the main generated income, capital was highly mobile and little retained within the economy. These economies remained largely under-monetarized, forcing them to rely on the credit provided by merchant networks.[5] Afghanistan's produce was almost solely agricultural, with pockets of relatively concentrated urbanization supported by surrounding sedentarized peasantry producing agricultural surplus. Yet with the important exceptions of the fruits from the Kabul, Hari Rud and Peshawar valleys, much of this surplus came in the form of dry grain, not a wealth-producing export sector of the economy. Although this sector proved a mainstay of the Durrani tax-base during the eighteenth century,[6] the breakdown of unified political order in the early nineteenth century alienated much of this surplus from central governmental coffers, forcing Afghan rulers to increasingly rely on its transit trade.

The main actors in this type of transit economy were merchant-traders, who thus played a key role in shaping the political economy. The merchants' political independence valued commercial as well as physical flexibility as cardinal virtues. Their ability to both survive and flourish in the face of commercial competition and political intransigence, if not hostility, was primarily a consequence of their adjustment strategies to changing market conditions. These strategies were based on commercial intelligence, a premium in the merchant-trader networks. Many of these networks maintained informal information orders far surpassing anything early colonial regimes could support either in terms of speed or quality of information dissemination. The bazaar rumours the British so disdainfully ignored after establishing their power in India sat at the heart of that system. As the economy was based in the main on credit and thus confidence, information was a key commodity, making it in many ways an information economy.

Earlier scholars derisively characterized this type of merchant-dominated, transit economy as 'peddler economies' and broadly created the impression it dominated the world outside Europe.[7] While recent scholarship has refuted such assertions, the negative connotations of these earlier arguments obscure the sophisticated credit networks and trade patterns developed in these transit economies.[8] They linked together regional economic blocs, and were thus effected by changes in those blocs. The breakdown of Afghanistan's transit economy was both a cause and consequence of the economic disruptions and realignments experienced by its trading partners through the eighteenth and early nineteenth centuries. Afghanistan's peripheralization marked its permanent exclusion from re-constituted trade networks in a fundamentally changed economic landscape. This happened again and again as European intrusion initially disrupted and then reconstituted major economic areas through colonial control, excluding the transit economies and trade networks formally supplying the larger economies. Afghanistan's experience was therefore a precursor of what awaited other colonial pariahs, once central to regional economic intercourse and subsequently excluded by European imperialism.

The Balkans, the Levant, Russian and Chinese Central Asia, and the Sudan had similar merchant-dominated transit economies exemplified by Afghanistan.[9] These were areas where penetration of central state authorities and power was limited, often physically restricted to cities as points of duty collection. Political authorities were increasingly dependent on those duties as external plunder opportunities constricted. When those duties failed to provide the necessary monies for the maintenance of political order, 'anarchy' inevitably ensued. Yet Afghanistan provides a case study not only for the economy of plunder, but for the process of peripheralization as well. Many of these areas were central transit areas of the old regional transit economies which European intrusion largely laid to rest. The slave trades in the Sokoto caliphate and Mahdist Sudan were particularly important economic activities for these regions, supplying not only local markets but also the Atlantic and Indian Ocean slave trades.[10] Increased colonial penetration and the subsequent curtailment of the trade economically and politically destabilized indigenous rulers. Such destabilization invited further colonial involvement in order to quell the consequent disorder.

These involvements came at a cost, however, which colonial states soon decided outweighed their potential benefits. Thus, rather than fully integrating these regions into the globalising economy of the nineteenth century, dominated as it was by rival European empires, these empires decided to cordon these areas off from their imperial orders. While the Afghan state was largely paid for in the late nineteenth century by the British subsidy and transformed into a 'fiscal colony' of British India, it was not integrated into the British imperial order.[11] Its fiscal subservience allowed the British a modicum of control whereby they purchased an acceptable level of order beyond their frontier, containing any potential disturbances outside the British imperial realm. The subsidy did not buy the Afghans in, but rather bought them off in order to keep them out. As in Afghanistan, British defeats in the Sudan prompted a re-assessment of imperial strategy, leading to the Sudan's temporary exclusion rather than integration into the imperial edifice.[12] Ultimately these regions suffered a fate similar to Afghanistan, with their indigenous economies destroyed through the movement of trade patterns and changing consumer tastes. Their economic collapse elicited a response from imperial powers, some of which were successful at establishing colonial regimes, and some of which failed. Yet even in the cases of colonial failure, these areas were forced into a position of dependency which shaped their subsequent political and economic evolution.

As with other areas of the Afghan story, there are massive gaps and silences in the historical record. One must therefore extrapolate from the records available, as well as from the broader trends affecting the region as a whole. The colonial archives offer a mixed picture of both spatial and temporal pockets of vibrancy juxtaposed with pockets of decline and stagnation. Given the extreme fluidity of the Central Asian caravan trade and the corridor character of Afghanistan in particular, this is unsurprising. Merchants easily re-directed their trade when political circumstances and economic opportunities warranted. This allowed some of the numerous trade corridors through Afghanistan and their associated nodal cities to boom while others simultaneously experienced severe economic decline. While the intensity of the decline varied from place to place, it was pervasive in absolute terms as Afghanistan found itself excluded from neighbouring markets. The seemingly incessant political instability of the first quarter of the nineteenth century, the Indian economy's deep recession in the 1820s–1830s, and the fundamental shifts in regional and global consumption cultures ensured the continued caravan trade served a shrinking market.

Afghanistan's economic health fundamentally depended on its South Asian neighbours, making it necessary to contextualize events beyond the Khyber with changes in South Asia. One of the transformative events in the South Asian economy, which had enormous ramifications beyond the Indus, was the East India Company's withdrawal of patronage from the Indian economy between 1820 and 1850.[13] This self-enforced removal compounded the pressures Company governance placed on the Indian economy. Its revenue demands were voracious, and the British administration prided itself on the variety of revenue settlements it authored to strip yet more surplus from the Indian cultivator. Much of the Company's appetite stemmed from the needs of its military establishment, and its structures of governance shared much with the military fiscalism of Mughal successor states which dominated the eighteenth century.[14] The pronounced commercial orientation of these successor states, allowing bankers increased access to state revenue flows controlled by scribal state bureaucracies, created new opportunities for capital investment which coincided with shifting patterns of consumption. One of the major recipients of such capital investment was the EIC, which was financed as much by indigenous as by British capital.[15]

The Company, however, definitively broke with the tradition of post-Mughal successor states, withdrawing from economic patronage from the late 1820s onwards. The Company's withdrawal restricted access to state fiscal resources, with the delineation of 'public' and 'private' resources separating 'indigenous capital from the institutions of state fiscalism'.[16] It compounded this by closing former Mughal mints while simultaneously raising its revenue demands in specie, creating a liquidity crisis in much of north India. By abrogating tax-farming, the Company virtually destroyed the economic basis of local elite consumption. It ceased procuring north Indian cloth, undermining the productive sector. At the same time, its establishment of political supremacy denied indigenous rulers the opportunity of plunder and war booty, which served as important stimuli to local economies. The burgeoning international depression and consequent trade crisis in the 1830s and 1840s meant the overall contraction of the Indian economy during this period thus retarded the growth of new consumption patterns. By the time this growth re-emerged in the mid-1840s, British manufactures flooded the Indian market creating new elite consumption patterns.[17]

The Company's effective withdrawal of state patronage from the South Asian economy severely distorted the Afghan transit economy, compounding the crisis it faced. The Company left the field to Indian merchants who were too under-capitalized and thus unable to meet the changing demands of the Indian and international markets.[18] Its withdrawal created a financial and cultural crisis unresolved until the inundation of the subcontinent with British manufactures. Consequently, the dependent Afghan economy was starved of South Asian capital which instead turned to opportunities within the north Indian economy created by the Company's retreat. This was evidenced by the changed migration patterns of Hindu merchant-bankers; for instance, in 1813 there were eighty documented *marwaris* merchants in Calcutta. By 1833, their number had risen to over 600.[19] By removing itself before the effects of England's industrialization began to be felt in the subcontinent, the Company created a void in the north Indian economic landscape. This void was filled by the Company's incessant revenue demands, which failed to either be satiated or abate. Thus the Afghan transit economy, formerly servicing a South Asian economy with key consumer goods such as horses, fruit and mercenaries, suffered from a collapse in demand and the diversion of resources to Company coffers.

The Afghan and Central Asian transit economies relied heavily on South Asian credit networks. Shikarpuri and Multani banking houses had, over the preceding two centuries, established an extensive financial network throughout Central Asia, Persia and Afghanistan.[20] Their representatives, known as *hindkis*, numbered as many as 8000 in early modern Afghanistan.[21] These merchants provided the credit system required by cash-starved economies. Most of these banking houses were family businesses, with the satellite branches scattered throughout the region and run by members originally sent out from these two cities. Shikarpuri and Multani merchant-bankers had an established presence as far afield as Astrakhan in southern Russia.[22]

These merchants represented two South Asian caste groups, *khattris* and *marwaris*, who generally divided their economic activities along these caste lines, with the former more exclusively involved in trading while the latter were in the main traders and local merchants.[23] These merchants concentrated on a niche market – local, short-distance trade – still profitable despite the collapse of the long-distance caravan trade. Their success in local trade patterns was partly attributable to their capital, but also to their partnership with local merchants. Business cooperatives and partnerships with Afghan merchants, who dominated the land routes through a 'virtual monopoly in transport animals in Multan, Kabul, Qandahar and Herat...', were especially important for those passing through the lands of the Durrani kingdom.[24]

The credit network provided by Shikarpuri and Multani bankers was the nervous system of Central Asian commerce. Charles Masson, writing from Kabul, insisted that 'every horse dealer and fruit seller settles his business in such a manner'.[25] Likewise, Mohan Lal visiting Shikarpur noted, 'you will see all the shopkeepers writing hoondees, or bills of exchange, which you can take in the name of their agents at Bombay, Sindh, the Panjab, Afghanistan, part of Persia, and Russia'.[26] By providing the ability to remit large sums of money through *hundis* to any major trading city in the Central Asian commercial corridor, they gave merchants the ability to trade on credit.[27] This was absolutely essential in a region where the security of trade routes was subject to abrupt and drastic change and merchants were guaranteed the loss of some of their merchandize. Further, the use of credit and bills of exchange in lieu of bullion allowed silver to be traded as a commodity, as well as currency, a significant innovation given the EIC demand.

The Company's insatiable demand for specie was the chief cause of the region's cash deprivation. An 1831 memo attributed the deteriorating terms of trade between India and Afghanistan/Central Asia to high demand for 'the manufactures of England and of the spices and other produce of China and the Easter Islands...'. Additionally, '[t]he European remittances are also a great drain upon them and their own consumption of silver in ornaments, hoarding, etc is very considerable.' These factors combined 'to keep the value of silver in the upper Provinces up at a high rate'.[28] Bombay annually sent nearly a crore (100 lakhs) of rupees to Jaipur, Amritsar, Patiala and other places to be minted, but none to Shikarpur.[29] The scarcity of bullion had differential effects throughout the region. While Bukhara and Kabul minted coins from bullion arriving with the transit trade, smaller centres, such as Kunduz, had very little money in circulation at all. What was in circulation were rupees 'of an Emperor of Delhi dating prior to the age of Nadir [Shah]'.[30] Yet even Bukhara and Kabul, the main centres of trade, were limited in their monetarization, often suffering from a lack of bullion. This lack often led to the debasement of coin, discouraging trade.[31]

The Hindu merchant-bankers shared the credit market with Afghan traders, as well as Armenian, Jewish, Georgian and Persian merchants. Like their *hindki* counterparts, these foreign merchants served as important financial, political and social intermediaries between Afghanistan and the larger world.

The Armenian Christians were particularly important for Europeans in their first dealings with the Afghan court, as well as in Lahore and Bukhara. They served as the conduit for initial European contact with many of the area's Muslim courts, making some Britons who believed the Armenians partisan to the cause of the Tsar nervous.[32]

A small community of Jewish merchants joined the Armenians as an important 'middlemen' minority mediating initial encounters, most notably through trade.[33] These merchant minorities 'helped to integrate various sectors of the Afghan economy while also liking local resources to distant markets'.[34] They also provided local potentates with important economic resources in the forms of loans, taxes and forced extortions. Their wealth, foreignness and status as religious minorities ensured all these groups suffered differing degrees of prosecution and violence. Their complete exclusion from the Durrani kingdom was as practically impossible as their complete integration. Pashtun rulers thus had to finely balance their cooperative dependence on such minorities with outright, forceful exploitation.

The Afghans demonstrated a greater willingness to extend credit than their Hindu counterparts. Arthur Conolly, during his travels to Quetta, remarked, he 'saw few bonds given; the Hindoos did not fail to demand them, but in their dealings with each other, the Affghaun [*sic*] merchants did no more than strike a hand in the presence of witnesses'.[35] Part of the reason for the Afghan merchants' greater willingness to extend credit was the protection afforded to them by their membership of the Islamic *umma*. Most of the cities of the Central Asian trade corridor maintained a differential tax rate for Muslim and non-Muslim traders, ensuring the actual movement of goods remained in the hands of Muslim caravan merchants. The *hindkis* offset this handicap, however, with their more extensive credit network. Afghan merchants could rival the Shikarpuri network only in parts, not over the entirety of the Central Asian trade corridor. Communally based financial and trade networks at times competed, and at other times cooperated with one another to service and profit from the Central Asian corridor trade. These networks specialized where necessary and generalized where possible, taking advantage of the political landscape to exploit economic opportunities.

Easy credit, coupled with high profit margins, accounts for the relative vibrancy of trade during a period of political instability. The willingness of Afghan merchants to grant credit was based, at least in part, on their ability to re-route trade in order to minimize risk. The need to minimize risk was reinforced by the absence of insurance in the Central Asian trade network,[36] an absence in marked contrast to neighbouring markets such as the Punjab where the Multani merchant-bankers employed insurance called *hurda*.[37] Yet merchants in the Central Asian trade, denied the formal institution of insurance, simply built it into their trading patterns.[38] They undertook riskier ventures, and more of them, promising higher profit returns if they succeeded. Shikarpur and Central Asian merchants expected a minimum profit margin of twenty-five to fifty per cent, while their European counterparts were satisfied with returns of less than ten per cent.[39] Central Asian merchants flooded the channels of trade in the expectation that their profit margins were high enough for the goods that did get through compensated for those seized and lost.

The paradoxical scarcity of bullion within and abundance of it flowing through Afghanistan accounts for the flourishing system of *hundi* credit operating throughout the Central Asian trade corridor. The bullion trade created the necessary confidence underwriting the credit system. Yet the credit economy was a fairly circumscribed, including only the merchant community, and occasionally travellers. Dr James Gerard, Alexander Burnes' travelling companion in 1831–1833, related his dealings with and reliance on *hindkis* for bills of credit to pay their expenses. He insisted the name of the East India Company was sufficient to instil confidence in merchants as far as Bukhara.[40] However Gerard portrayed the traders as sceptically amused when he expounded the values of national debt, a scepticism undoubtedly borne of rulers' proclivity to consider loans donations.[41] Consequently, the Central Asian credit network moved bullion to safer locations as quickly as possible, ensuring little was retained in the Afghan transit economy.

The mercantile independence of the region's trade system had important repercussions on Afghanistan's political stability because of its effects on governments' revenue streams. As the goods of the caravan trade fell out of favour in the Indian market and political stability disintegrated into an apparently chaotic abyss of tribal infighting, trade through Afghanistan suffered. Routes long serving the Central Asian and Persian caravan trade, as well as the Afghan trade, fell into disuse, replaced by routes through more stable areas, in some cases readily exploitable by new forms of cheaper technology such as steamboats. The permeability of Afghanistan as a trade corridor allowed merchants, especially networked merchants such as Shikarpuri bankers with connections throughout Central Asia, to redirect their merchandize away from unstable cities reached by unsafe routes. The complementarity of routes meant that trade could quickly shift to another route when political instability threatened.[42] Merchants were adept at adapting to fluid political and economic situations on the ground, which created limits as well as opportunities.[43]

The ability of merchants to redirect their trade was based on the character of their transport system – the *kâfilas*. Each *kâfila* was largely autonomous, with a *kafilabashi* or headman leading the conglomerate of merchants who joined the *kâfila* more or less independently. As a mostly self-contained unit, *kâfilas* were under no obligation to remain on a specific route or head for a certain destination. If news arrived the way ahead was unsafe, or that a different bazaar offered better prices, the *kafilabashi* of his own authority could change direction. The costs involved were minimal and the potential benefits very high. The pervasiveness of the Central Asian credit network facilitated both commercial and physical flexibility. Also, as insurance was generally not in use, there was no financial structure tying *kâfilas* to specific routes. Indeed, the lack of insurance encouraged merchants to be more risk-averse as they would have to absorb any losses themselves. While this made the trade system extremely flexible, it made the overall financial system of settled polities unstable.

With trade redirected at little cost or forewarning due to circumstances beyond the control of the bazaars expecting the arrival of *kâfilas*, market instability was endemic. This mercantile freedom created the classic boom and bust cycle of bazaar economies, where the arrival of *kâfilas* depressed prices by glutting the market, while prices steadily rose as time elapsed between the arrivals. The failure of a *kâfila* to materialize sparked a crisis for a trade community, and consequently the rulers who depended on the tax revenue. The inability of political rulers to control, much less direct the flow of trade, placed them at the mercy of the merchants. Long-term political success required the encouragement of trade, in itself requiring protection of property and safe passage through the region, not to mention a reasonable taxation regime. Afghan rulers, however, resorted to the self-defeating practice of seizing merchants and extorting money, as well as plundering caravans when under financial pressure. While this may have borne fruit with individuals, it was unsustainable as a system.

Afghan rulers regularly tapped into the Hindu bankers' credit network, negotiating loans when possible and extorting them when necessary.[44] Ahmad Shah's invasions of north India were financed by these bankers, repaid with the loot he absconded from India which was then circulated as finance capital in area trade.[45] Even the Company, which relied heavily on indigenous capital in its early days, utilized the credit facilities offered by the South Asian financial network.[46] The Kabul disaster of 1842 and subsequent Company withdrawal from Afghanistan did lasting damage not only to its political prestige, but to its credit-worthiness, pushing the South Asian credit network to the brink of collapse. As Hanifi has argued,

> The affairs in Kabul were transforming cooperative relations between North Indian bankers and colonial authorities into exchanges based on negative reciprocity. The anticipated and real losses of transnational merchant capital in Kabul as a result of the British occupation's collapse threatened to force the closure of a number of North Indian banking firms, which in turn seriously destabilized the fiscal integrity of the British government in India.[47]

When *hindkis* proved less than forthcoming as their capital was under threat, Afghan rulers turned to force. As confessional 'others', Hindu merchant-bankers could be despoiled by Muslim rulers with virtual impunity on the grounds of their infidel status. In at least one instance, three Hindu merchants from Ghazni died under torture as Dost Muhammad attempted to extract money from them to finance his *jihād* against Ranjit Singh.[48] Shikarpuri merchant-bankers reportedly 'contributed' Rs. 1,50,000 to Dost Muhammad's coffers in 1834–1835.[49] When pressed, however, Muslim rulers would not refrain from threatening Muslim merchants or even *mullahs* with torture. Dost Muhammad tortured to death a Muslim merchant, Subz Ali, for Rs. 15,000, while Mullah Rahim Shah was only spared a similar fate after the intervention of powerful friends and a 'contribution' of Rs. 4000.[50] Such measures, however, were a sign of desperation and served only to compound rulers' precarious financial situation by alienating those who underwrote the Afghan economy.

The Central Asian credit system, based on the diffuse network of Hindu merchant-bankers, was only part of the region's transit economy. Complementing their financial services were the mercantile activities of the traders who employed the *hindkis*' credit. The region's merchants were chiefly Afghans, with the Ghilzais especially prominent, amongst whom trade was even 'considered rather honorable'.[51] Afghan merchants largely controlled Bukhara's trade after 1820, frequenting the Russian trade fair at Nizhnii Novgorod, where they had 'been so much encouraged by the emperor and the greater part of the Russian trade to Bokhara has fallen into their hands of which the Uzbecks complain bitterly'.[52] As Muslims, all these merchant groups received preferential treatment in the nodal cities of the Central Asian trade corridor. But merchants' individual activities tended to concentrate on specific cities, rather than extensive routes. Few traders undertook the entire journey from Shikarpur and Multan to Bukhara. Instead, they regularly travelled truncated segments of the longer trade routes, such as Kabul to Bukhara, or Shikarpur to Kabul.

For the British, the most important of these merchant-trader groups were the Lohanis, whose homeland lay just south of Ghazni.[53] Often identified in colonial records as members of the *powindah* tribal group, the Lohanis were a nomadic Ghilzai Pashtun tribe whose annual migrations turned into a major trade expedition between Kabul and the cities of the Upper Indus.[54] Unlike with the Afghans, the colonial archives fail to detail their internal organization, their history or their cultural traditions despite their significant dealings with British authorities. Where they do appear extensively in the records is in their economic activities, especially their annual trading expeditions to India. Burnes described their massive annual migrations, dating from at least 1505, in the following terms:

all assemble here [Dera Ghazi Khan], in the end of April, their families having wintered on the banks of the Indus, to pass into Khorasan for the summer. They effect this order by three divisions or 'kirees,' which, I believe, simply mean migrations, and these bear the names of Nasseer, Kharoutee, and Muankhail, which is that of the branches of the tribes conducting them. The first is the most numerous, and with it, go from 5 to 60,000 head of sheep, but it is with the last that Hindoo merchants, and foreigners generally travel. The extensive nature of the traffic will be best explained by observing that the custom house books shew that 5140 camels laden with merchandize passed up this year, exclusive of those carrying the tents and baggage of the people. There are rated at the enormous number of 24,000 camels, the Nasseers having 17,000, the Muankhail 4000 and the Kharoutee 3000.[55]

Their annual caravan from the cities of the Upper Indus to Kabul, which Mohan Lal valued at Rs. 5,00,000, meant the Lohanis virtually dominated both the Multan and Shikarpur trade.[56] At Dera Ghāzī Khan, Dera Ismael Khan, Attock, Shikarpur, Multan and any number of bazaar towns along the river, they traded Afghan fruits, Central Asian silks and horses, Russian manufactures and bullion for British and Indian goods. Leech valued their annual purchases of English goods for the Kabul market at Multan at Rs. 6,00,000.[57] Many of them, dissatisfied with the terms and selection available, continued as far as Bombay before making the return journey to Kabul. Fearing plunder by the Warduks and Waziris as they travelled through the Gomal Pass, the Lohanis moved *en masse* with their goods, families and flocks, protected by thousands of armed men.[58]

The Lohanis provided the key transport link of the Central Asian trade, a fact the British clearly recognized.[59] Many of the participants of the Afghan and Central Asian transit trade sent their goods into the region with the annual Lohani migration *kâfila*, including Sayyid Muheen Shah whom the Company financed to explore the region's trade possibilities.[60] The British themselves relied on the Lohanis to convey the supplies of the Army of the Indus in 1839.[61] British efforts to establish an annual trade mart at Mithankot, part of the Indus Scheme, marked their attempt to incorporate the Lohani into a British trading system.[62] The idea, modelled on the great Russian fair at Nizhnii Novgorod, never rivalled the Tsar's political or commercial investment.[63]

The Russians reportedly invested more the £1,000,000 'for the purpose of damming, banking and otherwise improving' the site of the fair, as well as erecting permanent buildings as warehouses for goods.[64] The lack of British investment at least partly accounts for the lacklustre reaction of the Bombay merchants to scheme, who were anyway suffering from a severe economic downturn in the 1820s and 1830s. The Indus Scheme's collapse little affected the Lohanis' enthusiasm for trade with Company territories, and Alexander Burnes intended to introduce representatives of the group to the Governor-General during his trip to the Punjab in 1838.[65] Despite the courting of the British, the Lohanis retained their commercial independence and continued to play a central role in the caravan trade linking South and Central Asia through Afghanistan.

The Lohanis' semi-nomadic character contributed to their success as traders, making them key 'mediatory traders' who linked the various sedentary merchant groups based in the trade network's nodal cities.[66] Their good relations with other Pashtun, through whose land they passed, proved a key asset in their transportation predominance. This was augmented by their vast camel flocks which gave the Lohanis an independent source of capital. Their relationship with Shikarpuri merchant-bankers was therefore one of equals, and not creditor–debtor. The Lohanis and Shikarpuri merchants ensured and enjoyed the other's comparative advantage on different sides of the caravan passes, offering one another a kind of 'discriminate protection'.[67] The Lohanis, and other 'mediatory traders' like them, provided the key physical link between the nodal cities of the Central Asian trade corridor. Their political and economic independence allowed them to flourish even in times of instability, enabling the continued operation of the Afghan transit economy.

The commercial character of the Lohanis underscores some of the formative characteristics of the Afghan transit economy and Central Asian trading system. The merchant-traders who were the main economic actors remained autonomous, unbeholden to and where possible, uninvolved with any political authority. Within the merchant-trader community, the scope of particular communities' economic activities varied greatly. Some groups, such as the Shikarpuri and Multani bankers, were largely limited by circumstance and discrimination to the financial sector. Others, such as the Lohani, concentrated their skills and resources on the actual movement of goods. Afghan traders, like the Ghilzai, appeared best positioned to straddle both the finance and transport world, with their own communal finance network as well as transportation resources. These communally based trade networks enabled a trade which political instability and the lack of legal infrastructure might otherwise have discouraged. They provided individual traders with a necessary support network, allowing them to negotiate with merchant-traders from other communities with both the power and knowledge of larger communal backing. The Afghan transit economy, linking the Persian, Indian and Central Asian economies, depended on the financial connections these trader networks provided.

III.   Exogenous factors affecting the Afghan economy

Afghanistan's transit economy had long been a conduit of linkage between larger economic blocs in the region, as well as further afield. Its historic role as a transit corridor had survived earlier changes in global patterns of economic exchange, from the slow collapse of long-distance traffic on the famed Silk Road through to the rise and subsequent collapse of the neighbouring Safavid and Mughal Empires. Yet the changes shaping the global economy in the late eighteenth and early nineteenth centuries were of a categorically different magnitude than those of earlier epochs. Revolutions in transport, industry and finance coalesced as European colonial empires expanded around the world in order to reshape trading patterns and networks, fashioning arguably the first truly global economy.[68] Disparities in power, economic and political, between Europe and the rest of the world grew exponentially, and the requirements of European commerce began to shape the economic landscape of locales only remotely touched by its produce.[69] For Afghanistan, the eclipse, subjugation, and integration of the South Asian and Persian economies into a global one dominated by European, and more especially British trade, was to have a profound and long-lasting impact not only on its economic, but also on its political future.

The dislocations accompanying the re-alignment of global patterns of trade, especially changing patterns of silver consumption and supply, severely effected the Afghan economy. In the era before modern credit capitalism reigned supreme, money – the engine of international trade – was based on the value of American silver. As the foundation of the international financial system, fluctuations in the supply or production of American silver had repercussions worldwide. Silver was arguably the first global commodity spawning global patterns of trade. Mined in the Spanish American colonies of Peru and Mexico, purified with mercury from Habsburg mines in Europe, and then shipped around the world, by the late eighteenth century silver was the undisputed life-blood of the world economy. The remarkable changes in the American silver trade at the end of the eighteenth century had enormous, and as yet not fully understood, ramifications for the world's economies.

The largest Asian consumer of American silver by the late eighteenth century was China.[70] China's appetite for silver had important implications for both Asian and British imperial trade, and particularly the East India Company which monopolized the China trade until 1833. Early on, the Company found itself forced to export significant amounts of bullion to China in order to purchase Chinese goods.[71] Following the Company's assumption of the Bengal *dīwān* in 1765, the import of silver to India was discontinued in order to bolster the profitability of its Bengal governance. The Company's ban on silver imports and subsequent export of silver collected as tax revenue placed an enormous strain on the north Indian economy, leading some to declare a 'silver famine'.[72]

Yet such declarations do not fit with the reality of India's fiscal health in the early nineteenth century. In summarizing the yearly customs receipts for the China trade with Bombay, the former head of the Bombay customs house portrayed an annual credit of 'treasure' in Bombay's favour.[73] G.E. Trevelyan estimated Bombay's annual credit with China at Rs. 30,00,000–40,00,000, derived mainly from opium export.[74] Further, an examination of India's bullion balance sheet with both Britain and China between 1828 and 1840 shows that only in the years 1831–1833, years of depression in India, did India export bullion – to Britain. Even in the years of the First Opium War, India remained in the black with Chinese bullion imports.[75]

What allowed India to maintain a positive bullion balance *vis-à-vis* China while its economy was eclipsed by that of its imperial metropolitan centre? After all, by 1816, India suffered its first negative trade balance with Britain in textiles, and by 1837 it imported sixty-four million yards of cloth, its export mainstay.[76] While the introduction of opium into the China trade was undoubtedly a key factor, so too was the continued import of bullion into India overland from Chinese Turkistan through Ladakh and Afghanistan. The Elphinstone mission noted this movement of bullion, listing Dutch ducats from Russia and silver imprinted with Chinese stamps as regular items of the Bukhara trade.[77] Silver bullion passed as 'ingots are of pure silver...weighing from 105 to 110 tota and worth from 5.5 to 6 *tomans*'.[78] These *yamboos* (silver ingots) arrived 'chiefly from Yarkand either by way of Bokhara or Koondooz, and are used as bullion being melted up for the purpose immediately on importation here'. Minted separately by each Chinese province, the *yamboos* lacked a standard weight or value, although they averaged '195 rupees in Cabool'.[79]

Chinese and Indian demand for silver drove a circular pattern of consumption, moving eastwards by sea, and returning westwards overland through Central Asia and Afghanistan. Yet much of this silver originated from the Zacatecas mines in Mexico, the contemporary source of most of the world's money supply.[80] Mexican silver production reached all time highs at the end of the eighteenth century, with 24 million pesos minted in 1798.[81] By 1804, that number had risen to 27 million pesos and production did not fall until the wars of independence after 1810.[82] While seventy to eighty per cent of that silver was exported to Europe, at least half of the remainder was siphoned directly into the Asian trade via the Manila galleon.[83] Estimates vary widely, from the officially authorized export of 500,000 pesos annually to upward of 5,000,000 pesos a year at production's height.[84]

The Manila–China silver trade, virtually monopolized by the EIC traders after 1755, was estimated at over 1,000,000 Spanish dollars per annum through the eighteenth century, while in 1810 it was reportedly worth 1,550,000 Spanish dollars.[85] Joining the Manila silver was that brought directly from Europe, or rather Mexican silver re-exported from Europe, and Indian silver. Of the 195 tonnes of silver annually re-exported by Europe between 1776 and 1800, approximately forty tonnes was exported to the Asian trade by the EIC, while the Dutch East India Company, the VOC, exported an additional thirty-four tonnes. With twenty tonnes contributed by the Manila galleon, the annual Asian import of silver totalled ninety-four tonnes. This total, however, excludes the silver and gold which percolated to Central Asia through Russia. Despite these years being ones of almost constant European warfare, silver export from Europe dipped only slightly in real terms and virtually not at all in relative terms.[86] The trade was clearly significant to say the least.

China's appetite for silver exerted a considerable pull over the world economy. Between 1752 and 1800, 274 million Mexican pesos were imported to China, with the majority entering China after 1770. Chinese sources refer to a market-wide price inflation of goods coinciding with a massive influx of Spanish silver during this period.[87] The massive increase in American production, and Chinese silver intake, coincided with the north Indian silver 'famine', creating a vacuum for bullion in Central Asia.

North India's insatiable demand for bullion drove Afghanistan's through trade at least partly due to the economics of transport. The low weight to high value ratio made transport of bullion an attractive option for caravan merchants, with cost of transportation roughly equal to that of cloth. Contemporary sources valued the average camel load between 2000–3000 rupees and 4000 dollars, yet these estimates potentially represent a gross undervaluation.[88] In the case of silver ingots, a figure of Rs. 22,000 per camel is arguably more appropriate, based on the weight of the ingots themselves, their value, and Bactrian camels carrying capacity.[89] Shipping bullion overland was nearly as cheap and easy as doing so by sea, creating a viable market of exchange through Afghanistan.

Silver exported from China was joined by bullion pulled southwards from Russia to fulfil India's demand. Bukharan gold *tillas* imported by Kabul in the 1830s were reminted out of Russian, Dutch and Venetian gold ducats, themselves a mainstay of the Russo-Bukharan trade. Russia's limited indigenous gold production was augmented by the Baltic trade, which enjoyed a dramatic increase with the American Revolution.[90] Russia nonetheless suffered from a severe species shortage. The Tsarist government was so concerned by this shortage that not only did it restrict the export of bullion by merchants, but also restricted the export of coin by its own diplomatic missions to the region, forcing the Russian embassy to Bukhara in 1820 to exchange 72,000 Roubles for Dutch ducats in Moscow.[91] It was not until the early 1830s the government lifted the ban on the export of specie, and even then the amount exported by Persian and Central Asian merchants was a source of discomfort.[92]

One can only conjecture at the effect bullion shortages had on Russian policy towards Central Asia. Increased Russian efforts to establish some control over Central Asian trade at a time when Russian bullion was siphoned through the region towards India were likely more than coincidental. This bullion was purchased by Central Asian merchants whose trade at the 1840 fair at Nizhnii Novgorod accounted for forty per cent of Russia's national imports in value.[93] Like Afghanistan, Russia funnelled bullion to the Indian economy, whose insatiable appetite was largely spurred by the Company's revenue demands. But as Indian trade patterns turned to other channels of trade to receive wealth, Afghanistan increasingly found itself excluded and peripheralized from the South Asian economy.

In addition to the Chinese, Russian and Dutch bullion and coin noted by Elphinstone, Persia remitted a substantial amount of precious metals – gold, silver and jewels – to India via Afghanistan. Warren Hastings commented the plunder Nadir Shah treasure absconded with after sacking Delhi in 1739 financed Persian purchases of Company goods until the end of the eighteenth century, ensuring the Company's financial health.[94] Persia's outflow of goods and specie to India was largely financed by a significant inflow from its other trading partners. It imported significant amounts of bullion from Russia, with Armenian merchants introducing more than 300,000 gold ducats into Tabriz by 1821.[95] Persia, however, haemorrhaged bullion faster than Russia, with the Company estimating Persian exports to cover only a fifth of the cost of its Indian imports by the end of the eighteenth century. The balance was covered by bullion.[96] Virtually all of the imported bullion was re-exported to India, with £350,000 exported to India in 1809, and Rs. 34,17,994 (£290,000) arriving from Persia via the Gulf in 1821.[97] These exports through the Gulf failed to account for the unknown amount flowing into Afghanistan, at least some of which undoubtedly continued to India.

In Kabul and Bukhara, Persian, Chinese and Russian bullion flows converged. A limited amount of bullion was minted into rupees and *tillas* respectively, entering the Central Asian cash economy.[98] Dutch and Russian gold coming into the Central Asian trade through Astrakhan, Orenburg and Bukhara proved more important to Afghan financial flows than the dwindling Persian contribution. This bullion covered the trade imbalance created by the import of Indian products by Afghan, Indian and Lohani merchants to Bukhara.[99] Mir Izzat Ullah, Moorcroft's servant and the first demi-official British agent to visit Bukhara, commented on Hindu merchants' practice of buying bullion and sending it back to India, creating a great shortage throughout the region.[100]

The Company records listing the goods traded in Central Asia nearly all mention either Chinese silver ingots or Bukharan and Dutch gold, if not both. While few reports attempted to quantify this trade, those that do portray significant cash remittances. Robert Leech valued annual gold imports to Multan at Rs. 1,00,000, separately listing Rs. 50,000 Bukharan *tillas*. This Rs. 1,50,000 gold import was complemented by Rs. 1,00,000 in silver.[101] By the 1830s, Kabul annually received significant amounts of Bukharan gold *tillas* to cover its northern neighbour's trade deficit. In turn, it remitted this gold to India to cover its own balance of payments shortfall, amounting to as much as Rs. 2,00,000 annually.[102]

Afghanistan's transit economy was effected not only by the changing character of the Company's revenue demands, but also by changing patterns of consumption in its largest export market, India. These changes severely disrupted the Afghan transit economy, and consequently undermined the economic basis of political authority.[103] South Asian consumption patterns underwent a radical disruption with the intrusion of the Company and collapse of the Mughal Empire.[104] Pre-Company consumption goods possessed an ideological value which 'transcended them', while 'modern "positional" goods are self-referential to themselves and to the markets that create demand for them...'.[105] Political and cultural values of pre-Company consumption were mediated through patterns of consumption.[106] The breakdown of the Muslim empires undermined those values which soon found themselves in competition with the European norms espoused by the Company.

One of the most formidable of these norms was capitalism's adherence to market consumption, creating self-referential goods. The symbolism of consumption gave way to the economy of consumption. As one author has argued, 'the conspicuous consumption of the earlier political elite was replaced by the more austere life-style of the British bureaucrats'.[107] Thus India's ruling elite no longer consumed pomegranates from Kabul glorified in court poetry,[108] but cloths from Lancashire devoid of literary or broader cultural meaning. The Mughal rulers' 'political irredentism for Timurid homeland', expressed through 'nostalgic tastes for melons, dried apricots and almonds', was thus replaced by the new elites' efforts to Anglicize their consumption habits.[109]

While bullion had been, and remained a major consumption good in India, there were three other commodities of major importance in the Afghan transit trade. The first was Afghan fruit, which supplied virtually the entire region, most specifically north India. Although the collapse of the Mughal court culture deprived Afghan fruit of much of its symbolic and status value, British travellers hinted the trade continued to flourish. Arthur Conolly observed,

> The whole of Hindoostan is now supplied with dried and preserved fruits from Cabool.... Apples, quinces, and grapes are packed in cotton, and as they are easily damaged, the profit of them is uncertain; but pomegranates, pistachio nuts, almost and dried apricots, figs, raisins, &c., are brought without loss: the demand for them is certain and the profit good.[110]

Even the British continued to consider Kabul fruit a delicacy, although not the status good it once was under the Mughals. The British understood the Indus Scheme as an opportunity to rejuvenate and direct the fruit trade.[111] For instance, Lord Auckland ordered C.M. Wade to forward a diplomatic gift of Kabul fruit from Shah Shuja, newly installed on the Afghan throne, to Calcutta by steamer.[112] Leech estimated Multan annually imported Rs. 10,000 from Kabul, while Ahmedapur and Bhawalpur separately imported Rs. 10,000.[113]

Yet changes in the consumption patterns of north Indian elite had a devastating effect on demand for Afghan fruit. Compounding the fall in demand, political instability and continued warfare undoubtedly retarded production in some of Afghanistan's most fertile regions, such as the Peshawar and Hari Rud valleys. In at least one instance, the people of 'Lookisstan [*sic*]' reportedly cut down their fruit trees rather than pay the new tax levied by Dost Muhammad Khan to face the imminent British invasion.[114] What once had been not only a key economic resource for the Afghans, but more importantly a symbol of cultural refinement in South Asia literally withered on the vine. The public performance of consumption required new goods in order to satisfy the pretensions of a new power in South Asia. Kabul melons were replaced by English clocks, and with the change Indian elites abandoned the Timurid roots of Mughal culture for the Company's decidedly European ones.

The Central Asian horse market was the second market to collapse which had previously accounted for large amounts of trade, with Turkmen horses especially valued.[115] Company interest in the viability of import started in the early 1800s with the dispatch of William Moorcroft, Superintendent of the Company stud, to investigate Central Asian breeding grounds.[116] His death under suspicious circumstances dampened the Company's enthusiasm for the project. By the 1830s, virtually all of the Company's remounts were provided by its stud farms, shrinking the once important horse trade to a mere 600 annually imported to Bombay.[117] While some argued the Central Asian horse trade could provide a considerable savings over remounts from the stud farms, political instability, Company officers' preference for Arabian breeds and the downsizing of the Company's cavalry forces ensured the trade failed to recover in India.[118] The 'military revolution', catalysed by the Company's arrival and success on the subcontinent, ensured the demise of the horse in South Asian warfare, and thus its importance in Indian society.[119]

The 'military revolution' also caused the collapse of Afghanistan's third export mainstay – mercenaries. As discussed in Chapter Three, the early nineteenth century witnessed the reversal of a long-standing inflow of mercenaries, usually cavalrymen, into South Asia's military labour market from the Afghan lands. While this influx of military labour had proven essential for the Mughal successor states competing against one another in eighteenth-century India, the Company's establishment of its political paramountcy transformed these military labourers into a liability. Its successful reliance on European-trained sepoys who used infantry tactics and were employed for a fixed period heralded a sea change in the way warfare was prosecuted on the subcontinent. The freebooting Afghan mercenary entrepreneurs, offering their services to the highest bidder and receiving their pay out of war booty, were frequently left to fend for themselves during the off-seasons of between campaigns. Consequently, they too closely straddled the line separating military campaigning from simple brigandage for the Company's comfort. The regularization of military service by the Company, and its defeat of rival powers, most notably the Marathas, thus put large numbers of former mercenaries, many of them Afghans, out of work.

While this led to difficulties in maintaining order within Company territory, with bands of *dacoits* such as the *thugs* a widespread phenomenon through the 1830s, it also closed off the South Asian military labour market as a potential social safety valve for Afghan society.[120] This labour market had created opportunities for young men to prove their individual valour, as well as earn wealth in the form of booty unavailable in the comparatively poor territory of Afghanistan. With the closure of the market, tensions previously managed through the export of labour, and violence, returned to the Afghan lands. Competition for scarce resources assumed new violence as young men who formerly directed their ambition towards the north Indian plain, either as part of an Afghan raiding party or the South Asian military labour market, returned to face off against one another. Remittances from north India, previously a mainstay of the Afghan political economy, almost completely dried up. The violence marking the Afghan political landscape through much of the early nineteenth century thus coincided with the closure of the South Asian military labour market.

The collapse of Mughal-era commodity consumption created an opportunity for the EIC to substitute new consumption patterns in their place. The Company intentionally cultivated certain patterns while discouraging others. A prime example was the 1765 discontinuation of silver import to India, discouraging silver consumption, while simultaneously encouraging the rise of the opium trade. Opium became one of the most important and profitable parts of the Indian economy. For many Indian merchants, the opium trade served as a primary channel of capital accumulation, while for the British it largely financed their East Asia trade.[121] Its significance for Afghanistan was its exclusively Indian production chain. Unlike silver, it was cultivated and transited wholly through Company territory. The Company could therefore not only regulate supply, removed as it was from the political fortunes of neighbouring indigenous states, but it would also be the sole recipient of the tax receipts the trade generated. The Afghan transit economy was thus excluded from new South Asian trade patterns.

The British saw an opportunity to cultivate new patterns of consumption not only in South Asia, but also in Afghanistan and Central Asia which would place those markets in a position of dependency on British India. The Company initially sought to displace cheaper Russian imports from Afghan and Central Asian bazaars through superior quality and cheaper transport cost.[122] The key to the latter aim was the Indus Scheme.[123] The British wanted to cultivate the consumption of goods traditionally imported to Afghanistan and Central Asia, such as cloth, as well as create demand for new consumer goods such as tea.[124] The trade expedition of Sayyid Muheen Shah was an investigation into demands of Central Asian markets. His successful 'speculation' gave 'ground for believing that English manufactures when bought into competition with the Russian, would, in a few years, completely drive the latter from the markets, not only of Affghanistan [*sic*], but of all Central Asia'.[125] It was later followed by other efforts to gather commercial intelligence.

To cultivate a taste for British manufactures amongst the elite, the Company presented Afghan shahs with British-made telescopes, umbrellas, swords and pistols in place of the more traditional *khil'ats* (robes of honour).

While in ways the Company's preference of offering British manufactures as diplomatic presents was nothing extraordinary, when one considers its assertion of political authority within the Mughal moral universe, the decision assumes an entirely new significance. As well, the timing of the Company's decision to gift European manufactures reflected the changed attitudes within government circles. While there are a number of examples of European manufactures given to Afghan and Central Asian notables before 1830, the Company also continued to give South Asian gifts familiar to Indian and Muslim court norms. Elphinstone presented Shah Shuja an elephant with a *howdah* during his diplomatic mission in 1808–09,[126] while Governor-General Amherst's gifts to Shah Shuja in 1827 included Kashmiri shawls, Indian cloths and an elephant.[127] After 1830, similar examples are more difficult to locate and by 1843 the Company banned its officers from participating in South Asian gifting rituals, such as the giving of *nazr*.[128]

The problems facing the Company's cultivation of new consumption patterns amongst the Afghan elites were twofold. In cultural terms, the Company poorly understood the ritual importance and significance of many of the elite consumption goods it was trying to replace. These goods were often exchanged in what Bernardo Michael describes as 'ethnographic moments', where different cultures and expectations met with no clearly agreed mutual expectations, values and meanings between the participants. Such moments were thus a space for both misunderstanding and innovation where gifts 'uncoupled from their usual semantic moorings...remain[ed] entangled within multiple "webs of significance" spun by each participant'.[129]

One such moment was Elphinstone's reception at Shah Shuja's court. Despite the traditional exchange of *khil'ats*, the ritual of gifting quickly led to misunderstanding and miscommunication. The Afghans complained of the poverty of Elphinstone's gifts, to which he replied 'that the presents were not sent for their value but as a mark of friendship. These presents were got in a hurry and though they may be unworthy of a king they were the best procurable. Nothing can equal the meanness of this complaint...'.[130] He later ascribed the Afghans' complaints to their want of money, despite the fact the mission spent Rs. 2,31,565 (£28,945) on presents to members of Shuja's court.[131] In practical terms, the Afghans had nothing with which to pay for British and Indian imports. The collapse of the Indian market for Afghan exports and transit goods destroyed the main source of funds for the economy as a whole. The Company thus pursued a self-defeating policy, seeking to cultivate new consumption patterns while simultaneously compromising Central Asians' and Afghans' ability to pay for those patterns.

As both a supply and transit economy feeding the larger Indian economy, Afghanistan was particularly vulnerable to fluctuations in the Indian market. Shifts in Indian consumption patterns consequently meant shifts in the sources supplying those patterns. Such shifts could, and did, have devastating effects on secondary economies dependent on Indian demand. As Indian consumer culture moved away from goods originating in and transported through Afghanistan, the Afghan trade economy faced a crisis compounded by political instability engendered by trades' downward spiral. Afghanistan's relative poverty weakened internal demand. Local elites and courts were too poor to support much luxury demand.[132] Its splintered political society also meant the fracturing of the elites' resources. Moreover, the abandonment of Safavid and Timurid norms of legitimacy, and thus court ceremony in favour of a more religiously based concept of kingship, was matched, in the case of Dost Muhammad, by an increased austerity at court.[133] Dost Muhammad's financial distress led him to limit court spending to a meagre Rs. 5000 per month.[134]

Fundamental shifts in consumption patterns thus propelled the decline experienced by the Afghan economy. Exemplifying this process of decline were Kashmiri shawls, one of the most famous and important consumer goods formerly under Afghan control both in terms of production and transport to market.[135] A large and important pre-Company trade in the shawls was driven in the main by their ideological value.[136] Presentation of *khil'ats* was an important visual symbol in Muslim court culture.[137] While Kashmiri shawls did not replace *khil'ats*, they added an important dimension to the gift exchange of visible status goods. Their historically fine workmanship and the unique pashmina wool bolstered their ideological value.

Although Kashmiri shawls constituted one of the most important luxury trades throughout Asia, it suffered severe decline at the beginning of the nineteenth century. Wade reported the number of looms under the Mughals exceeded 30,000, while under the Durranis it had declined to about 18,000. By the 1830s, supposedly oppressive taxation and a fall in demand had reduced the number further to 6000.[138] The collapse of the wealthy Asian court cultures previously supporting the industry was for a short time replaced by European demand, especially French. That demand slackened, however, with the change in luxury taste and the rise of European substitutes, such as manufactured Scottish paisleys. What trade remained centred on the Persian court and the Ottoman *janissaries*. But the Qajars and the Ottomans, with the elimination of the *janissaries*, also eventually turned towards other luxury items as markers of status.[139]

The fall in demand for Kashmiri shawls, and underlying change in consumption culture, was partly a result of a supply shortage. The political instability of Afghanistan, as well as Chinese Turkistan and Ladakh, the key suppliers of pashmina wool, crippled the industry's output.[140] Apart from depressed production, overland transport through Afghanistan increasingly gave way to cheaper and safer sea routes via the Gulf.[141] Kashmir's permanent alienation from the Afghan throne with its loss to the Sikhs in 1818, with its annual remittance of Rs. 40,00,000 to the treasury, devastated the finances of the Afghan rulers.[142] Thus Afghan rulers were deprived of both Kashmir's direct economic resources, as well as the revenue of the important through trade. Political instability combined with concurrent shifts in global consumption patterns away from this once highly valued luxury good to devastate and exclude both the Afghan productive and transit economies. The fate of the Kashmiri shawl trade was repeated time and again, as nearly all the luxury goods Afghanistan's through trade supplied north Indian elite fell out of favour. In place of these Asian luxury goods, modern European positional goods gained ground, both forming and reflecting the Eurocentric tastes of a new Indian elite.

The collapse of demand in South Asia for Afghan goods, or even goods transported through Afghanistan, proved a devastating blow from which it did not economically recover. Combined with the closure of the north Indian plain as a raiding ground for the all-important plunder on which the Afghan political economy and order depended, this collapse propelled the Afghan political community into an almost perpetual state of economic crisis. South Asian demand was itself affected by massive changes taking place in the larger global economy, into which it was becoming more closely integrated. These same changes, however, sent Afghanistan on a course not of integration, but of exclusion. With little in the way of its own resources or products for changing consumer demand, Afghanistan also suffered from political instability which further undermined the one asset it could boast of – its centrality to routes of overland trade throughout the region. Thus as the globalising economy of the nineteenth century took deeper root in the colonies of European empires, Afghanistan was marginalized from an order it could not adapt to.

IV.   Conclusion

Afghanistan was home to a model of economy widespread throughout much of the world at the end of the eighteenth century. The following fifty years fundamentally transformed this Afghan model into a peripheralized and excluded appendage to the emerging modern global economy of the mid- and late nineteenth century. Can the transformation of that model economy reveal anything about what happened to other 'Afghan' economies coming into contact with European imperialism? Although every political society and economy is bound by its own peculiarities, Afghanistan's experiences represent a typology of both model and interaction. As a trade-based economy, Afghan-type economies depended on their trading partners. Events in those partners – political, economic or cultural – inevitably had repercussions on such transit trading societies.

The changes within Indian society during the first half of the nineteenth century are the archetype for similar changes which later occurred in other imperial colonies – the disruption of local economic patterns, the arrogation and attempted monopolization of political authority by the colonial state, and the transformation of indigenous culturally influenced patterns of consumption. For Afghanistan, these factors confluenced at the Khyber with the British ideology of free trade and ascendancy of the Forward School within policy circles. The Company's unwitting disruption of the Afghan political economy, combined with imperial ambitions and concerns of Indian security, compelled the British to attempt to integrate the 'Afghan' economy into the British imperial system. The failure of the imperialism of free trade to accomplish this led to the invasion of Afghanistan in the spring of 1839.

Unlike elsewhere, the British imperial economy had severely disrupted and undermined the Afghan political economy without constructing a viable alternative in its place. Denied the opportunity to either plunder or sell goods on the north Indian plain, the Afghan political economy quickly fell into disarray. Rather than inserting either their political paramountcy or economic dominance, the British refrained from exerting any meaningful influence over Afghanistan until 1839. This diffidence by the British marked Afghanistan's effective exclusion from the imperial world, a process repeated by other imperial powers in other colonial corners of the world. The external shocks experienced by the Afghan economy combined with internal political instability, resulting from the internalization of plunder, to marginalize this once central transit economy. Yet its marginalization did not relegate it to a position of impotence. The British found themselves time and again forced to engage with this peripheral frontier.

While local political instabilities combined with changes in consumption patterns to shrink a revived short-distance caravan trade through Afghanistan by the 1830s, deeper forces shaping the emerging imperial world political and economic order were at play. Afghanistan had been the central corridor for the shipment of massive amounts of goods and bullion between the gunpowder empires constituting the central heartland of the Islamic world. As the political order of the *dār al-Islām* collapsed, and the wealth and power of these empires were subjugated to European interests, Afghan trade routes slid towards redundancy. For a time, they continued to support themselves through a lively local trade. However, this too was financed by through trade mainly between India and Bukhara. When the Forward School decided to capture that trade, its days were necessarily numbered.

The disruptive effect of British ambitions not only profoundly displaced the consumption culture this trade serviced, but also systematically undermined the financial and political structure on which it rested. When the British found they could not successfully penetrate and dominate Central Asia and Afghanistan through trade channels alone, they resorted to military force. The British invasion, just as it was the result of a failure of British strategic calculations *vis-à-vis* the Sikhs, must be understood as a failure of their economic designs for the region, foremost amongst them the Indus Scheme. The British retreat in 1842 marked the end of British encouragement of Central Asian commerce until the late nineteenth century, with the EIC instead openly discouraging any connections, political or otherwise, beyond the Khyber. Unwilling or unable to participate in a political and economic order dominated by the British, the Afghans were marginalized from it, given the necessary resources only to contain its political instability internally, beyond British territories.

6

The Afghan Trade Corridor

I. Introduction

The Afghan model economy was bound together by a physical network of trade routes connecting the corridor cities of Central Asian caravan commerce. These routes were the sea-lanes of the Central Asian steppe, crossing deserts, mountains and the barren wastes of high plateaus to tie the distant cities of Central, South, East and West Asia together. The routes themselves were often ill-defined, passing through the vast rural tracts with tenuously established political order and questionable mercantile safety. Like their sea-faring counterparts, the merchants plying these routes required regular ports where they could re-supply for the onward journey and exchange goods. But the Central Asian and Afghan trade was a short-distance regional trade, allowing merchants to establish a profitable business transiting between two specific points on the Central Asian trade compass, rather than assuming the risk and inconvenience of longer journeys. These merchants remained, for the most part, fiercely independent of political loyalties or obligation. Yet their activities were central to the economic and political stability of the Afghan political community.

The story of caravan trading through the Central Asian/Afghan trade corridor during this period is central to understanding the evolution of the Afghan political entity and its relations with neighbouring economies and polities. While this was, in general, a period of economic decline and contraction, with destabilizing repercussions on centralized political authority in Afghanistan, for some it was also a period of growth and even vibrancy. Although the Afghans were excluded from the emerging globalized order of the nineteenth century, they were not eliminated altogether. Indeed, social, political and economic formations adapted to changing circumstances to preserve both their independence and viability. This story is therefore as much about the survival and constant contestation of indigenous political orders as about their eclipse. In spite of the encroachment of the British and Russian Empires, the Afghan political entity survived, although in a considerably altered form. Even more successfully, the merchant-traders of the Afghan trade corridor accommodated themselves to secure their continued dominance despite fundamental changes to the economic world in which they operated. The examination of this corridor thus offers an understanding of the conditions necessary for survival of politically and economically marginalized groups.

Afghanistan's trade routes were firmly anchored by the nodal cities of the Central Asian corridor which serviced them. This constellation of cities provided both markets in their own rights and convenient stopping points for merchants and goods on their way to the larger bazaars of India, China and Russia, as well as Persia. First amongst these was Bukhara. Its claim as the pre-eminent corridor city of Central Asian trade remained unchallenged throughout this period. Bukhara was the northern embarkation point for the caravan trade passing through Afghanistan, and thus lay at one end of a complicated network of routes. At the southern end of this corridor sat the cities of the Punjab, increasingly under British influence, and later direct control. To the west lay the cities of Persia, often little more than points of abeyance for onward trade. In the east, the cities of Chinese Turkistan – Kokan, Kashgar and Yarkand – stood as gateways to the large Chinese market.

In between these terminal points sat the cities of Afghanistan in its larger territorial and cultural sense – Meshad in Khorasan, Herat, Kabul, Kandahar, Balkh, Khulum, Kunduz, Shikarpur, Multan and Peshawar. The character of these cities offer insights into the trade patterns they anchored. And like the trade patterns they anchored, these cities were representative of urban centres supporting and servicing similar merchant-dominated trade economies. By offering a typology of these cities – transit/exchange cities and consumer/producer cities – followed by a detailed description of each, this chapter grounds the more theoretical discussion of the Afghan model in the physical reality of trade. Following the movement of trade southwards from Bukhara and continuing through to the cities of the Punjab plains, a clear picture emerges of a metaphorical sea of trade, criss-crossed by lanes of commerce. In turn, this sea was both shaped by, and itself shaped the contemporary local, regional and global political and economic changes taking place.

II.   Typology of caravan corridor cities

The Afghan corridor cities through which the Central Asian caravan commerce passed present archetypes of the different urban centres provisioning and living off the trade central to such transit economies. The following descriptions of these cities, detailing the general and characterizing the forms theory assumed in action, fills in the picture of what the Afghan corridor cities were like. Although the cities were fundamentally creatures of the circumstances creating them, they nonetheless illustrate the types of transit cities found anywhere the Afghan model economy dominated. The Afghan corridor cities were concurrently unified and separated by a multiplicity of factors, making any schematic division admittedly contrived. As the focus here is economic, in a broad sense of the word, their economic characteristics serve as the basis of division of city groups or typologies, where the members shared similar characteristics. Chief amongst the economic characteristics of these cities was their status as transit versus exchange cities.

Virtually all the cities involved in this trade were centres of transit. Most of the goods traded in their bazaars originated elsewhere and were on their way elsewhere to a final destination. There were some cities, however, where *kâfilas* halted more to break their journey than to trade. These were transit centres and included many of the smaller, less important cities such as Kunduz, Mazar-i Sharif and Peshawar. In contrast, the exchange cities, often referred to by the British as 'entrepots of trade', were where many merchant *kâfilas* both originated and ended. Bukhara, Kabul and Multan were foremost amongst these trading centres. They acted as funnels through which most Central Asian trade passed. In the main, they possessed large bazaars, credit facilities, and a level of political stability and economic security encouraging trade. Some of these entrepots additionally supported a small, but nonetheless significant consuming elite, in turn making them centres of consumption. In these cities, part of the trade goods passing through their bazaars remained and were consumed there. Bukhara and Kabul were the only two corridor cities with either the economic resources or political gravity to generate much of a consumer culture, with the former hosting a larger one than the latter.

The role each of these cities played was affected by their ecological environment and geographical locations. Rich lands yielding agricultural goods for the luxury export trade, such as pomegranates and grapes, surrounded Kabul, Herat, Peshawar and Bukhara. The fertility encompassing these cities stood in stark contrast to cities such as Quetta, Khulum and Meshad which often struggled to meet their own foodstuff requirements. While their location and ecological surroundings were not determinative of cities' economic fortunes or political character, these factors presented opportunities, as well as imposed limitations on productive capabilities. Despite the agricultural richness of the vale of Peshawar and the Hari Rud valley around Herat, near-continual warfare in both areas retarded output, ensuring them secondary positions in regional trade despite their potential wealth. The ordering presented here is meant to illustrate both differences and similarities between corridor cities, rather than creating a dialectic schematization. Most lay somewhere along the continuum rather than at the extremes of these classifications, even the supposedly ideal types of each category.

Although much of the importance of these ideal type cities rested on their economic activities, the urbanization of political authority throughout the region in general, and in Afghanistan in particular, made them centres of political power. As such, these cities resonate with ideas of 'city-states', inevitably inviting comparison to other societies where such political formations were prevalent, such as ancient Greece.[1] Yet as with earlier British comparisons of Afghan tribesmen to the clansmen of Highland Scotland, such comparisons, though superficially attractive, prove fundamentally flawed. Political authority in Afghanistan became centred in cities not because of their strength and stability, but rather out of economic necessity. This urbanization contravened the tribal norms of the Afghan socio-political universe, alienating political authority from those whom rulers claimed sovereignty over. Cities represented an alien political order and tradition, making them normatively incidental, rather than essential to Afghan tribal societies.[2] The urbanization of Afghan political authority and concurrent rise of 'city-states' was indicative of the fracturing of the Afghan political community. Their economic character remained paramount, making them centrally important to the Central Asian trade corridor and thus the Afghan model economy.

III.   Corridor cities of Central Asian caravan commerce

Bukhara: The centre of Central Asian commerce

Bukhara was the unrivalled centre of Central Asian trade, serving as the depot and entrepot of trade from Kabul, India, Russia, Persia and even Yarkand in Chinese Turkistan.[3] Even if merchants' goods were not destined for Bukhara's considerable bazaars, little of the region's trade missed its gates. Bukhara was the clearing house for all points on the Central Asian trade compass, becoming a focus of Anglo-Russian rivalry in the mid-nineteenth century. Its sheer volume of trade made Bukhara the quintessential exchange city. But its location in a fertile oasis, along with extensive horse breeding in its realms also made it an important centre of production.[4] The significant amount of exchange in its bazaars and wealth it generated, as well as a population of over 150,000 by the 1830s, making it the largest city in Central Asia, meant Bukhara claimed a sizeable consumer class.[5] Bukhara was thus the most important city in the Central Asian trading system and remained so until the ultimate decline of that system in the early twentieth century.[6] However, because of its location, economic activity and distinct cultural and political traditions, Bukhara differed significantly from the Afghan cities which were also part of the regional trade corridor.

At the beginning of the nineteenth century, Bukhara was a 'theocratic' city-state, asserting its authority over outlying areas southwards towards the Oxus. The rulers of Bukhara had to await the disintegration of the power of the Durrani Empire before establishing themselves firmly on the south side of the river, claiming Balkh as their protectorate.[7] Bukhara's government centred on its *amīr*, who sat as both the chief religious and secular authority. He ruled according to the *sharīa*, including in matters of economy such as duty rates, following the Hanafi School of Sunni Islam. A well-entrenched class of scholarly '*ulamā*' provided the governing bureaucracy enforcing the *amīr*'s commands. Of these, the *khushbegi,* or chief minister, was the most important and influential.[8] The Bukharans participated in the lively and profitable regional slave trade with the other Central Asian khanates, most notably Khiva. Persian Shias, as well as Russian Christians, were the main victims of this traffic, which remained a major economic mainstay in the region well into the latter half of the nineteenth century.[9]

Within the city itself, however, virtually all European travellers commented on the religious tolerance demonstrated by the authorities, especially towards merchants. The Russian mission of 1820, led by Baron von Meyendorff, noted 'Hindoos, Persians, Russians, and Armenians can all travel in Bokhara with safety as soon as the Government is satisfied as to their being *bona fide* merchants'.[10] This contrasts sharply with the mission's other observations concerning the presence of Russian slaves, as well as their failed attempts to purchase the freedom of some. Official tolerance extended to some middlemen minorities residing in the city more permanently, including the sizeable and long-standing Jewish community, numbering over 3000, who lived in Bukhara.[11] Though more temporary in their establishment, a community of over 300 Hindus, mainly merchants from Kabul, Multan and Shikarpur, resided there as well.[12] This group was central to the credit system underlying regional trade, offering and honouring *hundis* accepted by merchant houses in India and other points of their diaspora. The tolerance demonstrated by authorities is interesting, considering these merchants charged interest as high as twenty-five per cent on their loans, a decidedly un-Islamic practice the *amīr* could not have looked kindly upon.[13]

Afghan merchants, who migrated to Bukhara after the outbreak of civil war in Afghanistan in 1818, constituted an important segment of the trader community.[14] While these were in the main Ghilzai Pashtuns, Lohani traders also could have been included in their numbers.[15] Rising to dominance during the Afghan civil war, the Afghans virtually controlled Bukhara's external trade by the 1820s.[16] Their relocation and success attests to the willingness and ability of indigenous traders to exploit new opportunities as the political situation might dictate. It also underlines the importance of the networks maintained by diasporic communities which enabled far-flung members of the community to undertake long-distance commercial ventures. The merchants and their flexibility were essential elements to the survival of the Afghan social formation despite its exclusion from the colonial economic order.

Bukhara's market stability was partly a consequence of Russian encouragement, itself predicated on the recognition of the importance of value of Russo-Bukharan trade. To local merchants, Russian, Bukharan and Afghan alike, the trade was both profitable and relatively wealthy. Meyendorff valued the trade at eight million roubles in 1820, '…a very large sum for a population of three and a half millions...'.[17] The Russians estimated the regional economy beyond the Russo-Bukharan trade to have a 'fluctuating commercial capital' of between twelve and fifteen million roubles.[18] In 1835, Masson estimated its annual value at 1.6 million Bukharan *tillas*, or Rs. 125 lakhs, generating an annual customs revenue of 40,000 *tillas* for the Bukharan government.[19] In 1840, Central Asian trade goods, the majority of which originated in Bukhara, accounted for forty per cent of Russia's national imports.[20]

Almost all of this money circulated through the regional credit system in the form of *hundis*, apart from the bullion traded, capitalizing trade goods carried on the backs of camel caravans. The annual return *kâfila* from Bukhara to Orenburg consisted of at least 1300 Bactrian (double-humped) camels,[21] and possibly as many as 5000,[22] each carrying between 575 and 640 pounds.[23] The journey occupied between 55 and 65 days, roughly a third of the time it took for goods from Bukhara to reach the Russian trade fair at Nizhnii Novgorod.[24] In contrast, the return caravan from Russia to Bukhara was considerably smaller, estimated by Moorcroft to be a mere 600 camels.[25] P.B. Lord valued the Bukhara-Orenburg *kâfila* at an average of Rs. 3,00,000.[26] In order to accommodate all these goods, merchants and camels, Bukhara maintained at least fourteen caravanserais in 1820,[27] and even more by the time Burnes arrived in 1833.[28]

The main trade goods carried between Russia and Bukhara included various types of cloth, predictable given the caravan traders' economic need to carry goods with a high value to weight ratio, as well as cotton.[29] Additionally, goods such as leather, gold and silver lace, copper, cooking pots, satin, Russian-made Chinaware, dye, knives, scissors, needles, paper, locks, sugar, glass ware and beads were traded.[30] Tea was also imported from Russia, as well as China. British travellers believed it was a commodity market they could easily capture with cheaper shipping costs up the Indus and thence overland via Kabul.[31] In return, Bukharan merchants, as well as a growing number of Afghan merchants travelling with the Bukharan caravans to Orenburg or the Russian fair at Nizhnii Novgorod, traded numerous types of indigenous cloths, including Kashmiri shawls, fruit, horses, tea and imports from China, as well as a number of other goods. The balance of trade favoured the Central Asian merchants, at least until the onset of the industrial revolution in Russia in the second half of the nineteenth century.[32] These merchants also left Russia with significant amounts of specie and coinage.

Although Russo-Bukharan trade was paramount to the city's economic fortunes, Bukharan trade with Kabul, and thence with India, accounted for a substantial volume. The Meyendorff mission thought Bukharan trade with Kabul equal to its intercourse with Russia.[33] Burnes noted that Bukhara annually received about 2000 camels, the same number India annually sent Kabul, with approximately 500 camels carrying indigo.[34] He inferred this volume to be historically low, as the *amīr* of Bukhara maintained no relations with Dost Muhammad Khan or any of the other Afghan chiefs who succeeded the disintegrating Durrani Empire.[35] Charles Masson valued the annual southern trade at twenty-five lakhs, accounting for a fifth of Bukhara's total foreign trade.[36]

British policy-makers seem to have been convinced the trade flowing southwards from Bukhara to Kabul was more significant, not least because it carried Russian goods into a market many adherents of the Forward School considered within the British political frontier. These men blamed the 'closure' of the Indus for this, the volume of Russian trade in the Afghan kingdom.[37] Yet Russian policy-makers were equally concerned at the competition from British goods in the Central Asia, as well as Persian trades.[38] The presence of both Russian and British goods in Bukhara and Kabul served to underline the former's centrality in regional trade patterns, as well as the fact those patterns tied to these cities into a larger economic world.

Bukhara to Kabul: The backbone of Afghan caravan commerce

From Bukhara, caravans bound for Kabul, Persia and India headed in roughly one of two directions. The first took them west, often through Khiva and thence southwards to Meshad. Raiding Turkmen tribes and the relative lawlessness of this route made it precarious at best, however, the average annual caravan trade to Turkistan from Bukhara consisted of over 1000 camels.[39] The preferred route headed in a southerly direction towards Kabul via Balkh, Mazar-i Sharif, Khulum, Kunduz and Bamian. The cities lying between Kabul and Bukhara did not in themselves represent major trade entrepots, but rather important stations on the way to larger markets. Balkh, one of the oldest cities in Central Asia, was little more than a collection of ruins by the beginning of the nineteenth century.[40] Despite its small population, numbering 8000–10,000, it was the site of continuous confrontation between the *amīr* of Bukhara and Mir Murad Beg, the ruler of Kunduz.[41] Mazar-i Sharif, the great shrine city, served as Balkh's trading centre. Yet contemporary sources made little mention of Mazar's value as an entrepot. Rather, both Balkh and Mazar served merely as transit points along the caravan routes.

Political instability contributed to the degradation of the area's productive capacity, in spite of the fact the largest and most important irrigation system on the Oxus watered the area.[42] What little wealth there was generally went to the shrine at Mazar-i Sharif, which increasingly assumed governmental responsibilities in the absence of any other temporal authority. The head of the shrine in Mazar was invested with not only religious, but political authority as well, making it unique amongst Central Asian corridor cities.[43] Nowhere else in Afghanistan did the historical marriage of political and religious authority survive. Indeed, the further one moved south from Bukhara, itself ruled by an *amīr* in cooperation with the '*ulamā*', the more secular the character of political authority. Mazar's political neighbour, the _khān_ of Kunduz, aptly demonstrates this. Nonetheless, these disparate city-states, with radically different forms of political authority and organization, remained economically bound together. Representative of cities found throughout similar transit economies, these cities formed an integral part of the Afghan economy and the political order sustained by it.

Kunduz and Khulum: At the confluence of trade routes

In contrast to the head of Mazar-i Sharif's Hazrat Ali shrine, Mir Murad Beg, the ruler of Kunduz who controlled much of northeastern Afghanistan and Badakhshan after the mid-1820s, based his legitimacy on his tribal, rather than religious credentials.[44] Murad Beg acted and ruled as an Uzbek tribal chief, dominating the area from Bamian to Balkh, at times in confrontation, and alternately, in cooperation with Dost Muhammad Khan.[45] Kunduz, his centre of power, was universally described as a place of ill climate, poorly situated in a marshland making disease endemic. Josiah Harlan quoted a 'notorious Persian proverb which says, "When tired of life go to Kundooz [sic]"'.[46] Despite its poor climate, Kunduz supported a significant amount of commercial activity, with approximately 1500 houses arranged around a bazaar of 346 shops.[47] Caravans from Chinese Turkistan laden with tea, silks and silver passed through Kunduz on their way to the larger markets of Bukhara and Kabul. Kunduz's location made it an important transit and exchange centre for the China trade and consequently a centre of exchange. As such, it attracted a multi-ethnic merchant community with a prominent Hindu contingent. Murad Beg's chief vizier was a Hindu named Atma Ram, originally a shopkeeper from Peshawar who had 'risen from the meanest origins among the Uzbek'.[48]

Despite Mir Murad Beg's oft-repeated reputation for rapacity, demonstrated by his forcible relocation of Badakhshanis to the marshlands around Kunduz where many perished, he maintained a markedly benign attitude towards trade.[49] According to Burnes, '[t]he trader passes through the dominions of Koondooz without molestation'. Taxes were kept low to encourage trade, and even completely rescinded on certain high value articles such as Kashmiri shawls. Through such policies, Kunduz retained a competitive advantage over alternate trade routes.[50] P.B. Lord, deputed by Burnes to Mir Murad Beg during his mission to Kabul, recorded that Atma Ram farmed the taxes for Rs. 40,000, later adjusted to Rs. 60,000, relying mainly on duties from the Kabul/Bukhara _kâfilas_.[51] Murad Beg's political fortunes remained intimately bound to his success as an essential element of the Afghan transit economy. His authority rested on his ability to gather and distribute plunder from taxing passing _kâfilas_, thus his better treatment of traders than his own subjects.[52]

Much of the southbound trade from Bukhara missed Kunduz for its more commercially sophisticated neighbour, Khulum. Edward Stirling described

Khulum in the 1820s as 'the entrepot between Bokhara and Cabul'. Like Kunduz, Khulum retained a community of wealthy Hindu merchants who played an important role in the through trade.[53] With over 8000 homes, it was considerably larger than its political senior Kunduz.[54] The fact much Bukharan trade missed Kunduz meant that although it served as Mir Murad Beg's political power centre, Khulum, the major transit point for a number of caravan routes, served as his economic engine. Joining the southbound Bukharan caravans in Khulum were goods from the Chinese caravans which first stopped in Kunduz. As a place where major routes converged, Khulum offered the most sophisticated services for traders in northern Afghanistan.

From Khulum, caravans entered the Bamian region, the first area under the direct control of Kabul, though at times precariously so. Dost Muhammad's authority was largely limited to annual tribute, and often challenged by the independent pretensions of Hadji Khan, the so-called 'vakeel' of Bamian.[55] In general though, this little affected the caravan trade as both protagonists recognized its continuing importance as a source of revenue and wealth. Passage through the valley of the giant Buddhas was therefore usually uneventful, save minor plundering by the Hazaras inhabiting the hills between Bamian and Kabul.[56]

Kabul: The centre of the Afghan economy

Beyond Bamian, traders and their goods finally reached the most important city in Afghanistan and the hub of inter-regional trade – Kabul. Although the disintegration of the Durrani Empire and descent into civil war denuded Kabul of political supremacy over the rest of Afghanistan, it retained an economic paramountcy bolstered by the lacklustre fortunes of other Afghan cities and the dynamic leadership of Dost Muhammad Khan. Kabul's pre-eminence thus rested on its physical centrality, which transformed it into the main exchange entrepot of the Afghan transit trade. It lay in the midst of an extremely fertile valley which historically produced fruits exported to India, turning it into an important production centre. The profits from the fruit trade previously supported a small, but significant consumer class. But the changes in Indian elite tastes and the poverty engendered by years of endemic instability undermined Kabul's consumption, drastically shrinking it by the 1820s. With the renewal of trade links following the peace established by Dost Muhammad, Kabuli consumption, especially of manufactured cloths, began to rebound.

As an important and relatively large urban centre, Kabul's population was diverse, differentiating it from the more homogeneous Pashtun tribal lands over which it claimed suzerainty. As such a cosmopolitan place, Kabul bred an urban society of distinct behavioural mores distinguishing it from rural surroundings. Mohan Lal, the Kashmiri *munshi* accompanying Burnes in 1833, referred to the drinking habits of the population as a whole, and the sexual promiscuity of the women, citing a local proverb, '[T]he flour of

Peshawar is not without a mixture of barley, and the women of Kabul are not without lovers.' The city was home to significant numbers of Pashtun, Hindus, Lohanis, Qizilbash, Armenians and Georgians. Kabul's ethnic diversity was closely mirrored by its religious pluralism, with communities of Christians, mostly Armenian and Georgian merchants, Jews, as well as upwards of 2000 Hindu merchants and shop-keepers.[57] From as early as the 1780s, European travellers noted Hindus, Christians and Jews practised their religion without fear of molestation or retribution.[58] The stresses of later political upheavals curbed some of the city's toleration, but in rather unexpected ways. Largely excluded from this sense of religious pluralism was Kabul's Shi'a Qizilbash minority. But these sectarian tensions were fundamentally grounded in political rivalry veiled in the rhetoric of religious controversy.

As in Bukhara, the city's protection of non-Muslim minorities created the environment necessary for a booming merchant and trade economy. George Forster commented merchants received ample aegis in Kabul 'with a spirit rarely seen in a Mahometan country'.[59] The bazaar was described as a bustling cornucopia of goods from throughout the region, including Indian cloths, Chinese and Russian tea, Central Asian horses – all paid for with re-minted American silver and Bukharan gold *tillas*. Dr James Gerard's account of the main bazaar in Kabul portrays a bustling city:

> when the bazar[*sic*] opens, one is amply gratified by a scene, which for luxury and real comfort, activity of business, variety of objects, and foreign physiognomy, has no living model in India. The fruits which we had seen out of season at Peshawar loaded every shop; the masses of snow for sale, threw out refreshing chill, and sparkled by the sun's heat: the many strange faces and strange figures, each speaking in the dialect of his nation, made up a confusion more confounded than that of any Babel, but with this difference, that here the mass of human beings were intelligible to each other, and the work of communication and commerce went on. The covered part of the bazar, which is entered by lofty portals, dazzled my sight, even quite as much as the snow of the Himalayan peaks, when reflected against the setting sun. In these stately corridors, the shops rise in benches above each other, the various articles with their buyers and sellers, regularly arranged in tiers, representing so many living strata.[60]

Gerard's 1833 description, documenting a city recently emerged from a long period of civil war and reduced in political influence, is considerably more colourful than Forster's 1783 journal recording his visit during Kabul's reign as capital of the still formidable Durrani Empire.

In spite of the collapse of Afghanistan's traditional Indian export markets of mercenaries, fruit and horses, the period following the Afghan civil war witnessed a resurgence of trade between India, Afghanistan and Central

Asia. Burnes insisted that prior to 1816, Kabul had largely been supplied with cloths and European manufactures from Russia via Bukhara.[61] With the stability brought about by the firm establishment of Dost Muhammad Khan in Kabul by 1826, however, 'a commercial revolution, almost unobserved, has gradually changed the channels of commerce'.[62] Under the reign of Dost Muhammad, receipts from the customs house increased by over Rs. 50,000 in six years, a twenty-five per cent rise chiefly attributable to an increase in the volume of British goods imported from India.

Dost Muhammad's resumption of control over the customs house created a windfall in duty receipts. Whereas previously the annual return averaged around Rs. 82,000, under his direct control that amount rose to Rs. 2,22,000, with only Rs. 15,000–20,000 of the increase attributable to higher duties.[63] In 1834, Dost Muhammad collected Rs. 2,98,000 in customs receipts from a total of Rs. 101.2 lakhs, or £993,331 worth of goods.[64] The resumption of hostilities with the Sikhs negatively impacted Kabul's economy, closing trade routes and forcing Dost Muhammad to extract contributions from merchants.[65] Yet despite these higher duties, and threat of having their goods looted by the regime, not to mention Afghan tribesmen, the traders continued to come.

Kabul's vibrant commercial activity enabled Shikarpuri bankers to offer *hundis* at an average rate of six per cent, 'lower by half than is common among the Native Governments of India'.[66] Much of Kabul's success may be attributed to the confidence inspired by Dost Muhammad Khan after years of turmoil and instability. Burnes reported that although Dost Muhammad no longer observed the *sharīa* duty rate of one to forty, merchant confidence remained high.[67] Much of their willingness was born of the centrality of Kabul's position in regional trade patterns, a consideration obviously more powerful than the disincentive provided by Kabul's fourteen duty collection points.[68] Kabul's location, combined with the stability of Dost Muhammad's reign, ensured its continued economic success until the destruction of its bazaar by the Company's Army of Retribution in 1842.

British interest in the Central Asian trade, Kabul's position as a hub of that trade, its proximity to British territory and the importance of its ruler ensured British agents regularly reported a detailed picture of the city's commerce. Comprehensive reports of the goods for sale in the Kabul bazaar include both prices and profit margins.[69] The Company financed trade missions to Kabul, clandestinely, to ascertain demand for products from British India and their competitiveness. It selected Sayyid Muheen Shah, a merchant-trader from the Pishin valley who assisted Arthur Conolly on his overland journey through Afghanistan, for a commercial expedition to the Kabul market.[70] He was granted an interest-free loan of Rs. 12,000 with which to purchase goods in India for sale in the Kabul bazaar. He returned with a profit of almost Rs. 5000, trading nearly wholly in cloths.[71] Having discussed the prevailing conditions in the Kabul bazaar with the Sayyid on his return, C.M. Wade wrote to his superiors that with the exception of velvets and woollens in the Bukhara trade, British goods would face little difficulty displacing Russian manufactures in the Afghan and Central Asian markets.[72]

Previous restrictions on imports from India had disappeared by the 1830s, making Indian cloth, indigo, cotton and sugar, as well as European manufactures Kabul's chief imports.[73] By the early 1830s, it was claimed Kabul imported Rs. 3,00,000 worth of British goods and Rs. 2,00,000 worth of Russian goods,[74] although Leech claimed the Lohanis alone imported Rs. 6,00,000 annually from India.[75] These goods were carried to Kabul in caravans of between 600 and 2000 camels, almost exclusively driven by the Lohanis.[76] But the Bukharan trade nonetheless remained both important and profitable, with Naib Badruddin, the largest Kabuli merchant, importing Rs. 1,00,000 worth of silk from Bukhara in 1835 from an original investment of Rs. 40,000–50,000 made two years previously.[77]

Charles Masson's letters regularly reported the arrival, and at times delay of *kâfilas* to Kabul and the consequences in both the bazaar and government finances.[78] His detailed letters offered descriptions of what must have been fairly typical *kâfila* traffic:

> During the month [of September] two kafilas have arrived from Bokhara comprising 150 camil [*sic*], horse and mule loads of merchandize among which were forty of silk raw and thrown, thirty of wool, twenty of chirss, three or four of naukah, two of tea and the remainder of sundries as cohineal, gold thread and lace, wire, needles, paper, china ware, silver (Jamn Kashgari) and dye stuffs Isher gul Zullil and bub-gung one kaffila comprising 70 loads has arrived from Peshawar, consisting of bingbis, coarse cotton fabrics, leather, felts, matting times & etc with three packages of Kashmir shawls. From Kandahar small ass kafilas or rather straggling parties about 20 individuals have reached bringing spices, drugs, and manufactured goods brought from Bombay with tobacco, figs & etc the produce of Kandahar. A very large kafila from Kabul has proceeded to Turkistan of above 500 loads, the bulk indigo, and British manufactured goods, with cloths of India, fabric, spices salamunaniac & etc.[79]

The largest of these *kâfilas*, the annual Lohani migration from the Indus which Burnes numbered as high as 17,000 animals, yielded substantial tax receipts for the ruler of Kabul.[80] For the year 1837/1838, the Lohanis imported thirty-eight different types of cloth yielding Rs. 9732 in taxes. Taxed at the rate of Rs. 1 per Rs. 40 of value, the Lohani *kâfila* carried goods valued at Rs. 3,89,280. This, however, did not include the 1007 camel loads of indigo valued at Rs. 140 each and yielding an additional Rs. 20,140 in taxes. In total, the annual Lohani *kâfila* was worth Rs. 5,30,260, yielding Rs. 29,872 in taxes to Dost Muhammad Khan.[81]

Tax receipts from the Lohani *kâfilas* were the foundation of the contracting Afghan political economy which Kabul's rulers were prisoners of. Dost Muhammad desperately needed these trade receipts. Duties set too high, however, discouraged traffic.[82] Most rulers reacted to falling trade duty receipts with a dual strategy, forcefully extorting from those least able to resist it, while concurrently creating an incentive structure to encourage trade. In at least one instance, Dost Muhammad decided to shift the tax burden away from the caravan merchants and to the Kabul bazaar traders instead.[83] He regularly forced loans from the more permanent commercial population of Kabul.[84] Another strategy he adopted to encourage greater trade, and thus trade receipts, was to announce those *kâfilas* arriving before Naw Ruz would be subject to reduced duty rates and their *kafilabashis* granted *khil'ats*.[85] These were all strategies of fiscal survival by a man continually struggling to renew his political legitimacy.

Kabul to India: A porous border

Onwards from Kabul, trade passed along two major corridors, each with an assortment of actual routes. The first led to Kandahar via Ghazni. The intermittent warfare between the Sikhs and Dost Muhammad Khan throughout the 1830s meant much of the trade between Kabul and India followed this circuitous road, passing through Baluchistan before reaching Kandahar or Shikarpur and Multan. Ghazni itself, formerly the centre of Afghan power under the Ghilzais, was of negligible commercial importance. It had fallen under the suzerainty of Kabul and was governed by one of Dost Muhammad's sons. Ghazni was one of six major collection points for Kabul transit duties. In 1834, Rs. 80,000 in taxes was collected off Rs. 32 lakhs of goods which passed through the town. In comparison, Kabul collected Rs. 1,40,000 from Rs. 56 lakhs of trade goods in the same year.[86] Ghazni was thus a point of transit for the Kabul economy.

Its importance to the Kabul political economy notwithstanding, Ghazni had contracted from its former extent of ten miles to little more than one by the 1830s.[87] Its reduced state and dilapidation made Ghazni little more than a transit point for caravans on their way to Kandahar, Kabul or India via the Gomal Pass. The city suffered from the often-strained relations between Kabul and Kandahar, not to mention the political and commercial instability of the latter. Yet despite Ghazni's poor economic fortunes, it continued to support a significant, if small, Hindu trader community. Masson records that Dost Muhammad sequestered twenty-one of these merchants and extracted Rs. 30,000 to finance his *jihād* against Ranjit Singh.[88] Most merchants thus avoided the route, heading southwards to India through a series of passes allowing them to bypass Ghazni and its points of duties collection.

From Ghazni, caravans heading to the Indus trading cities of Shikarpur and Multan ran the gauntlet of the Gomal Pass, through Waziri territory. The Waziri tribesmen had a reputation as hostile predators, opportunistically attacking passing caravans, even those who paid their transit tolls, protection money by another name. Only well-armed and sizeable caravans used this route, in practice limiting traffic to the annual great Lohani *kâfilas*. Describing their annual passage through the Gomal in the late 1830s, A.C. Gordon stated the Lohani migrations were accompanied by between 4000 and 15,000 men in order to protect the participants against raiding tribesmen, especially the Waziris with whom they were perpetually at odds. Additionally, the Lohanis played upon the Waziris reverence for *sayyids* and *pīrs* by including well-known *sayyids* in their *kâfilas*.[89] The Lohanis' singular significance in Afghanistan's corridor trade, however, elevated this otherwise avoided route to one of the most important in the Central Asian trade corridor.

The other major trade corridor from Kabul proceeded eastwards towards Jalalabad and then on to Peshawar via the Khyber Pass. Reportedly known as the 'Switzerland of Khorrasan [*sic*]' according to Masson, Jalalabad was a lively city with a considerable amount of its own agricultural produce, including rice, sugar cane, dates, grape, figs, plums and pomegranates.[90] Like Ghazni, it fell under Kabul's political paramountcy, providing the Kabul exchequer with Rs. 3,50,000 of revenue, mainly from land taxes.[91] Yet in terms of trade and mercantile activity, Jalalabad was relatively poor. It produced only Rs. 12,000 in duty receipts, from a trade total of Rs. 48 lakhs of trade goods.[92] And despite his expectations of a lakh of rupees, Dost Muhammad's extractions from the small Hindu trading community produced an anaemic Rs. 26,000.[93]

Lying on the road between Kabul and Peshawar, rather than at the crossroads of different routes, Jalalabad, like Ghazni, was little more than a transit point on the way to centres of exchange. The city was populated by 'mostly descendants of Indian people... [who] speak also the Hindusthani languages...'.[94] The Elphinstone mission estimated the population to be about 2000 families, a number Burnes later revised downwards to 2000 people.[95] From Jalalabad to Peshawar, caravans chose one of three passes, the Khyber being the most famous, easiest, but also usually the most dangerous. Travellers and merchants had the option of river transport to Peshawar, floating down the Kabul River on rafts of inflated hides.[96] Clearing the last passes of the Hindu Kush, merchants emerged onto the north Indian plain and thus directly entered the massive Indian economy.

Peshawar: The 'frontier effect'

Emerging from the Khyber onto the Peshawar plain, one was presented with a city described in 1785 as 'large, very populous and opulent'.[97] When Elphinstone visited the Afghan winter capital, its population exceeded 75,000 and produced an annual revenue of between Rs. 5,50,000 and Rs. 7,50,000.[98] By the 1830s, however, it was described as poor and ragged in appearance, ravaged by a long period of sustained warfare and plunder. Its population had shrunk by a third, while its revenue suffered an even sharper decline to only Rs. 30,000 per annum.[99] Peshawar, like Kabul, was home to a diverse population. Its proximity to India contributed to its high proportion of Indian inhabitants. Forster noted the presence of a significant community of Jews, who like their Kabul compatriots, enjoyed considerable protection by the political authorities.[100] Forty years later, Mohan Lal also noted the protection benefiting religious minorities during his visit in 1833.[101] Perhaps paradoxically, Peshawar was also described 'the most learned city of Muhammadans'.[102]

Both Forster and Moorcroft considered the Peshawar they visited, under the control of the Kabul powers, as the centre of trade between India and Afghanistan.[103] During their visits, Peshawar was an entrepot similar to Bukhara, sitting as it did as the gateway to the South Asian market. It sustained a large agricultural output, on par with that of Kabul, providing the north Indian market with fruits and in return consuming a substantial amount of cloth and other imports. This situation had changed dramatically by the time Burnes visited the city in the 1830. Following its sacking by the Sikhs in 1819, Peshawar 'ceased to be an entrepot of trade for the merchants have deserted a neighbourhood which was overtaxed by the chief, and continually alarmed by the demonstrations of Ranjit Singh who lately burned its' palace and laid waste to its' fields'.[104] The Sikh destruction of the city and its surrounding agricultural lands severely curtailed Peshawar's prosperity. The Afghan-Sikh rivalry dominating much of the 1830s discouraged *kâfila* traffic along the routes between Kabul and Peshawar, much to the latter's detriment.

According to the British, Peshawar's fall from grace lay in the punitive policies of the Sikh kingdom. Burnes blamed a Rs. 60 per horse tax on goods transported to Lahore for the decimation of trade through Peshawar.[105] Ranjit generally claimed Peshawar's then-limited agricultural output as tribute, depriving the city of any independent wealth base. Politics therefore trumped ecology and location, turning the formerly rich vale largely into an economic wasteland and unstable frontier. Peshawar's decline is illustrative of the processes at work in the Afghan transit economy and the vulnerabilities of both cities and rulers. Political instability discouraged *kâfila* traffic, compounding both Afghan and Sikh financial strains. As with Kabul, this instability was, at least initially, caused partly by the collapse of the north Indian fruit market Peshawar supplied. Peshawar's failed transition to the internalization of plunder merged with external shocks to undermine its economic base and propel it into a cycle of political instability. This cycle was temporarily halted with the establishment of Sikh supremacy, but only broken with the British assumption of control.

Meshad and the economics of pilgrimage

The eastern corridor from Bukhara to Kabul represented only one of the two major caravan corridors through which merchants transported their goods. The western corridor, beginning at Bukhara and bearing southwest through Meshad, Herat and Kandahar, was the other main trade route.[106] This route connected Central, South and West Asia. The first major mart on this route westwards out of Bukhara was the Central Asian khanate of Khiva. However, tense relations between Bukhara and Khiva, which the Russians attempted to exploit in their favour, exerted a chilling effect on direct trade between the two cities.[107] Khiva's involvement in Central Asian trade patterns appears to have largely focused on slaves and plunder, with the Russians and the Persians being the main victims.[108] Khivan merchants did, however, regularly attend Nizhnii Novgorod. But their success was at times hostage to the poor political relations marking Russo-Khivan intercourse. On one occasion, Tsar Nicholas ordered the goods of the Khivan merchants attending the fair to be seized in response to the poor treatment Russian traders received at the hands of the Khivan khan.[109]

With Khiva proving at times a fickle trading mart, many of the westward caravans were bound for Meshad in northeastern Persia. To fully appreciate the importance of this link between Bukhara and Meshad, one needs to contextualize the trade between these two cities in an overall picture of Persian trade. Total Persian trade in 1801 amounted to Rs. 134 lakhs (£1.34 million), with Afghan trade accounting for Rs. 40 lakhs. Direct Persian trade with Bukhara was estimated at a mere Rs. 5,00,000, but at least some of the Rs. 40 lakhs of Afghan trade was undoubtedly diverted to Bukhara.[110] Save with India, the balance of trade favoured Persia. To cover its trade deficit with India, Persia was forced to export bullion.

While most of the Indian trade and thus bullion transfers were shipped via the Gulf, a significant amount passed overland via Afghanistan and Central Asia. Indeed, by the time of his visit in 1832, Mohan Lal declared, '[t]he trade of Bokhara with Persia has rendered Mashad the most populous and wealthy city in Khorasan'.[111] Meshad was the key transit city for Khorasan trade and funnelled goods both into and out of Persia. It was a major transit and exchange centre, with the large number of pilgrims visiting the Imam Reza shrine augmenting the bazaaris' trade. The Imam Reza shrine, like the Hazrat Ali shrine in Mazar-i Sharif, served as a wealth repository for the city and bred a limited consumer culture. Like its Afghan counterparts, Meshad's economic vitality was constrained by Persia's political instability, as well as its agricultural poverty.[112] The slave raiding Turkmen tribes also hurt Meshad's economy, largely depopulating its hinterland.[113]

The region's instability, as well as the plundering by both rulers and desert tribesmen, significantly increased the risk faced by caravan merchants. That risk could be minimized by re-routing trade, a practice often employed by merchants even when it required more time to reach desired markets. The ability to quickly and cheaply re-route to safer roads was essential to the economic survival of the merchant-trader community on the periphery. Burnes noted that most merchants preferred to send their goods to Meshad from Kabul via Bukhara, rather than face the exactions of the Kandahar *sardārs* and Kamran in Herat.[114] Yet alternative avenues of trade were not always open. Although the road from Balkh to Meshad was an easy sixteen-day journey, the depredations of Turkmen raiders and difficult relations with the khan of Khiva often closed it.[115] This, in turn, stopped the trade between Meshad and Kabul, which in 1834 was reportedly non-existent.[116] Like many of the Central Asian trade corridor's nodal cities, Meshad's tenure as a regional entrepot fundamentally depended on the safety of the routes feeding it, as well as its own taxation regime. Unfavourable circumstances in either quickly altered its economic fortunes.

Estimates of Meshad's population varied widely, from 45,000 to 100,000, with Arthur Conolly and Joseph Wolff, who visited within two years of each other, disagreeing by as much as 55,000.[117] Alexander Burnes' travelling companion, Dr Gerard, recorded the merchant investment in the *kâfila* with which they travelled from Bukhara to Meshad to be Rs. 15,000–20,000.[118] The number of caravans regularly travelling between Meshad and Bukhara, not to mention Herat or caravans from the Persian heartland, may only be speculatively guessed at. But Meshad's numerous caravanserais, 'at least twenty-five or thirty', compared with Bukhara's fourteen, indicate a large volume of trade passing through the city's gates.[119]

James Fraser captured a comprehensive, if concise picture of the city's trade during his visit in the early 1820s,

> The commerce of Mushed [*sic*] is considerable; for though the consumption of foreign articles, or the export of its own, amounts to nothing large, it has become an entrepot for the produce of all surrounding countries, and rich caravans are daily arriving from Bockhara, Khyvah, Herat, Yezd, Cashan, Ispahan, &c. &c. &c. and a constant interchange of commodities must be taking place.[120]

In addition to the merchants, Meshad's importance as a pilgrimage centre with the shrine of Imam Reza, drew more than 100,000 pilgrims annually.[121] These pilgrims regularly came laden with one or two mules of trading goods.[122] They added to a trade estimated at 500,000 *tomans* a year, a number based on customs receipts which captured only a small percentage of the city's actual trading activity.[123] The failure of customs agents to capture more of the trade passing through the city underscores the transitory nature of the Central Asian caravan trade. For cities like Meshad, this was a wealth mover, not a wealth producer.

Herat: Poverty to prosperity and back again

Caravans moving east from Meshad were inevitably bound for Herat, Khorasan's other great entrepot. Herat alternated between Persian and Afghan control, interspersed with bouts of *de jure* and *de facto* independence. When Forster passed through the city in the mid-1780s, he found a city with only two caravanserais, little more than 100 Hindu merchants, and a smattering of Jews.[124] By the mid-1810s, the city had reportedly exploded to a population of over 100,000. In this later period, under the rule of *Shahzadeh* Firuzuddin, Herat housed twenty caravansaries supporting a robust trade which paid for thirty public baths and six religious colleges.[125] Firuzuddin's reign came to an abrupt end, however, with the arrival of Shah Mahmud and *Shahzadeh* Kamran in 1819. Their rule proved disastrous for the city, with its population contracting to around 40,000 by the 1820s. Under Kamran, Herat suffered two Persian expeditions against it, the second of which ostensibly prompted the British invasion of Afghanistan in 1839. Herat, more than any other city, therefore went through a typological evolution over this period. Starting as a relatively poor transit city, it transformed into a major entrepot and production hub, and reverted to its earlier status as a poor transit centre.

Travellers to Herat under Kamran's reign described a city of roughly 4000 homes, with 1200 shops and a population of between 45,000 and 60,000, with reportedly 1000 Hindu merchant-bankers, a notable increase from Forster's day. Mohan Lal insisted the political authority in the city lay with the Persian minority despite the Afghans constituting two-thirds of the population.[126] Subsequent tensions between Herat and Persia tell a different story however. Connolly, whose own visit barely preceded Lal's, indicated the economic power of the city rested with the Hindu merchants, many of whom he presumed to be rich based on their willingness to stay in spite of the abuse they regularly received from their Muslim neighbours.[127] By the late 1830s, however, the principal Shikarpuri merchant-bankers had been driven away, and their business was conducted instead by local agents.[128]

The treatment Hindu merchant-bankers received in Herat contrasted sharply with what they experienced in the region's other cities. The difference, however, is largely explained by Herat's position on an unstable frontier with Persia. Persian and Afghan rulers both fell back on the standard of religious dogma to rally support for their constant struggle for supremacy of Herat, and more broadly over Khorasan. As in Kabul though, such religious rhetoric often disguised other tensions fuelling the conflict. Islam enabled these rulers to build larger coalitions to support their narrow interests.[129] The *Risalah-i Mazarat-i Harat*, a book published in 1892, listed over 300 *ziâratgah* (shrines) within the old city itself, giving at least the outward appearance of religiosity.[130] Despite the prominence of the architecture of Islam in the city, Herat's rulers and population had a reputation for impiety.[131]

The countryside surrounding Herat was extremely lush, watered by the Hari Rud River which supported considerable agricultural production. Almost 450 villages surrounded Herat, drawing on eight large canals and over 120 *qanats*, and producing over 68,000 *kharwārs* (ass loads) of grain.[132] The agricultural wealth both required and encouraged a more centralized social structure to mobilize community resources in order to ensure continued productivity. In addition to grain, poppy cultivation was widespread and important, with the opium it produced transported to Bukhara and beyond.[133] Yet because this sizeable local produce mainly supported local trade, it failed to provide the buying power for foreign goods. The logic of a low weight to high value ratio meant most local agricultural produce was consumed locally, a fact that was true throughout much of Afghanistan.

Like Kabul, Herat was an important centre of fruit production, with Claude-Auguste Court recording over thirty-two varieties of grapes grown locally.[134] In contrast to Kabul though, Herat was physically too far removed for fresh fruit to reach India. It lacked the snow which preserved Kabul's fruit on its southbound journey.[135] Nor was there much demand for luxury foreign goods amongst Afghan elite. Forster noted a small quantity of European goods, mainly French arriving from the Persian Gulf, but also remarked on the limited demand for them.[136] While European goods may have been in slight demand, regional trade supported a caravan economy requiring at least seven major caravanserais in Herat. Of these seven, one was occupied solely by Hindu merchants, whose interests lay in medium-distance, regional trade. A second was occupied by Afghan and Bukharan merchants, whose presence also indicate the continuation of a sizeable distance trade.[137]

Herat's caravanserais, however, were of secondary importance when compared to its bazaar. Built in the fifteenth century during Herat's tenure as capital of the Timurid Empire, the bazaar likely served as a proto-type for those of Ishfahan and Bukhara, from whence many of the goods sold in it came.[138] The bazaar sat in the heart of the walled city, at the *charsu* where the four main roads converge. Charles Masson described it as 'ample and extensive',[139] while Mohan Lal insisted it demonstrated the city's former greatness and importance as the trading mart of Khorasan, although he noted its derelict state.[140] As with so many of the region's large trading centres, the bazaar of Herat was the scene of an eclectic gathering of 'Persians from Meshed, Moguls from Turbut, Tartars from Bokhara, Kurds, Afghans, Seesstannees and Belooches', not to mention Hindus and Jews.[141] This scene of vibrant commerce, apparently flourishing under the auspices of Firozuddin at the beginning of the nineteenth century, was strangled by the exactions and capricious rule of Kamran after the mid-1820s.

Under Firozuddin, Bukharan caravans filled with gold sand and silver arrived two to three times a year, while there was a steady stream of commerce from both Kandahar and Meshad. But his successors increased the transit duties to onerous levels. Apart from the normal one in forty duty levied on entering the city, caravans had to pass through five duty collection points in transit, collecting a hefty Rs. 23 per camel. Yet even under the depressed state of Kamran's rule, the Bukhara caravans alone were responsible for 600 *tomans* of tax revenue annually.[142] Much of that commerce, including the Kashmiri shawls Leech valued at one crore of rupees, was later diverted via the Gulf. The indigo trade with Multan and Shikarpur, formerly worth Rs. 10,00,000 annually, plummeted to barely Rs. 10,000 under Kamran.[143]

Merchants travelling northwards from India, however, still found a profitable market for their goods, selling piece goods for four times their

Bombay price.[144] But these merchants were virtually all Shikarpuri, remitting their profits as quickly as possible to avoid Kamran's taxation. Like Dost Muhammad though, he recognized this was not a viable long-term strategy.[145] Kamran treated the population of Herat with equal disdain, selling 6000 Seistanis and Baluchis to Turkmen slavers in return for horses following the suppression of their revolt.[146] Like so many other corridor cities, Herat transited, rather than generated or retained wealth. Other routes benefited thus from what Herat itself once did – 'distractions prevalent elsewhere', be they in the form of banditry, oppressive taxation or political instability.[147]

Herat's economic peripheralization was representative of that experience by the larger Afghan transit economy of which it was a part. The internalization of plunder discouraged *kâfila* traffic which avoided Herat for safer and friendlier treatment in Kabul. Such a fall in trade forced Herat's rulers to plunder its agricultural wealth, formerly the basis of its productive status in regional trade patterns, and even its population. This plundering in turn severely retarded agricultural output, as it did in the vale of Peshawar. Compounding these internal pressures were changes in north India's sumptuary patterns, one of a number of external shocks buffeting the Afghan economy. The consequent instability proved inviting for the Persians and their Russian patrons, drawing them into a series of attempts to conquer Herat. These attempts eventually required the British to act, launching the First Afghan War. Thus despite its economic marginality, Herat remained important to the imperial centres.

Kandahar: The heavy hand of government

Kandahar, the original capital of the Durrani Empire, was the southern funnel point for caravan routes out of Afghanistan. It received trade not only from the west, with caravans arriving from Herat and beyond, but also served as a gateway for Kabul trade. As such, Kandahar should have been an entrepot of considerable wealth and importance. But political instability and the highest duty rates of any corridor city transformed it to a market best avoided. The area's arid climate encouraged dry farming of grains, in contrast to the fruits of the Hari Rud and Kabul valleys which constituted the bulk of produce exported to India. The low price of grain exhibits the city's difficulties. Grain's cheapness was not so much a result of its surplus, but rather a consequence of the *sardārs* forcing cultivators to sell at ruinously low prices.[148] Kandahar's ecological aridity was therefore compounded by its politically-induced poverty.

The Elphinstone mission reported a city of approximately 5000 houses and a population in which Afghans constituted only one quarter, the remainder being Tajiks, *fārsīwāns* ('Persian speakers') and 'many Hindoos'.[149] But despite its centrality to trade, by the 1820s Kandahar was a dilapidated city suffering from chronic instability and misgovernment. Court's journal described an impoverished city where the debasement of coin, a five per cent tax on foreign coinage, and an exit tax on all goods ravaged its fortunes. Failure to faithfully declare for either of these taxes led to seizure of all property.[150] Unlike the standard two and a half per cent allowed by the *sharīa* and charged in most cities of the Central Asian trade corridor, duties in Kandahar were as high as ten per cent, a fourfold increase.[151] By the end of the decade, the Kandahar *sardārs* had increased duty rates to twenty-five per cent.[152] More damning still was the regular mistreatment of merchants and forced extortion of money by authorities. Charles Masson spoke of 'all merchants and traders who had been seized in their houses or shops and dragged before the *darbār* for the purpose of extorting money. This was not an occasional, or monthly, but a daily occurrence ...'.[153] Profit margins must have been high for traders, especially Hindus, to remain in the city.

Even though the mercantile community regularly received such rough treatment, the bazaars of Kandahar contained over 400 shops, 'omitting the small ones' and were 'exceedingly well-filled'.[154] Masson thought Kandahar 'perhaps the best arranged city in Central Asia'.[155] Agricultural production provided Kandahar's *sardārs* much of their annual Rs. 9,50,000 lakhs of revenue.[156] Yet the sense of decline remained palpable, especially when comparing sources from the 1830s with those of a generation before. Visiting Kandahar in the 1780s, George Forster painted an animated picture trade, where Turkmen merchants from Bukhara and Samarkand mingled with Hindu traders from Multan and Shikarpur. All enjoyed 'liberty and protection', rather than being subjected to the daily extortions described by Masson fifty years later.[157]

The caravans entering the city gates from Herat, Kabul or Quetta, although significantly diminished by the 1830s, remained the life-blood of Kandahar's trade. Mohan Lal credited much of Kandahar's trade wealth to goods from Bombay, travelling via Shikarpur and Baluchistan, a journey of fourteen days. Thence, 'the route of the Luhanis [*sic*], who provide the largest proportion of merchandize to Kabul and Turkistan, is the only one by which the commercial intercourse is conducted. It leaves Candahar on the west, and proceeds straight to Ghazni ...'.[158] Kandahar's trade with Herat was minimal. Kamran's unfriendly mercantile policies, Persia's well-known ambitions for Herat, and the enmity with which the Herat and Kandahar rulers held each other reduced the flow of trade between these two cities to a mere trickle.[159] The Kandahar *sardārs* suffered from the flexibility and independence of the Afghan trade network, making their political authority precarious. As their unfriendly mercantile policies discouraged trade, merchants' attentions focused on the cities of Upper Sind, reached via Quetta and the narrow defiles of the Bolan.

Southwards to India

Quetta stood as little more than a glorified village throughout the entirety of this period. Totalling no more than 400 small houses, it was populated by Afghans, Baluchis and Hindus. The latter group, constituting about a fourth of the population, was exclusively engaged in trade, described as 'more considerable than a stranger would be apt to imagine from the appearance of the place'.[160] Besides the passage of caravans between India and Central Asia/Afghanistan, Quetta provided merchants a market in which to exchange goods and thus truncate their journeys. Quetta was therefore a small exchange centre, not the entrepot of larger cities such as Kabul and Bukhara. It was most similar to Khulum, a transit centre offering sufficient facilities for trade to those not wanting to continue their journeys. As such, it represented an important transitional corridor city, a frontier mediating the movement between different ecological and political zones.

Many of the caravans passing through Quetta originated from or were bound for Shikarpur and Multan, the great trading cities of Upper India and financial anchors of the Central Asian trade well into the mid-nineteenth century. These cities lay on the South Asian side of the southern passes – the Bolan and Sanghar, leading to Quetta and Kandahar respectively. The Gomal Pass, accessing Ghazni and central to the Bukharan trade, spilled onto the Indus Plain just above them. They served as gateways into the north Indian markets, a status formerly shared with Peshawar. Shikapur and Multan were important centres of exchange and thus served as key entrepots linking the South Asian trade economy with the Central Asian one. Although on the Indus, neither city boasted much in the way of exportable agricultural output. They were nonetheless productive centres of a different kind, providing the financial network on which Central Asian trade so heavily relied. Their service-based and service-exporting economies distinguished them from other cities of the caravan trade in productive terms, but their role as centres of trade firmly grounded them in the typologies prevalent throughout the region.

Over the course of the eighteenth century, Shikarpur transformed itself into a hub of finance, becoming the financial heart of regional trade.[161] With a population of around 30,000, a tenth of whom were Afghans granted lands by the Durrani monarchs,[162] it was the 'focus of all the money transactions of Western Asia'.[163] While its trade remained less than that of Multan, in its bazaar of almost 900 shops business was brisk.[164] Mohan Lal described it by writing, '[a]fter passing though lanes closely peopled, I stepped into the large bazar[sic], and found it full. There was no shop in which I did not observe half a dozen Khatri [sic] merchants, who appeared to me to have no time to speak to the purchasers'.[165] Yet the political instability of its northern neighbours and contests for its control between the Afghans, Sikhs, Sindis and the British combined with the massive disruptions in the Indian economy to sharply reduce regional trade by the beginning of the nineteenth century.

Masson blamed the waning of Shikarpur's trade on continued bad governance and instability after it fell out of the orbit of the Durrani Empire during the Afghan civil war.[166] The Amirs of Sind, whose control of Shikarpur and the Indus steadily strengthened with their growing independence of collapsing Durrani power, effectively strangled trade with high duties.[167] When the Sikhs wrested control of Shikarpur away from Hyderabad, they did little to relieve its heavy tax burden. Yet despite reputedly 'onerous' duties on even the smallest articles of consumption, Shikarpur's trade remained robust. The value of its trade with countries west of the Indus and Sutlej was estimated in the early 1830s at Rs. 52,92,000, of which over Rs. 30,00,000 was in silver, and Rs. 12,00,000 in English goods.[168]

By the late 1830s though, after becoming the focus of intense Anglo-Sikh rivalry and suffering from the downturn in both the South and Central Asian economies, the city's trade amounted to an anaemic Rs. 2,10,000. High duties, capturing over a quarter of the total value of trade, were at least partly responsible for the contraction of commerce.[169] Yet contemporary descriptions of bustling business in the city's bazaars reinforce the idea that though trade declined, it did so in a relative, not necessarily absolute sense. Indeed, Leech's report on trade provides a much more vibrant, as well as detailed picture of its economic activity at the same time Burnes' report depicts it as having severely contracted.[170] Much of the reason for this continued flourishing in the face of contracting trade lay in its sophisticated credit system. While the regional network of Shikarpuri bankers consisted of largely autonomous branches in a cooperative structure, virtually all of them remitted their wealth to India via Shikarpur.

Shikarpur's periodic trading rival was the city of Multan. Described by the Elphinstone mission as a city in decline with 5000–6000 indifferent houses,[171] Masson recorded a similar impression during his visit in the 1820s. He wrote that the bazaars exhibited

> but little of that bustle or activity which might be expected in a city of so much reputed commerce .... Although miserable decreased in trade since it fell into the hands of the Seiks, its bazar [sic] continues well supplied, there are numerous Bankers, and many manufactures are carried on ...[172]

Leech painted a rather different picture a decade later. By then, the city boasted four customs houses, twenty-two bazaars housing over 4600 shops and a population of 80,000.[173] Leech's report indicates a relative rebound in the prosperity of the city's trade, undoubtedly in part the result of a quarter century of peace under Sikh sovereignty. Yet both Leech and Masson echoed the official attitude of the Company establishment, blaming the Sikhs for discouraging Multani trade rather than crediting them with establishing the necessary political stability for it to flourish. Such attitudes cultivated British hostility towards Sikh ambitions on the left bank of the Indus.

Ironically, Multan's rivalry with Shikarpur was financed by Shikarpuri as well as Lohani merchants. Multan's export trade with Khorasan and Turkistan was valued at Rs. 5,50,000, similar to Shikarpur's. But its import trade amounted to a meagre Rs. 15,000.[174] The valuable silk trade constituting a cornerstone of Multan's economic wealth nearly all originated in Central Asia, imported from Bukhara. Of such great importance was this silk that without it, Multan 'would not become the rival of the markets of Hindusthan, the Panjab, and Khorasan'.[175] The dominance of Lohani merchants in Multan gave it direct access to the Bukhara market, regularly supplying it via the southbound caravan from Kabul. Multan therefore stood as the southern gateway into the Central Asian trade. Yet its commercial fame notwithstanding, its role as a gateway as opposed to repository of trade condemned to poverty, as attested to by the paucity of its imports.

Thus even the richest cities of the Central Asian corridor trade found their fortunes waning and their wealth declining as political instability combined with re-alignments in global trade patterns to largely exclude them from the emerging world economy of the nineteenth century. While its location at the geographic heart of Asia meant that Afghanistan had once been central to major international trading routes, the growth of a world economy out of European colonial empires based on maritime patterns of trade turned that former asset into a liability. Not only were the channels of trade reoriented by the force of colonialism, but so too were the goods which flowed through them. No longer were the mercenaries, horses or fruits which Kabul, and the other Afghan cities of this trade corridor, offered neighbouring empires of much value in South Asian bazaars. Instead, the British attempted to transform the Afghan lands as a market of sale, rather than supply.

IV. Conclusion

The corridor cities of the Central Asian caravan trade were the arteries of the crumbling Islamic universe through which the all important short-distance caravan trade continued to percolate. These cities provided anchor points for the *kâfila* routes where merchants could exchange goods, avail themselves of the pervasive *hundis* credit system and break their long journeys. The multiplicity of these cities and the routes which fed them, however, made them subject to the capricious confidence of the *kafilabashis*. Political instability in the cities themselves, unsafe roads or even weak markets discouraged approaching caravans whose self-sufficient autonomy allowed them to easily re-direct their trade to friendlier destinations at relatively little cost.

Not only was the economic vibrancy of these cities subject to the decisions of merchants on the road, but so too was the political stability of their rulers. Caravans represented an important source of revenue to the rulers' treasuries they could ill afford to alienate in the long term through poor treatment or high taxation. The convergence of interest between merchants and Afghan rulers created the nexus of the Afghan political economy. The caravans were the life-blood of the Afghan polity and the increasing difficulties they faced with the structural economic changes taking place on a global scale propelled their political beneficiaries towards an impending crisis by the late 1830s. This caravan-based transit economy formed the core of the Afghan model economy, seen in different manifestations, though always with the same essential characteristics, throughout the contemporary world.

Afghanistan was far from the only trade corridor in the early nineteenth-century global economy, though few proved as geographically important and politically unstable. Yet far from the land of chaos and economic stagnation, a complex and dynamic economy appears to have dominated the Afghan political landscape. Contrary to expectations, political turmoil failed to destroy trade through Afghanistan, but instead simply re-routed it. This can be explained by Afghanistan's unique position. As the central corridor connecting the major economies of Asia, there were few, if any, realistic alternative routes available outside Afghanistan. Yet inside Afghanistan, there existed a plethora of routes along which trade could be quickly and efficiently re-routed to avoid trouble. Thus despite the crisis of the Afghan political economy, and its subsequent destabilization of Afghan political authority, viable social formations survived and indeed prospered in this periphery.

During the first decade of the nineteenth century, the last years of the life of the Durrani Empire, trade suffered from the dislocation caused by both an increasingly unstable internal political environment as well as external economic and political shocks. Political upheaval in Persia and Company competition largely destroyed Persian trade through Afghanistan. Likewise, the Durrani's other great trading market, India, having just recovered from the convulsion of the Second Anglo-Maratha War, was undergoing a period of consolidation under the auspices of British power uninterested in either the politics or trade of countries beyond the Indus. The collapse of American silver mining adversely effected the Chinese economy, in turn reducing the circulation of bullion through the Afghan trade corridor. Political instability, influencing all its neighbours, not to mention Afghanistan itself, hampered trade. Thus contextual events fill the silence of written records regarding Afghan trade during these years.

With the increase in political instability following Shah Shuja's fall in 1810 and the outbreak of the Afghan civil war in 1818, a clear pattern of trade through Afghanistan materialized. The hostilities of the civil war focused primarily on the eastern reaches of Afghanistan, around Kabul and Kandahar. This left Herat relatively unscathed, a situation bolstered by amicable relations with the new Qajar dynasty of Persia. Predictably, trade flowed through the western marches of Afghanistan, enriching the city of Herat and its rulers and breeding stability with its tax receipts. With the ascendancy of Dost Muhammad Khan in Kabul and the establishment of Muhammadzai authority throughout eastern Afghanistan, the situation changed dramatically. The peace and stability Herat had enjoyed for nearly fifteen years migrated east to Kabul and Kandahar, while the instability previously besetting these areas arrived at Herat with Shah Mahmud and his son *Shahzadeh* Kamran. Herat's cordial relations with Persia ended, and Kamran's constant intrigues against the successful Muhammadzai to the east condemned Herat to a perpetual state of hostility.

To the east though, Kabul and Kandahar were trying to rebuild. Dost Muhammad Khan appreciated the need for stability after such a long struggle for succession and did his utmost to encourage the return of merchants to his realms. The stability of eastern Afghanistan remained largely intact, save for the Peshawar plain, until the late 1830s. This stability encouraged a dramatic resumption of trade with India. The trade routes thus migrated with political stability, abandoning Herat in the west in favour of Kabul in the east. The hostilities between Dost Muhammad and Ranjit Singh eventually closed the Khyber and the more direct routes to Hindustan from Kabul. Here again though, the trade patterns simply followed the path of least resistance and flowed along the longer, more stable routes via the Gomal or Bolan.

Complementing the physical reorientation of the trade patterns was the change in goods carried along these routes. While indigenous cloth was the most important item carried at the beginning of the period, by the time of the British invasion in 1839, European-manufactured cloths had assumed pride of place. Afghanistan's historic export of fruit continued to meet the much-diminished demand of Indian markets; however, the horse and mercenary trades collapsed, replaced by a southward flow of bullion to cover the balance of payments deficit. Most importantly, the replacement of indigenous trade goods with European ones had far-reaching political ramifications in an era when the flag followed trade. British policy-makers came to see the cheap British cloths and manufactured goods exported to Afghanistan and Central Asia in a relatively small trade as central to the stability of the empire, at least their Indian empire. Lohani merchants seeking to realize a profit of twenty-five to thirty per cent had little idea that when they sold Lancaster cloth in the bazaars of Kabul, the workings of political economy would be so palpably felt by Government House in Calcutta.

Company free trade policy was designed to establish British political hegemony and thus stability. By flooding the indigenous markets with cheap British and Indian manufactures, the Company hoped the resultant market share would create a dependency on these goods. Such economic dependence would inevitably invite political influence, securing British hegemony in Afghanistan. Free trade was therefore a strategic formula for the creation of dependency and consequent British political control. But it was also the rhetorical language of governmentality during this period. Free trade and its *laissez-faire* prescriptions for governance limited the universe of action and imagination for British policy-makers. Practically, the transitory nature of the region's trade mitigated against the establishment of British influence. Just as the key participants of the Afghan model transit economy remained aloof of the control of and obligation to Afghan *sardārs*, these merchants' independence stood at odds with British ideas of political economy. In the end, the British decided to act more directly, invading Afghanistan.

The Afghan model economy and its participants serviced a political and economic world collapsing in the face of changes rendered by the emerging global imperial order. The British attempt to integrate Afghanistan into the new global order was destined to fail precisely because it undermined the foundations of Afghan political economy. More profoundly though, it was destined to fail because assumptions created by the combination of the Elphinstonian episteme and contemporary British norms of governance created policy prescriptions ill-suited to the Afghan political reality. Colonial knowledge failed colonial action, but in doing so it noted, without understanding, the deeper trends shaping the global political and economic order contributing to that failure. The British withdrawal from Afghanistan in 1842, marking their abandonment of attempts to integrate the Afghan political entity into the emerging imperial global order, led to its political and economic peripheralization.

Conclusion

The 'Failure' of the Afghan Political Project

I. The creation of 'Afghanistan'

Before it was a palpable reality, 'Afghanistan' was a conceptual construct of the East India Company's (EIC) colonial imagination. That construct proved extremely important as the Company projected its understanding of the Afghan political universe onto a kingdom in profound crisis. The dissolution of the neighbouring Mughal and Safavid Empires, combined with the expansion of European empires in the area, set in motion the disintegration of regional patterns of trade and economic intercourse which the Afghan lands had formerly been central to. The Afghan political entity was thrown into crisis with the collapse of the Islamic political order which had formerly incubated it.

As the successor states of eighteenth-century South Asia gave way to the power of the EIC, a newly independent Afghan polity found itself faced with an alien type of government. The Company represented and constructed a new order, global in scope, based on European norms and embodied by the British Empire. In a practical sense, the Company itself was responsible for the failure of the Afghan political universe to assume the shape of a Weberian state that the British based their expectations on. The establishment of Company order on the north Indian plain, as well as that of Ranjit Singh, closed off this rich store of treasure as a resource for Afghan political authority. The plundering polity model on which Ahmad Shah Abdali founded the Durrani Empire in 1747 thus broke down and subsequent Afghan leaders were forced to internalize their pursuit of plunder. This entailed its own complications.

With the plundered resources of the Gangetic Plain alienated, Afghan shahs employed other idioms of authority to legitimate their rule. The three idioms defining the Afghan political universe to which they turned were tribe, Islam and royalism. These were the normative orders on which political authority rested, representing what David Edwards has termed the 'moral fault lines' of the Afghan political community.[1] Ahmad Shah's successors attempted to build

163

their rule upon these three constructs of authority, turning to any possible combination as power slipped from their grasp. Yet the Afghan political universe prevented the emergence of a stable combination of these orders. This was not because of some inherent flaw or contradiction in that universe, but was instead due to its eclipse and exclusion from a global order which emerged during the course of the nineteenth century based on European imperialism.

The establishment of Company paramountcy in north India did not simply prevent the Afghans from mounting their regular raids for plunder. More profoundly, it reshaped the face of South Asia's political and economic order as it integrated India into a world system authored and dominated by the British. The British brought with them new modalities of power, not only philosophically in the form of the European state, but also practically with the force of European arms. Likewise, as the British integrated India into an empire increasingly defined by and dependent on it, the ties binding the pre-colonial economic order frayed. In Afghanistan's case, this meant that its role as a transit corridor linking the economies of West, Central, East and South Asia became less and less important to the economies it connected. Afghanistan was thus impoverished as patterns of trade and economic intercourse migrated to fit the demands of the new world economy integrated through the European imperial order.

For a time, the British attempted to integrate the Afghans into that order as well. Their conceptual framework produced for them the requisite knowledge and understanding required to render the Afghans a part of their expanding empire, or so they believed. Initially, they attempted to do this diplomatically, dispatching an embassy and commercial missions to the Afghan kingdom. When these failed, the British decided their interests required the forcible integration of the Afghan kingdom into their imperial order. They thus invaded Afghanistan. But the subsequent occupation went deeply wrong, and the British Empire found itself faced with its most ignoble defeat. The British thereafter abandoned their attempts to integrate Afghanistan into their imperial order, save to the extent of containing disorder within itself and outside the British realm. Afghanistan was thus marginalized and excluded from the global imperial order which largely defines the world we live in today.

Much of the subsequent history of Afghanistan centres on the repeated failure to construct a stable and lasting ideological edifice upon which to build a modern Weberian state. The Afghans have never squared the circle of the competing normative orders of tribe, Islam and royalism shaping their socio-political universe. At times, elements of the Afghan political community have been able to erect elements of a state on one or a mixture of these normative orders, extracting acceptance from other groups through force. Such was the success of Abdur Rahman Khan and the short-lived success of the Taliban. Yet the twenty-three years of civil war, from the Saur Revolution in 1978 until the American-sponsored victory of the Northern Alliance in 2001, demonstrated the brittle fragility of the Afghan political settlement. Just as the Russian invasion of 1979 exacerbated the 'moral fault lines' within the Afghan political community, so too did the British occupation of 1839–1842.

II. The argument revisited

The preceding pages have argued the marginalization of the Afghan political entity from the emerging global order was the result of a British conceptual framework which conditioned imperial understandings and actions. This framework created expectations of how the Afghans should act as a modern state, but ones which the colonial state could not enforce because its power in the area was largely absent. The Afghan state, however, could not emerge along these lines because of a crisis of Afghan political authority and its consequent 'incoherence'. This thesis has been elucidated along four key axes of argument, focusing on the construction of the colonial imagination, the 'Great Game', the internal dynamics of Afghan political society, and the nature of the Afghan economy. The first chapter addressed the creation of the colonial understandings and the Elphinstonian episteme through which Afghanistan was subsequently conceived. It then discussed the continuing grip held by Anglo-Russian rivalry known as the 'Great Game' over the popular imagination as well as academic historiography.

Chapter 2 argued that the Game's focus on European activity in the area, to the detriment of indigenous agency, fails to reflect the reality documented in the archives. While the Game most certainly did exist with a real physical manifestation in the late nineteenth century, for the early nineteenth century, it was little more than a paper chase, with the movement of Russian troops largely restricted to the imagination of the British 'official mind'. The currency and power of the myth of the Great Game has been buttressed by the weight of the colonial archive and tradition of subsequent historiography understanding the archive on its own terms. But the same records documenting British fears of Russian incursions clearly contextualize those fears with British worries of internal disgrace in India. They voice British concern over the rise of Ranjit's kingdom of the Punjab, with its large European-trained army and successful expansion throughout northwest India.

British fears of Ranjit's ambitions led to the development of a complex strategy of Sikh containment resting on the integration of the Afghans into the Company's strategic orbit. The third chapter looked at the nature of Anglo-Sikh relations and their effect on British actions towards Afghanistan. Yet in developing this strategy of containment, the British limited their understandings of its object, the Afghans, in a narrow and constrained way. They treated the Kingdom of Kabul, or rather the 'city-states' which occupied its former lands by the 1820s, similar to indigenous political entities they had previously encountered on the Indian subcontinent. But this was patently not the case, a fact the British realized to their detriment too late in the day. British attempts to recruit the Afghans into their Sikh containment strategy led them to encourage hostilities between the Sikhs and Afghans, which they then tried to manage. That management failed, however, largely because the British did not appreciate the conflict's importance to the contending parties. With that failure the British were forced to directly intercede, not to counter an ephemeral Perso-Russian threat at Herat, but to secure an Afghan buffer against Sikh ambitions. The death of Ranjit Singh and Afghan rebellion undermined the British intervention, forcing them to withdraw and excluding Afghanistan from their strategic framework and larger global order.

The British failure of 1842 was a consequence of a series of policy miscalculations themselves caused by poor institutional understandings of the Afghan political entity. The nature of that entity was internally fractious, and Chapter Four outlined the contours of the fault lines along which it fractured. Afghanistan's social ecology was bound by Afghan concepts of political community, which faced severe challenges at the beginning of the nineteenth century, problematizing the evolution of their political order. With the collapse of the former 'gunpowder empires' and establishment of Sikh and EIC power in north India, the Afghans were set adrift in a world which no longer afforded them the opportunities they were either familiar with or culturally accustomed to. Afghan leaders thus attempted to redefine the language of power, drawing on the normative orders of the Afghan socio-political universe to construct a legitimatory discourse of political authority. Yet the mutual contradictions of tribe, Islam and royalism, once subsumed by the success of plunder, proved too much. As leaders employed one normative order to legitimate themselves, they faced the disqualifying judgments of another. The British strategy of influence, and later intervention, stepped into this quagmire. Their interactions only served to exacerbate the contradictions of the Afghan socio-political universe.

Chapters Five and Six examined the Afghan political economy and its breakdown over the course of this period. They constructed a model typology representative of other economies similarly peripheralized on the frontiers of empire. The Afghan economy was a transit economy, dominated by merchant-traders who moved goods through Afghanistan on the backs of camel caravans, producing few exportable goods and retaining little wealth. Yet its location, as the crossroad between South, Central, East and West Asia, ensured virtually all of the region's trade passed through it. The merchant-traders driving Afghanistan's trade economy came from a variety of communities and dealt freely with one another. Communal solidarity gave these otherwise highly vulnerable merchants a skeletal safety network throughout the region which encouraged trade. They all relied on the extensive credit network which paid for trade in cash-starved Central Asia and Afghanistan. The mobility of these merchants, as well as their wider networks, gave them a large amount of independence from political authorities, a fact which Afghan rulers were acutely aware of.

The fragmentation of political authority in Afghanistan, combined with the multiplicity of routes between markets, made it essentially a trade corridor anchored by a number of nodal cities. These cities alternately prospered and declined, depending on market conditions and their political environments. The caravan trade continued to prosper despite the collapse of long-distance, intercontinental trade under pressure from European maritime trade. Through Afghanistan transited Indian cloths, Chinese-minted American silver, Venetian ducats, British and Russian manufactures, Chinese tea, and Kashmiri shawls. These goods traded hands in exchange cities such as Kabul, Bukhara and Meshad, eventually supplying markets on all points of the inter-Asian trade compass. At times, the caravans carrying these goods were plundered by unruly tribesmen, or even economically desperate rulers. All the nodal cities in the trade corridor relied on these caravans, and the rulers' authority was especially susceptible to their decision to frequent other marts. Rulers had to find the right balance between extortion and encouragement to ensure they extracted enough out of the caravans to secure their rule without discouraging trade in their bazaars.

The reliance of Afghan rulers on the tax receipts from these caravans forced them to urbanize their political authority. But this urbanization divorced them from the tribal values of most of their subjects while at the same time providing them only a poor Islamic institutional infrastructure. The unstable nature of this transit trade was further compounded by the collapse of Afghanistan's former export markets, most importantly India. Changes in Indian sumptuary patterns, sparked by the Company's intrusion, undercut demand for Afghan fruits, horses and mercenaries. Leadership of the Afghan political community thus increasingly relied upon a contracting transit trade passing through urban centres which lay outside the tribal normative order and failed to offer adequate resources for the establishment of Islamic authority. The decline and eclipse of the Afghan model economy, with its consequences for the evolution of Afghan political authority, provides a case study for other frontier areas on the margins of the emerging global order marginalized by circumstances.

III. Implications

In 1842, the kingdom of the Afghans most closely fit the repeated British trope of a place of pure anarchy and chaos separated from civilization by the rugged Khyber Pass and the force of Company arms. Yet the state of political turmoil was as much the result of British activities in the area as internal Afghan discord. The Afghans had successfully expelled the forces of a foreign invader whose continued presence offended their Islamic and tribal sensibilities. While these forces withdrew, however, the order they represented remained and deepened. The world the Afghans had once been an integral part of had disintegrated. The presence of British forces was simply a testament to the completion of that process, rather than a harbinger of its beginnings.

The Afghans' violent expulsion of Company sepoys marked their rejection of British attempts to co-opt and integrate their kingdom into the emerging global order constructed on the edifice of the British Empire. Rebuffed in their strategic designs, the British moved from integrating Afghanistan into their imperial system as a buffer state to isolating and excluding it. If the Afghan tribesmen would not be loyal subjects, or at the very least willing pawns, they would be outcasts ignored by the colonial state. They were a marginal and violent people inhabiting a marginal and harsh land. Their isolation from the order and civilization of the British Empire and the global political order it embodied thus became not simply justifiable, but imperative. Afghanistan was to be excluded, later appended and always constrained, a consequence of its own inability to change.

Yet the marginalization of Afghanistan was an outcome predicated on more than British strategic imperatives. The British exclusion of Afghanistan resulted from their failure to integrate it into their imperial order. The origins of this failure lay in the projection of the colonial understandings onto a political entity in the midst of a profound crisis, at least partly of the EIC's own making. That crisis meant that the previous examples of political order which they inherited through experience and proximity no longer fit the new world the Afghans independently inhabited. The Afghans thus needed to redefine the nature of their own political order and the foundations on which it rested. But the diverse entities within the Afghan social ecology were largely self-referential, excluding other normative orders and thus communities. The Afghans failed to form a consensus about the foundations of a unified political community, meaning these alternate social formations remained the centre of Afghan society. While some leaders imposed consensus through force, constructing elements of a modern state on one or a combination of the Afghan normative orders, such successes proved fleeting.

The 'failure' narrative of the Afghan state offers an easy and inaccurate rhetorical category in which to place the evolution of Afghan politics. It ignores the emergence and vibrancy of various communal and social formations inhabiting Afghanistan's social ecology in the midst of that identity crisis. These formations proved incredibly resilient in the face of radical change engendered by internal and external events, and remained viable despite their effective exclusion from the emerging global order. Yet their marginalization did not prevent them from forging linkages with that global order, often forced through the disruptive intrusion of European imperial powers. These social formations became increasingly insular and particularistic at a time when deeper connections were drawing them into an ever-more globalized world. While this may have proved beneficial for the

Afghans during times of external threat, it made the creation of an all-Afghan political consensus all the more difficult.

While the British may have altered their strategies of containment of the Afghan political entity as the nineteenth century wore on, and even temporarily abandoned them to again attempt to forcibly integrate it into their imperial order, they always returned to the same conclusion. It was cheaper and easier to isolate the Afghans in the rugged territories beyond the British Indian frontier than to make them a part of the British Empire. The British developed strategies of frontier governance which put the onus of the maintenance of order on the tribesmen themselves.[2] They paid the Afghan rulers a regular subsidy which served as the financial basis for the Anglo-Durrani state, turning it into a fiscal colony.[3] Even the tribal areas falling under formal British jurisdiction were largely isolated and contained, divided into tribal agencies where a political officer relied on chiefs to ensure order. When that order broke down, the British launched punitive raids, at times on a massive scale, into these tribal territories.[4] When the Afghan state was involved, as in 1919, they likewise responded violently. In the end, however, the colonial state retreated, leaving the Afghans to themselves, but keeping them out of the settled districts and thus civilization.

Central to containing Afghanistan and its disorder outside of British territory was the delineation of the Afghan state. Afghanistan's borders were defined by the British and Russians in a space of roughly twenty years at the end of the nineteenth century. Afghans, or rather representatives of the Afghan state, were often intentionally excluded from this process of boundary demarcation, and thus the genesis of the Afghan state as a territorial entity.[5] Afghan rulers, dependent on the British subsidy from the mid-nineteenth through to the early twentieth century, were expected to act within the limits deemed acceptable by the colonial state. When they exceeded these, the British demonstrated themselves willing to intervene, even if their interventions proved both costly and ineffectual in terms of the accomplishment of British aims and protection of their interests. More broadly though, as the Afghans were subsumed into an international system shaped by European empires, they were expected to act in accordance with the forms of that system. The international system which took root in the nineteenth century left little space for non-state actors in the inter-state realm. This obviously led to tensions and frictions, as European colonial powers sought to channel their interactions through institutions which many societies lacked.

Yet, this is not to say these societies did not have traditions of political order, or indeed statehood. Rather, the attributes and competences which the European concept of state entailed differed markedly from those current in many other areas of the world. European-defined states thus had little traction in the historical or political memory of many peoples over which they came to dominate. The European-conceived state became embedded in many societies through the colonial experience. While much recent historiography of colonialism has demonstrated the truly hybrid nature of most colonial states, in all the relationship between indigenous and exogenous forms and concepts of political order was inherently unequal. This was also true of Afghanistan, a para-colonial state, or rather a state created but not occupied by the colonial order. Afghanistan was thus created as a statal space without the 'benefit', as it were, of colonial domination. It was expected to act as a state, but was deprived of the colonial institutions of statehood. The colonial concept proved to have limited penetration of the Afghan political universe when uncoupled from colonial force.

IV.   The colonial legacy

What can be taken from the experiences of Afghanistan in the early nineteenth century? How should it inform the perspective on Afghanistan's present, if at all? Do the events and processes analysed in the preceding chapters only have relevance to Afghanistan and its immediate neighbours, or are there larger lessons to be drawn? These are all complicated questions with multifaceted answers which this book has only tentatively begun to address. This conclusion offers an opportunity to reflect on some of the work's broader implications, and how those implications may help move forward our understanding of the modern global order, as well as modern Afghanistan.

First, Afghanistan's past not only informs understandings of its present, but also offers a lens through which to view other areas historically situated on the edges of expanding empires. The larger processes at work in Afghanistan's peripheralization, as well as the timing of Afghanistan's colonial encounter, uniquely position it as a case study against which other, later experiences, such as the Sudan, Balkans and the Levant, may be compared. As European empires expanded through the nineteenth century, and the modern global order which they represented evolved and came to be more firmly established, more and more areas previously central to older regional systems were marginalized. A combination of their political recalcitrance and perceived instability, as well as their economic poverty and reliance on transit trade, initially encouraged reluctant imperial involvement, and sometimes intrusion.

When these involvements failed, the imperial centres decided to cut their losses and isolate such areas as beyond their territories. By doing so, the empires excluded these areas from the emerging global order based on their own imperial systems, retarding the viability of these areas' political and economic independence. Yet the exclusion of such areas did not denude them of their ability to affect imperial centres, and peripheries alike. As areas which lost out in the realignment of regional and global politico-economic power structures, they continued to affect those structures, although mostly in a negative way. Effective exclusion required the dedication of money and resources, and remained incomplete. Examining those who lost not only reveals much about these peripheralized areas themselves, but also reflects on those who gained at their expense and who worked so hard to exclude them.

Second, for Afghanistan itself, an examination of its past deepens reflections on its present. The problems facing the formation of an Afghan state date from the inception of Afghan political independence in 1747, which was accompanied by a profound reconstitution of the regional and global political and economic orders. But the trajectory of events in the early nineteenth century has not determined their course in the late twentieth or even early twenty-first century. While notable parallels may be drawn between past British, and Russian, involvement in Afghanistan and present American involvement, these are unique events which were the outcome of a specific set of temporal circumstances.

Recognizing this, it is the contention of this argument that the internal problems facing the Afghan political community at the beginning of the nineteenth century largely remain in place. The 'ideological incoherence' of the Afghan political order remains unresolved, with no settled indigenous consensus on which a lasting state structure may be constructed. This does not mean the Afghan political order is in some way deficient. Rather, the implication is that as constituted, largely through the efforts of neighbouring colonial powers, the creation of a modern Afghan state remains problematic at best. Perhaps greater 'ideological coherence' and stability would come of a geographic division and reconstitution of the lands of Afghanistan in some different political constellation. But such excursions into the realm of the counterfactual lay beyond the scope of this enquiry. The concern here is what is, not what might have been, or indeed might someday be.

> ...why is it that non-European colonial countries have no historical alternative but to try to approximate the given attributes of modernity when that very process of approximation means their continued subjection under a world order which only sets their tasks for them and over which they have no control?[6]

Partha Chatterjee's observation seems particularly pressing, and potentially dangerous in the case of Afghanistan. Afghanistan as a state is a wholly colonial creation. The state, as it was forced to evolve in Afghanistan, was thus foreign in conception and definition. It is, in Chatterjee's words, a wholly 'derivate discourse'. Is it any surprise, then, it remains relatively stillborn within the Afghan political order? Is it time to reconsider the Afghan state, or indeed the concept of 'Afghanistan' itself? Such questions will undoubtedly be dismissed by some as naive. Yet is the expectation the Afghans will necessarily mould themselves to the forms of the international system any more realistic, especially given the survival and viability of alternative social formations throughout the colonial period?

The colonial legacy lingers still, with international relations giving primacy to the state. Yet what about political societies where the state does not monopolize political space, but is one of a number of competing actors, and potentially a very weak one at that? The international community, like the colonial system from which it has evolved, proves equally ill-equipped to deal with such societies. In cases such as Afghanistan, the international community has time and again sought to reconstitute state structures rather than deal with alternate social formations fulfilling its role. The international community in part justifies this stance by portraying these alternate formations as usurping and undermining the role of the state, ensuring political instability and chaos. And yet often these formations create and ensure stability as alternative centres of governmental authority.

It is the challenge and attempted usurpation by the state of their areas of competence which engenders political violence and social chaos. In the eyes of many in the international community, these social formations are categorically negative. Their only proper role is subordinate to the state, not in place of it. Thus tribal and religious formations need to be subjugated by the state. This subordination ideally happens through co-optation and political bargaining, integrating these formations and the groups they represent into the political settlement of the state. Alternatively, they must be coerced into recognition of the state's sovereignty. Either way, the displacement of these alternate social formations entails a radical reordering of Afghanistan's social ecology. Such reordering would necessarily be an act of state-sponsored violence. State construction is by its very nature an act of violence, be it epistemic or actual in expression.

Yet is this antagonistic and totalizing narrative, with the logic of 'state failure', the only way to understand these alternative social formations and the role they play? Is 'state failure' as catastrophically damning for indigenous inhabitants as for the international community? The survival, if not thriving, of communities in the midst of 'state failure' suggests the answer to both these questions to be negative. Perhaps it would be more fruitful for the international community to invest in creating space for these formations within it, rather than focusing efforts on a manifestation of political authority – the state – the very essence of which is to at best subsume, at worst supplant these alternative social communities.

This is not to argue that these alternative social formations have been in any way superior to the state. In innumerable ways, both the state and these alternative social communities have a poor record providing for the general good of Afghan society. The moral superiority of either seems a dubious proposition under any circumstances. Rather, this conclusion seeks to problematize the present of the Afghan state with the diverse pasts of its political communities. Unless the international community's state-building activities fundamentally engage with the issue of the social consensus underpinning the Afghan state, its investment runs the very real risk of coming to naught.

And so we have seemingly come full circle. The problems which beset the transformation of the kingdom of Kabul into the state of Afghanistan remain unresolved. The legitimatory and consensual basis of the Afghan state has yet to be agreed upon by, and clearly elaborated to, a consenting populace. Members of Afghanistan's multiple political and social formations continue to look outside the state for the meeting of their needs. At times this takes the form of open revolt, arguably such as with the continuing presence of the Taliban in the southern provinces. More generally though, it assumes an attitude of distrust and indifference amongst the populace at large. How this will ultimately turn out is beyond the brief of the historian. Accordingly, it must be left to future generations of historians to tell us whether the efforts to construct a stable, Weberian Afghan state is any more successful in the twenty-first century than it was in the nineteenth century.

Epilogue

> History sometimes spins an interesting tale, doesn't it, and such a tale is being spun today.... [I]s the United States firmly committed to the future of Afghanistan? That's what they want to know. My answer is, absolutely. It's in our nation's interest that Afghanistan develop into a democracy. It's in the interests of the United States of America for there to be examples around the world of what is possible, that it's possible to replace tyrants with a free society in which men and women are respected.... And so my message to the people of Afghanistan is, take a look at this building. It's a big, solid, permanent structure, which should represent the commitment of the United States of America to your liberty. I firmly believe the work that we're doing together is laying the foundation of peace for generations to come.[1]
>
> *President Bush's remarks dedicating the new*
> *U.S. embassy in Kabul*

On Wednesday, the 1st of March 2006, President George W. Bush became the first U.S. President since Dwight Eisenhower to visit Afghanistan. The President's visit occurred under considerably different circumstances than his predecessor's. Security concerns ensured his visit remained a guarded secret virtually until his plane landed in Kabul. In the short time President Bush had to catch a cloistered glimpse of the reality he understood the United States to be shaping in Afghanistan, he laid out both his vision for Afghanistan's future and in so doing the problems it will likely continue to face. Bush's reference to the U.S. embassy as 'big, solid, permanent' echoes the language employed by the international community to describe its vision of the Afghan state it is presently constructing. The embassy building is a physical manifestation of the architecture of power, just as the international community it represents seek to be the architects of Afghan state power.

This is a well-trodden path powerful members of the international community have previously pursued, generally ending in disastrous results. Yet is this time different? Is Bush right in claiming he, and the broader international community, are 'laying the foundation of peace for generations to come'? Only time will tell the ultimate success or failure of current efforts to overcome the long-standing lack of the consensual legitimacy of the

Afghan state. But the current efforts of the international community do not necessarily inspire the confidence and hope President Bush suggested. As the violence and casualties increase in Afghanistan, the public discussion has moved from highlighting Afghanistan as a success story to decrying it as an evolving disaster. Perhaps the American President would have been wise to note that the ISAF headquarters, just across the street from the US embassy, sits on the grounds of the British cantonment from the First Afghan War.

The problems first faced by centralizing state agents then have continued to plague efforts to establish the sovereign authority of the Afghan state through to the present day. True, there have been significant moments of stability and arguably prosperity for the Afghan state. The reign of Abdur Rahman Khan in the late nineteenth century, Shah Aminullah in the early twentieth century, and Zahir Shah's post-war rule and Daud's rule up to 1978 were generally marked by stability, if not always peace. Yet these moments proved fleeting. As soon as the state, and its underlying legitimatory discourse, faced significant challenges, it crumbled. Abdur Rahman Khan's state succumbed to tribal infighting and instability. Aminullah was overthrown by an Islamic revivalist. Daud fell to an internal coup, supported by the Soviets who were later overwhelmed by a religiously inspired resistance movement. Once the state lost its power to effectively coerce consent, that consent was withdrawn.

The space of the state receded and was filled by alternative social formations which at times attempted to co-opt the state itself. One is therefore left with the story of an ineffectual and incomplete state, the legitimacy of which was never based on a social or political consensus. The state 'failed' because its roots in Afghan society were simply too shallow.

In the midst of yet another failure of the Afghan state, following the Soviet invasion, Afghan civil war, and rise of the Taliban, the international community has now stepped into the breach. It is attempting, through a massive infusion of aid, to deepen the roots of the state in Afghan society. But in doing so, is it addressing the lack of consensus within the Afghan political community which has doomed so many previous state-building attempts? The international community's focus on state institutions rather than state competence, coupled with its virtually non-existent knowledge of current Afghan society, should not inspire confidence. Is international aid simply a modern manifestation of the British subsidy policy which under-wrote the survival of the Afghan state in the later half of the nineteenth century? Will the structures being constructed prove as brittle as their predecessors when world's attention inevitably moves from Afghanistan? If so, will the international community again treat Afghanistan as a 'barbarian beyond', a source of instability and danger full of opium, warlords and pre-modern tribalism?

Just as the East India Company (EIC) created, maintained and invested itself into multiple understandings and misunderstandings of Afghan society and political culture, so too does the international community today. The international community appears set to repeat the Company's mistakes because the Afghans poorly fit their prescriptions and expectations of statehood. Equating the 'failure' of the Afghan state with the 'failure' of Afghan political society is precisely the narrow logic dominating current discourse. Such logic is teleological in origin and implication. It unnecessarily privileges the state as the guarantor of order, looking at its failure as the result of disorder and chaos. Yet the state and political society have been historically distinct, and remain so today in Afghanistan. This at least partly explains the weakness of the former.

In the midst of the state failure detailed in this book, one cannot escape the realization of the continued existence of alternative social formations on the periphery of the state which moved in to fulfil its functions with its collapse. Unsurprisingly, these alternative social formations congealed around the normative orders shaping the Afghan political universe. When possible, they attempted to co-opt the state. When necessary, they substituted it. These alternative social formations – *qaum, khel,* religious *ṭarīqats,* and communities of itinerant traders – met the needs of their members, to varying extents of success and with varying degrees of competence. They thus engendered the loyalty, through coercion and consent, which the state lacked. These formations represented viable alternatives to state control, remaining powerful sources of identity and authority for many of Afghanistan's inhabitants. Their existence, character and role need be historically recognized and engaged with, not simply as challengers of state authority, but as independent bases of community. More practically, their continued importance in the lives of many Afghans needs to be reconciled with the present state-building agenda of the international community. Without such recognition and reconciliation, the efforts of the past decade and suffering of the people of Afghanistan may very well be for naught.

Notes

Introduction

1. On the Muslim 'gunpowder empires', see Marshall Hodgson, The Venture of Islam: Gunpowder Empires and Modern Times, Vol. III (1974). On the Ahmad Shah Abdali and the founding of the Durrani Empire, see Ganda Singh, *Ahmad Shah Durrani: Father of Modern Afghanistan* (1959); Fayz Muhammad Katib, *Siraj Al-Tavarikh* (Hijra 1372 (1993/1994)).
2. Arnold Fletcher, *Afghanistan: Highway of Conquest* (1965).
3. See, for example, Shah Mahmoud Hanifi, 'Inter-Regional Trade and Colonial State Formation in 19th Century Afghanistan' (University of Michigan).
4. The 'Pashtun' are also referred to as the 'Pukhtun', the former being the softer usage of the southern dialect of Pashto while the latter is the harder usage of the northern dialect of Pukhto. I use Pashtun and Pashto throughout.
5. See, for instance, V. Gregorian, *The Emergence of Modern Afghanistan* (1969); M.E. Yapp, *Strategies of British India: Britain, Iran and Afghanistan 1798–1850* (1980); Edward Ingram, *Britain's Persian Connection, 1798–1828* (1992); Louis Dupree, *Afghanistan* (1980).
6. Examples of this newer literature include, Christine Noelle, *State and Tribe in Nineteenth Century Afghanistan: The Reign of Amir Dost Muhammad Khan, 1826–1863* (1997); Zalmay Gulzad, *External Influences and the Development of the Afghan State in the Nineteenth Century* (1994).
7. See, for instance, C.A. Bayly, *Empire and Information* (2002); Douglas Peers, *Between Mars and Mammon: Colonial Armies and the Garrison State in Early Nineteenth-Century India* (1995); J.S. Grewal, *The Sikhs of the Punjab* (1998).
8. See, for example, Bernard Cohn, *Colonialism and Its Forms of Knowledge: The British in India* (1996); Eugene Irschick, *Dialogue and History: Constructing South India 1796–1895* (1994).
9. See, for instance, C.A. Bayly, *The Birth of the Modern World, 1780–1914* (2004); Kenneth Pomeranz and Steven Topik, *The World That Trade Created: Society, Culture and the World Economy, 1400-the Present* (1999).
10. Nicholas Dirks, *Castes of Mind: Colonialism and the Making of Modern India* (2001); David Ludden, 'Orientalist Empiricism: Transformation of Colonial Knowledge,' in *Orientalism and the Postcolonial Predicament* (1993); Ronald Inden, 'Orientalist Constructions of India', *Modern Asian Studies*.
11. Weber defined a state as having a central political authority controlling a definite territorial and enjoying a monopoly of the legitimate violence.

1 The power of colonial knowledge

1. For a summary of Elphinstone's mission, see S.R. Bakshi, 'Elphinstone's Mission to Kabul', *Journal of Indian History*. The British had previously dispatched diplomatic correspondence to Timur Shah in the late eighteenth century via an itinerant *sayyid*, Ghulam Muhammad. Robert Nichols, *Settling the Frontier: Law, Land and Society in the Peshawar Valley, 1500–1900* (2001), 81.

2. For a discussion of colonial knowledge, see Nicholas Dirks, *Castes of Mind: Colonialism and the Making of Modern India* (2001); Bernard Cohn, *Colonialism and Its Forms of Knowledge: The British in India* (1996); Eugene Irschick, *Dialogue and History: Constructing South India 1796–1895* (1994).
3. Matthew Edney, *Mapping an Empire: The Geographical Construction of British India, 1765–1843* (1990), 40–1.
4. For a discussion of 'colonial information order', see C.A. Bayly, *Empire and Information* (2002).
5. Elphinstone's *Account* was similar in intellectual genesis, though decidedly smaller in scale, to the French *Description de l'Egypte* published in twenty-three volumes between 1809 and 1823. Edward Said, *Orientalism* (2003), 84–7.
6. Ronald Inden defines a 'hegemonic text' in the following terms:

> [It] is not concerned with narrow and internalist issues of the discipline itself but with the broader questions of [Afghanistan's] place in the world and history, issues in which those outside of the discipline, the active subjects of the world – business and government leaders – and the more passive subjects of the world's history, the populace at large, are interested. It is, furthermore, an account that is seen, during the period of its predominance, to exercise leadership in a field actively and positively and not one that is merely imposed on it. A hegemonic text is also totalizing – it provides an account of every aspect of [Afghan] life. It accounts for all the elements that the relevant knowing public wants to know about.

Ronald Inden, 'Orientalist Constructions of India', *Modern Asian Studies*, 417. While Inden's discussion of Orientalist texts is useful, Norbert Peabody's critique does an excellent job identifying its shortcomings. Norbert Peabody, 'Tod's *Rajast'han* and the Boundaries of Imperial Rule in Nineteenth Century India', *Modern Asian Studies*.
7. David Ludden, 'Orientalist Empiricism: Transformation of Colonial Knowledge', in *Orientalism and the Postcolonial Predicament* (1993), 259.
8. See, for instance, A. Burnes, *Travels into Bokhara; Together with a Narrative of a Voyage on the Indus* (2003; reprint, 1834).
9. Mountstuart Elphinstone, *An Account of the Kingdom of Caubul*, Vol. 1 (1991; reprint, 1838), 284.
10. Martha McLaren, *British India and British Scotland, 1780–1830: Career Building, Empire Building, and a Scottish School of Thought on Indian Governance* (2001), 120.
11. Ibid., 66.
12. For a description of that universe, see George Stocking, Jr. *Victorian Anthropology* (1987), 8–45.
13. Martha McLaren, *British India and British Scotland, 1780–1830: Career Building, Empire Building, and a Scottish School of Though on Indian Governance* (2001), 30, 64.
14. James Tod's *Annals and Antiquities of Rajast'han* is another example of the philosophical histories produced by early generations of scholar administrators. See generally Norbert Peabody, 'Tod's *Rajast'han*, and the Boundaries of Imperial Rule in Nineteenth Century India', *Modern Asian Studies*.
15. Mountstuart Elphinstone, *An Account of the Kingdom of Caubul*, Vol. 1 (1991; reprint, 1838), vi–vii; Jane Rendall, 'Scottish Orientalism: From Robertson to James Mill', *The Historical Journal*, 50.
16. Elphinstone to Colebrooke, 16 December 1811, Edinburgh, *Minto Papers*, Ms. 11727.

17. Ibid.
18. Elphinstone to Lord Minto, 20 November 1811, Edinburgh, *Minto Papers*, Ms. 11722.
19. For a discussion of how the eighteenth-century values colouring Elphinstone's writings affected other areas of Company policy, notably the Bengal Permanent Settlement, see Ranajit Guha, *A Rule of Property for Bengal: An Essay on the Idea of Permanent Settlement* (1963).
20. See George Stocking, *Victorian Anthropology* (1987), 10–20. One must bear in mind Frederic Cooper's admonition not to homogenize 'Enlightenment values' into a totalizing monolith, but rather to recognize the complexity of the Enlightenment past. Frederick Cooper, *Colonialism in Question: Theory, Knowledge, History* (2005), 3–33.
21. Jane Rendall, 'Scottish Orientalism', *The Historical Journal*, 45.
22. See generally G. Alder, *Beyond Bokhara: The Life of William Moorcroft, Asian Explorer and Pioneer, Veterinary Surgeon, 1767–1825* (1985).
23. See generally McLaren, *British India and British Scotland, 1780–1830: Career Building, Empire Building, and a Scottish School of Though on Indian Governance* (2001); Douglas Peers, *Between Mars and Mammon: Colonial Armies and the Garrison State in Early Nineteenth-Century India* (1995).
24. Eric Stokes, *The English Utilitarians and India* (1959), 9.
25. Thomas Metcalf, *Ideologies of the Raj* (1994), 26–7.
26. Notes on the Hazaras of Bisut, 1838, IOR, London, *Masson Papers*, MSS.Eur.E166/MSS.Eur.J643; Hassan Poladi, *The Hazaras* (1989).
27. Masson did publish a few volumes of his travels. Charles Masson, *Narrative of a Journey to Kalat, Including an Account of the Insurrection at That Place in 1840; and a Memoir on Eastern Balochistan* (1843); Masson, *Narrative of Various Journey in Baloochistan, Afghanistan and the Punjab*, Vol. 3 (1974).
28. A. Burnes, *Travels into Bokhara; Together with a Narrative of a Voyage on the Indus* (2003; reprint, 1834); Burnes, *Cabool: Being a Personal Narrative of a Journey to and Residence in That City, in the Years 1836, 7 and 8* (1842).
29. William Moorcroft and George Trebeck, *Travels in India: Himalayan Provinces of Hindustan and the Punjab in Ladakh and Kashmir in Peshawar, Kabul, Kunduz, and Bokhara from 1819 to 1825* (2000; reprint, 1841). For a discussion of the process of publication involved with Moorcroft's journals, see John Keay, *When Men and Mountains Meet: The Explorers of the Western Himalayas, 1820–75* (1977; reprint in 2000), 44–5.
30. He places this generational shift in the 1840s. David Washbrook, 'India, 1818–1860: The Two Faces of Colonialism', in *Oxford History of the British Empire* (1999), 417.
31. Observations on the Political State and Resources of Afghanistan, 23 January 1835, NAI, New Delhi, *Foreign Department, Political Consultations*, No. 46.
32. See generally Michael Fisher, *Indirect Rule in India: Residents and the Residency System* (1991), 316–74.
33. C.A. Bayly, *Empire and Information* (2002), 6–9, 212–46; David Ludden, 'Orientalist Empiricism: Transformation of Colonial Knowledge', in *Orientalism and the Postcolonial Predicament* (1993), 267–8.
34. David Ludden, 'India's Development Regime', in *Colonialism and Culture* (1992), 256.
35. Between 1849 and 1899, the Punjab government undertook 64 military expeditions against the tribes. Lal Baha, *N.-W.F.P. Administration under British Rule, 1901–1919* (1978), 5.

36. Scots accounted for over fifty per cent of Europeans in a number of fields in India. Ian J. Barrow, *Making History, Drawing Territory: British Mapping in India, C. 1756–1905* (2003), 26; Linda Colley, *Britons: Forging the Nation* (1992), 369.

37. See, for example, Edward Stirling, *Some Considerations on the Political State of the Intermediate Countries between Persia and India, with Reference to the Project of Russia Marching an Army through Them* (1835), 32; Arthur Conolly, *Journey to the North of India, over the Land from England through Russia, Persia and Afghanistan*, Vol. 2 (1834), 121–2.

38. Mountstuart Elphinstone, *An Account of the Kingdom of Caubul*, Vol. 1 (1991; reprint, 1838), 231.

39. Ibid., 255.

40. Elphinstone recognized the limits of the analogy on this point. Ibid., 217.

41. See Elphinstone's description of Afghan internal governance, in which he stressed the value of individual independence. Ibid., 229–33.

42. Robert Dodgshon, *From Chiefs to Landlords: Social and Economic Change in the Western Highlands and Islands, C. 1493–1820* (1998), 41.

43. Igor Kopytoff, 'The Internal African Frontier: Cultural Conservatism and Ethnic Innovation', in *Frontiers and Borderlands: Anthropological Perspectives* (1999), 40–1.

44. See, for example, Papers Respecting Afghanistan and the Countries between the Indus and the Caspian, 1831, IOR, London, *Secret & Political*, L/PS/19/26, Memorandum of Information Regarding Afghanistan and Central Asia, 23 August 1831, IOR, London, *Secret and Political*, L/P&S/19/26.

45. Jane Rendall, 'Scottish Orientalism: From Robertson to James Mill', *The Historical Journal*, 66. See also Jeremy Black, 'Gibbon and International Relations', in *Edward Gibbon and Empire* (1997). For Elphinstone's sympathetic description of the Afghans' tribal institutions, see Mountstuart Elphinstone, *An Account of the Kingdom of Caubul*, Vol. 1 (1991; reprint, 1838), 231–5.

46. J.W. Burrow, Rosamond McKitterick and Roland Quinault, 'Epilogue', in *Edward Gibbon and Empire* (1997).

47. R.D. Choksey, *Mountstuart Elphinstone: The Indian Years, 1795–1827* (1971), 101. Gibbon's writings on Rome continued to influence British administrators and officers through the nineteenth century, with Winston Churchill's *The Story of the Malakand Field Force* making numerous references and allusions to Gibbon. Roland Quinault, 'Winston Churchill and Gibbon', in *Edward Gibbon and Empire* (1997).

48. Jane Rendall, 'Scottish Orientalism: From Robertson to James Mill', *The Historical Journal*.

49. Robert Nichols closely associates early nineteenth-century description of Afghan society with Fredrik Barth's and Akbar Ahmed's late twentieth-century descriptions and analyses of Pashtun society. Robert Nichols, *Settling the Frontier: Law, Land and Society in the Peshawar Valley, 1500–1900* (2001), 81–6.

50. Eugene Irschick, *Dialogue and History: Constructing South India, 1796–1895* (1994), 1–14.

51. Neamat Ullah, *History of the Afghans* (1976). For a discussion of the uses of this text, see Bernt Glatzer, 'War and Boundaries in Afghanistan: Significance and Relativity of Local and Social Boundaries', *Weld des Islams*, 387.

52. Nicholas Dirks, *Castes of Mind: Colonialism and the Making of Modern India* (2001), 43–60.

53. Punjab and Countries Westward of the Indus [Area Covered 60–78 E. Long 24–40 N. Lat], 1809, IOR, X/9972.

54. Mountstuart Elphinstone, *An Account of the Kingdom of Caubul,* Vol. 1 (1991; reprint, 1838), xiv.
55. Like most maps of the time, Macartney's map was produced from a route survey.
56. This was true throughout the British Empire. As John Comaroff notes in reference to South Africa, 'For the British, in fact, command without cartography did not actually amount to colonialism at all'. John Comaroff, 'Governmentality, Materiality, Legality, Modernity: On the Colonial State in Africa', *African Modernities: Entangled Meanings in Current Debates,* 116.
57. Ian J. Barrow, *Making History, Drawing Territory: British Mapping in India, C. 1756–1905* (2003), 12–3.
58. Ibid., 31.
59. On the issue of language, see Bernard Cohn, *Colonialism and Its Forms of Knowledge: The British in India* (1996), 16–56.
60. Mountstuart Elphinstone, *An Account of the Kingdom of Caubul* (1815), iii–iv.
61. C.A. Bayly, 'Knowing the Country: Empire and Information in India', *Modern Asian Studies,* 16.
62. Mountstuart Elphinstone, *An Account of the Kingdom of Caubul,* Vol. 2 (1991; reprint, 1838), 181–214.
63. On national traditions of scholarship focusing on certain ethnic groups in Afghanistan, see Nigel Allan, 'Defining Place and People in Afghanistan', *Post-Soviet Geography and Economics,* 556–7.
64. See, for example, 'Afghanistan: The Problem of Pashtun Alienation', *ICG Asia Reports* (Kabul/Brussels: International Crisis Group), 5 August 2003, No. 62.
65. B.D. Hopkins, 'The Bounds of Identity: The Goldsmid Mission and the Delineation of the Perso-Afghan Border in the Nineteenth Century', *Journal of Global History,* 236–8.
66. Thongchai Winichakul, 'Maps and the Formation of the Geo-Body of Siam', in *Asian Forms of the Nation* (1996), 76–7; Graham Clarke, 'Blood, Territory and National Identity in Himalayan States', in *Asian Forms of the Nation* (1996), 217.
67. This image was especially prevalent in the late nineteenth century. See, for example, Winston Churchill, *The Story of the Malakand Field Force: An Episode of Frontier War* (1989).
68. R. Gopalakrishnan, *The Geography and Politics of Afghanistan* (1982), 108.
69. For the case of Iran, see Firoozeh Kashani-Sabet, *Frontier Fictions: Shaping the Iranian Nation, 1804–1946* (1999).
70. On indigenous ideas of territoriality, see David Edwards, *Heroes of the Age: Moral Fault Lines on the Afghan Frontier* (1996), 82–8; Nigel Allan, 'Defining Place and People in Afghanistan', *Post-Soviet Geography and Economics.*
71. For descriptions of the *hamsāya,* see Mountstuart Elphinstone, *An Account of the Kingdom of Caubul,* Vol. 1 (1991; reprint, 1838), 228; Memoir Chiefly Relating to the Revenue and Trade of the Kingdom of Caubul, 1808, IOR, London, *Elphinstone Papers,* MSS.Eur.F88.366; Report on the Durranee Tribes, 19 April 1841, IOR, London, *Secret & Political,* L/PS/18/C5. *Hamsāya* resemble a form of individual adoption modern anthropologists refer to as 'milk kinship'. Peter Parkes, 'Alternative Social Structures Foster Relations in the Hindu Kush: Milk Kinship Allegiance in Frontier Mountain Kingdoms of Northern Pakistan', *Comparative Studies in Society and History.*
72. Scholars have argued this happened with caste as well. See generally Susan Bayly, *Caste, Society and Politics in India from the Eighteenth Century to the Modern Age* (1999), 97–143.

73. R.D. Choksey, *Mountstuart Elphinstone: The Indian Years, 1795–1827* (1971), 101.
74. Sketch of the Doorraunee History, 1809, IOR, London, *Elphinstone Papers*, MSS. Eur.F88.367.
75. Genealogy of Afghans, Watermark 1843, IOR, London, *Kaye & Johnson: People of Afghanistan and Topographical papers*, MSS.Eur.E166. Masson noted that 'historians' numbered the Afghan tribes between 395 and 397. Who these 'historians' were is not clear.
76. Ibid.
77. Paul Georg Geiss, *Pre-Tsarist and Tsarist Central Asia: Communal Commitment and Political Order in Change* (2003), 55. See also Sneath's critique of Geiss in particular, and the idea of fictive kinship more generally. David Sneath, *The Headless State: Aristocratic Order, Kinship Society and Misrepresentations of Nomadic Inner Asia* (2007), Chapter 2.
78. Ibn Khaldun, *The Muqaddimah: An Introduction to History* (1958).
79. Bernt Glatzer, 'War and Boundaries in Afghanistan: Significance and Relativity of Local and Social Boundaries', *Weld des Islams* 397–9.
80. Akbar S. Ahmed, *Pukhtun Economy and Society: Traditional Structure and Economic Development in Tribal Society* (1980), 129.
81. See Charles Lindholm (ed.), *Frontier Perspectives: Essays in Comparative Anthropology* (1996).
82. See, for example, Meerza Geramy Khaun to Mahummud Aly Khaun, 29 March 1811, NAI, New Delhi, *Foreign Department, Political Consultations*, No. 35, Fraser, 1st Assistant Resident at Delhi in Charge, to Edmonstone, 13 April 1811, NAI, New Delhi, *Foreign Department, Political Consultations*, No. 18, Translated Extract of a Letter from Meer Keramat Ali to Captain Wade Dated 31 October 1833, 25 March 1834, NAI, New Delhi, *Foreign Department, Secret Consultations*, No. 9, Intelligence from Candahar: Candahar, Cabul, Herat, Persia and Bokhara Affairs, Trans. J.H. Lovett, 18 July 1800, IOR, London, *Home & Misc.*, H/474(4). For a discussion of the structure of violence and its implications in Pashtun society, see David Edwards, *Heroes of the Age: Moral Fault Lines on the Afghan Frontier* (1996), 64–5.
83. See General and Geographical Memoir, 1833, IOR, London, *Secret and Political*, L/PS/19/47; Journal, 1811–1817, IOR, London, *Elphinstone Papers*, MSS.Eur.F88.370; Private Notes, 1827, IOR, London, *Masson Papers*, MSS.Eur.B218; Journal – Kabul, 1824, IOR, London, *Moorcroft Papers*, MSS.Eur.D250, Vol. 3.
84. Fredrik Barth, 'Pathan Identity and Its Maintenance', in *Ethnic Groups and Boundaries: The Social Organization of Cultural Difference* (1969).
85. Ibid., 132.
86. Rob Hager, 'State, Tribe and Empire in Afghan Inter-Polity Relations', in *The Conflict of Tribe and State in Iran and Afghanistan* (1983), 85.
87. Hastings Donnan and Thomas M. Wilson, *Borders: Frontiers of Identity, Nation and State* (1999), 25.
88. See R.O. Christensen, 'Tribesmen, Government and Political Economy on the North-West Frontier', in *Arrested Development in India: The Historical Dimension* (1988).
89. Akbar S. Ahmed, 'An Aspect of the Colonial Encounter in the North-West Frontier Province', *Asian Affairs*, 319.
    See, for example, Report on the Durranee Tribes, 19 April 1841, IOR, London, *Secret & Political*, L/PS/18/C5.
90. See generally M.E. Yapp, 'Tribes in the Khyber, 1838–1842', in *The Conflict of Tribe and State in Iran and Afghanistan* (1983).

91. The Afghan experience was not unique. See, for example, Robert M. Utley, *The Last Days of the Sioux Nation* (1963); Jean Comaroff, 'The Empire's Old Clothes: Fashioning the Colonial Subject', in *Cross-Cultural Consumption: Global Markets, Local Realities* (1996).

92. M.E. Yapp, 'Tribes in the Khyber, 1838–1842', in *The Conflict of Tribe and State in Iran and Afghanistan* (1983).

93. See P.C. Salzman, 'Tribal Chiefs as Middlemen: The Politics of Encapsulation', *Anthropological Quarterly*.

94. On the frontier policy of tribal subsidies, see C. Collin Davies, *The Problem of the North-West Frontier 1890–1908: With a Survey of Policy since 1849* (1974).

95. Bernt Glatzer, 'War and Boundaries in Afghanistan', *Weld des Islams*, 14.

96. Hastings Donnan and Thomas M. Wilson, *Borders: Frontiers of Identity, Nation and State* (1999), 33; Bernt Glatzer, 'War and Boundaries in Afghanistan', *Weld des Islams*, 11.

97. Mountstuart Elphinstone, *An Account of the Kingdom of Caubul*, Vol. 1 (1991; reprint, 1838), 219–21; Fredrik Barth, *Political Leadership among Swat Pathans* (1959), 81; P.B. Golden, *An Introduction to the Turkic Peoples. Ethnogenesis and State Formation in Medieval and Early Modern Eurasia and the Middle East* (1992), 4–5.

98. The first book of Elphinstone's first volume was dedicated to Afghanistan's geography and ecology, preceding any discussion of its inhabitants, history or government. Mountstuart Elphinstone, *An Account of the Kingdom of Caubul*, Vol. 1 (1991; reprint, 1838), 112–95.

99. On Afghanistan's agricultural productivity during the early years of the Durrani Empire, see Yuri V. Gankovsky, 'The Durrani Empire: Taxes and Tax System', in *Afghanistan: Past and Present* (1981).

100. Rob Hager, 'State, Tribe and Empire in Afghan Inter-Polity Relations', in *The Conflict of Tribe and State in Iran and Afghanistan* (1983), 94.

101. See generally Christine Noelle, *State and Tribe in Nineteenth Century Afghanistan: The Reign of Amir Dost Muhammad Khan, 1826–1863* (1997).

102. See Chapter IV.

103. See, for instance, Adam Kuper, *The Invention of Primitive Society* (1988); Lawrence Rosen, *The Culture of Islam: Changing Aspects of Contemporary Muslim Life* (2002); Sneath, *The Headless State: Aristocratic Order, Kinship Society and Misrepresentations of Nomadic Inner Asia* (2007), especially Chapter 2.

2 The myth of the 'Great Game'

1. M.E. Yapp argues the term 'the Great Game' did not come into popular usage until after the Second World War and was not commonly used by either its players or contemporary observers. M.E. Yapp, 'The Legend of the Great Game', *Proceedings of the British Academy*. Cf. Yapp's interpretation with Karl Meyer's, which claims the term was first used in the 1840s by Arthur Conolly. Karl Meyer and Shareen Brysac, *Tournament of Shadows: The Great Game and the Race for Empire in Asia* (1999), xxiii.

2. Fayz Muhammad's *Siraj Al-Tavarikh* portrays the activities of nearly all Europeans in the area as Company-inspired, seeking to pre-empt the establishment of Russian influence. Fayz Muhammad Katib, *Siraj Al-Tavarikh* (Hijra 1372 (1993/1994)), 161–72.

3. See Edward Ingram, *The Beginning of the Great Game in Asia, 1828–1834* (1979); Edward Ingram, *Commitment to Empire: Prophecies of the Great Game, 1797–1800*

(1981); Edward Ingram, *In Defence of British India: Great Britain in the Middle East, 1775–1842* (1984).

4. See generally M.S. Anderson, *The Eastern Question, 1774–1923: A Study in International Relations* (1966).

5. Yapp, *Strategies of British India: Britain, Iran and Afghanistan, 1798–1850* (1980).

6. Note on Commerce of Afghanistan/Note on Trade of Cabul, 5 September 1836, NAI, New Delhi, *Foreign Department, Political Consultations*, Nos. 9–19.

7. See Eric Stokes, *The English Utilitarians and India* (1959), 1–46.

8. Maj. J. Stewart, an ardent proponent of the Russian threat, argued that '[w]ith the navigation of the Indus, our commerce would no doubt gradually and silently advance towards Central Asia. But let it be left to private enterprise, let government have nothing to do with it'. J. Stewart's Memorandum on the Russian Danger, 22 June 1830, *The correspondence of Lord William Cavendish Bentinck: Governor-General of India, 1828–1835*, No. 230: Enclosure in 2 August letter Bentinck to Lord Ellenborough.

9. Thomas Metcalf argues the impeachment trial of Warren Hastings, a rallying point for Company opponents, served as a social dialogue regarding the justification of British rule of India, and by implication the larger thesis of British governance. Thomas Metcalf, *Ideologies of the Raj* (1994), 26–7. See also Nicholas Dirks, *The Scandal of Empire: India and the Creation of Imperial Britain* (2006), Sudipta Sen, *Empire of Free Trade: The East India Company and the Making of the Colonial Marketplace* (1998), 121–65.

10. See generally Douglas Peers, *Between Mars and Mammon: Colonial Armies and the Garrison State in Early Nineteenth-Century India* (1995).

11. For a good summary of the debate surrounding the so-called 'Age of Reform', see David Washbrook, 'Progress and Problems: South Asian Economic and Social History, c. 1720–1860', *Modern Asian Studies*.

12. Arthur Conolly, *Journey to the North of India, over the Land from England through Russia, Persia and Afghanistan*, Vol. 2 (1834), 65–6.

13. Henry Pottinger, *Travels in Beloochistan and Sinde* (1816), 360–1.

14. Bentinck's Minute on North-West India, 1 June 1833, *The Correspondence of Lord William Cavendish Bentinck: Governor-General of India 1828–1835*, No. 597.

15. Wade to Prinsep, 27 February 1832, PPA, Lahore, *Records of the Ludhiana Agency*, No. 138.9.

16. Bentinck to R. Campbell, 15 December 1831, *The correspondence of Lord William Cavendish Bentinck: Governor-General of India, 1828–1835*, No. 383.

17. See, for instance, J.G. Ravenshaw to Bentinck, 10 December 1832, *The correspondence of Lord William Cavendish Bentinck: Governor-General of India 1828–1835*, No. 530.

18. Papers Respecting Afghanistan and the Countries between the Indus and the Caspian, 1831, IOR, London, *Secret & Political*, L/PS/19/26.

19. Douglas Peers, *Between Mars and Mammon: Colonial Armies and the Garrison State in Early Nineteenth-Century India* (1995), 38.

20. Ibid., 56, 216–7, 228. See also M.E. Yapp, 'British Perceptions of the Russian Threat to India', *Modern Asian Studies*.

21. See, for example, Campbell, Asst. Resident at Katmandu, to Macnaghten, 5 February 1838, NAI, New Delhi, *Foreign Department, Political Consultations*, No. 14; Lord to Wade, 27 November 1838, PPA, Lahore, *Records of the Ludhiana Agency*, No. 110.25;

Hodgson, Resident at Katmandu to Macnaghten, 26 December 1839, NAI, New Delhi, *Foreign Department, Secret Consultations*, No. 141.

22. See generally Kim Wagner, *Thuggee: Banditry and the British in Early Nineteenth Century India* (2007).

23. Sir Charles Metcalfe to Bentinck, 9 October 1831, *The correspondence of Lord William Cavendish Bentinck: Governor-General of India 1828–1835*, No. 361. Metcalfe's opposition was partly borne of his concern about internal Indian order and belief that its maintenance is where money should be directed. Douglas Peers, *Between Mars and Mammon: Colonial Armies and the Garrison State in Early Nineteenth-Century India* (1995), 54. Elphinstone also later denounced Auckland's decision to invade Afghanistan. Karl Meyer and Shareen Brysac, *Tournament of Shadows: The Great Game and the Race for Empire in Asia* (1999), 93–4.

24. C.A. Bayly, *Empire and Information* (2002), 10–56.

25. See generally Anand Yang, 'A Conversation of Rumors: The Language of Popular "Mentalites" in Late Nineteenth-Century Colonial India', *Journal of Social History*.

26. Specifically in relation to Afghanistan, see C.A. Bayly, *Empire and Information* (2002), 128–40.

27. Note on Commerce of Afghanistan/Note on Trade of Cabul, 5 September 1836, NAI, New Delhi, *Foreign Department, Political Consultations*, Nos. 9–19.

28. Its arguable role in the Mutiny of 1857 is a case in point. C.A. Bayly, *Empire and Information* (2002), 315–30.

29. For a discussion of contemporary South Asian bazaars, *qasbahs* and urban centres, see C.A. Bayly, *Rulers, Townsmen and Bazaars: Northern Indian Society in the Age of British Expansion, 1770–1870* (2003).

30. One of the most important and influential of these anti-Russian propaganda tracts was John McNeill, *Progress and Present Position of Russia in the East* (1836).

31. See, for example, Note on Commerce of Afghanistan/Note on Trade of Cabul, 5 September 1836, NAI, New Delhi, *Foreign Department, Political Consultations*, Nos. 9–19; Memorandum of Information Regarding Afghanistan and Central Asia, 23 August 1831, IOR, London, *Secret and Political*, L/P&S/19/26.

32. Papers Respecting Afghanistan and the Countries between the Indus and the Caspian, 1831, IOR, London, *Secret & Political*, L/PS/19/26.

33. Ibid.

34. Cf., for example, A Report on the Countries between India and Russia, 5 May 1833, IOR, London, *Secret & Political*, L/PS/19/44; Notice on Herat, with a Sketch of the State of Affairs in the Surrounding Counties (Burnes to Wade), 7 February 1838, IOR, London, *Secret & Political*, L/PS/5/130.

35. Extract Bengal Political Consultations – Governor General Minute: Employment of Abbas Koolie Khan to Transmit Intelligence from Cabul, 26 October 1807, IOR, London, *Board's Collections*, F/4/247/5565.

36. See, for instance, Elphinstone to Edmonstone, 9 June 1810, NAI, New Delhi, *Foreign Department, Political Consultations*, No. 12; Strachey to Edmonstone: Secret Department Dispatch Dated 6 August, 14 July 1810, IOR, London, *Bengal Proceedings*, P/BEN/SEC/226, No. 5. Bayly refers to the successes of this system. C.A. Bayly, 'Knowing the Country: Empire and Information in India', *Modern Asian Studies*, 16, 21.

37. For a description, see Metcalfe to John Adam, 15 May 1813, NAI, New Delhi, *Foreign Department, Political Consultations*, No. 17; Metcalfe to John Adam, 10 December 1813, NAI, New Delhi, *Foreign Department, Political Consultations*, No. 43. See also C.A. Bayly, *Empire and Information* (2002), 128–35.

38. The Company heavily relied upon the commercial intelligence provided by the diasporic network of Indian merchants and bankers operating throughout the region. Wade to Metcalfe, 7 April 1826, NAI, New Delhi, *Foreign Department, Political Consultations*, No. 13.

    See also C.A. Bayly, 'Knowing the Country: Empire and Information in India,' *Modern Asian Studies*, 16. The British mission to Persia at times had it own news-writers stationed in western Afghanistan. The only records from these news-writers available are the extracts occasionally forwarded to Calcutta from Tehran. See, for example, Copy of a Letter from the Persia Envoy Extraordinary: McNeill to Macnaghten, 22 January 1837, IOR, London, *Secret & Political*, L/PS/5/127, No. 57.

39. Mir Kiramat Ali Who Had Been Appointed Newswriter at Kandahar Is Allowed His Travelling Expenses from Calcutta to Kandahar, July 1832–March 1834, IOR, London, *Board's Collections*, F/4/1466/57654. This was reportedly at the higher end of salaries. C.A. Bayly, 'Knowing the Country: Empire and Information in India', *Modern Asian Studies*, 26.

40. The immediate cause of Karamat Ali's removal was his failure to report for an extended period of time, although it was later discovered he had been embezzling from the bills of exchange sent him by Wade. Resources of Afghanistan, 30 March 1835, NAI, New Delhi, *Foreign Department, Political Consultations*, No. 46.

41. See Wade's instructions to Karamat Ali. Wade to Secretary to Gov't, 5 September 1832, IOR, *Board's Collections*, F/4/1466/57654.

42. Strachey's rather polite rebuke of Sayyid Nujjuf Aly, the Company's news-writer in Herat and his counterpart in Kandahar for their 'discovery' by local authorities is indicative of these men's positions in local courts. Strachey to Edmonstone, Secretary to the Government: Secret Department Dispatch 30 June, 7 June 1810, IOR, London, *Bengal Proceedings*, P/BEN/SEC/225, No. 9.

43. John S. Galbraith, 'The "Turbulent Frontier" As a Factor in British Expansion', *Comparative Studies in Society and History*.

44. J.A. Norris, *The First Afghan War, 1838–1842* (1967), 195–96, 208.

45. See, for example, Burnes to Macnaghten, 26 January 1838, IOR, London, *Secret & Political*, L/PS/5/130.

46. Masson recorded his wanderings for the Bushire resident, David Wilson, who forwarded them to Calcutta. Letter from the Resident at Bushire, Major David Wilson, to the Bombay Government, Forwarding the Memo of Charles Masson on Parts of Afghanistan and the Independent Punjab, 11 September 1830, IOR, London, *Board's Collections*, F/4/1399/55442A. On Masson, see generally Gordon Whitteridge, *Charles Masson of Afghanistan: Explorer, Archaeologist, Numismatist and Intelligence Agent* (2002).

47. Gerard to C.E. Trevelyan, 19 June 1834, NAI, New Delhi, *Foreign Department, Secret Consultations*, No. 4; Wade to Macnaghten, 19 June 1834, NAI, New Delhi, *Foreign Department, Secret Consultations*, No. 1. See also Whitteridge, *Charles Masson of Afghanistan: Explorer, Archaeologist, Numismatist and Intelligence Agent* (2002), 124. On Wade, see generally Erach Rustam Kapadia, 'The Diplomatic Career of Sir Claude Wade: A Study of British Relations with the Sikhs and Afghans, July 1823–March 1840' (University of London).

48. To get a sense of Masson's feelings regarding his Company service and his personal interests, see generally *Pottinger Papers*, London, PRO, FO/705/32. Masson resigned from Company service in October 1838, apparently much disgusted by

his treatment. His detention on the orders of William Macnaghten following the revolt in Khelat largely explains the vindictive tone of his memoirs. See Charles Masson, *Narrative of a Journey to Kalat, Including an Account of the Insurrection at That Place in 1840; and a Memoir on Eastern Balochistan* (1843), 167–83.

49. Masson to H. Pottinger, 30 November 1835, PRO, London, *Pottinger Papers*, FO/705/32; Masson to H. Pottinger, 18 October 1838, PRO, London, *Pottinger Papers*, FO/705/32.

50. See, for example, Observations on the Political State and Resources of Afghanistan, 23 January 1835, NAI, New Delhi, *Foreign Department, Political Consultations*, No. 46.

51. Masson's correspondence with Henry Pottinger, the political agent in Sind, is regularly peppered with diatribes against Wade, whom he clearly loathed and Pottinger distrusted. See, for instance, H. Pottinger to Masson, 16 September 1838, PRO, London, *Pottinger Papers*, FO/705/32.

52. Masson's original dispatches, as well as those of his predecessor Karamat Ali, have disappeared, leaving only Wade's forwarded copies, which themselves lack any regularity to his superiors in Calcutta.

53. Quoted in Michael Fisher, 'The Office of Akhbar Nawis: The Transition from Mughal to British Forms', *Modern Asian Studies*, 66.

54. Correspondence Relating to Persia and Afghanistan, 1834–1839, 1839, IOR, London, *Secret and Political*, L/PS/20/C1. See also J.A. Norris, *The First Afghan War, 1838–1842* (1967), 221–4, 417–23.

55. While it was within Wade's authority to edit Masson's and Burnes' intelligence reports, it was not within his prerogative to interfere with communication between foreign heads of state and the Governor-General. Personal communication with Jean Marie La Font. New Delhi, 4 December 2003.

56. See, for example, Wade to Colebrooke, 13 February 1829, NAI, New Delhi, *Foreign Department, Political Consultations*, No. 26; Prinsep to Wade, 14 May 1831, PPA, Lahore, *Records of the Ludhiana Agency*, No. 115.79.

57. Extract of a Letter from Mr Masson to Captain Wade Dated 9 April 1835, 24 August 1835, NAI, New Delhi, *Foreign Department, Political Consultations*, No. 63.

58. See, for instance, Moorcroft to Swinton, 26 July 1822, NAI, New Delhi, *Foreign Department, Political Consultations*, No. 56; Nesselrode to Runjeet Singh, 10 October 1823, NAI, New Delhi, *Foreign Department, Political Consultations*, No. 25.

59. This traveller, who unlike Stephan remains nameless despite appearing in greater detail in the archives, turned out to be a Jewish trader from the Caucuses travelling through Central Asia and onto Chinese Turkistan. Lord to Burnes, 11 April 1838, IOR, London, *Secret & Political*, L/PS/5/130; Burnes to Macnaghten, 26 January 1838, IOR, London, *Secret & Political*, L/PS/5/130.

60. Macnaghten to H.T. Prinsep, 27 August 1838, IOR, London, *Secret & Political*, L/PS/5/133; Macnaghten to Wade, 27 August 1838, PPA, Lahore, *Records of the Ludhiana Agency*, No. 121.87.

61. Wade to Hawkins, 24 August; 7, 13 September 1830, PPA, Lahore, *Records of the Ludhiana Residency*, No. 98.114–6.

62. Douglas Peers, *Between Mars and Mammon: Colonial Armies and the Garrison State in Early Nineteenth-Century India* (1995), 230.

63. It must be emphasized this number is limited to archivally documented individuals. Of those, the bulk, over 100 Indians in the Company's military service, came as escorts to the embassy of Mountstuart Elphinstone. This list

includes the following individuals: George Forster, Mountstuart Elphinstone, Richard Strachey (Elphinstone mission), Lt. John Macartney (Elphinstone mission), Mr Tickel (Elphinstone mission), Captain Raper (Elphinstone mission), Mr Robert Alexander (Elphinstone mission), Lt. Christie, Lt. Henry Pottinger, William Moorcroft, George Trebeck (Moorcroft's companion), Charles Masson (a.k.a. John Lewis), Lt. Arthur Conolly, Alexander Burnes, Dr James Gerard (Burnes companion, 1831), Lt. P.B. Lord (Burnes mission, 1836–8), Lt. John Wood (Burnes mission, 1836–8), Josiah Harlan (an American formerly in the Company's service). In addition to these individuals were a number of deserters and European 'adventurers' in pursuit of service with native powers.

64. See, for example, From Prince Ayoob to Mr Metcalfe, Resident at Dihlee Received in April 1813, 15 May 1813, NAI, New Delhi, *Foreign Department, Political Consultations*, No. 16; Futteh Khan to Governor-General, 10 June 1814, NAI, New Delhi, *Foreign Department, Political Consultations*, No. 7. A son of Tipu Sultan reportedly visited Kabul and urged Shah Mahmud to ally himself with the Company. Metcalfe to John Adam, 15 May 1813, NAI, New Delhi, *Foreign Department, Political Consultations*, No. 17.

65. For Moorcroft's recall orders, see Amherst to Secret Committee, 9 January 1824, IOR, London, *Secret & Political*, L/PS/6/34.

66. The Company seemed more concerned that Moorcroft's activities would be seen as officially sanctioned rather than recovering its prestige. Metcalfe to Wade, 7 April 1826, NAI, New Delhi, *Foreign Department, Political Consultations*, No. 13.

67. Bentinck to Robert Campbell, 11 May 1831, *The correspondence of Lord William Cavendish Bentinck: Governor-General of India 1828–1835*, No. 319.

68. Lord Clare to Bentinck, 31 July 1831, *The Correspondence of Lord William Cavendish Bentinck: Governor-General of India 1828–1835*, No. 344; Lord Clare to Bentinck, 24 September 1831, Oxford University Press, *The Correspondence of Lord William Cavendish Bentinck: Governor-General of India 1828–1835*, No. 357.

69. Douglas Peers, *Between Mars and Mammon: Colonial Armies and the Garrison State in Early Nineteenth-Century India* (1995), 211.

70. Even Bentinck, despite his warm assessment of Ranjit, recognized the danger of his ambitions for the Company. He consequently kept parallel negotiations with the Amirs of Sind for the opening of the Indus a secret from Ranjit. Peter Auber to Bentinck, 10 May 1832, *The correspondence of Lord William Cavendish Bentinck: Governor-General of India 1828–1835*, No. 442.

71. See, for example, Lord Ellenborough to Bentinck, 12 January 1830, *The correspondence of Lord William Cavendish Bentinck: Governor-General of India 1828–1835*, No. 175; Bentinck to R. Campbell, 15 December 1831, Oxford University Press, *The Correspondence of Lord William Cavendish Bentinck: Governor-General of India 1828–1835*, No. 383.

72. Bentinck wanted to deploy steamers on the Indus, possibly two from the Bombay Presidency. Bentinck's Minute on Steam Navigation, 8 June 1833, *The Correspondence of Lord William Cavendish Bentinck: Governor-General of India 1828–1835*, No. 599; Lord Clare to Bentinck, 10 May 1833, Oxford University Press, *The Correspondence of Lord William Cavendish Bentinck: Governor-General of India 1828–1835*, No. 587.

73. Secret Committee to G.G., 12 January 1830, IOR, London, *Secret & Political*, L/PS/5/543.

74. Masson viciously derided the Indus Scheme in his memoir, pointing out the Indus had never been 'closed'. Charles Masson, *Narrative of Various Journey in Baloochistan, Afghanistan and the Punjab*, Vol. 3 (1974), 432–3.

75. 'The Indus Navigation Treaty of 1832 and Supplementary Indus Navigation Treaty of 1834' in Anil Chandra Banerjee, *Anglo-Sikh Relations: Chapters from J.D. Cunningham's 'History of the Sikhs'* (1949), 155–60.

76. See, for example, Mackeson to Wade, 20 January 1834, PPA, Lahore, *Records of the Ludhiana Agency*, No. 105.27; Report on the Establishment of an Entrepot of Fair for the Indus Trade, 18 January 1838, IOR, London, *Secret & Political*, L/PS/5/130. For more on the Lohani traders, see Chapter 5.

77. Sayyid Muheen Shah, who reported these numbers, blamed the high cost of transport engendered by the insecurity of the road. His duty bill totalled only twelve per cent of his total cost. Letter from the G.G's Secretary, 13 March 1832, IOR, London, *Secret & Political*, L/PS/5/42.

78. Ranjit was to receive Rs. 155 ans. 4 for territories on the right bank of the Indus and Rs. 67 ans. 15 pie. 9 for territories on the left bank. Anil Chandra Banerjee, *Anglo-Sikh Relations: Chapters from J.D. Cunningham's 'History of the Sikhs'* (1949), 155–60.

79. See, for example, Wade to Prinsep, 27 February 1832, PPA, Lahore, *Records of the Ludhiana Agency*, No. 138.9.

80. Fraser to G.R. Clerk, 28 December 1832, PPA, Lahore, *Records of the Ambala Agency*, No. 32.135; Macnaghten to G.R. Clerk, 16 December 1832, PPA, Lahore, *Records of the Ambala Agency*, No. 32.126.

81. Wade to Macnaghten, 20 October 1837, NAI, New Delhi, *Foreign Department, Political Consultations*, No. 67.

82. J.G. Ravenshaw to Bentinck, 11 April 1832, *The Correspondence of Lord William Cavendish Bentinck: Governor-General of India 1828–1835*, No. 430.

83. See, for example, Notes on the Invasion of India, 19 August 1825, NAI, New Delhi, *Foreign Department, Secret Consultations*, Nos. 3–4; John McNeill, *Progress and Present Position of Russia in the East* (1836); Maj. Gen. Sir S.F. Whittingham to Bentinck, 18 August 1834, *The correspondence of Lord William Cavendish Bentinck: Governor-General of India 1828–1835*, No. 763.

84. For an overview of Russian progress in Afghanistan and Central Asia up to the nineteenth century, see Mikhail Volodarsky, 'The Russians in Afghanistan in the 1830s', *Central Asian Survey*.

85. B.D. Hopkins, 'Race, Sex and Slavery: "Forced Labour" In Central Asia and Afghanistan in the Early Nineteenth Century', *Modern Asian Studies*.

86. See, for instance, Burnes to Macnaghten, 20 October 1837, IOR, London, *Secret & Political*, L/PS/5/129.

87. Macnaghten to Wade, 19 March 1833, NAI, New Delhi, *Foreign Department, Secret Consultations*, No. 41.

88. Burnes to Ruhum Dil Khan, 3 July 1839, NAI, New Delhi, *Foreign Department, Secret Consultations*, No. 35.

89. See, for instance, Memorandum of Information Regarding Afghanistan and Central Asia, 23 August 1831, IOR, London, *Secret and Political*, L/PS/19/26; Note on Commerce of Afghanistan/Note on Trade of Cabul, 5 September 1836, NAI, New Delhi, *Foreign Department, Political Consultations*, Nos. 9–19.

90. Bentinck endorsed the dispatch of a European commercial agent to Kabul as early as 1833. Bentinck's Minute on North-West India, 1 June 1833, *The correspondence of Lord William Cavendish Bentinck: Governor-General of India 1828–1835*, No. 597.

91. For Burnes' original instructions, see Minute, 5 September 1836, NAI, New Delhi, *Foreign Department, Political Consultations*, Nos. 9–19.
92. See Macnaghten to Burnes, 15 May 1837, NAI, New Delhi, *Foreign Department, Secret Consultations*, No. 21.
93. Shah Mahmoud Hanifi, 'Inter-Regional Trade and Colonial State Formation in 19th Century Afghanistan' (University of Michigan), 126.
94. See, for instance, Peter Hopkirk, *The Great Game: On Secret Service in High Asia* (1990), 132–4.
95. Burnes to McNeill, 6 June 1837, IOR, London, *McNeill Papers*, Mss.Eur. D1165/2.
96. Wade to Gov't, 13 February 1832, cited in Anil Chandra Banerjee, *Anglo-Sikh Relations: Chapters from J.D. Cunningham's 'History of the Sikhs'* (1949), 42.
97. Douglas Peers, *Between Mars and Mammon: Colonial Armies and the Garrison State in Early Nineteenth-Century India* (1995), 56–7.
98. J.S. Grewal, *The Sikhs of the Punjab* (1998), 123.
99. Charles Joseph Hall, 'The Maharaja's Account Books. State and Society under the Sikhs: 1799–1849' (University of Illinois), 210, 40.
100. Douglas Peers, *Between Mars and Mammon: Colonial Armies and the Garrison State in Early Nineteenth-Century India* (1995), 231.
101. See, for example, Private Letter to Governor-General from a Camp near Ooch, 12 May 1837, IOR, London, *Masson Correspondence*, MSS.Eur.E161.3/MSS.Eur. J633:3(ii).
102. For a general overview of the Punjab under Ranjit Singh, see J.S. Grewal, *The Sikhs of the Punjab* (1998), 99–128.
103. For a copy of the treaty, see Anil Chandra Banerjee, *Anglo-Sikh Relations: Chapters from J.D. Cunningham's 'History of the Sikhs'* (1949).
104. Ibid., lvi; Anil Chandra Banerjee, *The Khalsa Raj* (1985), 95.
105. J.S. Grewal, *The Sikhs of the Punjab* (1998), 95.
106. Indu Banga, 'Formation of the Sikh State, 1765–1845', in *Five Punjabi Centuries: Polity, Economy, Society and Culture, C. 1500–1990* (1997), 95.
107. On the Punjab at the end of the Mughal era, see Muzaffar Alam, *The Crisis of Empire in Mughal North India: Awadh and the Punjab, 1707–1748* (1986), 134–203.
108. J.S. Grewal, *The Sikhs of the Punjab* (1998), 109. Hall argues this overestimates the true financial income of the Punjab state. Charles Joseph Hall, 'The Maharaja's Account Books. State and Society under the Sikhs: 1799–1849' (University of Illinois), 205–06.
109. Indu Banga, 'Formation of the Sikh State, 1765–1845', in *Five Punjabi Centuries: Polity, Economy, Society and Culture, C. 1500–1990* (1997), 94.
110. Salaries were, however, usually kept in six months arrears. Charles Joseph Hall, 'The Maharaja's Account Books. State and Society under the Sikhs: 1799–1849' (University of Illinois), 235.
111. Ibid.
112. Indu Banga, 'Formation of the Sikh State, 1765–1845', in *Five Punjabi Centuries: Polity, Economy, Society and Culture, C. 1500–1990* (1997), 92.
113. Ibid.; Charles Joseph Hall, 'The Maharaja's Account Books. State and Society under the Sikhs: 1799–1849' (University of Illinois), 10–11. On 'segmentary states', see Burton Stein, 'The Segmentary State in South Indian History', in *Realm and Region in Traditional India* (1977), Aidan Southall, 'The Segmentary State in Africa and Asia', *Comparative Studies in Society and History*.

114. Sir Percy Sykes later judged that

> [t]his policy was distinctly short-sighted since it depended upon the loyalty but also on the power, life and health of Ranjit Singh, who had ruined his health by debauchery and drink and had already been struck with paralysis in 1834. ... Surely to make paralytic Ranjit Singh the sheet anchor of the British policy was most unwise.

Percy Sykes, *A History of Afghanistan*, Vol. 1 (1940), 398–9.
115. W.H. Macnaghten to Bentinck, 26 December 1831, *The Correspondence of Lord William Cavendish Bentinck: Governor-General of India 1828–1835*, No. 390.
116. Bentinck's Minute on Military Policy, 13 March 1835, *The Correspondence of Lord William Cavendish Bentinck: Governor-General of India 1828–1835*, No. 810.
117. Charles Joseph Hall, 'The Maharaja's Account Books. State and Society under the Sikhs: 1799–1849' (University of Illinois), 198.
118. Ibid., 205–06.
119. Anil Chandra Banerjee, *The Khalsa Raj* (1985), 107.
120. Bikrama Jit Hasrat, *Anglo-Sikh Relations, 1799–1849: A Reappraisal of the Rise and Fall of the Sikhs* (1968), 156–7.
121. For Metcalfe and his contemporaries view on what he calls 'Indian militarism', see generally Douglas Peers, *Between Mars and Mammon: Colonial Armies and the Garrison State in Early Nineteenth-Century India* (1995).
122. Minute by Sir Charles Metcalfe, Secretary to Gov't, 2 June 1833, quoted in Secret Letter from Bengal, 6 June 1833, IOR, London, *Secret & Political*, L/PS/5/43.
123. Dayal Dass, *Charles Metcalfe and British Administration in India* (1988), 48–53; D.N. Panigrahi, *Charles Metcalfe in India: Ideas and Administration* (1968), 18–20.
124. Douglas Peers, *Between Mars and Mammon: Colonial Armies and the Garrison State in Early Nineteenth-Century India* (1995), 31; Dayal Dass, *Charles Metcalfe and British Administration in India* (1988), 192–6.
125. Metcalfe to Auckland, 15 October 1836, BL, London, *Auckland Papers*, Add.Mss.37689.
126. Auckland to Hobhouse, 7 October 1836, BL, London, *Auckland Papers*, Add.Mss.37689.
127. Minute, 5 September 1836, NAI, New Delhi, *Foreign Department, Political Consultations*, Nos. 9–19. William Macnaghten's accompanying instructions reinforced Auckland's point. See Macnaghten to Wade, 3 October 1836, NAI, New Delhi, *Foreign Department, Secret Consultations*, No. 18; Wade to Macnaghten, 1 August 1838, NAI, New Delhi, *Foreign Department, Secret Consultations*, No. 33.
128. Auckland to Metcalfe, 24 September 1836, BL, London, *Auckland Papers*, Add.Mss.37689.
129. 'It was part of request that the Dentist should bring a set of teeth with him and thus if we satisfy him we shall hear no more of his jaw'. Auckland to Metcalfe, 15 October 1836, BL, London, *Auckland Papers*, Add.Mss.37689.
130. Report by Captain C.M. Wade on Amherst's Meeting with Maharaja Ranjit Singh Report of the Proceedings During the Mission from the Governor-General to Maharaja Runjeet Singh by Captain C.M. Wade to Sir Charles Metcalfe, 1 August 1827, IOR, London, *Amherst Papers*, Mss. Eur. F140/155.
131. On Sikh difficulties with Peshawar, see, for example, Notes on Afghanistan, 1824, IOR, London, *Moorcroft Papers*, MSS.Eur.G30.5ff/MSS.Eur.K362; Wade to Colebrooke, 22 May 1829, NAI, New Delhi, *Foreign Department*, No. 10; Wade

to Colebrooke, 30 May 1829, NAI, New Delhi, *Foreign Department, Political Consultations*, No. 17.

132. On Sikh actions against Sayyid Barelwi, see Murray to Wade, 30 March 1827, NAI, New Delhi, *Foreign Department, Political Consultations*, No. 33; Wade to Hawkins, 17 November 1830, PPA, Lahore, *Records of the Ludhiana Agency*, No. 98.131; Wade to Martin, 21, 31 March 1831, PPA, Lahore, *Records of the Ludhiana Agency*, Nos. 98.159–60.

133. From Kelim Ullah to Captain Wade Received the 30th of July, 19 September 1834, NAI, New Delhi, *Foreign Department, Ootacamund Secret Consultations*, No. 1; Wade to Macnaghten, 26 August 1834, NAI, New Delhi, *Foreign Department, Ootacamand Secret Consultations*, No. 4.

134. See, for example, Mackeson to Wade, 16 November 1837, IOR, London, *Secret & Political*, L/PS/5/129.

135. Report by Captain C.M. Wade on Amherst's Meeting with Maharaja Ranjit Singh, Report of the Proceedings During the Mission from the Governor-General to Maharaja Runjeet Singh by Captain C.M. Wade to Sir Charles Metcalfe, 1 August 1827, IOR, London, *Amherst Papers*, Mss. Eur. F140/155.

136. On Company attitudes towards Afghanistan, see British Indifference to Afghan Civil War, 10 November; 9 October 1830, IOR, London, *Secret & Political*, L/PS/6/244; L/PS/6/42.

137. On Dost Muhammad's overtures to Governor-General Bentinck, see Arrival at Ludhiana of an Agent from Sirdar Sultan Muhammed Khan of Peshawar. Letters Subsequently Sent to the Governor-General (Lord Bentinck) by Sultan Muhammad Khan and by Dost Muhammad of Kabul, July 1832–March 1834, IOR, *Board's Collection*, F/4/1466/57656.

On Shah Shuja's attempts to gain Company support in efforts to regain his throne, see, for instance, Metcalfe to John Adam, Acting Chief Secretary to Government, 10 May 1816, NAI, New Delhi, *Foreign Department, Political Consultations*, No. 10; Murray to Metcalfe, 31 October 1816, NAI, New Delhi, *Foreign Department, Political Consultations*, No. 32; Shah Shuja, the Ex-King of Kabul, Is Refused an Audience with the Governor-General, Lord Amherst – His Request for Assistance to Regain His Throne Is Likewise Declined – Question Whether He Should Be Granted an Increase in Stipend – His Secret Negotiations with Maharaja Ranjit Singh, March 1826–February 1829, IOR, London, *Board's Collections*, F/4/1181/30743(3).

138. Michael Ignatieff's suggestion that the United States is currently embarked on creation of a version of 'empire lite' thus has historical antecedents. See Michael Ignatieff, *Empire Lite: Nation-Building in Bosnia, Kosovo and Afghanistan* (2003).

139. Arms Purchased by Shah Shuja at Delhi Are Exempted from Transit Duty – His Plans to Return to Kabul to Regain His Kingdom, September 1832–March 1834, IOR, London, *Board's Collections*, F/4/1466/57660, No. 57660.

140. See, for instance, Further Papers Regarding the Negotiations between Shah Shuja and Ranjit Singh – the Bengal Government Decline to Support Any Attempt by Shah Shuja to Regain His Kingdom, May 1829–November 1830, IOR, London, *Board's Collections*, F/4/1325/52479.

141. Remarks Upon Afghanistan, 26 August 1834, NAI, New Delhi, *Foreign Department, Ootacamund Secret Consultations*, No. 5.

142. Shuja had been attempting to negotiate Ranjit's support for years. In 1829, when it appeared Shuja was seriously contemplating a campaign for the throne, the two reached a formula regarding Peshawar which remained

essentially the same throughout future negotiations – namely that Ranjit would become overlord of Peshawar. On this first negotiation, see Wade to J.E. Colebrooke, Delhi Resident, 20 February 1829, NAI, New Delhi, *Foreign Department, Political Consultations*, No. 17; Wade to Colebrooke, 12 June 1829, NAI, New Delhi, *Foreign Department, Political Consultations*, No. 27; Wade to Colebrooke, 12 June 1829, NAI, New Delhi, *Foreign Department, Political Consultations*, No. 25.

143. For reports of Shuja's defeat, including Dost Muhammad's pursuit of him to Khelat, see Pottinger to Wade, 25 July 1834, PPA, Lahore, *Records of the Ludhiana Agency*, No. 105.56/268; Wade to Macnaghten, 13 August 1834, PPA, Lahore, *Records of the Ludhiana*, No. 140.63.

144. Christine Noelle, *State and Tribe in Nineteenth Century Afghanistan: The Reign of Amir Dost Muhammad Khan, 1826–1863* (1997), 11–17.

145. See, for example, Mackeson to Wade, 10 April 1838, PPA, Lahore, *Records of the Ludhiana Agency*, No. 110.62; Extract of a Letter from Mr Masson to Captain Wade Dated Camp Bassul 13 April 1834, 7 September 1835, NAI, New Delhi, *Foreign Department, Political Consultations*, No. 36. Although *sardār* of Peshawar under Ranjit Singh, Sultan Muhammad Khan approached the Company, as well as received approaches by Dost Muhammad. Wade to Macnaghten, 5 July 1832, PPA, Lahore, *Records of the Ludhiana Agency*, No. 138.29, Arrival at Ludhiana of an Agent from Sirdar Sultan Muhammed Khan of Peshawar. Letters Subsequently Sent to the Governor-General (Lord Bentinck) by Sultan Muhammad Khan and by Dost Muhammad of Kabul, July 1832–March 1834, IOR, *Board's Collection*, F/4/1466/57656. Ranjit likewise dispatched envoys to Dost Muhammad's camp, including the American Josiah Harlan. Banerjee, *Anglo-Sikh Relations: Chapters from J.D. Cunningham's 'History of the Sikhs'*, 52.

146. See, for instance, Observations on the Political State and Resources of Afghanistan, 23 January 1835, NAI, New Delhi, *Foreign Department, Political Consultations*, No. 46.

147. Wade to Macnaghten, 13 February 1835, PPA, Lahore, *Records of the Ludhiana Agency*, 141.9.

148. Wade to Macnaghten, 23 January 1835, NAI, New Delhi, *Foreign Department, Political Consultations*, No. 45.

149. For Dost Muhammad's attempts to get British mediation, see, for example, Wade to Macnaghten, 1 February 1833, PPA, Lahore, *Records of the Ludhiana Agency*, No. 140.6; Extract of a Letter from Mr Masson to Captain Wade Dated 20 February Regarding the Probable Course of Events in Case of the Triumph or Defeat of Dost Mohamed Khan, and the Reliance of That Chief and His Family on the Mediation of the British Government Together with the Advantages of Such a Mediation to the British, 6 July 1835, NAI, New Delhi, *Foreign Department, Political Correspondence*, No. 16. Ranjit Singh was understandably more reserved about his desire to countenance Company mediation. See, for instance, Wade to Colebrooke, 4 September 1829, NAI, New Delhi, *Foreign Department, Political Consultations*, No. 20; Wade to Macnaghten, 20 April 1835, NAI, New Delhi, *Foreign Department, Political Consultations*, No. 36.

150. See Minute, 5 September 1836, NAI, New Delhi, *Foreign Department, Political Consultations*, Nos. 9–19; Macnaghten to Burnes, 20 October 1837, NAI, New Delhi, *Foreign Department, Political Consultations*, No. 79.

151. Tripartite Treaty, 26 September 1838, NAI, New Delhi, *Foreign Department, Secret Consultations*, No. 6.

152. For an example of British attitudes, see Macnaghten to Burnes, 9 May 1838, NAI, New Delhi, *Foreign Department, Political Consultations*, No. 76.
153. See, for example, Wade to Macnaghten, 14 February 1838, NAI, New Delhi, *Foreign Department, Political Consultations*, No. 56.
154. Auckland made this clear in his Minute of 1837. Minute by the Governor-General, 11 September 1837, NAI, New Delhi, *Foreign Department, Political Consultations*, No. 42.
155. For the British mediating position, see Macnaghten to Ameer Dost Mohamed Khan, 29 May 1839, NAI, New Delhi, *Foreign Department, Secret Consultations*.
156. Dost Muhammad received Vitkevich in line with advice he received from Burnes. Burnes to Macnaghten, 18 February 1838, IOR, London, *Secret & Political*, L/PS/5/130.

3   Anglo-Sikh relations and South Asian warfare

1. There is relatively little recent historiography about this period of the Punjab's history. See, for example, Glushan Lall Chopra, *The Panjab as a Sovereign State* (1960), Bikrama Jit Hasrat, *Anglo-Sikh Relations, 1799–1849: A Reappraisal of the Rise and Fall of the Sikhs* (1968).
2. Burnes to Wade, 7 April 1837, PPA, Lahore, *Records of the Ludhiana Agency*, 108.18.
3. See, for example, McNeill to Viscount Palmerston, 15 December 1837, IOR, London, *Secret & Political*, L/PS/9/104.
4. See, for instance, Notes on the Invasion of India, 19 August 1825, NAI, New Delhi, *Foreign Department, Secret Consultations*, Nos. 3–4.
5. See, for example, Abstract of Intelligence from Cabul from 3 to 25 December 1832, 19 March 1833, NAI, New Delhi, *Foreign Department, Secret Consultations*, No. 31; Wade to Macnaghten, 21 December 1832, PPA, Lahore, *Records of the Ludhiana Agency*, No. 138.70; J.A. Norris, *The First Afghan War, 1838–1842* (1967), 66–7.
6. For a sense of how the British ambassador in Persia and the Home Government viewed Russian participation in the siege of Herat, see McNeill to Viscount Palmerston, 30 December 1837, IOR, London, *Secret & Political*, L/PS/9/104; McNeill to Palmerston, 30 June 1837, PPA, Lahore, No. 119.51. Interestingly, Burnes and McNeill, the British envoy to the Persian court, both initially advocated supporting Dost Muhammad Khan. See On the Indus above Mooltan, Confidential Letter from Burnes to McNeill, June 6 1837, IOR, London, *Masson Correspondence*, MSS. Eur.E161.3/MSS.Eur.J633:3(iv), Letter from McNeill to Captain Burnes in Cabool, Including Translations of Various Despatches from the Shah's Court, 13 March 1837, IOR, London, *Masson Correspondence*, MSS.Eur.E161.3/MSS.EUR.J633:3(iii).
7. Extract of a Letter from Mr Masson to Captain. Wade Dated 2 February, 15 May 1837, NAI, New Delhi, *Foreign Department, Secret Consultations*, No. 7; Wade to Macnaghten, 15 May 1837, NAI, New Delhi, *Foreign Department, Secret Consultations*, No. 7. See also Fayz Muhammad Katib, *Siraj Al-Tavarikh* (Hijra 1372 (1993/1994)), 176–7.
8. Extract of a Letter from Mr Masson to Captain Wade Dated 7th May, 7 August 1837, NAI, New Delhi, *Foreign Department, Political Consultations*, No. 86; Extract of a Letter from Mr Masson to Captain Wade Dated 18 May, 7 August 1837, NAI, New Delhi, *Foreign Department, Political Consultations*, No. 91.

9. Wade to Macnaghten, 12 June 1837, NAI, New Delhi, *Foreign Department, Secret Consultations*, No. 8.

10. Burnes to Macnaghten, 4 September 1837, IOR, London, *Secret & Political*, L/PS/5/129.

11. Wade to Macnaghten, 20 October 1837, NAI, New Delhi, *Foreign Department, Political Consultations*, No. 67.

12. Macnaghten to Wade, 27 December 1837, PPA, Lahore, *Records of the Ludhiana Agency*, No. 119.91.

13. See, for example, Wade to Macnaghten, 12 June 1837, NAI, New Delhi, *Foreign Department, Secret Consultations*, No. 8; Wade to Macnaghten, 17 July 1837, NAI, New Delhi, *Foreign Department, Political Consultations*, No. 33.

14. For an example of Burnes' relations with Dost Muhammad, see Burnes to Macnaghten, 27 December 1837, NAI, New Delhi, *Foreign Department, Political Consultations*, No. 12.

15. Auckland to Dost Mohamed Khan, 9 May 1838, NAI, New Delhi, *Foreign Department, Political Consultations*, No. 75.

16. Macnaghten to Burnes, 9 May 1838, NAI, New Delhi, *Foreign Department, Political Consultations*, No. 76.

17. Burnes to Macnaghten, 18 February 1838, IOR, London, *Secret & Political*, L/PS/5/130; Burnes to Macnaghten, 25 April 1838, IOR, London, *McNeill Papers*, MSS.Eur.D1165/13.

18. Shortly after his public disavowal, Vitkevich was found dead in St. Petersburg. It was officially ruled a suicide, but speculation to the contrary persists. Karl Meyer and Shareen Brysac, *Tournament of Shadows: The Great Game and the Race for Empire in Asia* (1999), 84–5, 106.

19. On Shuja's reception in Kandahar, see Macnaghten to T.H. Maddock, Official Secretary to Govt of India, 6 June 1839, BL, London, *Broughton Papers*, Add. 36474; Burnes to Auckland, 25 April 1839, BL, London, *Broughton Papers*, Add. 36474.

    On Auckland's tone, see Minute by the Governor-General, 11 September 1839, NAI, New Delhi, *Foreign Department, Secret Consultations*, No. 18.

20. See, for example, Macnaghten to T.H. Maddock, 4 September 1839, NAI, New Delhi, *Foreign Department, Secret Consultations*, No. 227.

21. Lord Bentinck formed a poor opinion of Shah Shuja, contending that 'he has no energy of character'. Bentinck to C. Marjoribanks, 26 February 1833, *The Correspondence of Lord William Cavendish Bentinck: Governor-General of India 1828–1835*, No. 557. For an idea of officers' attitudes, see J.A. Norris, *The First Afghan War, 1838–1842* (1967), 335.

22. Shah Mahmoud Hanifi, 'Inter-Regional Trade and Colonial State Formation in 19th Century Afghanistan' (University of Michigan), 126.

23. See, for instance, Detail of Town Duties of Candahar Carried to HM's Credit in the Revenue Account, WM1839, RAS, London, *Rawlinson Papers*, Box 3, VII, Report on the Durranee Tribes, 19 April 1841, IOR, London, *Secret & Political*, L/PS/18/C5.

24. M.E. Yapp, 'The Revolutions of 1841–2 in Afghanistan', *Bulletin of the School of Oriental and African Studies*, 345.

25. The treaty, recognizing Sikh claims over Peshawar, required the Sikhs to assist the Company's expedition. While the grudgingly helped force the Khyber, the Lahore *darbār* in the main refused to aid the British expedition. Maddock to Clerk, Political Agent Loodhiana, 16 October 1839, NAI, New Delhi, *Foreign Department, Secret Consultations*, No. 116.

26. Auckland to George Clerk, 23 May 1841, BL, London, *Auckland Papers*, Add. Mss. 37705.
27. See generally M.E. Yapp, 'The Revolutions of 1841–2 in Afghanistan', *Bulletin of the School of Oriental and African Studies*.
28. John William Kaye, *History of the War in Afghanistan*, Vol. 1 (1851), 615. Interestingly, in at least one case in Kandahar, British authorities turned to the '*ulamā*' to soothe public outrage over relations between a European soldier and an Afghan woman. Macnaghten to T.H. Maddock, Official Secretary to Govt of India, 6 June 1839, BL, London, *Broughton Papers*, Add. 36474.
29. Peter Hopkirk, *The Great Game: On Secret Service in High Asia* (1990), 261–6.
30. On the other survivors, see Linda Colley, *Captives: The Story of Britain's Pursuit of Empire and How Its Soldiers and Civilians Were Held Captive by the Dream of Global Supremacy, 1600–1850* (2003), 347–66.
31. Declaration on the Part of the Right Honorable the Governor-General of India, 24 October 1838, NAI, New Delhi, *Foreign Department, Oot. Political Consultations*, No. 8, Macnaghten to Ameer Dost Mohamed Khan, 29 May 1839, NAI, New Delhi, *Foreign Department, Secret Consultations*.
32. See, for example, Abstract Translation of a Letter from Ruhum Dil Khan to the Address of Lieut. Colonel Sir Alexander Burnes, 3 July 1839, NAI, New Delhi, *Foreign Department, Secret Consultations*, No. 35; Lord to Wade, 12 June 1839, NAI, New Delhi, *Foreign Department, Secret Consultations*, No. 75A.
33. C.A. Bayly, *Empire and Information* (2002), 174.
34. The Company's victory over the Peshwa in the Third Anglo-Maratha War in 1818 is usually viewed as establishing the Company's unrivalled supremacy in the subcontinent. This sense of mastery was underlined by the Company's attitudes towards participation in South Asian court ceremony. See Gail Minault, 'The Emperor's Old Clothes: Robing and Sovereignty in Late Mughal and Early British India', in *Robes of Honour: Khil'at in Pre-Colonial and Colonial India* (2003).
35. See generally Dirk H.A. Kolff, *Naukar, Rajput and Sepoy: The Ethnohistory of the Military Labour Market in Hindustan, 1450–1850* (1990).
36. Jos Gommans, *The Rise of the Indo-Afghan Empire* (1999), 135–43; Jos Gommans, 'Indian Warfare and Afghan Innovation During the Eighteenth Century', in *Warfare and Weaponry in South Asia, 1000–1800* (2001).
37. On the Company army and warfare, see generally Seema Alavi, *Sepoys and the Company: Tradition and Transition in North India, 1770–1830* (1995).
38. C.A. Bayly, 'The British Military-Fiscal State and Indigenous Resistance: India 1750–1820', in *The Imperial State at War: Britain from 1689 to 1815* (1994).
39. Crow to Jonathon Duncan, 7 May 1800, IOR, London, *Home & Misc.*, H/333(24).
40. On the 'military revolution', see Geoffrey Parker, *The Military Revolution: Military Innovation and the Rise of the West* (1988).
41. On the idea of military fiscalism in South Asia, see generally Douglas Peers, *Between Mars and Mammon: Colonial Armies and the Garrison State in Early Nineteenth-Century India* (1995).
42. Rohan D'Souza, 'Crisis before the Fall: Some Speculations on the Decline of the Ottomans, Safavids and Mughals', *Social Scientist*.
43. See Chapter 4.
44. Thomas Barfield, 'Problems in Establishing Legitimacy in Afghanistan', *Iranian Studies*, 271.
45. M.E. Yapp, 'The Revolutions of 1841–2 in Afghanistan', *Bulletin of the School of Oriental and African Studies*, 339.

46. On the role of negotiation in South Asian warfare, see Jos Gommans, 'Indian Warfare and Afghan Innovation During the Eighteenth Century', in *Warfare and Weaponry in South Asia, 1000–1800* (2001).

47. Martha McLaren, *British India and British Scotland, 1780–1830: Career Building, Empire Building, and a Scottish School of Thought on Indian Governance* (2001), 58, 103.

48. David Washbrook, 'India, 1818–1860: The Two Faces of Colonialism', in *Oxford History of the British Empire* (1999), 405.

49. For a detailed discussion of the Company military model, see Seema Alavi, 'The Makings of Company Power: James Skinner in the Ceded and Conquered Provinces, 1802–1840', in *Warfare and Weaponry in South Asia, 1000–1800* (2001).

50. See, for example, Wade to W. Murray, 29 April 1824, PPA, Lahore, *Records of the Ambala Agency*, Nos. 24.79–81.

51. See, for instance, Princep's instructions to Wade to take five European mercenaries in Lahore into custody if they were deserters. Interestingly, they claimed and proved to be Russian, a fact which raised considerably less concern than if they had been Company deserters. Prinsep to Wade, 14 May 1831, PPA, Lahore, *Records of the Ludhiana Agency*, No. 115.79.

52. See Andre Wink, *Land and Sovereignty in India: Agrarian Society and Politics under the Eighteenth Century Maratha Svarajya* (1986). Such peripheral areas later caused difficulty to Abdur Rahman Khan when he attempted to establish a centralized Afghan state in the late nineteenth century. He termed such areas *yaghistan* ('land of rebellion'). David Edwards, *Heroes of the Age: Moral Fault Lines on the Afghan Frontier* (1996), 27.

53. For a short biographical sketch of many of the European mercenaries, see Charles Grey, *European Adventurers of Northern India, 1785–1849* (1929).

54. Elliot to W. Murray, 24 July 1812, PPA, Lahore, *Records of the Ambala Agency*, No. 23.128. For a list of Europeans in Ranjit's service, see Particulars of Several Europeans and Others Who Have Proceeded to Lahore with the View of Entering Runjeet Singh's Service, and Who Have since Generally Quitted That Country, 1830–32, IOR, London, *Boards Collections*, F/4/1344/53436; Glushan Lall Chopra, *The Panjab as a Sovereign State* (1960), 144–5.

55. See, for example, Wade to Prinsep, 25 September 1831, PPA, Lahore, *Records of the Ludhiana Agency*, No. 137.30.

56. For a detailed discussion of these officers, see Jean-Marie LaFont, *Fauj-I-Khas: Maharaja Ranjit Singh and His French Officers* (2002).

57. During his visit to the Punjab in 1837, Sir Henry Fane, Commander-in-Chief, estimated the *Khalsa*'s strength between sixty and seventy battalions, 700 artillery pieces and a large cavalry contingent of up to 4000 men. Bikrama Jit Hasrat, *Anglo-Sikh Relations, 1799–1849: A Reappraisal of the Rise and Fall of the Sikhs*, (1968), 150–1. Wade estimated Ranjit's forces to be considerably smaller, not exceeding 25,000 men excluding garrisons. C.M. Wade to Captain Benson, 11 December 1831, *The Correspondence of Lord William Cavendish Bentinck: Governor-General of India 1828–1835*, No. 381. For the most comprehensive overview of Ranjit's military establishment, see Charles Joseph Hall, 'The Maharaja's Account Books. State and Society under the Sikhs: 1799–1849' (University of Illinois), 198–240.

58. Report by Captain C.M. Wade on Amherst's Meeting with Maharaja Ranjit Singh, Report of the Proceedings During the Mission from the Governor-General to Maharaja Runjeet Singh by Captain C.M. Wade to Sir Charles Metcalfe, 1 August 1827, IOR, London, *Amherst Papers*, Mss. Eur. F140/155.

59. Emily Eden, *Up the Country: Letter Written to Her Sister from the Upper Provinces of India* (1978), 209–10. See also J.A. Norris, *The First Afghan War, 1838–1842* (1967), 241–2.

60. Macnaghten to Wade, 2 October 1832, PPA, Lahore, *Records of the Ludhiana Agency*, No. 116.34; Journal of a Journey of a French Officer in 1826, 1841, IOR, London, *Secret & Political*, L/PS/20/G10/3.

61. Messr. Court, who formerly served a Persian prince, had enquired about joining the Russian service from a fellow French officer on General Yermaloff's staff. Bentinck to Charles Grant, 1 May 1832, *The Correspondence of Lord William Cavendish Bentinck: Governor-General of India 1828–1835*, No. 436. Count Simonovich, the Russian Envoy to the Persian Court in Tehran, had served in Napoleon's forces until 1815, after which he entered the Tsar's service. His service brought him into contact with some of Ranjit Singh's French officers, a fact the British were aware of. Personal communication with Jean-Marie La Font. New Delhi, 4 December 2003.

62. Messr. Ventura maintained running correspondence with the Governor-General Lord Auckland. He offered, on two or three occasions, his services to the Company, but was discouraged by Wade. Wade to Macnaghten, 25 June 1836, PPA, Lahore, *Records of the Ludhiana Agency*, No. 142.39.

63. See, for example, Auckland to Charles Metcalfe, 7 January 1836, BL, London, *Auckland Papers*, Add.Mss.37689.

64. On the Present Political State of Afghanistan: Extract from Mr Moorcroft's Letter to Mr Swinton, 28 September 1824, IOR, London, *Home & Misc*, H/664(24), No. 822/4.
    See also Robert Nichols, *Settling the Frontier: Law, Land and Society in the Peshawar Valley, 1500–1900* (2001), 91.

65. Notes on Afghanistan, 1824, IOR, London, *Moorcroft Papers*, MSS.Eur.G30.5ff/MSS.Eur.K362.

66. Pottinger to Wade, 7 August 1834, PPA, Lahore, *Records of the Ludhiana Agency*, No. 105.63; Wade to Macnaghten, 13 August 1834, PPA, Lahore, *Records of the Ludhiana*, No. 140.63. Dost Muhammad originally employed Abd al-Samad Khan Tabrizi, a former personal servant of Muhammad Ali Mirza who had left Persia in search of mercenary employment. He organized a force of 1000 regular foot. Fayz Muhammad Katib, *Siraj Al-Tavarikh* (Hijra 1372 (1993/1994)), 155.

67. Rohan D'Souza, 'Crisis before the Fall: Some Speculations on the Decline of the Ottomans, Safavids and Mughals', *Social Scientist*, 23–4.

68. See, for example, Moorcroft to Swinton, 10 October 1813, NAI, New Delhi, *Foreign Department, Political Consultations*, No. 40; Murray to Wade, 30 March 1827, NAI, New Delhi, *Foreign Department, Political Consultations*, No. 33.

69. See generally Josiah Harlan, *A Memoir of India and Avghanistan* (1842); Josiah Harlan, *Central Asia: Personal Narrative of Josiah Harlan, 1823–1841* (1939); Ben Macintyre, *Josiah the Great: The True Story of the Man Who Would Be King* (2004).

70. 'Mr Fast is an Englishman. He was formerly in the Honourable Company's military service and is a son of Brigadier Fast at Delhi.' Wade to Macnaghten, 3 July 1837, NAI, New Delhi, *Foreign Department, Political Consultations*, No. 30.
    Mr Dicks was described as an 'East Indiaman' who accompanied Shah Shuja from Ludiana on his 1834 expedition to reclaim his throne. Apparently, he deserted Shuja in Sind, seeking employment on better terms with the Amirs of Sind. Wade to Macnaghten, 18 July 1834, NAI, New Delhi, *Foreign Department, Ootacamand Secret Consultations*, No. 6.

Fayz Muhammad Katib's chronicle portrays Campbell and Dick as agents of the EIC, planted by Wade and Mackeson. Fayz Muhammad Katib, *Siraj Al-Tavarikh* (Hijra 1372 (1993/1994)), 161–3, 72.

Mr Campbell mainly commanded Dost Muhammad's cavalry detachments. Extract of a Letter from Mr Masson to Captain Wade Dated the 9th April 1835, 24 August 1835, NAI, New Delhi, *Foreign Department, Political Consultations*, No. 63. None of these European mercenaries appear to have fought the British during their invasion in 1839, although Mr Harlan and Mr Campbell remained in the Dost's employment for at least part of the time.

71. See generally Jean-Marie LaFont, *Fauj-I-Khas: Maharaja Ranjit Singh and His French Officers* (2002).
72. Prinsep to Wade, 14 May 1831, PPA, Lahore, *Records of the Ludhiana Agency*, No. 115.79; Wade to Colebrooke, 27 February 1829, NAI, New Delhi, *Foreign Department, Political Consultations*, No. 12.
73. Campbell to Macnaghten, 23 May 1833, NAI, New Delhi, *Foreign Department, Secret Consultations*, No. 18.
74. This included Mr Borowski, a Tsarist officer of Polish origin who led the battalion of Russian deserters during the 1832–3 expedition. He commanded the Shah's forces during the siege until killed on 24 June 1838. Macnaghten to Wade, 6 November 1832, PPA, Lahore, *Records of the Ludhiana Agency*, No. 116.37; J.A. Norris, *The First Afghan War, 1838–1842* (1967), 180. Borowski had been in Bombay in the early 1830s and was thought by authorities there to have been a Russian spy. Lord Clare to Bentinck, 8 January 1832, *The Correspondence of Lord William Cavendish Bentinck: Governor-General of India 1828–1835*, No. 394.
75. Memo of Advices in Secret Letters from Bengal Relative to the Threatened Invasion of India by Zemaun Shah, 3 October–25 January 1798–1800, IOR, London, *Home & Misc.*, H/481(7).
76. Wade to Macnaghten, 19 February 1835, NAI, New Delhi, *Foreign Department, Political Consultations*, No. 8; Wade to Macnaghten, 1 August 1838, NAI, New Delhi, *Foreign Department, Secret Consultations*, No. 16.
77. For an example of the tribute terms, see Wade to Colebrooke, 12 June 1829, NAI, New Delhi, *Foreign Department, Political Consultations*, No. 27; Wade to Colebrooke, 30 May 1829, NAI, New Delhi, *Foreign Department, Political Consultations*, No. 17.
78. Bikrama Jit Hasrat, *Anglo-Sikh Relations, 1799–1849: A Reappraisal of the Rise and Fall of the Sikhs* (1968), 152.
79. Wade to Macnaghten, 20 April 1835, NAI, New Delhi, *Foreign Department, Political Consultations*, No. 36.
80. See, for instance, Fayz Muhammad Katib, *Siraj Al-Tavarikh* (Hijra 1372 (1993/1994)), 87, 110, 150–1.
81. Extract of a Letter from Mr Masson to Captain Wade Dated the 2nd February, 15 May 1837, NAI, New Delhi, *Foreign Department, Secret Consultations*, No. 7; Dost Mohamed to Wade, 15 May 1837, NAI, New Delhi, *Foreign Department, Secret Consultations*, No. 8.
82. See generally Marc Gaborieau, 'The *Jihād* of Sayyid Ahmad Barelwi on the North West Frontier: The Last Echo of the Middle Ages? Or a Prefiguration of Modern South Asia', in *Sufis, Sultans and Feudal Orders: Professor Nurul Hasan Commemoration Volume* (2004); Robert Nichols, *Settling the Frontier: Law, Land and Society in the Peshawar Valley, 1500–1900* (2001), 94–104.
83. The later British labelling of Sayyid Ahmad Barelwi as a 'Wahabi' was largely politically motivated and theologically misinformed. See Ashraf Ghani, 'Islam

and Statebuilding in a Tribal Society', *Modern Asian Studies*; Christine Noelle, 'The Anti-Wahabi Reaction in Nineteenth Century Afghanistan', *The Muslim World*.

84. See, for example, Wade to Hawkins, 24 August; 7, 13 September 1830, PPA, Lahore, *Records of the Ludhiana Residency*, No. 98.114–6; Wade to Hawkins, 17 November 1830, PPA, Lahore, *Records of the Ludhiana Agency*, No. 98.131. Yar Muhammad Khan, leading *sardār* of Peshawar and one time ally of Sayyid Ahmad's, died fighting the Sayyid's revolt. Chopra, *The Panjab as a Sovereign State*, 27; Katib, *Siraj Al-Tavarikh*, 153.

85. See, for instance, Mackeson to Wade, 25 February 1838, PPA, Lahore, *Records of the Ludhiana Agency*, No. 110.49.

86. Wade to Macnaghten, 11 June 1838, IOR, London, *Secret & Political*, L/PS/5/131.

87. For an example of British efforts defining the Indian moral universe in terms of indigenous language of legitimacy, see Extract from the Opinion of Mohamedan Law Officers Respecting the Legal Effect of the Transactions between Meer Roostum and Ali Morad, in Papers Presented to Parliament, Relative to Sind, 1844, PRO, London, *Ellenborough Papers*, PRO/30/12/15/5.

88. Robert Nichols, *Settling the Frontier: Law, Land and Society in the Peshawar Valley, 1500–1900* (2001), 96; Wade to C.T. Metcalfe, Delhi Resident, 30 March 1827, NAI, New Delhi, *Foreign Department, Political Consultations*, No. 32. Fayz Muhammad Katib claims Sayyid Ahmad was a regular trooper in the EIC cavalry. Fayz Muhammad Katib, *Siraj Al-Tavarikh* (Hijra 1372 (1993/1994)), 150.

89. Anil Chandra Banerjee, *The Khalsa Raj* (1985), 99.

90. Marc Gaborieau, 'The *Jihād* of Sayyid Ahmad Barelwi on the North West Frontier: The Last Echo of the Middle Ages? Or a Prefiguration of Modern South Asia', in *Sufis, Sultans and Feudal Orders: Professor Nurul Hasan Commemoration Volume* (2004), 30.

91. Extract of a Letter from Mr Masson to Captain Wade Dated 31 October 1836, 6 February 1837, NAI, New Delhi, *Foreign Department, Political Consultations*, No. 14; Copy of a Dispatch from Loodhiana Political Agent on a Mission to Lahore, 7 January 1837, IOR, London, *Secret & Political*, L/PS/5/127, No. 46.

92. Marc Gaborieau, 'The *Jihād* of Sayyid Ahmad Barelwi on the North West Frontier: The Last Echo of the Middle Ages? Or a Prefiguration of Modern South Asia', in *Sufis, Sultans and Feudal Orders: Professor Nurul Hasan Commemoration Volume* (2004), 34.

93. Extract of a Letter from Mr Masson to Captain Wade Dated at Kabul 20th Mahomedan Month Barat 1250, 30 March 1835, NAI, New Delhi, *Foreign Department, Political Consultations*, No. 46; Masson to H. Pottinger, 20 September 1834, PRO, London, *Pottinger Papers*, FO/705/32.

94. Extract of a Letter from Mr Masson to Captain Wade Dated 20 February, 1 June 1835, NAI, New Delhi, *Foreign Department, Political Consultations*, No. 31.

95. Extract of a Letter from Mr Masson to Captain Wade Dated 20 February 1835, 25 May 1835, NAI, New Delhi, *Foreign Department, Political Consultations*, No. 30.

96. Anil Chandra Banerjee, *Anglo-Sikh Relations: Chapters from J.D. Cunningham's 'History of the Sikhs'* (1949), 52.

97. Extract of a Letter from Mr Masson to Captain Wade Dated 20 February 1835, 25 May 1835, NAI, New Delhi, *Foreign Department, Political Consultations*, No. 30; Extract of a Letter from Mr Masson to Captain Wade Dated 20 February, 1 June 1835, NAI, New Delhi, *Foreign Department, Political Consultations*, No. 31.

98. See generally Olivier Roy, *Islam and Resistance in Afghanistan* (1986).

99. See Chapter 4.

100. 'I should much regret it, but in a contest between the two [Dost Muhammad Khan and Maharaja Ranjit Singh], if forced to side with either, I would assuredly side with him [Maharaja Ranjit Singh]'. Minute by the Governor-General, 11 September 1837, NAI, New Delhi, *Foreign Department, Political Consultations*, No. 42.

4 Ontology of the Afghan political community

1. Mountstuart Elphinstone, *An Account of the Kingdom of Caubul*, Vol. 1 (1991; reprint, 1838), 235.
2. David Edwards, *Heroes of the Age: Moral Fault Lines on the Afghan Frontier* (1996).
3. Ibid., 3, 216.
4. C.A. Bayly coined this term. C.A. Bayly, *Imperial Meridian: The British Empire and the World, 1780–1830* (1989), 33–54; On British fears, see, for example, Copy of a Letter from Dhely Addressed to Hussien Alli Khan, Munshee of the Residency, 26 October 1798, IOR, London, *Bengal Proceedings*, P/BEN/SEC/50, Enclosure no. 18; Sec Dept dispatch 23 November, Notes on Cabul, Afghans, Abdallis, Timur Shah, Zemaun Shah, nd, IOR, London, *Home & Misc.*, H/605(1).
5. Shah Mahmoud Hanifi's important work has detailed this process under the reign of Abdur Rahman Khan. Shah Mahmoud Hanifi, 'Inter-Regional Trade and Colonial State Formation in 19th Century Afghanistan' (University of Michigan); Shah Mahmoud Hanifi, 'Impoverishing a Colonial Frontier: Cash, Credit and Debt in Nineteenth Century Afghanistan', *Iranian Studies*.
6. For an alternative visions of the state, specific to the Asian context, see Hans Antlon and Stein Tonnesson, eds., *Asian Forms of the Nation* (1996).
7. See generally B.D. Hopkins, 'The Bounds of Identity: The Goldsmid Mission and the Delineation of the Perso-Afghan Border in the Nineteenth Century', *Journal of Global History*.
8. See, for instance, Thomas Barfield, 'Problems in Establishing Legitimacy in Afghanistan', *Iranian Studies*.
9. Edwards refers to these three elements as honour, Islam and rule. David Edwards, *Heroes of the Age: Moral Fault Lines on the Afghan Frontier* (1996), 219.
10. Burton Stein, 'State Formation and Economy Reconsidered', *Modern Asian Studies*, 388.
11. See Ashraf Ghani, 'Islam and Statebuilding in a Tribal Society', *Modern Asian Studies*; Asta Olesen, 'The Political Use of Islam in Afghanistan During the Reign of Amir Abdur Rahman (1880–1901)', in *Contributions to Islamic Studies* (1987).
12. Although Barfield argues that '[T]he Durrani Empire was not a Pashtun tribal confederacy but a centralized military regime that depended on paid mercenaries and subject tribes who could be mobilized only through their own leaders who also expected to be rewarded', I contend the 'subject tribes', whose loyalty was ensured through regular plunder, made it a tribal confederacy. Thomas Barfield, 'Problems in Establishing Legitimacy in Afghanistan', *Iranian Studies*, 270.
13. The Durrani shahs did not treat the Durrani tribes as either equals or partners in governance. Ibid., 271.
14. Shah Mahmoud Hanifi, 'Inter-Regional Trade and Colonial State Formation in 19th Century Afghanistan' (University of Michigan), 255–98.
15. For a description of the workings of the *jirga*, see Mountstuart Elphinstone, *An Account of the Kingdom of Caubul*, Vol. 1 (1991; reprint, 1838), 215, 222–6.

16. In the election of Ahmad Shah, a noted *darwêsh*, Muhammad Sabir Shah, played the decisive role. Ganda Singh, *Ahmad Shah Durrani: Father of Modern Afghanistan* (1959), 25–9. Dost Muhammad repeated this show of charismatic religious selection by having the son of the *mīr wā'iẓ* (chief religious officer of Kabul) similarly nominate him; Christine Noelle, *State and Tribe in Nineteenth Century Afghanistan: The Reign of Amir Dost Muhammad Khan, 1826–1863* (1997), 15–16; See also Fayz Muhammad Katib, *Siraj Al-Tavarikh* (Hijra 1372 (1993/1994)), 12–13. Another Afghan leader to adopt the title *amīr al-mu'minīn* was Mullah Omar, leader of the Taliban. Ahmed Rashid, *Taliban: Militant Islam, Oil and Fundamentalism in Central Asia* (2000), 20.

17. Akbar S. Ahmed, *Pukhtun Economy and Society: Traditional Structure and Economic Development in Tribal Society* (1980), 90; Asta Olesen, *Islam and Politics in Afghanistan* (1995), 34.

18. Elphinstone insisted that '... although it [Pashtun society] encourages *little* [*italics original*] disorders, it affords an effectual security against the general revolutions and calamities to which despotic countries in Asia are so frequently subject'. Mountstuart Elphinstone, *An Account of the Kingdom of Caubul*, Vol. 1 (1991; reprint, 1838), 231–2.

19. This requirement, however, did not apply to the Qizilbash. Burnes to Macnaghten, 14 October 1837, IOR, London, *Secret & Political*, L/PS/5/129; Asta Olesen, *Islam and Politics in Afghanistan* (1995), 36–7.

20. Elphinstone described a number of offices and their responsibilities. Mountstuart Elphinstone, *An Account of the Kingdom of Caubul*, Vol. 2 (1991; reprint, 1838), 262–5, 277–8.

21. See Burnes to Macnaghten, 27 December 1837, NAI, New Delhi, *Foreign Department, Political Consultations*, No. 12; Observations on the Political State and Resources of Afghanistan, 23 January 1835, NAI, New Delhi, *Foreign Department, Political Consultations*, No. 46.

22. See generally Sarah Ansari, *Sufi Saints and State Power: The Pirs of Sind, 1843–1947* (1992).

23. Popular disaffection with the *'ulamā'* was arguably a consequence not simply of their association with the state, but more importantly with their position of privilege that association protected. M.E. Yapp, 'The Revolutions of 1841–2 in Afghanistan', *Bulletin of the School of Oriental and African Studies*, 342–3, 366.

24. Paysheet for Mullahhs and Syads, WM1839, RAS, London, *Rawlinson Collection*, Box 3, VII. When the Kabul revolt started in the early winter of 1841, the official religious leadership was sidelined by the more dynamic leadership of Sufi *sayyids* and *pirs*. J.A. Norris, *The First Afghan War, 1838–1842* (1967), 361–90.

25. Thomas Barfield, 'Problems in Establishing Legitimacy in Afghanistan', *Iranian Studies*, 270.

26. See, for example, Kuzilbash Influence in Afghanistan, 31 January 1836, NAI, New Delhi, *Foreign Department, Political Consultations*, Nos. 36–40.

27. See Memorandum Regarding the Present Chiefs of Cabool and Candahar, 1838, IOR, London, *Secret & Political*, L/PS/5/131; Wade to Macnaghten, 27 August 1832, NAI, New Delhi, *Foreign Department, Secret Consultations*, No. 25.

28. Said Amir Arjomand, *The Shadow of God and the Hidden Imam: Religion, Political Order, and Societal Change in Shi'ite Iran from the Beginning to 1890* (1984), 12.

29. See generally Michael Axelworthy, *The Sword of Persia: Nader Shah, from Tribal Warrior to Conquering Tyrant* (2006). The Timurid legacy continued to exert a strong influence over the political culture of South Asia in the form of the Mughals who

themselves were originally Timurids. Likewise, although Timurid state had given way to a succession of Chingizid states in Central Asia by 1500, it still exerted an important resonance over political culture.

30. Said Amir Arjomand, *The Shadow of God and the Hidden Imam: Religion, Political Order, and Societal Change in Shi'ite Iran from the Beginning to 1890* (1984), 94–5.
31. See Mullah Muhammad Baqir Majlisi, 'The Fountainhead of Life (Extracts), in *Two Seventeenth Century Tracts on Kingship'*, in *Authority and Political Culture in Shi'ism* (1988); Mullah Muhsin Fayd Kashani, 'The Kingly Mirror, in *Two Seventeenth Century Tracts on Kingship'*, in *Authority and Political Culture in Shi'ism* (1988).
32. See generally Peter Christensen, 'The Qajar State', in *Contributions to Islamic Studies: Iran, Afghanistan and Pakistan* (1987); Hamid Algar, *Religion and State in Iran, 1785–1906* (1969).
33. Peter Avery, 'Nadir Shah and the Afsharid Legacy', in *The Cambridge History of Iran: From Nadir Shah to the Islamic Republic* (1991), 11.
34. See generally Ernest Tucker, 'Explaining Nadir Shah: Kingship and Royal Legitimacy in Muhammad Kazim Marvi's Tarikh-I Alam-Ara-Yi Nadiri', *Iranian Studies*.
35. Said Amir Arjomand, *The Shadow of God and the Hidden Imam: Religion, Political Order, and Societal Change in Shi'ite Iran from the Beginning to 1890* (1984), 221.
36. See Ernest Tucker, 'Nadir Shah and the Ja'fari Madhhab Reconsidered', *Iranian Studies*.
37. For an idea of Nadir's relationship with those chiefs, see Peter Avery, 'Nadir Shah and the Afsharid Legacy', in *The Cambridge History of Iran: From Nadir Shah to the Islamic Republic* (1991), 35–6.
38. John Perry describes Nadir's supporters as 'free-booters' – Sunni Afghans and Uzbeks on whom he based his authority. J.R. Perry, 'The Zand Dynasty', in *The Cambridge History of Iran* (1991), 65. Perhaps Peter Avery's verdict is nearer the mark when he writes, 'Gratitude turned into dismay when he tried to obfuscate the religious differences on which Iran's identity had come to rest, and when his "Timurid" ambitions and consequent craving for conquest blinded him to the country's need for peace and stability'. Peter Avery, 'Nadir Shah and the Afsharid Legacy', in *The Cambridge History of Iran: From Nadir Shah to the Islamic Republic* (1991), 57. Ernest Tucker argues the consequences of Nadir's departure from Shi'a orthodoxy were surprisingly mild. Ernest Tucker, 'Nadir Shah and the Ja'fari Madhhab Reconsidered', *Iranian Studies*, 164.
39. See generally Ernest Tucker, 'Nadir Shah and the Ja'fari Madhhab Reconsidered', *Iranian Studies*.
40. See generally Ernest Tucker, 'Explaining Nadir Shah: Kingship and Royal Legitimacy in Muhammad Kazim Marvi's Tarikh-I Alam-Ara-Yi Nadiri', *Iranian Studies*.
41. There is an important debate about the strength of the Safavid monarchy, *vis-à-vis* both the *'ulamā'* and Persian tribes. Peter Christensen, 'The Qajar State', in *Contributions to Islamic Studies: Iran, Afghanistan and Pakistan* (1987), 6–7.
42. Peter Avery, 'Nadir Shah and the Afsharid Legacy', in *The Cambridge History of Iran: From Nadir Shah to the Islamic Republic* (1991), 37.
43. Ibid., 54.
44. For a description of the riches of Delhi when Nadir conquered it in 1739, see Michael Axelworthy, *The Sword of Persia: Nader Shah, from Tribal Warrior to Conquering Tyrant* (2006), 1–17.
45. C.A. Bayly, *Imperial Meridian: The British Empire and the World, 1780–1830* (1989), 39.

46. Ganda Singh, *Ahmad Shah Durrani: Father of Modern Afghanistan* (1959), 32–5.
47. Mountstuart Elphinstone, *An Account of the Kingdom of Caubul*, Vol. 2 (1991; reprint, 1838), 284.
48. Ibid., 283–4.
49. Ibid., 281–2.
50. See generally Christine Noelle, *State and Tribe in Nineteenth Century Afghanistan: The Reign of Amir Dost Muhammad Khan, 1826–1863* (1997).
51. See, for example, Report on the Durranee Tribes, 19 April 1841, IOR, London, *Secret & Political*, L/PS/18/C5; Notice on the Affairs of Candahar in 1838. With a Sketch of the Preceding Dooranee History, 8 July 1838, IOR, London, *Secret & Political*, L/PS/5/131.
52. Letters from George Forster to Henry Dundas, 9 June 1785, IOR, London, *Home & Misc.*, H/685(3).
53. Mountstuart Elphinstone, *An Account of the Kingdom of Caubul*, Vol. 2 (1991; reprint, 1838), 258–61.
54. For a description of the *tiyūl* system, see Memoir Chiefly Relating to the Revenue and Trade of the Kingdom of Caubul, 1808, IOR, London, *Elphinstone Papers*, MSS. Eur.F88.366. Part of the reason behind Timur Shah's move from Kandahar to Kabul was that the majority of the land around Kandahar had been distributed as *tiyūls*.
55. See, for instance, Substance of a Diary of News Received from Kandahar, 11 February 1810, IOR, London, *Bengal Proceedings*, P/BEN/SEC/225, No. 5: Secret Department dispatch 5 June, Elphinstone to Minto, 13 April 1810, IOR, London, *Bengal Proceedings*, P/BEN/SEC/225, No. 22: in Secret Department dispatch of 2 May.
56. Dost Mohamed to Wade, 15 May 1837, NAI, New Delhi, *Foreign Department, Secret Consultations*, No. 8.
57. Abstract of News from Peshowr – Received 13 May 1810, 5 June 1810, NAI, New Delhi, *Foreign Department, Secret Consultations*, No. 6; Elphinstone to Minto, 13 April 1810, IOR, London, *Bengal Proceedings*, P/BEN/SEC/225, No. 22: in Secret Department dispatch of 2 May.
58. Extract of a Letter from Mr Masson to Captain Wade Dated 2 June, 22 February 1836, NAI, New Delhi, *Foreign Department, Political Consultations*, No. 29.
59. Macnaghten to T.H. Maddock, Official Secretary to Govt of India, 6 June 1839, BL, London, *Broughton Papers*, Add. 36474.
60. Ochterlony to Lushington, 17 April 1810, PPA, Lahore, *Records of Luhiana Agency*, No. 10.57.
61. Mir Izzat Ullah, 'Travels Beyond the Himalaya', *Journal of the Royal Asiatic Society of Great Britain and Ireland*, 336–7.
62. Dispatch from Moorcroft to George Swinton, 6 June 1825, IOR, London, *Secret & Political*, L/PS/5/109.
63. For a description of the taxation regime in Herat, see Mohan Lal, *Travels in the Panjab, Afghanistan, & Turkmenistan to Balk, Bokhara, and Herat; and a Visit to Great Britain and Germany* (1846), 261–2. For a more general picture of taxation under Dost Muhammad Khan, see Extract of Letters from Mr Masson to Captain Wade from 27 June to 29 July 1836, 21 November 1836, NAI, New Delhi, *Foreign Department, Political Consultations*, No. 32; Extract of a Letter from Mr Masson to Captain Wade Dated the 2 June, 22 February 1836, NAI, New Delhi, *Foreign Department, Political Consultations*, No. 29.
64. Fredrik Barth, 'Pathan Identity and Its Maintenance', in *Ethnic Groups and Boundaries: The Social Organization of Cultural Difference* (1969), 129.

65. Asta Olesen, 'The Political Use of Islam in Afghanistan During the Reign of Amir Abdur Rahman (1880–1901)', in *Contributions to Islamic Studies* (1987), 66, 69.

66. Akbar S. Ahmed, 'Tribes and States in Waziristan', in *The Conflict of Tribe and State in Iran and Afghanistan* (1983), 5–7; Fredrik Barth, 'Pathan Identity and Its Maintenance', in *Ethnic Groups and Boundaries: The Social Organization of Cultural Difference* (1969), 119–20.

67. See Sergie Andreyev, 'History and Doctrine of the Rawshani Movement' (University of Oxford).

68. David Edwards, *Heroes of the Age: Moral Fault Lines on the Afghan Frontier* (1996), 192.

69. Herat was in a state of severe decline by the end of the nineteenth century. Mohan Lal, *Travels in the Panjab, Afghanistan, & Turkmenistan to Balk, Bokhara, and Herat; and a Visit to Great Britain and Germany* (1846), 244–70. Mountstuart Elphinstone, *An Account of the Kingdom of Caubul*, Vol. 1 (1991; reprint, 1838), 249–50, 283. The *madrasas* of Bukhara were the main centre of Islamic learning for Afghan *mullahs*. Burnes depicted the level of learning as rather low, largely limited to repetition of texts. A. Burnes, *Travels into Bokhara; Together with a Narrative of a Voyage on the Indus*, Vol. 3 (Lahore: Sang-e-meel Publications, 2003), 141–2.

70. Mountstuart Elphinstone, *An Account of the Kingdom of Caubul*, Vol. 1 (1991; reprint, 1838), 282.

71. A. Burnes, *Travels into Bokhara; Together with a Narrative of a Voyage on the Indus* (2003; reprint, 1834), 142.

72. Letter from the Resident at Bushire, Maj. David Wilson, to the Bombay Government, Forwarding the Memo of Charles Masson on Parts of Afghanistan and the Independent Punjab, 11 September 1830, IOR, London, *Board's Collections*, F/4/1399/55442A.

73. David Edwards, *Heroes of the Age: Moral Fault Lines on the Afghan Frontier* (1996), 134, Mountstuart Elphinstone, *An Account of the Kingdom of Caubul*, Vol. 1 (1991; reprint, 1838), 228.

74. Information from Kabul Received at Pishawar on the 5 May, 17 July 1839, NAI, New Delhi, *Foreign Department, Secret Consultations*, No. 41.

75. Edwards briefly discusses the different types of Islamic offices found within Pashtun tribal society. David Edwards, *Heroes of the Age: Moral Fault Lines on the Afghan Frontier* (1996), 253, n. 8.

76. Mountstuart Elphinstone, *An Account of the Kingdom of Caubul*, Vol. 2 (1991; reprint, 1838), 277–8.

77. David Edwards, *Heroes of the Age: Moral Fault Lines on the Afghan Frontier* (1996), 135.

78. See Robert McChesney, *Waqf in Central Asia* (1991), 231–56.

79. Fredrik Barth, *Political Leadership among Swat Pathans* (1959), 57.

80. David Edwards, *Heroes of the Age: Moral Fault Lines on the Afghan Frontier* (1996), 256, n. 15.

81. Ibid., 137.

82. See, for example, Mountstuart Elphinstone, *An Account of the Kingdom of Caubul*, Vol. 1 (1991; reprint, 1838), 288–9, Dispatch from Moorcroft to George Swinton, 6 June 1825, IOR, London, *Secret & Political*, L/PS/5/109.

83. Notes on the Hazaras of Bisut, 1838, IOR, London, *Masson Papers*, MSS.Eur.E166/MSS.Eur.J643.

84. See, for instance, Sketch of the Doorraunee History, 1809, IOR, London, *Elphinstone Papers*, MSS.Eur.F88.367; A Memoir on the Uzbek State of Kundooz and the Power of Its Present Ruler Mahomed Murad Beg, 1838, IOR, London, *Reports and Papers, Political, Geographical, & Commercial, Submitted to Government*, V3320.

85. Observations on the Trade of Kabul, 2 November 1835, NAI, New Delhi, *Foreign Department, Political Consultations*, No. 56; Pottinger to Macnaghten, 26 June 1839, NAI, New Delhi, *Foreign Department, Secret Consultations*, No. 123.

86. Mountstuart Elphinstone, *An Account of the Kingdom of Caubul*, Vol. 1 (1991; reprint, 1838), 248–61. See also Margaret Ann Mills, *Oral Narrative in Afghanistan: The Individual Tradition* (1990). Mohan Lal attended a public recitation of the story of Karbala by Shi'a *mullahs* outside Herat during Muharram. Mohan Lal, *Travels in the Panjab, Afghanistan, & Turkmenistan to Balk, Bokhara, and Herat; and a Visit to Great Britain and Germany* (1846), 244.

87. M. Nazif Shahrani, 'Local Knowledge of Islam and Social Discourse in Afghanistan and Turkestan in the Modern Period', in *Turko-Persian in Historical Perspective* (1991), 168–70.

88. The absence of urban *'ulamā'* is meant in a comparative, rather than absolute sense. Contemporary European observers remarked on the learning and influence of *mullahs* on the urban populaces. These *'ulamā'* were often associated with the state, although not necessarily supportive of it. Elphinstone to Minto, nd 1809, IOR, London, *Bengal Proceedings*, P/BEN/SEC/219, Enclosure No. 6; Sec Dept dispatch 19 April; Mohan Lal, *Travels in the Panjab, Afghanistan, & Turkmenistan to Balk, Bokhara, and Herat; and a Visit to Great Britain and Germany* (1846), 44, Mountstuart Elphinstone, *An Account of the Kingdom of Caubul*, Vol. 1 (1991; reprint, 1838), 282–8.

89. The main Sufi orders prominent in Afghanistan were the *Qaderiya, Naqsshibandiya, Chishtiya* and *Suhrawardiya*. Asta Olesen, *Islam and Politics in Afghanistan* (1995), 44–8.

90. See generally Francis Robinson, 'Perso-Islamic Culture in India from the 17th Century to the Early 20th Century', in *Turko-Persia in Historical Perspective* (1991); Ira Lapidus, 'Islamic Revival and Modernity: The Contemporary Movements and the Historical Paradigms', *Journal of the Economic and Social History of the Orient*.

91. Francis Robinson, 'Perso-Islamic Culture in India from the 17th Century to the Early 20th Century', in *Turko-Persia in Historical Perspective* (1991), 120.

92. See generally Qeyamuddin Ahmad, *The Wahabi Movement in India* (1966); Marc Gaborieau, 'The *Jihād* of Sayyid Ahmad Barelwi on the North West Frontier: The Last Echo of the Middle Ages? Or a Prefiguration of Modern South Asia', in *Sufis, Sultans and Feudal Orders: Professor Nurul Hasan Commemoration Volume* (2004). Barbara Metcalf characterizes Barelwi's *jihād* as 'an expression of post-Mughal state building...given meaning by the rich Islamic tradition of warrior-saints and the Mahdi'. Barbara Metcalf, *Islamic Revival in British India: Deoband 1860–1900* (1982), 62.

93. See Edward's discussion of the similar challenges faced by the Mullah of Hadda at the end of the nineteenth century. David Edwards, *Heroes of the Age: Moral Fault Lines on the Afghan Frontier* (1996), 193.

94. Wade to Macnaghten, 7 October 1837, IOR, London, *Secret & Political*, L/PS/5/129; Wade to Martin, 21, 31 March 1831, PPA, Lahore, *Records of the Ludhiana Agency*, Nos. 98.159–60.

95. Akbar S. Ahmed, *Pukhtun Economy and Society: Traditional Structure and Economic Development in Tribal Society* (1980), 70.

96. For British and Sikh efforts at communicating with Afghan leaders through Muslim functionaries, see Pottinger to McNeill, 28 September 1837, IOR, London, *Secret & Political*, L/PS/20/A7/1; Macnaghten to T.H. Maddock, 4 September 1839, NAI, New Delhi, *Foreign Department, Secret Consultations*, No. 227.

97. See, for example, Wade to Macnaghten, 12 June 1837, NAI, New Delhi, *Foreign Department, Secret Consultations*, No. 8; Abstract Translation of a Letter from Ruhum Dil Khan to the Address of Lieut. Colonel Sir Alexander Burnes, 3 July 1839, NAI, New Delhi, *Foreign Department, Secret Consultations*, No. 35.

98. Christine Noelle, 'The Anti-Wahabi Reaction in Nineteenth Century Afghanistan', *The Muslim World*, 23. Sayyid Ahmad Barelwi's two learned companions, *Maulvi* Ismail and *Maulvi* Abdul Hye, were both natives of Delhi and former servants of the Nawab of Ameer Khan. Wade to C.T. Metcalfe, Delhi Resident, 30 March 1827, NAI, New Delhi, *Foreign Department, Political Consultations*, No. 32.

99. Mountstuart Elphinstone, *An Account of the Kingdom of Caubul*, Vol. 2 (1991; reprint, 1838), 283–4.

100. One such example of royal pretence was a letter in which he addressed the Ottoman sultan, Mustafa III, as '*biradar*'. Jos Gommans, *The Rise of the Indo-Afghan Empire* (1999), 49–51.

101. Muhmood Shah to Minto, 11 February 1811, Edinburgh, *Minto Papers*, Ms. 11586; Translation: Substance of a Written Agreement Delivered to Runjeet Sing on the Part of Zeman Shah through His Vakeel Hurry Sing on the 12th of Sheval During His Stay at Lahore, 9 March 1800, IOR, London, *Bengal Proceedings*, P/BEN/SEC/79, Enclosure No. 87; Sec Dept dispatch 30 December; Shah Mahmud to Governor-General, 29 March 1811, NAI, New Delhi, *Foreign Department, Political Consultations*, No. 37.

102. An Account of the Nations Subject to the King of Caboul with Information Regarding the Neighbouring States – in Two Parts – by Mr Elphinstone, 23 July 1812, IOR, London, *Elphinstone Papers*, MSS.Eur.E92/MSS.Eur.K247.

103. Wade to Macnaghten, 1 August 1838, NAI, New Delhi, *Foreign Department, Secret Consultations*, No. 16. Interestingly though, in writing to the Governor-General, Ranjit did refer to Dost Muhammad with the latter title. Wade to Macnaghten, 3 January 1838, NAI, New Delhi, *Foreign Department, Political Consultations*, No. 28.

104. Macnaghten to T.H. Maddock, 4 September 1839, NAI, New Delhi, *Foreign Department, Secret Consultations*, No. 227.

105. Dost Muhammad was reportedly present at his murder. Fayz Muhammad Katib, *Siraj Al-Tavarikh* (Hijra 1372 (1993/1994)), 83.

106. *Shahzadeh* Kamran had all the Durrani *sardārs* participate in Fath Khan's execution so that none of them could ally with his Barakzai brothers because of the blood debt. Ibid., 139.

107. See, for example, Hawkins to W. Murray, 16 January 1830, PPA, Lahore, *Records of the Ambala Agency*, No. 30.8.

108. Christine Noelle, *State and Tribe in Nineteenth Century Afghanistan: The Reign of Amir Dost Muhammad Khan, 1826–1863* (1997), 14–7. See also Fayz Muhammad Katib, *Siraj Al-Tavarikh* (Hijra 1372 (1993/1994)), 147–8.

109. Copy of a Letter from the Persia Envoy Extraordinary: McNeill to Macnaghten, 22 January 1837, IOR, London, *Secret & Political*, L/PS/5/127, No. 57. It was claimed Shah Shuja's mother was also a Qizilbash woman from Nishapur in Persia. Wade to Hawkins, 12 March 1830, NAI, New Delhi, *Foreign Department, Secret Consultations*, No. 7.

110. Dost Muhammad received Barelwi at court, but declined to offer anything more than moral support. Christine Noelle, 'The Anti-Wahabi Reaction in Nineteenth Century Afghanistan', *The Muslim World*, 45.

111. Dispatch to the Secret Committee, 5 March 1835, NAI, New Delhi, *Foreign Department*, No. 2; Wade to Macnaghten, 19 February 1835, NAI, New Delhi, *Foreign Department, Political Consultations*, No. 8.

112. Masson to H. Pottinger, 20 September 1834, PRO, London, *Pottinger Papers*, FO/705/32.

113. Extract of a Letter from Mr Masson to Captain Wade Dated at Kabul 20th Mahomedan Month Barat 1250, 30 March 1835, NAI, New Delhi, *Foreign Department, Political Consultations*, No. 46; Wade to Macnaghten, 19 February 1835, NAI, New Delhi, *Foreign Department, Secret Consultations*, No. 7.

114. For a history of the Prophet's cloak, see Robert McChesney, *Waqf in Central Asia* (1991), 222–7; Fayz Muhammad Katib, *Siraj Al-Tavarikh* (Hijra 1372 (1993/1994)), 37–9.

115. On the reading of the *khutba*, see Wade to Macnaghten, 19 February 1835, NAI, New Delhi, *Foreign Department, Political Consultations*, No. 8. On the coins, see Fayz Muhammad Katib, *Siraj Al-Tavarikh* (Hijra 1372 (1993/1994)), 178.

116. Extract of a Letter from Mr Masson to Captain Wade Dated the 20th of February 1835, 25 May 1835, NAI, New Delhi, *Foreign Department, Political Consultations*, No. 30. Fayz Muhammad places the number at 60,000. Fayz Muhammad Katib, *Siraj Al-Tavarikh* (Hijra 1372 (1993/1994)), 178–9.

117. M.E. Yapp, 'The Revolutions of 1841–2 in Afghanistan', *Bulletin of the School of Oriental and African Studies*, 339.

118. Extract of a Letter from Mr Masson to Captain Wade, Dated 31 May, 14 December 1835, NAI, New Delhi, *Foreign Department, Political Consultations*, No. 64.

119. See M.E. Yapp, 'The Revolutions of 1841–2 in Afghanistan', *Bulletin of the School of Oriental and African Studies*.

120. Ashraf Ghani, 'Islam and Statebuilding in a Tribal Society', *Modern Asian Studies*, 270. See also Christine Noelle, 'The Anti-Wahabi Reaction in Nineteenth Century Afghanistan', *The Muslim World*, 70–4; Asta Olesen, 'The Political Use of Islam in Afghanistan During the Reign of Amir Abdur Rahman (1880–1901)', in *Contributions to Islamic Studies* (1987), 66–70. Barfield argues the most important innovation during this period was the participation of peripheral segments of Afghan society, marking the birth of mass politics. Thomas Barfield, 'Problems in Establishing Legitimacy in Afghanistan', *Iranian Studies*, 273–4.

5   Camels, Caravans and Corridor Cities

1. See, for example, K.N. Chaudhuri, *The Trading World of Asia and the East India Company* (1978); N. Steensgaard, *The Asian Trade Revolution of the Seventeenth Century: The East India Companies and the Decline of the Caravan Trade* (1974). For a good summary of debates surrounding the decline of the so-called 'gunpowder empires' see Rohan D'Souza, 'Crisis before the Fall: Some Speculations on the Decline of the Ottomans, Safavids and Mughals', *Social Scientist*.

2. Ira Lapidus has argued

The decline of the Muslim empires can be understood in terms of the internal life cycles of such regimes, but the conjunctions suggest a common external factor:

the rise of the capitalist economy and the progressive capture of world trade by European nations. Though the decline of organized Muslim states sometimes preceded, sometimes intersected with, and sometimes was precipitated by the rising power of European states, in general it may be fair to say that the growing control of Europe over world trade, though not absolute, undermined the economic productivity, trading profits and the revenue base of the Muslim empires, induced inflationary change, and opened the way to internal political conflicts for control of the domestic economies of Muslim regions.

Ira Lapidus, 'Islamic Revival and Modernity: The Contemporary Movements and the Historical Paradigms', *Journal of the Economic and Social History of the Orient*, 450.

3. Important exceptions to this include Jos Gommans, *The Rise of the Indo-Afghan Empire* (1999); Scott Levi, *The Indian Trade Diaspora in Central Asia and Its Trade, 1550–1900* (2002).

4. For a picture of overland trade networks and routes, see Scott Levi, 'India, Russia and the Eighteenth Century Transformation of the Central Asian Caravan Trade', *Journal of Economic and Social History of the Orient*; Claude Markovits, *The Global World of Indian Merchants, 1750–1947: Traders of Sind from Bukhara to Panama* (2000); S.F. Dale, *Indian Merchants and Eurasian Trade, 1600–1750* (1994).

5. Hanifi depicts the *hundi* system in Afghanistan as a means of debt servicing which widely dispersed the cumulative debt of Afghan society. Shah Mahmoud Hanifi, 'Impoverishing a Colonial Frontier: Cash, Credit and Debt in Nineteenth Century Afghanistan', *Iranian Studies*, 204, 15.

6. See Yuri V. Gankovsky, 'The Durrani Empire: Taxes and Tax System,' in *Afghanistan: Past and Present* (1981).

7. See, for instance, Fernand Braudel, *Capitalism and Material Life, 1400–1800* (1973).

8. See, for example, Andre Gunder Frank, *Reorient: Global Economy in the Asian Age* (1998); Immanuel Wallerstien, *The Modern World-System* (1974); C.A. Bayly, *The Birth of the Modern World, 1780–1914* (2004).

9. See, for instance, Michael Kaser, 'Economic Continuities in Albania's Turbulent History', *Europe-Asia Studies*; Gabriel Warburg, 'Mahdism and Islamism in Sudan', *International Journal of Middle East Studies*; Paul E. Lovejoy and J.S. Hogendorn, 'Revolutionary Mahdism and Resistance to Colonial Rule in the Sokoto Caliphate, 1905–06', *The Journal of African History*.

10. Douglas H. Johnson, 'Economic and Political Aspects of the Slave Trade in Ethiopia and the Sudan in the Second Half of the Nineteenth Century', *The International Journal of African Historical Studies*; James L.A. Webb, 'The Horse and Slave Trade between the Western Sahara and Senegambia', *The Journal of African History*.

11. See Shah Mahmoud Hanifi, 'Inter-Regional Trade and Colonial State Formation in 19th Century Afghanistan' (University of Michigan); Shah Mahmoud Hanifi, 'Impoverishing a Colonial Frontier: Cash, Credit and Debt in Nineteenth Century Afghanistan', *Iranian Studies*.

12. See generally P.M. Holt, *The Mahdist State in the Sudan, 1881–1898: A Study of Its Origins, Development and Overthrow* (1979).

13. David Washbrook, 'Progress and Problems: South Asian Economic and Social History, C. 1720–1860', *Modern Asian Studies*, 79.

14. See C.A. Bayly, 'The British Military-Fiscal State and Indigenous Resistance: India 1750–1820', in *The Imperial State at War: Britain from 1689 to 1815* (1994);

Douglas Peers, *Between Mars and Mammon: Colonial Armies and the Garrison State in Early Nineteenth-Century India* (1995), 106–43, 184–242.

15. David Washbrook, 'South Asia, the World System, and World Capitalism', in *South Asia and World Capitalism* (1990), 72–3.

16. David Washbrook, 'Progress and Problems: South Asian Economic and Social History, C. 1720–1860', *Modern Asian Studies*, 80.

17. C.A. Bayly, *Rulers, Townsmen and Bazaars: Northern Indian Society in the Age of British Expansion, 1770–1870* (2003), 263–302.

18. C.A. Bayly, 'Age of Hiatus: The North Indian Economy and Society, 1830–50', in *Indian Society and the Beginnings of Modernization* (1976), 95.

19. Thomas A. Timberg, 'Hiatus and Incubator: Indigenous Trade and Traders, 1837–1857', in *Trade and Finance in Colonial India, 1750–1860* (1995), 252, 62.

20. S.F. Dale, 'Indo-Russian Trade in the 18th Century', in *South Asia and World Capitalism* (1990), 149; Claude Markovits, *The Global World of Indian Merchants, 1750–1947: Traders of Sind from Bukhara to Panama* (2000), 38.

21. Scott Levi, *The Indian Trade Diaspora in Central Asia and Its Trade 1550–1900* (2002), 178. Hanifi goes even further, arguing they accounted for six to twelve per cent of the nineteenth-century Afghan population. Shah Mahmoud Hanifi, 'Impoverishing a Colonial Frontier: Cash, Credit and Debt in Nineteenth Century Afghanistan', *Iranian Studies*, 201, n. 7.

22. See generally Scott Levi, *The Indian Trade Diaspora in Central Asia and Its Trade 1550–1900* (2002).

23. S.F. Dale, *Indian Merchants and Eurasian Trade, 1600–1750* (1994), 59–60
    See also G.D. Sharma, 'The Marwaris: Economic Foundations of an Indian Capitalist Community', in *Business Communities of India: A Historical Perspective* (1984); Thomas Timberg, *The Marwaris: From Traders to Industrialists* (1978); J.S. Grewal, 'Business Communities of Punjab', in *Business Communities of India: A Historical Perspective* (1984); Bhagat Singh, 'Trade and Commerce under Maharaja Ranjit Singh', in *Maharaja Ranjit Singh: Politics, Society and Economy* (1984).

24. S.F. Dale, *Indian Merchants and Eurasian Trade, 1600–1750* (1994), 63.

25. Masson to H. Pottinger, 16 January 1837, PRO, London, *Pottinger Papers*, FO/705/32.

26. Mohan Lal, *Travels in the Panjab, Afghanistan, & Turkmenistan to Balk, Bokhara, and Herat; and a Visit to Great Britain and Germany* (1846), 438.

27. The equivalent system used by Muslim money-lenders is called the *hawala* system. See generally Divya Sharma, 'Historical Traces of Hundi, Sociocultural Understanding and the Criminal Abuses of Hawala', *International Criminal Justice Review*.

28. Papers Respecting Afghanistan and the Countries between the Indus and the Caspian, 1831, IOR, London, *Secret & Political*, L/PS/19/26.

29. Ibid.

30. A Report on the Countries between India and Russia, 5 May 1833, IOR, London, *Secret & Political*, L/PS/19/44.

31. Letter from the Resident at Bushire, Maj. David Wilson, to the Bombay Government, Forwarding the Memo of Charles Masson on Parts of Afghanistan and the Independent Punjab, 11 September 1830, IOR, London, *Board's Collections*, F/4/1399/55442A.

32. See, for example, Journal – Kabul, 1824, IOR, London, *Moorcroft Papers*, MSS.Eur. D250, Vol. 3; Macnaghten to Wade, 27 August 1838, PPA, Lahore, *Records of the Ludhiana Agency*, No. 121.87.

33. Mountstuart Elphinstone, *An Account of the Kingdom of Caubul*, Vol. 1 (1991; reprint, 1838), 420–1; A. Burnes, *Travels into Bokhara; Together with a Narrative of a Voyage on the Indus* (2003; reprint, 1834), 69.

34. Shah Mahmoud Hanifi, 'Impoverishing a Colonial Frontier: Cash, Credit and Debt in Nineteenth Century Afghanistan', *Iranian Studies*, 215.

35. Arthur Conolly, *Journey to the North of India, over the Land from England through Russia, Persia and Afghanistan*, Vol. 2 (1834), 168–9.

36. On the Trade of Bahawalpur, 25 September 1837, NAI, New Delhi, *Foreign Department, Political Consultations*, No. 92; Mohan Lal, *Travels in the Panjab, Afghanistan, & Turkmenistan to Balk, Bokhara, and Herat; and a Visit to Great Britain and Germany* (1846), 412; Commercial Information Regarding Bhawal Khan's Country, 25 September 1837, NAI, New Delhi, *Foreign Department, Political Consultations*, No. 87.

37. Lal to Mackeson on Multan Commerce, 9 May 1836, NAI, New Delhi, *Foreign Department, Political Consultations*, No. 42.

38. Dale refers to the practice of Safavid, Mughal and even Nadirite *radhars*, or highway police, using local tolls merchants paid to compensate those whose goods were robbed on the road. S.F. Dale, *Indian Merchants and Eurasian Trade, 1600–1750* (1994), 39.

39. See, for instance, On the Trade of Bahawalpur, 25 September 1837, NAI, New Delhi, *Foreign Department, Political Consultations*, No. 92; Burnes to Macnaghten, 20 March 1839, NAI, New Delhi, *Foreign Department, Secret Consultations*, No. 164.

40. Letter from Herat, 26 March 1833, IOR, London, *Gerard Papers*, MSS.Eur.C951.

41. Ibid.

42. S.F. Dale, *Indian Merchants and Eurasian Trade, 1600–1750* (1994), 46.

43. Scott Levi, *The Indian Trade Diaspora in Central Asia and Its Trade 1550–1900* (2002), 177.

44. Afghan rulers regularly extorted forced loans from members of the merchant community. See, for example, 'Extract of a Letter from Mr Masson to Captain Wade Dated at Kabul 20th Mahomedan Month Barat 1250', 30 March 1835, NAI, New Delhi, *Foreign Department, Political Consultations*, No. 46; 'Report on the Trade between Shikarpoor and Herat', 1838, IOR, London, *Reports and Papers, Political, Geographical, & Commercial, Submitted to Government*, V3320.

45. Claude Markovits, *The Global World of Indian Merchants, 1750–1947: Traders of Sind from Bukhara to Panama* (2000), 61.

46. David Washbrook, 'Progress and Problems: South Asian Economic and Social History, C. 1720–1860', *Modern Asian Studies*, 79–85.

47. Shah Mahmoud Hanifi, 'Impoverishing a Colonial Frontier: Cash, Credit and Debt in Nineteenth Century Afghanistan', *Iranian Studies*, 207.

48. Masson to Wade, 10 August 1835, NAI, New Delhi, *Foreign Department, Political Consultations*, No. 29.

49. Extract of a Letter from Mr Masson to Captain Wade, Dated 31 May, 14 December 1835, NAI, New Delhi, *Foreign Department, Political Consultations*, No. 64.

50. Masson to H. Pottinger, 20 September 1834, PRO, London, *Pottinger Papers*, FO/705/32.

51. Tajiks and Lohanis were also prominent trading groups. Memoir Chiefly Relating to the Revenue and Trade of the Kingdom of Caubul, 1808, IOR, London, *Elphinstone Papers*, MSS.Eur.F88.366.

52. On the Commerce of Central Asia, 6 June 1833, IOR, London, *Secret & Political*, L/PS/19/45. Other merchant groups were also present at the annual fair, including Turkmen traders from Khiva. Copy of a Dispatch from the Political Agent at Loodiana, 27 June 1837, IOR, London, *Secret & Political*, L/PS/5/128, No. 29.
53. Mohan Lal, *Travels in the Panjab, Afghanistan, & Turkmenistan to Balk, Bokhara, and Herat; and a Visit to Great Britain and Germany* (1846), 76–7.
54. S.F. Dale, *Indian Merchants and Eurasian Trade, 1600–1750* (1994), 52–3, 62.
55. Trade of the Upper Indus or Derajat, 5 August 1837, IOR, London, *Reports and Papers, Political, Geographical, & Commercial, Submitted to Government*, V3320.
56. The Ghilzais regularly visited Multan as well. On the Trade of Bahawalpur, 25 September 1837, NAI, New Delhi, *Foreign Department, Political Consultations*, No. 92.
57. Report on the Commerce of Multan, 1838, IOR, London, *Reports and Papers, Political, Geographical, & Commercial, Submitted to Government*, V3320.
58. Gordon, Assistant Political Agent on a Deputation to Dera Ismail Khan to Maddock, 2 October 1839, NAI, New Delhi, *Foreign Department, Secret Consultations*, No. 81. See also Christine Noelle, *State and Tribe in Nineteenth Century Afghanistan: The Reign of Amir Dost Muhammad Khan, 1826–1863* (1997), 282–3.
59. See, for example, Observations on the Trade of Kabul, 2 November 1835, NAI, New Delhi, *Foreign Department, Political Consultations*, No. 56; Report on the Commerce of Multan, 1838, IOR, London, *Reports and Papers, Political, Geographical, & Commercial, Submitted to Government*, V3320.
60. Wade to Macnaghten, 18 April 1836, PPA, Lahore, *Records of the Ludhiana Agency*, No. 142.25. On Sayyid Muheen Shah's trading expedition, see Shah Mahmoud Hanifi, 'Inter-Regional Trade and Colonial State Formation in 19th Century Afghanistan' (University of Michigan), 208–23.
61. Carriage Supply Furnished by Lohanis, 24 September 1838, NAI, New Delhi, *Governor General's dispatch to Secret Committee*, No. 23; Auckland to the Lohanee Merchants Sarwur Khane, Ameer Khan, 1838, IOR, London, *Secret & Political*, L/PS/5/133.
62. See, for instance, Assembly of Lohanis at Mithenkot, 8 May 1834, NAI, New Delhi, *Foreign Department, Secret Consultations*, Nos. 16–8.
63. The efforts of the Russian Finance Minister E.F. Kankrin to establish trading companies for the Central Asian trade in order to compete with the British in the late 1830s could have been a Russian response to the Indus Scheme. The efforts came to naught, however, as unlike their Lohani counterparts, the Central Asian merchants were not interested in the proposed scheme. Anne Lincoln Fitzpatrick, *The Great Russian Fair: Nizhnii Novgorod, 1840–90* (1990), 86.
64. A Memoir on the Uzbek State of Kundooz and the Power of Its Present Ruler Mahomed Murad Beg, 1838, IOR, London, *Reports and Papers, Political, Geographical, & Commercial, Submitted to Government*, V3320. For a contemporary description of the fair, see Burnes to Macnaghten, 20 October 1837, IOR, London, *Secret & Political*, L/PS/5/129. On the fair generally, see Anne Lincoln Fitzpatrick, *The Great Russian Fair: Nizhnii Novgorod, 1840–90* (1990).
65. Burnes to Macnaghten, 11 October 1837, PPA, Lahore, *Records of the Ludhiana Agency*, No. 108.41.
66. S.F. Dale, *Indian Merchants and Eurasian Trade, 1600–1750* (1994), 64.
67. Claude Markovits, *The Global World of Indian Merchants, 1750–1947: Traders of Sind from Bukhara to Panama* (2000), 66–7.

68. See generally C.A. Bayly, '"Archaic" And "Modern" Globalization in the Eurasian and African Arena, Ca. 1750–1850', in *Globalization in World History* (2002); C.A. Bayly, *Imperial Meridian: The British Empire and the World, 1780–1830* (1989); C.A. Bayly, *The Birth of the Modern World, 1780–1914* (2004), 23–120.

69. See, for instance, Andre Gunder Frank, *Reorient: Global Economy in the Asian Age* (1998); Kenneth Pomeranz, *The Great Divergence: China, Europe and the Making of the Modern World Economy* (2000).

70. See generally Dennis Owen Flynn, 'Cycles of Silver: Global Economic Unity through the Mid-Eighteenth Century', *Journal of World History*.

71. 'Three Reports of the Select Committee Appointed by the Court of Directors to Take into Account the Export Trade from Great Britain to the East Indies, China, Japan and Persia' (London: East India Company) 1793, No. 11.

72. See, for example, C.A. Bayly, 'Age of Hiatus: The North Indian Economy and Society, 1830–50', in *Indian Society and the Beginnings of Modernization* (1976).

73. Statement of the Annual Imports from, and Exports to China, under the Following Heads for the Last 38 Years, 12 October 1839, PRO, London, *Ellenborough Papers*, PRO/30/12/15/5.

74. Papers Respecting Afghanistan and the Countries between the Indus and the Caspian, 1831, IOR, London, *Secret & Political*, L/PS/19/26.

75. K.N. Chaudhuri, 'India's Foreign Trade and the Cessation of the East India Company's Trading Activities, 1828–40', in *Trade and Finance in Colonial India* (1995), 312–14.

76. Scott Levi, *The Indian Trade Diaspora in Central Asia and Its Trade 1550–1900* (2002), 242.

77. Memoir Chiefly Relating to the Revenue and Trade of the Kingdom of Caubul, 1808, IOR, London, *Elphinstone Papers*, MSS.Eur.F88.366.

78. Various Notes, 1809, IOR, London, *Elphinstone Papers*, MSS.Eur.F88.372.

79. Description of Articles, Mostly Russian, Found in the Bazar of Cabool, and Brought to It by Way of Bokhara, 7 February 1838, IOR, London, *Reports and Papers, Political, Geographical, & Commercial, Submitted to Government*, V3320.

80. M.N. Pearson, 'Asia and World Precious Metal Flows in the Early Modern Period', in *Evolution of the World Economy, Precious Metals and India* (2001), 42.

81. D.A. Brading and Harry E. Cross, 'Colonial Silver Mining: Mexico and Peru', *The Hispanic American Historical Review*, 576.

82. D.A. Brading, 'Mexican Silver-Mining in the Eighteenth Century: The Revival of Zacatecas', *The Hispanic American Historical Review* (1970), 665–6, 668.

83. Ward Barrett, 'World Bullion Flows, 1450–1800', in *The Rise of Merchant Empires: Long-Distance Trade in the Early Modern World, 1350–1750* (1990), 245.

84. Ibid., 248.

85. The silver export to India that same year was calculated at 1,100,000 Spanish dollars. Serafin D. Quiason, *English 'Country Trade' With the Philippines, 1644–1765* (1966), 78–9.

86. Ward Barrett, 'World Bullion Flows, 1450–1800', in *The Rise of Merchant Empires: Long-Distance Trade in the Early Modern World, 1350–1750* (1990), 251.

87. P. Kuhn, *Soulstealers: The Chinese Sorcery Scare of 1768* (1990), 37–8.

88. Papers Respecting Afghanistan and the Countries between the Indus and the Caspian, 1831, IOR, London, *Secret & Political*, L/PS/19/26. It is interesting, as well, that Trevelyan and Conolly denominated the amounts in dollars (presumably Mexican silver dollars), emphasizing both the presence and pre-eminence of American silver in Asia.

89. 148 ingots weighing on average 1.768 kilograms and worth Rs. 150 each. This discrepancy may be accounted for by the fact that Trevelyan likely referred to transportation cost south of the Hindu Kush, coupled with the preference of merchants to spread their risk, making it unlikely any camel would actually be laden with so much bullion.

90. See generally Hans Christian Johansen, *Shipping and Trade between the Baltic Area and Western Europe 1784–95* (1983).

91. Carl Hermann Scheidler, *A Journey from Orenburg to Bokhara in the Year 1820* (1870), 2; Scott Levi, *The Indian Trade Diaspora in Central Asia and Its Trade 1550–1900* (2002), 241.

92. Anne Lincoln Fitzpatrick, *The Great Russian Fair: Nizhnii Novgorod, 1840–90* (1990), 82–5.

93. Ibid., 85.

94. C.A. Bayly, ' "Archaic" And "Modern" Globalization in the Eurasian and African Arena, Ca. 1750–1850', in *Globalization in World History* (2002), 60.

95. A.K.S. Lambton, 'Persian Trade under the Early Qajars', in *Islam and the Trade of Asia* (1970), 236. Persian merchants, who in the main were actually Armenians, proved as much a headache to Tsarist authorities as their Central Asian counterparts. The terms of trade, however, were more favourable for Russia in the Persian case, with Persia absorbing forty per cent of all Russian exports to Asia during the late 1820s and early 1830s. Anne Lincoln Fitzpatrick, *The Great Russian Fair: Nizhnii Novgorod, 1840–90* (1990), 81–4.

96. 'Three Reports of the Select Committee Appointed by the Court of Directors to Take into Account the Export Trade from Great Britain to the East Indies, China, Japan and Persia' (London: East India Company) 1793, No. 11.

97. A.K.S. Lambton, 'Persian Trade under the Early Qajars', in *Islam and the Trade of Asia* (1970), 236.

98. Mohan Lal, *Travels in the Panjab, Afghanistan, & Turkmenistan to Balk, Bokhara, and Herat; and a Visit to Great Britain and Germany* (1846), 107.

99. S.F. Dale, *Indian Merchants and Eurasian Trade, 1600–1750* (1994), 28.

100. Mir Izzat Ullah, 'Travels Beyond the Himalaya', *Journal of the Royal Asiatic Society of Great Britain and Ireland*, 69.

101. Report on the Commerce of Multan, 1838, IOR, London, *Reports and Papers, Political, Geographical, & Commercial, Submitted to Government*, V3320.

102. Description of Articles, Mostly Russian, Found in the Bazar of Cabool, and Brought to It by Way of Bokhara, 7 February 1838, IOR, London, *Reports and Papers, Political, Geographical, & Commercial, Submitted to Government*, V3320.

103. For a discussion of the importance of sumptuary patters, see C.A. Bayly and Susan Bayly, 'Eighteenth Century State Forms and the Economy', in *Arrested Development in India: The Historical Dimension* (1988).

104. On the politics of consumption, see generally Arjun Appadurai, 'Introduction: Commodities and the Politics of Value', in *The Social Life of Things: Commodities in Cultural Perspective* (1986). On the role of consumption in colonial societies, see, for example, Jean Comaroff, 'The Empire's Old Clothes: Fashioning the Colonial Subject', in *Cross-Cultural Consumption: Global Markets, Local Realities* (1996).

105. C.A. Bayly, ' "Archaic" and "Modern" Globalization in the Eurasian and African Arena, Ca. 1750–1850', in *Globalization in World History* (2002), 52.

106. Ibid.

107. Dietmar Rothermund, 'Problems of India's Arrested Economic Growth under British Rule', in *Arrested Development in India: The Historical Dimension* (1988), 5.

108. See, for example, Babur, *The Baburname* (1996).
109. S.F. Dale, *Indian Merchants and Eurasian Trade, 1600–1750* (1994), 22; Thomas A. Timberg, 'Hiatus and Incubator: Indigenous Trade and Traders, 1837–1857', in *Trade and Finance in Colonial India, 1750–1860* (1995), 251–2.
110. Arthur Conolly, *Journey to the North of India, over the Land from England through Russia, Persia and Afghanistan*, Vol. 2 (1834), 227–8.
111. See, for example, Wade to Keramet Ali, 7 January 1835, NAI, New Delhi, *Foreign Department, Political Consultations*, No. 58A.
112. Maddock to Wade, 30 January 1840, PPA, Lahore, *Records of the Ludhiana Agency*, No. 126.25.
113. Report on the Commerce of Multan, 1838, IOR, London, *Reports and Papers, Political, Geographical, & Commercial, Submitted to Government*, V3320; Commercial Information Regarding Bhawal Khan's Country, 25 September 1837, NAI, New Delhi, *Foreign Department, Political Consultations*, No. 87. Shikarpur was reported to export Rs. 10,000 annually. Trade between Shikarpoor and Marwar, 25 September 1837, NAI, New Delhi, *Foreign Department, Political Consultations*, No. 90.
114. Copy of a Letter from Ghoolam Khan Populozye Dooranee to Captain Burnes Dated 19 July, 14 November 1838, NAI, New Delhi, *Foreign Department, Secret Consultations*, No. 52.
115. The Mughals annually imported 21,000 Turkic horses during the last decade of Akbar's reign. Shireen Moosvi, *The Economy of the Mughal Empire, c. 1595: A Statistical Survey* (1987), 378. Dale thinks this potentially as a gross under-estimation. S.F. Dale, *Indian Merchants and Eurasian Trade, 1600–1750* (1994), 25–6. On the importance of the trade in eighteenth-century South Asia, see Jos Gommans, *The Rise of the Indo-Afghan Empire* (1999), 68–103.
116. Moorcroft encouraged strengthening the Company's stock by importing Central Asian breeds. Bengal Government Recommend the Court of Directors to Procure Certain Arms as Presents for the Chiefs of Lahore, Kabul and Bokhara, January 1816–October 1817, IOR, London, *Board's Collections*, F/4/605/15012.
117. Papers Respecting Afghanistan and the Countries between the Indus and the Caspian, 1831, IOR, London, *Secret & Political*, L/PS/19/26. Burnes estimated the annual horse import to Shikarpur at 500–800. Presumably, most of those mounts went on to Bombay. On the Commerce of Shikarpoor and Upper Sinde, 5 June 1837, NAI, New Delhi, *Foreign Department, Political Consultations*, No. 60. The Elphinstone mission noted the decline in the horse trade, but attributed it to political instability rather than reduced demand. Memoir Chiefly Relating to the Revenue and Trade of the Kingdom of Caubul, 1808, IOR, London, *Elphinstone Papers*, MSS.Eur.F88.366. P.B. Lord, dispatched to Turkistan in 1838 as part of the Burnes mission, blamed the decline of the horse trade in India on the Company stud farm. Prospects of Trade with Turkistan in Reference to the Contemplated Establishment of an Annual Fair on the Banks of the Indus, 22 February 1838, IOR, London, *Secret & Political*, L/PS/5/130. Wade blamed the decline in horse trade on the high duties placed on it by Ranjit Singh. Although this alone could not account for the decline, Wade hit upon an important strategic and symbolic consideration of the Lahore *darbār*. Ranjit's disruption of the trade with Company territories reserved the higher quality Turkic horses for his own needs, leaving the Company with its weakly Ghazipur mounts. Wade to Metcalfe, 20 April 1827, NAI, New Delhi, *Foreign Department, Political Consultations*, No. 7;

Murray to Wade, 20 April 1827, NAI, New Delhi, *Foreign Department, Political Consultations*, No. 7.

118. Trevelyan argued the remount provided by the Company stud farm at Ghazipur cost between Rs. 1000 and Rs. 1200, while superior Turkic horses could be purchased for Rs. 500. Papers Respecting Afghanistan and the Countries between the Indus and the Caspian, 1831, IOR, London, *Secret & Political*, L/PS/19/26. Burnes, however, thought the cost of Turkic horses to be as high as the Company stud due to high cost of transit. General and Geographical Memoir, 1833, IOR, London, *Secret and Political*, L/PS/19/47.

119. According to Barfield, this was equally important for Afghan society as demonstrated in the First Afghan War. Thomas Barfield, 'Problems in Establishing Legitimacy in Afghanistan', *Iranian Studies*, 274–5. The trade nonetheless remained extremely important for the Bukharan economy. See, for instance, General and Geographical Memoir, 1833, IOR, London, *Secret and Political*, L/PS/19/47; Journal – Kabul, 1824, IOR, London, *Moorcroft Papers*, MSS.Eur.D250, Vol. 3.

120. On *thugs* and *dacoits* of this era, see Kim Wagner, *Thuggee: Banditry and the British in Early Nineteenth Century India* (2007).

121. Claude Markovits, *The Global World of Indian Merchants, 1750–1947: Traders of Sind from Bukhara to Panama* (2000), 14.

122. Letter from the GG's Secretary, 13 March 1832, IOR, London, *Secret & Political*, L/PS/5/42; Josiah Harlan, *Central Asia: Personal Narrative of Josiah Harlan, 1823–1841* (1939), 132. Charles Masson argued the attention of Russian merchants to the demands of the market partly accounted for their success. Observations on the Trade of Kabul, 2 November 1835, NAI, New Delhi, *Foreign Department, Political Consultations*, No. 56.

123. Memorandum of Information Regarding Afghanistan and Central Asia, 23 August 1831, IOR, London, *Secret and Political*, L/P&S/19/26.

124. For an idea of the goods traded, see, for instance, Moorcroft to Metcalfe, 10 October 1823, NAI, New Delhi, *Foreign Department, Political Consultations*, No. 36; Description of Articles, Mostly Russian, Found in the Bazar of Cabool, and Brought to It by Way of Bokhara, 7 February 1838, IOR, London, *Reports and Papers, Political, Geographical, & Commercial, Submitted to Government*, V3320.

125. Letter from the GG's Secretary, 13 March 1832, IOR, London, *Secret & Political*, L/PS/5/42.

126. Fayz Muhammad Katib, *Siraj Al-Tavarikh* (Hijra 1372 (1993/1994)), 106–7.

127. Stirling (Persian Secretary) to Wade, 1 June 1827, NAI, New Delhi, *Foreign Department, Political Consultations*, No. 115. I have found no such examples regarding Afghanistan after 1830.

128. Gail Minault, 'The Emperor's Old Clothes: Robing and Sovereignty in Late Mughal and Early British India', in *Robes of Honour: Khil'at in Pre-Colonial and Colonial India* (2003), 134.

129. Bernardo A. Michael, 'When Soldiers and Statesmen Meet: 'Ethnographic Moments' on the Frontiers of Empire, 1800–1815,' in *Khil'at in Pre-Colonial and Colonial India* (2003), 89–90.

130. R.D. Choksey, *Mountstuart Elphinstone: The Indian Years, 1795–1827* (1971), 113.

131. Elphinstone to Edmonstone, 3 August 1809, IOR, London, *Home & Misc.*, H/657–9.

132. For a description of the court maintained by the Kandahar *sardārs*, see Letter from the Resident at Bushire, Maj. David Wilson, to the Bombay Government, Forwarding the Memo of Charles Masson on Parts of Afghanistan and the

Independent Punjab, 11 September 1830, IOR, London, *Board's Collections*, F/4/1399/55442A. For an idea of the expenditure of the Lahore *darbār*, see Charles Joseph Hall, 'The Maharaja's Account Books. State and Society under the Sikhs: 1799–1849' (University of Illinois).

133. On Dost Muhammad's court culture, see, for example, Burnes to Macnaghten, 27 December 1837, NAI, New Delhi, *Foreign Department, Political Consultations*, No. 12; Josiah Harlan, *A Memoir of India and Afghanistan* (1842), 146–8. To compare the austerity of Dost Muhammad's *darbār* with that of his predecessor Shah Shuja, see Elphinstone to Minto, 19 March 1809, IOR, London, *Bengal Proceedings*, P/BEN/SEC/219, Enclosure No. 5; Sec Dept Despatch of 29 April.

134. Christine Noelle, *State and Tribe in Nineteenth Century Afghanistan: The Reign of Amir Dost Muhammad Khan, 1826–1863* (1997), 263. In contrast, Shah Shuja received Rs. 50,000 per annum during his exile in Company territories. See, for instance, Relative to the circumstances under which a stipend of Rs. 50,000 PAnn: (including a sum of Rs. 1500 PMo granted to his wife in 1815) was assigned for the maintenances of Shuja-oll-Moolk, the exiled King of Cabul, during the period of his residence at Lodhianah, where a house was also provided for his accommodation at an expense of Rs. 5000, 1817, IOR, London, *Board's Collection*, F/4/600/14445.

135. For the best description of the manufacture of Kashmir shawls, see Moorcroft to Swinton, 10 October 1823, NAI, New Delhi, *Foreign Department, Political Consultations*, No. 29.

136. For a discussion of their later ideological construction by the colonial state, see Michelle Maskiell, 'Consuming Kashmir: Shawls and Empires, 1500–2000', *Journal of World History*.

137. See generally Steward Gordon, ed., *Robes and Honour: Khil'at in Pre-Colonial India and Colonial India* (2003).

138. Wade to Prinsep, 27 February 1832, PPA, Lahore, *Records of the Ludhiana Agency*, No. 138.9.

139. Ibid.; C.A. Bayly, *The Birth of the Modern World, 1780–1914* (2004), 105.

140. For a discussion of this trade, see Janet Rizvi, *Transhimalayan Caravans: Merchant Princes and Peasant Traders in Ladakh* (2001), 59–60.

141. Mohan Lal, *Travels in the Panjab, Afghanistan, & Turkmenistan to Balk, Bokhara, and Herat; and a Visit to Great Britain and Germany* (1846), 277.

142. Memoir Chiefly Relating to the Revenue and Trade of the Kingdom of Caubul, 1808, IOR, London, *Elphinstone Papers*, MSS.Eur.F88.366.

6   The Afghan trade corridor

1. John Prevas, *Xenophon's March: Into the Lair of the Persian Lion* (2002), 36.

2. Many anthropologists argue that tribes and cities are mutually dependent in this type of instance. See Thomas Barfield, 'Tribe and State Relations: The Inner Asian Perspective', in *Tribes and State Formation in the Middle East* (1990); Ernest Gellner, 'Tribalism and State in the Middle East', in *Tribes and State Formation in the Middle East* (1990).

3. See, for instance, Moorcroft to Swinton, 20 September 1822, NAI, New Delhi, *Foreign Department, Political Consultations*, No. 76; Memorandum Respecting Rhubarb, 10 October 1823, NAI, New Delhi, *Foreign Department, Political Consultations*, No. 33.

4. For contemporary descriptions of the city, see generally A. Burnes, *Travels into Bokhara; Together with a Narrative of a Voyage on the Indus* (2003; reprint, 1834), 124–52, 241–54, 335–48; Mohan Lal, *Travels in the Panjab, Afghanistan, & Turkmenistan to Balk, Bokhara, and Herat; and a Visit to Great Britain and Germany* (1846), 120–43; James G. Gerard, 'Continuation of the Route of Lt. A. Burnes and Dr Gerard, from Peshawar to Bukhara', *Journal of the Royal Asiatic Society of Bengal*.

5. Burnes to the Secretary of the Right Honorable Governor-General of India, 24 December 1832, NAI, New Delhi, *Foreign Department, Secret Consultations*, No. 31. Joseph Wolff, passing through Bukhara shortly before Burnes, estimated the population at 180,000. Joseph Wolff, *Travels and Adventures* (1861), 343–4.

6. For an overview of the Central Asian economy in the nineteenth century, see Paul Georg Geiss, *Pre-Tsarist and Tsarist Central Asia: Communal Commitment and Political Order in Change* (2003), 126–237.

7. Josiah Harlan, *Central Asia: Personal Narrative of Josiah Harlan, 1823–1841* (1939), 29–30; A Memoir on the Uzbek State of Kundooz and the Power of Its Present Ruler Mahomed Murad Beg, 1838, IOR, London, *Reports and Papers, Political, Geographical, & Commercial, Submitted to Government*, V3320. See Jonathan Lee, *The Ancient Supremacy: Bukhara, Afghanistan and the Battle for Balkh, 1731–1901* (1996), 92–281.

8. Supplementary Notice on the States of Toorkistan, 11 April 1838, NAI, New Delhi, *Foreign Department, Political Consultations*, No. 34; Burnes to the Secretary of the Right Honorable Governor-General of India, 24 December 1832, NAI, New Delhi, *Foreign Department, Secret Consultations*, No. 31.

9. See generally B.D. Hopkins, 'Race, Sex and Slavery: "Forced Labour" In Central Asia and Afghanistan in the Early Nineteenth Century', *Modern Asian Studies*.

10. Carl Hermann Scheidler, *A Journey from Orenburg to Bokhara in the Year 1820* (1870), 59. See also Letter from Meshad, 10 October 1832, IOR, London, *Gerard Papers*, MSS.Eur.C951. Later observers found that Bukhara's tolerance for non-Sunni subjects notably diminished. A Memoir on the Uzbek State of Kundooz and the Power of Its Present Ruler Mahomed Murad Beg, 1838, IOR, London, *Reports and Papers, Political, Geographical, & Commercial, Submitted to Government*, V3320; Supplementary Notice on the States of Toorkistan, 11 April 1838, NAI, New Delhi, *Foreign Department, Political Consultations*, No. 34.

11. Mohan Lal, *Travels in the Panjab, Afghanistan, & Turkmenistan to Balk, Bokhara, and Herat; and a Visit to Great Britain and Germany* (1846), 127. Scheidler, commenting the Jewish community of Bukhara was the largest in Central Asia, estimated their number at around 4000, with 300 houses in the city. Carl Hermann Scheidler, *A Journey from Orenburg to Bokhara in the Year 1820* (1870), 41. Wolff estimated their number at 15,000, although this seems a gross-overstatement. He may have included the Afghan community in their number as part of the Pashtun claim to be one of the lost tribes of Israel. Joseph Wolff, *Travels and Adventures* (1861), 343–4.

12. Carl Hermann Scheidler, *A Journey from Orenburg to Bokhara in the Year 1820* (1870), 35. Visiting the city around 1812, Mir Izzat Ullah claimed the Hindu merchants came mainly from Shikarpur and Kabul, staying in Bukhara for only six months to two years. Mir Izzat Ullah, 'Travels Beyond the Himalaya', *Journal of the Royal Asiatic Society of Great Britain and Ireland*, 337.

13. Mir Izzat Ullah, 'Travels Beyond the Himalaya', *Journal of the Royal Asiatic Society of Great Britain and Ireland*, 339.

14. Carl Hermann Scheidler, *A Journey from Orenburg to Bokhara in the Year 1820* (1870), 35–6.
15. Scheidler specifically mentioned the Ghilzai in his memoirs. Ibid.
16. On the Commerce of Central Asia, 6 June 1833, IOR, London, *Secret & Political*, L/PS/19/45.
17. Carl Hermann Scheidler, *A Journey from Orenburg to Bokhara in the Year 1820* (1870), 50. Scheidler's estimate undoubtedly included all Bukhara's dependent territories, while the smaller population total cited earlier was restricted to the city itself. Conolly repeated this amount in 1834, likely taken from Scheidler or Meyendorff. He placed the value of eight million roubles at £333,333, however, it is unclear whether that would be the value in 1820 or 1834. Arthur Conolly, *Journey to the North of India, over the Land from England through Russia, Persia and Afghanistan*, Vol. 2 (1834), 230–1.
18. Carl Hermann Scheidler, *A Journey from Orenburg to Bokhara in the Year 1820* (1870), 50.
19. Observations on the Trade of Kabul, 2 November 1835, NAI, New Delhi, *Foreign Department, Political Consultations*, No. 56. In 1809, Macartney reported the annual duty to be around seven lakhs of *tillas*. Memoir of a Map of Cabul and the Adjacent Countries, 1809, IOR, London, *Home & Misc.*, H/659.
20. Anne Lincoln Fitzpatrick, *The Great Russian Fair: Nizhnii Novgorod, 1840–90* (1990), 85.
21. On the Commerce of Central Asia, 6 June 1833, IOR, London, *Secret & Political*, L/PS/19/45. On the different types of camels used in the area's trade, see Major Parsons, Deputy-Commissary-General, to H. Torrnes, Esq., 3 February 1839, PRO, London, *Ellenborough Papers*, PRO/30/12/33/2.
22. Mir Izzat Ullah, 'Travels Beyond the Himalaya', *Journal of the Royal Asiatic Society of Great Britain and Ireland*, 332. Most European observers estimated the size of the caravan at around 3000. Arthur Conolly, *Journey to the North of India, over the Land from England through Russia, Persia and Afghanistan*, Vol. 2 (1834), 230–1; Private Letter from Lord in Koondooz to Burnes, 30 January 1838, IOR, London, *Secret & Political*, L/PS/5/130.
23. This was 150 pounds more than the single humped dromedary used in India could carry on average. Carl Hermann Scheidler, *A Journey from Orenburg to Bokhara in the Year 1820* (1870), 50; General and Geographical Memoir, 1833, IOR, London, *Secret and Political*, L/PS/19/47.
24. Anne Lincoln Fitzpatrick, *The Great Russian Fair: Nizhnii Novgorod, 1840–90* (1990), 81–2.
25. Moorcroft to Swinton, 20 September 1822, NAI, New Delhi, *Foreign Department, Political Consultations*, No. 76.
26. Private Letter from Lord in Koondooz to Burnes, 30 January 1838, IOR, London, *Secret & Political*, L/PS/5/130.
27. Carl Hermann Scheidler, *A Journey from Orenburg to Bokhara in the Year 1820* (1870), 37.
28. A. Burnes, *Travels into Bokhara; Together with a Narrative of a Voyage on the Indus* (2003; reprint, 1834), 139.
29. Levi argues Russia imported less than five per cent of its cotton overland by the time of the British occupation of Afghanistan in the 1840s. Scott Levi, *The Indian Trade Diaspora in Central Asia and Its Trade 1550–1900* (2002), 246.
30. Papers Respecting Afghanistan and the Countries between the Indus and the Caspian, 1831, IOR, London, *Secret & Political*, L/PS/19/26.

31. Letter from Meshad, 10 October 1832, IOR, London, *Gerard Papers*, MSS.Eur.C951. Moorcroft commented that British manufactures were more cheaply imported overland from Russia than via India and Afghanistan. Moorcroft to Swinton, 20 September 1822, NAI, New Delhi, *Foreign Department, Political Consultations*, No. 76.

32. Anne Lincoln Fitzpatrick, *The Great Russian Fair: Nizhnii Novgorod, 1840–90* (1990), 81–6; Scott Levi, *The Indian Trade Diaspora in Central Asia and Its Trade 1550–1900* (2002), 241; A. Burnes, *Travels into Bokhara; Together with a Narrative of a Voyage on the Indus* (2003; reprint, 1834), 367–77.

33. Carl Hermann Scheidler, *A Journey from Orenburg to Bokhara in the Year 1820* (1870), 50.

34. On the Commerce of Central Asia, 6 June 1833, IOR, London, *Secret & Political*, L/PS/19/45.

35. A Report on the Countries between India and Russia, 5 May 1833, IOR, London, *Secret & Political*, L/PS/19/44.

36. Observations on the Trade of Kabul, 2 November 1835, NAI, New Delhi, *Foreign Department, Political Consultations*, No. 56.

37. See, for example, Memorandum of Information Regarding Afghanistan and Central Asia, 23 August 1831, IOR, London, *Secret and Political*, L/P&S/19/26.

38. Anne Lincoln Fitzpatrick, *The Great Russian Fair: Nizhnii Novgorod, 1840–90* (1990), 86.

39. On the Commerce of Central Asia, 6 June 1833, IOR, London, *Secret & Political*, L/PS/19/45.

40. Josiah Harlan described Balkh as having two caravansaries and an 'unendowed *madrasa*', used as a guesthouse. Josiah Harlan, *Central Asia: Personal Narrative of Josiah Harlan, 1823–1841* (1939), 28. See also A. Burnes, *Travels into Bokhara; Together with a Narrative of a Voyage on the Indus* (2003; reprint, 1834), 110–13; Memoir of a Map of Cabul and the Adjacent Countries, 1809, IOR, London, *Home & Misc.*, H/659.

41. Memoir Chiefly Relating to the Revenue and Trade of the Kingdom of Caubul, 1808, IOR, London, *Elphinstone Papers*, MSS.Eur.F88.366. Moorcroft, who actually visited Balkh, estimated its population at no more than 1000 houses. William Moorcroft and George Trebeck, *Travels in India: Himalayan Provinces of Hindustan and the Punjab in Ladakh and Kashmir in Peshawar, Kabul, Kunduz, and Bokhara from 1819 to 1825* (2000; reprint, 1841), 494.

42. Edward Stirling, *Some Considerations on the Political State of the Intermediate Countries between Persia and India, with Reference to the Project of Russia Marching an Army through Them* (1835), 46; Mir Izzat Ullah, *Travels in Central Asia by Meer Izzut-Oollah* (1872), 81–2.

43. Josiah Harlan, *Central Asia: Personal Narrative of Josiah Harlan, 1823–1841* (1939), 32–3. See generally Robert McChesney, *Waqf in Central Asia* (1991), 217–56.

44. See generally A Memoir on the Uzbek State of Kundooz and the Power of Its Present Ruler Mahomed Murad Beg, 1838, IOR, London, *Reports and Papers, Political, Geographical, & Commercial, Submitted to Government*, V3320, Descriptive List of Chiefs of Uzbeg States in Central Asia, 29 April 1839, BL, London, *Broughton Papers*, Add. 36470.

45. Dost Muhammad and Mir Murad Beg often clashed over control of Bamian. See Extract of a Letter from Mr Masson to Captain Wade Dated at Kabul 5 December 1836, 5 June 1837, NAI, New Delhi, *Foreign Department, Political Consultations*, No. 46; Wade to Macnaghten, 12 February 1833, NAI, New Delhi, *Foreign Department, Secret Consultations*, Nos. 19–20.

46. Josiah Harlan, *Central Asia: Personal Narrative of Josiah Harlan, 1823–1841* (1939), 44.

47. Prospects of Trade with Turkistan in Reference to the Contemplated Establishment of an Annual Fair on the Banks of the Indus, 22 February 1838, IOR, London, *Secret & Political*, L/PS/5/130; A Memoir on the Uzbek State of Kundooz and the Power of Its Present Ruler Mahomed Murad Beg, 1838, IOR, London, *Reports and Papers, Political, Geographical, & Commercial, Submitted to Government*, V3320.

48. A Report on the Countries between India and Russia, 5 May 1833, IOR, London, *Secret & Political*, L/PS/19/44; Mohan Lal, *Travels in the Panjab, Afghanistan, & Turkmenistan to Balk, Bokhara, and Herat; and a Visit to Great Britain and Germany* (1846), 100–1.

49. Translation of a Letter in Reply from Meer Moorad Beg, the Chief of Koondooz to the Address of the Late Dr Gerard Received at Cabool, 1834, IOR, London, *Secret & Political*, L/PS/5/129.

50. A Report on the Countries between India and Russia, 5 May 1833, IOR, London, *Secret & Political*, L/PS/19/44.

51. A Memoir on the Uzbek State of Kundooz and the Power of Its Present Ruler Mahomed Murad Beg, 1838, IOR, London, *Reports and Papers, Political, Geographical, & Commercial, Submitted to Government*, V3320.

52. James G. Gerard, 'Continuation of the Route of Lt. A. Burnes and Dr Gerard, from Peshawar to Bukhara', *Journal of the Royal Asiatic Society of Bengal*, 10.

53. Edward Stirling, *Some Considerations on the Political State of the Intermediate Countries between Persia and India, with Reference to the Project of Russia Marching an Army through Them* (1835), 48. See also Mir Izzat Ullah, *Travels in Central Asia by Meer Izzut-Oollah* (1872), 79.

54. Mir Izzat Ullah, *Travels in Central Asia by Meer Izzut-Oollah* (1872), 80.

55. Masson to H. Pottinger, 1 January 1833, PRO, London, *Pottinger Papers*, FO/705/32; Notice on Herat, with a Sketch of the State of Affairs in the Surrounding Counties (Burnes to Wade), 7 February 1838, IOR, London, *Secret & Political*, L/PS/5/130.

56. See, for example, Wade to Macnaghten, 13 September 1837, IOR, London, *Secret & Political*, L/PS/5/129.

57. Mohan Lal, *Travels in the Panjab, Afghanistan, & Turkmenistan to Balk, Bokhara, and Herat; and a Visit to Great Britain and Germany* (1846), 73–4.

58. G. Forster, *A Journey from Bengal to England through the Northern Parts of India, Kashmir, Afghanistan and Persia* (1798), 68.

59. Ibid., 72, 88.

60. James G. Gerard, 'Continuation of the Route of Lt. A. Burnes and Dr Gerard, from Peshawar to Bukhara', *Journal of the Royal Asiatic Society of Bengal*, 3.

61. Secret Letter from Bengal, 6 June 1833, IOR, London, *Secret & Political*, L/PS/5/43.

62. Ibid.; On the Commerce of Central Asia, 6 June 1833, IOR, London, *Secret & Political*, L/PS/19/45.

63. On the Political State of Cabool, 26 November 1837, IOR, London, *Reports and Papers, Political, Geographical, & Commercial, Submitted to Government*, V3320.

64. Observations on the Trade of Kabul, 2 November 1835, NAI, New Delhi, *Foreign Department, Political Consultations*, No. 56.

65. See, for example, Extract of a Letter from Mr Masson to Captain Wade Dated 30 August 1836, 9 January 1837, NAI, New Delhi, *Foreign Department, Political Consultations*, No. 45; Burnes to Macnaghten, 27 December 1837, NAI, New Delhi, *Foreign Department, Political Consultations*, No. 12.

66. On the Political State of Cabool, 26 November 1837, IOR, London, *Reports and Papers, Political, Geographical, & Commercial, Submitted to Government*, V3320.
67. Ibid.
68. Christine Noelle, *State and Tribe in Nineteenth Century Afghanistan: The Reign of Amir Dost Muhammad Khan, 1826–1863* (1997), 284.
69. See, for example, Description of Articles, Mostly Russia, Found in the Bazar of Cabool and Brought to It by Way of Bokhara, 11 April 1838, NAI, New Delhi, *Foreign Department, Political Consultations*, No. 30.
70. Minute by GG, 25 November 1831, NAI, New Delhi, *Foreign Department, Secret Consultations*, No. 2. For a more comprehensive discussion of Sayyid Muheen Shah's trading activities, see Shah Mahmoud Hanifi, 'Inter-Regional Trade and Colonial State Formation in 19th Century Afghanistan' (University of Michigan), 208–22.
71. Results of Muhim Shah's Commercial Speculation, 17 August 1835, NAI, New Delhi, *Foreign Department, Political Consultations*, Nos. 70–3.
72. Wade to Macnaghten, 17 August 1834, PPA, Lahore, *Records of the Ludhiana Agency*, No. 140.66.
73. On the Commerce of Central Asia, 6 June 1833, IOR, London, *Secret & Political*, L/PS/19/45.
74. Geographical Memoir to Accompany Papers Respecting Afghanistan and Persia Printed by Order of the House of Commons, 1839, PRO, London, FO/95/654. Mohan Lal, *Travels in the Panjab, Afghanistan, & Turkmenistan to Balk, Bokhara, and Herat; and a Visit to Great Britain and Germany* (1846), 78.
75. Report on the Commerce of Multan, 1838, IOR, London, *Reports and Papers, Political, Geographical, & Commercial, Submitted to Government*, V3320.
76. Mohan Lal, *Travels in the Panjab, Afghanistan, & Turkmenistan to Balk, Bokhara, and Herat; and a Visit to Great Britain and Germany* (1846), 76–7; On the Commerce of Central Asia, 6 June 1833, IOR, London, *Secret & Political*, L/PS/19/45.
77. Masson to Wade, 10 August 1835, NAI, New Delhi, *Foreign Department, Political Consultations*, No. 29.
78. See, for example, Extract of a Letter from Mr Masson to Captain Wade Dated the 10 May 1835, 12 October 1835, NAI, New Delhi, *Foreign Department, Political Consultations*, No. 70.
79. Copy of a Dispatch from the Political Agent at Loodhiana, on a Mission to Lahore, 1 January 1837, IOR, London, *Secret & Political*, L/PS/5/127, No. 30. Quoting Masson to Wade 30 September 1836.
80. Burnes claimed in total the Lohani migrations moved over 24,000 camels through the Gomal Pass in three separate *kâfilas*. Harlan estimated the Lohani total significantly lower at 10,000. Trade of the Upper Indus or Derajat, 5 August 1837, IOR, London, *Reports and Papers, Political, Geographical, & Commercial, Submitted to Government*, V3320; Josiah Harlan, *A Memoir of India and Avghanistan* (1842), 59.
81. Taxes Levied on Indian Goods Taken by Lohanee Merchants to Cabul, 26 September 1838, NAI, New Delhi, *Foreign Department, Political Consultations*, Nos. 10–11.
82. See, for instance, Extract of a Letter from Mr Masson to Captain Wade Dated the 3 August 1837, 16 October 1837, NAI, New Delhi, *Foreign Department, Political Consultations*, No. 84.
83. Masson to Wade, 3 August 1837, IOR, London, *Secret & Political*, L/PS/5/129.
84. See, for example, Copy of a Dispatch from Loodianah Political Agent, 5 August 1837, IOR, London, *Secret & Political*, L/PS/5/127, No. 13; Extract of Letters from Mr Masson to Captain Wade from 27 June to 29 July 1836, 21 November 1836, NAI, New Delhi, *Foreign Department, Political Consultations*, No. 32.

85. Copy of a Dispatch from the Political Agent at Loodhiana, 27 June 1837, IOR, London, *Secret & Political*, L/PS/5/128, No. 20.

86. Observations on the Trade of Kabul, 2 November 1835, NAI, New Delhi, *Foreign Department, Political Consultations*, No. 56.

87. Mohan Lal, *Travels in the Panjab, Afghanistan, & Turkmenistan to Balk, Bokhara, and Herat; and a Visit to Great Britain and Germany* (1846), 329–30. See also G.T. Vinge, *A Personal Narrative of a Visit to Ghuzni, Kabul, and Afghanistan and of a Residence at the Court of Dost Muhamed with Notices of Ranjit Singh, Khiva and the Russian Expedition* (1999), 120–35.

88. Extract of a Letter from Mr Masson to Captain Wade Dated the 20 February 1835, 25 May 1835, NAI, New Delhi, *Foreign Department, Political Consultations*, No. 30; Extract of a Letter from Mr Masson to Captain Wade Dated at Kabul 20th Mahomedan Month Barat 1250, 30 March 1835, NAI, New Delhi, *Foreign Department, Political Consultations*, No. 46.

89. Gordon, Assistant Political Agent on a Deputation to Dera Ismail Khan to Maddock, 2 October 1839, NAI, New Delhi, *Foreign Department, Secret Consultations*, No. 81.

90. Masson's description of Jalalabad as part of Khorasan highlights Afghanistan's cultural and political hybridity, belonging both to the South Asian and Persian spheres. Letter from the Resident at Bushire, Maj. David Wilson, to the Bombay Government, Forwarding the Memo of Charles Masson on Parts of Afghanistan and the Independent Punjab, 11 September 1830, IOR, London, *Board's Collections*, F/4/1399/55442A.

91. Observations on the Political State and Resources of Afghanistan, 23 January 1835, NAI, New Delhi, *Foreign Department, Political Consultations*, No. 46.

92. Observations on the Trade of Kabul, 2 November 1835, NAI, New Delhi, *Foreign Department, Political Consultations*, No. 56.

93. Copy of a Dispatch from the Political Agent at Loodhiana, 27 June 1837, IOR, London, *Secret & Political*, L/PS/5/128, No. 20.

94. Letter from the Resident at Bushire, Maj. David Wilson, to the Bombay Government, Forwarding the Memo of Charles Masson on Parts of Afghanistan and the Independent Punjab, 11 September 1830, IOR, London, *Board's Collections*, F/4/1399/55442A.

95. Memoir Chiefly Relating to the Revenue and Trade of the Kingdom of Caubul, 1808, IOR, London, *Elphinstone Papers*, MSS.Eur.F88.366; A. Burnes, *Travels into Bokhara; Together with a Narrative of a Voyage on the Indus* (2003; reprint, 1834), 57.

96. Mohan Lal, *Travels in the Panjab, Afghanistan, & Turkmenistan to Balk, Bokhara, and Herat; and a Visit to Great Britain and Germany* (1846), 461.

97. Forster's Route from Jamboo to Astracan, 12 July 1785, IOR, London, *Forster Papers*, MSS.Eur.B14/MSS.Eur.K115.

98. Memoir Chiefly Relating to the Revenue and Trade of the Kingdom of Caubul, 1808, IOR, London, *Elphinstone Papers*, MSS.Eur.F88.366.

99. On the Commerce of Central Asia, 6 June 1833, IOR, London, *Secret & Political*, L/PS/19/45.

100. G. Forster, *A Journey from Bengal to England through the Northern Parts of India, Kashmir, Afghanistan and Persia* (1798), 50.

101. Mohan Lal, *Travels in the Panjab, Afghanistan, & Turkmenistan to Balk, Bokhara, and Herat; and a Visit to Great Britain and Germany* (1846), 44.

102. Joseph Wolff, *Travels and Adventures* (1861), 365.

103. G. Forster, *A Journey from Bengal to England through the Northern Parts of India, Kashmir, Afghanistan and Persia* (1798), 50; William Moorcroft and George Trebeck, *Travels in the Himalaya Provinces of Hindustan and the Panjab; in Ladakh and Kashmir; in Peshawar, Kabul, Kunduz and Bokhara*, Vol. 2 (1841), 338.

104. On the Commerce of Central Asia, 6 June 1833, IOR, London, *Secret & Political*, L/PS/19/45.

105. Ibid., Burnes to Macnaghten, 4 September 1837, IOR, London, *Secret & Political*, L/PS/5/129.

106. For a contemporary summary of the settlement centres laying between Bukhara and Herat, see Notice on Herat, with a Sketch of the State of Affairs in the Surrounding Counties (Burnes to Wade), 7 February 1838, IOR, London, *Secret & Political*, L/PS/5/130. See generally Jonathan Lee, *The Ancient Supremacy: Bukhara, Afghanistan and the Battle for Balkh, 1731–1901* (1996).

107. Wade to Macnaghten, 14 May 1834, PPA, Lahore, *Records of the Ludhiana Agency*, 140.35.

108. For an example of Turkmen raiding activities in the area of transCaspia, see Supplementary Notice on the States of Toorkistan, 11 April 1838, NAI, New Delhi, *Foreign Department, Political Consultations*, No. 34.

109. Copy of a Dispatch from the Political Agent at Loodiana, 27 June 1837, IOR, London, *Secret & Political*, L/PS/5/128, No. 29.

110. A.K.S. Lambton, 'Persian Trade under the Early Qajars', in *Islam and the Trade of Asia* (1970), 235.

111. Mohan Lal, *Travels in the Panjab, Afghanistan, & Turkmenistan to Balk, Bokhara, and Herat; and a Visit to Great Britain and Germany* (1846), 193.

112. For an idea of Persia's internal situation, see, for example, Campbell to Macnaghten, 23 May 1833, NAI, New Delhi, *Foreign Department, Secret Consultations*, No. 18; Ellis to Viscount Palmerstone, 29 April 1836, IOR, London, *Secret & Political*, L/PS/9/99.

113. Notice on Herat, with a Sketch of the State of Affairs in the Surrounding Counties (Burnes to Wade), 7 February 1838, IOR, London, *Secret & Political*, L/PS/5/130.

114. Burnes to Macnaghten, 20 March 1839, NAI, New Delhi, *Foreign Department, Secret Consultations*, No. 164.

115. Notice on Herat, with a Sketch of the State of Affairs in the Surrounding Counties (Burnes to Wade), 7 February 1838, IOR, London, *Secret & Political*, L/PS/5/130; Copy of a Dispatch from the Political Agent at Loodhiana, 27 June 1837, IOR, London, *Secret & Political*, L/PS/5/128, No. 20.

116. Abstract of Intelligence from Cabul Dated 23 April to 24 May 1833, 3 January 1834, NAI, New Delhi, *Foreign Department, Secret Consultations*, No. 2.

117. Arthur Conolly, *Journey to the North of India, over the Land from England through Russia, Persia and Afghanistan*, Vol. 2 (1834), 225; Joseph Wolff, *Travels and Adventures* (1861), 312.

118. Letter from Meshad, 10 October 1832, IOR, London, *Gerard Papers*, MSS.Eur.C951.

119. J.B. Fraser, *Narrative of a Journey into Khorasan* (1825), 460.

120. Ibid., 468.

121. Papers Respecting Afghanistan and the Countries between the Indus and the Caspian, 1831, IOR, London, *Secret & Political*, L/PS/19/26.

122. Arthur Conolly, *Journey to the North of India, over the Land from England through Russia, Persia and Afghanistan*, Vol. 2 (1834), 292.

123. Ibid.

124. G. Forster, *A Journey from Bengal to England through the Northern Parts of India, Kashmir, Afghanistan and Persia* (1798), 134–5. Fayz Muhammad insists it was from this merchant community that Eldred Pottinger, the British officer who organized Herat's defences during the 1838 Persian siege, raised the necessary funds. Fayz Muhammad Katib, *Siraj Al-Tavarikh* (Hijra 1372 (1993/1994)), 184.

125. Journal of a Journey of a French Officer in 1826, 1841, IOR, London, *Secret & Political*, L/PS/20/G10/3; Abstract of the Routes of Lieuts. Christie and Pottinger, 8 September 1810, IOR, London, *Secret & Political*, L/PS/9/67.

126. Mohan Lal, *Travels in the Panjab, Afghanistan, & Turkmenistan to Balk, Bokhara, and Herat; and a Visit to Great Britain and Germany* (1846), 303–4.

127. Arthur Conolly, *Journey to the North of India, over the Land from England through Russia, Persia and Afghanistan*, Vol. 2 (1834), 44–5.

128. Report on the Trade between Shikarpoor and Herat, 1838, IOR, London, *Reports and Papers, Political, Geographical, & Commercial, Submitted to Government*, V3320.

129. Shah Mahmud and Kamran regularly used the Persian's status as infidel Shi'as to rally support from neighbouring Hazaras, and occasionally Bukhara and Khiva. See, for instance, Translation of the Contents of a Letter from Rutteen Chund to Moolla Hidict Oolla Khan – Dated Umrustsur the 17th of Rubbee A.H. 1241 Corresponding with the 31st October Ad 1825, 2 December 1825, NAI, New Delhi, *Foreign Department, Political Consultations*, No. 21.

130. Heinz Gaube, *Iranian Cities* (1979), 44.

131. Mohan Lal, *Travels in the Panjab, Afghanistan, & Turkmenistan to Balk, Bokhara, and Herat; and a Visit to Great Britain and Germany* (1846), 271.

132. Arthur Conolly, *Journey to the North of India, over the Land from England through Russia, Persia and Afghanistan*, Vol. 2 (1834), 6–7.

133. Mohan Lal, *Travels in the Panjab, Afghanistan, & Turkmenistan to Balk, Bokhara, and Herat; and a Visit to Great Britain and Germany* (1846), 275.

134. Journal of a Journey of a French Officer in 1826, 1841, IOR, London, *Secret & Political*, L/PS/20/G10/3.

135. James G. Gerard, 'Continuation of the Route of Lt. A. Burnes and Dr Gerard, from Peshawar to Bukhara', *Journal of the Royal Asiatic Society of Bengal*, 3.

136. G. Forster, *A Journey from Bengal to England through the Northern Parts of India, Kashmir, Afghanistan and Persia* (1798), 120.

137. Letter, 30 March 1833, IOR, London, *Gerard Papers*, MSS.Eur.C941.

138. Heinz Gaube, *Iranian Cities* (1979), 36–8.

139. Letter from the Resident at Bushire, Maj. David Wilson, to the Bombay Government, Forwarding the Memo of Charles Masson on Parts of Afghanistan and the Independent Punjab, 11 September 1830, IOR, London, *Board's Collections*, F/4/1399/55442A.

140. Letter, 30 March 1833, IOR, London, *Gerard Papers*, MSS.Eur.C941.

141. Letter from the Resident at Bushire, Maj. David Wilson, to the Bombay Government, Forwarding the Memo of Charles Masson on Parts of Afghanistan and the Independent Punjab, 11 September 1830, IOR, London, *Board's Collections*, F/4/1399/55442A.

142. Mohan Lal, *Travels in the Panjab, Afghanistan, & Turkmenistan to Balk, Bokhara, and Herat; and a Visit to Great Britain and Germany* (1846), 261–2, 277.

143. Report on the Trade between Shikarpoor and Herat, 1838, IOR, London, *Reports and Papers, Political, Geographical, & Commercial, Submitted to Government*, V3320.

144. Mohan Lal, *Travels in the Panjab, Afghanistan, & Turkmenistan to Balk, Bokhara, and Herat; and a Visit to Great Britain and Germany* (1846), 318.

145. Letter from Meshad, 10 October 1832, IOR, London, *Gerard Papers*, MSS.Eur.C951.

146. Notice on Herat, with a Sketch of the State of Affairs in the Surrounding Counties (Burnes to Wade), 7 February 1838, IOR, London, *Secret & Political*, L/PS/5/130; Copy of a Letter from Political Agent at Loodhiana, 21 May 1837, IOR, London, *Secret & Political*, L/PS/5/127, No. 56.

147. Letter from the Resident at Bushire, Maj. David Wilson, to the Bombay Government, Forwarding the Memo of Charles Masson on Parts of Afghanistan and the Independent Punjab, 11 September 1830, IOR, London, *Board's Collections*, F/4/1399/55442A.

148. Extract of a Letter from Mr Masson to Captain Wade Dated at Kabul 5 December 1836, 5 June 1837, NAI, New Delhi, *Foreign Department, Political Consultations*, No. 46.

149. Memoir Chiefly Relating to the Revenue and Trade of the Kingdom of Caubul, 1808, IOR, London, *Elphinstone Papers*, MSS.Eur.F88.366. Although he did not estimate the population's size, Rawlinson offered a similar breakdown of the Kandahar populace. Report on the Durranee Tribes, 19 April 1841, IOR, London, *Secret & Political*, L/PS/18/C5.

150. Journal of a Journey of a French Officer in 1826, 1841, IOR, London, *Secret & Political*, L/PS/20/G10/3.

151. Mohan Lal, *Travels in the Panjab, Afghanistan, & Turkmenistan to Balk, Bokhara, and Herat; and a Visit to Great Britain and Germany* (1846), 231.

152. Report on the Trade between Shikarpoor and Herat, 1838, IOR, London, *Reports and Papers, Political, Geographical, & Commercial, Submitted to Government*, V3320.

153. Letter from the Resident at Bushire, Maj. David Wilson, to the Bombay Government; Forwarding the Memo of Charles Masson on Parts of Afghanistan and the Independent Punjab, 11 September 1830, IOR, London, *Board's Collections*, F/4/1399/55442A.

154. Mohan Lal, *Travels in the Panjab, Afghanistan, & Turkmenistan to Balk, Bokhara, and Herat; and a Visit to Great Britain and Germany* (1846), 302.

155. Letter from the Resident at Bushire, Maj. David Wilson, to the Bombay Government, Forwarding the Memo of Charles Masson on Parts of Afghanistan and the Independent Punjab, 11 September 1830, IOR, London, *Board's Collections*, F/4/1399/55442A.

156. Observations on the Political State and Resources of Afghanistan, 23 January 1835, NAI, New Delhi, *Foreign Department, Political Consultations*, No. 46.

157. G. Forster, *A Journey from Bengal to England through the Northern Parts of India, Kashmir, Afghanistan and Persia* (1798), 103.

158. Mohan Lal, *Travels in the Panjab, Afghanistan, & Turkmenistan to Balk, Bokhara, and Herat; and a Visit to Great Britain and Germany* (1846), 317–18.

159. See, for instance, Pottinger to McNeill, 28 September 1837, IOR, London, *Secret & Political*, L/PS/20/A7/1; Macnaghten to Wade, 13 November 1837, IOR, London, *Secret & Political*, L/PS/5/129.

160. Arthur Conolly, *Journey to the North of India, over the Land from England through Russia, Persia and Afghanistan*, Vol. 2 (1834), 166–7.

161. Burnes claimed Timur Shah transformed Shikarpur into the Central Asian financial centre after 1786. On the Commerce of Shikarpoor and Upper Sinde, 5 June 1837, NAI, New Delhi, *Foreign Department, Political Consultations*, No. 60.

162. Ibid. For a general description of Shikarpur, see Journal to Shikarpur, 26 April 1836, PPA, Lahore, *Records of the Ludhiana Agency*, No. 107.4; Lal to Mackeson, 1 August 1836, NAI, New Delhi, *Foreign Department, Political Consultations*, No. 34.

163. Report on the Establishment of an Entrepot of Fair for the Indus Trade, 18 January 1838, IOR, London, *Secret & Political*, L/PS/5/130.

164. On the Commerce of Shikarpoor and Upper Sinde, 5 June 1837, NAI, New Delhi, *Foreign Department, Political Consultations*, No. 60.

165. Mohan Lal, *Travels in the Panjab, Afghanistan, & Turkmenistan to Balk, Bokhara, and Herat; and a Visit to Great Britain and Germany* (1846), 438.

166. Letter from the Resident at Bushire, Maj. David Wilson, to the Bombay Government, Forwarding the Memo of Charles Masson on Parts of Afghanistan and the Independent Punjab, 11 September 1830, IOR, London, *Board's Collections*, F/4/1399/55442A.

167. Memorandum of Information Regarding Afghanistan and Central Asia, 23 August 1831, IOR, London, *Secret and Political*, L/PS/19/26.

168. Papers Respecting Afghanistan and the Countries between the Indus and the Caspian, 1831, IOR, London, *Secret & Political*, L/PS/19/26.

169. The customs duties were farmed for Rs. 64,000 annually. On the Commerce of Shikarpoor and Upper Sinde, 5 June 1837, NAI, New Delhi, *Foreign Department, Political Consultations*, No. 60.

170. *Cf.* Trade between Shikarpoor and Marwar, 25 September 1837, NAI, New Delhi, *Foreign Department, Political Consultations*, No. 90; On the Commerce of Shikarpoor and Upper Sinde, 5 June 1837, NAI, New Delhi, *Foreign Department, Political Consultations*, No. 60.

171. Memoir Chiefly Relating to the Revenue and Trade of the Kingdom of Caubul, 1808, IOR, London, *Elphinstone Papers*, MSS.Eur.F88.366; Elphinstone to Minto, 1 February 1809, IOR, London, *Bengal Proceedings*, P/BEN/SEC/215, No. 4; in correspondence of 20 March, No. 53.

172. Letter from the Resident at Bushire, Maj. David Wilson, to the Bombay Government; Forwarding the Memo of Charles Masson on Parts of Afghanistan and the Independent Punjab, 11 September 1830, IOR, London, *Board's Collections*, F/4/1399/55442A.

173. Report on the Commerce of Multan, 1838, IOR, London, *Reports and Papers, Political, Geographical, & Commercial, Submitted to Government*, V3320.

174. Journal from Multan to Mithenkot, 1 August 1836, NAI, New Delhi, *Foreign Department, Political Consultations*, No. 33; Lal to Mackeson on Multan Commerce, 9 May 1836, NAI, New Delhi, *Foreign Department, Political Consultations*, No. 42, Commercial Information Regarding Bhawal Khan's Country, 25 September 1837, NAI, New Delhi, *Foreign Department, Political Consultations*, No. 87.

175. Mohan Lal, *Travels in the Panjab, Afghanistan, & Turkmenistan to Balk, Bokhara, and Herat; and a Visit to Great Britain and Germany* (1846), 393–5.

Conclusion

1. See David Edwards, *Heroes of the Age: Moral Fault Lines on the Afghan Frontier* (1996).

2. One such example is the Frontier Crimes Regulation, which still regulates the Federally Administered Tribal Areas of Pakistan. See generally C. Collin Davies, *The Problem of the North-West Frontier 1890–1908: With a Survey of Policy since*

1849 (1974); James W. Spain, 'Political Problems of a Borderland', in *Pakistan's Western Borderlands: The Transformation of a Political Order* (1979); Garry Alder, *British India's Northern Frontier, 1865–95: A Study in Imperial Policy* (1963).

3. Shah Mahmoud Hanifi, 'Inter-Regional Trade and Colonial State Formation in 19th Century Afghanistan' (University of Michigan), Shah Mahmoud Hanifi, 'Impoverishing a Colonial Frontier: Cash, Credit and Debt in Nineteenth Century Afghanistan', *Iranian Studies*.

4. Between 1849 and 1899, the colonial state undertook 62 expeditions against the Afghan tribes inhabiting its territory. Lal Baha, *N.-W.F.P. Administration under British Rule, 1901–1919* (1978), 5. The operations against the Faqir of Ipi in the 1937 tied down more than 40,000 troops on the frontier. Milan Hauner, 'One Man against the Empire: The Faqir of Ipi and the British in Central Asia on the Eve of and During the Second World War', *Journal of contemporary history*, 192.

5. See R. Gopalakrishnan, *The Geography and Politics of Afghanistan* (1982), 70–113.

6. Chatterjee, *Nationalist Thought and the Colonial World: A Derivative Discourse* (1986), 10.

Epilogue

1. This speech was given on 1 March 2006. 'President and Mrs Bush dedicate U.S. embassy building in Afghanistan'. http://www.whitehouse.gov/news/releases/2006/03/20060301-4.html. Last accessed 25/07/2007.

Glossary of Foreign Terms

Abdali – original name of the tribe which Ahmed Shah Abdali led; the name was changed to 'Durrani' following his assumption of the office of shah in 1747

amīr – 'commander', Arabic title employed by Afghan leaders; Dost Muhammad Khan was the first to assume this title

amīr al-mu'minīn – 'leader of the faithful', adopted by Dost Muhammad Khan in 1835 when he declared a *jihād* against the Sikhs

'asabiyah – kinship solidarity or clan spirit which Ibn Khaldun argued was the source of tribal unity

bālā hiṣār – 'high castle/fort'; citadel overlooking Kabul

Barakzai – clan of the Durrani tribe which displaced the ruling Suddozai clan in the Afghan civil war

crore – unit of 10 million rupees

dār al-ḥarb – 'world of war' denoting non-Muslim lands

dār al-Islām – 'world of Islam' denoting Muslim lands

Darî – dialect of Persian spoken in Afghanistan

darbār – ruler's court

darwêsh – holy man

dīwān – Mughal administrative and tax unit

Durrani – 'Pearl of pearls'; name adopted by Ahmed Shah on his assumption of Afghan leadership and bestowed to his tribesmen

fārsī – Persian dialect spoken in Iran

fārsīwān – 'Persian speakers'; Afghan ethnic group denoted by their use of the *Fārsī* dialect of Persian

fatwā – a religious ruling propagated by the *'ulamā'*

firengi – European foreigners

fitna – 'rebellion'; term employed by Andre Wink to denote rebellious lands on the periphery of empire which affected central authority

ghāzī – Islamic religious warrior

hamsāya – 'neighbour'; Afghan ethnic group 'adopted' by tribes

hindkis – Hindu merchant-banker, generally from Multan or Shikarpur

hundis – bills of exchange/credit

jāgīr – land grant based on military tenure used in the Mughal Empire

jazâ'ilchî – 'musket men'; Afghan tribesmen using *jazâ'ils*, long-barrelled smooth-bore rifles

jihād – 'struggle'; often understood as 'holy war', there is a differentiation between a 'greater' (internal) and 'lesser' (external) *jihād*

jirga – Pashtun tribal council

kâfila – caravan

kafilabashi – head of caravan

Kāfir – 'unbeliever'; title generally bestowed to non-Muslims. In the Afghan context, the *Kaffirs* of *Kaffiristan*, now known as the *Nuristanis* of *Nurisitan*, are believed to be the country's original inhabitants. They inhabit a remote and mountainous region in the extreme east of the country.

Khalsa Dal – Ranjit Singh's army; *khalsa* is a Punjabi military order *khān* – title of tribal leader

kharwār – 'ass loads'; unit of measure for grain

khattris – trader community originally from the Punjab who played an important role in the Central and South Asian financial network

khel – 'tribe'

khil'at – robe of honour presented in Muslim courts

Khirqa-i mubaraka – piece of the Prophet's cloak given to Ahmed Shah by the rulers of Bukhara; later employed by Dost Muhammad, and more recently Mullah Omar of the Taliban to legitimate their rule

khutba – prayer read in the name of the ruler at Friday prayers

lakh – unit of 100,000

madrasa – Islamic religious school

malik – tribal leader

marwaris – trader/banker community originally from Jiasalmer in Rajastan who played a key role in the Central/South Asian financial network

mian – religious leader claiming descent from the Prophet

mīr – title for a tribal leader amongst Uzbeks and Hazara

mīr wā'iz – head religious authority of Kabul

Naqshbandiyah – popular Sufi sect in Afghanistan

pādshāh – term similar to *shah-i shah*, or 'king of kings'

Pashtünwâlî – Pashtun tribal code

pīr – 'elder'; title usually reserved for senior Sufi

powinda – migratory trader community better known as the Lohanis who dominated the transit trade from the Punjab to Kabul

qaum – 'tribe'; basic term of community

qazī – government-appointed Islamic judge

Qizilbash – 'red headed'; Persianized Shia community of Turkic origin who served as the bureaucratic class in Kabul

ryot – 'peasant'; term generally used in South Asia

Saddozai – Ahmed Shah's clan within the Durrani tribe; original *shahs* of Afghanistan but lost their royal office with the victory of the Barakzai in the Afghan civil war

sardārs – Afghan nobles

sayyid – religious leader claiming descent from the Prophet

shâh – Persian for 'king'

Shahzadeh – 'son of king'; prince

sharīa – Islamic religious law based on the Koran and Hadith

tarbûrwâlî – agnatic cousin rivalry structuring violence in Pashtun society

tarīqat – Sufi brotherhood

tilla – Bukharan unit of gold currency

tiyūl – Afghan jaghir

toman – Persian unit of currency

'ulamā' – Islamic religious scholars [sing. *'ālim*]

waqf – Islamic religious endowment

yamboo – silver ingots

Yusufzai – westernmost Pashtun tribe inhabiting the Swat valley

zîâratgah [sing. *Ziyarat*] – religious shrines, generally tombs of Sufi saints

Unpublished Sources

India Office Records (IOR), London

Elphinstone Papers
Gerard Papers, Forster Papers
Masson Papers
McNeill Papers
Moorcroft Papers

Secret Letters and Enclosures from India (Secret and Political):
    L/P&S/5
    L/P&S/6
    L/P&S/9
    L/P&S/18
    L/P&S/19
    L/P&S/20
Board's Collection
Home & Miscellaneous Series
Survey of India Maps
Bengal Proceedings

British Library (BL), London

Broughton Papers Add.
Auckland Papers Add.

Public Records Office (PRO), London

Persian Papers FO/95, FO/539
Pottinger Papers
Ellenborough Papers

National Archives of India (NAI), New Delhi

Foreign Department Proceedings:
    Political Consultations
    Secret Consultations
    Ootacamand Secret Consultations

Punjab Provincial Archives (PPA), Lahore

Records of the Ludiana Agency
Records of the Ambala Agency
Records of the Delhi Agency
Press list of old records in the Punjab Secretariat, Lahore (1915)

Royal Asiatic Society (RAS), London

Rawlinson Papers

National Library of Scotland (NLS), Edinburgh

Minto Papers

Contemporary Published Works

Press List of Old Records in the Punjab Secretariat. Vols. I–VI. Lahore: The Superintendent, Government Printing, Punjab, 1915.

A. Burnes. *Cabool: Being a Personal Narrative of a Journey to and Residence in That City, in the Years 1836, 7 and 8.* London, 1842.

——. *Travels into Bokhara; Together with a Narrative of a Voyage on the Indus.* 3 vols. Lahore: Sang-e-meel Publications, 2003. Reprint, 1834.

Arthur Conolly. *Journey to the North of India, over the Land from England through Russia, Persia and Afghanistan.* 2nd revised ed. 2 vols. London: Richard Bentley, 1834.

Mountstuart Elphinstone. *An Account of the Kingdom of Caubul.* 2nd ed. 2 vols. Karachi: Indus Publications, 1991. Reprint, 1838.

——. *An Account of the Kingdom of Caubul.* London: Longman, Hurst, Rees, Orme and Brown, 1815.

J.P. Ferrier. *History of the Afghans.* London: John Murray, 1858.

J.B. Fraser. *Narrative of a Journey into Khorasan.* London: Longman, Hurst, Rees, Orme, Brown and Green, 1825.

Josiah Harlan. *A Memoir of India and Avghanistan.* Philadelphia: J. Dobson, 1842.

——. *Central Asia: Personal Narrative of Josiah Harlan, 1823–1841.* London: Luzac & Co., 1939.

John William Kaye. *History of the War in Afghanistan.* 2 vols. London: Richard Bentley, 1851.

Muhammad Hayat Khan. *Afghanistan and Its Inhabitants.* Translated by H. Priestly. 2nd ed. Lahore: Sang-e-Meel Publications, 1999.

Alexis Krausse. *Russia in Asia.* 2nd ed. London: Curzon Press, 1899. Reprint, 1973.

Mohan Lal. *Journal of a Tour through the Punjab, Afghanistan, Turkistan, Khorasan, and Part of Persia, in Company with Lieut. Burnes and Dr Gerard.* Calcutta, 1834.

——. *Life of the Amir Dost Mohammed Khan of Kabul.* Oxford: Oxford University Press, 1978.

——. *Travels in the Panjab, Afghanistan, & Turkmenistan to Balk, Bokhara, and Herat; and a Visit to Great Britain and Germany.* London: Wm. H. Allen & Co., 1846.

Charles Masson. *Narrative of a Journey to Kalat, Including an Account of the Insurrection at That Place in 1840; and a Memoir on Eastern Balochistan.* London: Richard Bentley, 1843.

——. *Narrative of Various Journey in Baloochistan, Afghanistan and the Punjab.* 3 vols. Karachi: Oxford University Press, 1974. Reprint, 1843.

John McNeill. *Progress and Present Position of Russia in the East.* London: John Murray, 1836.

William Moorcroft and George Trebeck. *Travels in the Himalaya Provinces of Hindustan and the Panjab; in Ladakh and Kashmir; in Peshawar, Kabul, Kunduz and Bokhara.* 2 vols. London: John Murray, 1841.

William Moorcroft and George Trebeck. *Travels in India: Himalayan Provinces of Hindustan and the Panjab in Ladakh and Kashmir in Peshawar, Kabul, Kunduz, and*

Bokhara from 1819 to 1825. 2 vols. New Delhi: Low Price Publications, 2000. Reprint, 1841.

Leopold von Orlich. *Travels in India, Including Sinde and the Punjab.* Translated by H. E. Lloyd. 2 vols. London: Longman, Brown Green & Longmans, 1845.

W.G. Osborne. *The Court and Camp of Runjeet Singh, Oxford in Asia Historical Reprints.* Karachi: Oxford University Press, 1973. Reprint, 1840.

Henry Pottinger. *Travels in Beloochistan and Sinde.* London: Longman, Hurst, Rees, Orme and Brown, 1816.

J.A. Robinson. *Notes on the Nomad Tribes of Eastern Afghanistan.* 2nd ed. Quetta: Nisa Traders, 1980. Reprint 1932.

Lady Sale. *A Journal of the Disasters in Affghanistan, 1841–2.* Lahore: Sang-e-Meel Publications, 1999. Reprint, 1843.

Carl Hermann Scheidler. *A Journey from Orenburg to Bokhara in the Year 1820.* Translated by C.E.F. Chapman. Edited by B.v. Meyendorf. Calcutta: Foreign Department Press, 1870.

Edward Stirling. *Some Considerations on the Political State of the Intermediate Countries between Persia and India, with Reference to the Project of Russia Marching an Army through them.* London: Whittaker and Co., 1835.

Edward Stirling. *The Journals of Edward Stirling in Persia and Afghanistan, 1828–1829.* Edited by J. Lee. Naples: Institutio Universatario Orientale, 1991.

Mir Izzat Ullah. *Travels in Central Asia by Meer Izzut-Oollah.* Translated by C.P.D. Henderson. Calcutta: Foreign Department Press, 1872.

Neamat Ullah. *History of the Afghans.* Translated by B. Dons. 2 vols. Karachi: Indus Publications, 1976.

G.T. Vinge. *A Personal Narrative of a Visit to Ghuzni, Kabul, and Afghanistan and of a Residence at the Court of Dost Muhamed with Notices of Ranjit Singh, Khiva and the Russian Expedition.* Lahore: Sang-e-Meel Publications, 1999.

Joseph Wolff. *Travels and Adventures.* London: Saunders, Otley & Co., 1861.

John Wood. *A Journey to the Source of the Oxus.* 2nd ed. *Oxford in Asia Historical Reprints.* Karachi: Oxford University Press, 1976. Reprint, 1872.

Bibliography

Secondary Literature

Qeyamuddin Ahmad. *The Wahabi Movement in India*. Calcutta: Firma K.L. Mukhopadhyay, 1966.

Akbar S. Ahmed. 'An Aspect of the Colonial Encounter in the North-West Frontier Province'. *Asian Affairs* 9 (Old Series 65), no. 3 (1978): 319–27.

——. *Pukhtun Economy and Society: Traditional Structure and Economic Development in Tribal Society*. London: Routledge, 1980.

——. *Religion and Politics in Muslim Society: Order and Conflict in Pakistan*. Cambridge: Cambridge University Press, 1983.

——. 'Tribes and States in Waziristan'. In *The Conflict of Tribe and State in Iran and Afghanistan*, edited by R. Tapper, London: Croom Helm, 1983, 192–209.

Muzaffar Alam. *The Crisis of Empire in Mughal North India: Awadh and the Punjab, 1707–1748*. Delhi: Oxford University Press, 1986.

Seema Alavi. 'The Company Army and Rural Society: The Invalid Thanah, 1780–1830'. *Modern Asian Studies* 27, no. 1 (1993): 147–78.

——. *Sepoys and the Company: Tradition and Transition in North India, 1770–1830*. New Delhi: Oxford University Press, 1995.

——. 'The Makings of Company Power: James Skinner in the Ceded and Conquered Provinces, 1802–1840'. In *Warfare and Weaponry in South Asia, 1000–1800*, edited by J. Gommans and D.H.A. Kolff, New Delhi: Oxford University Press, 2001, 275–310.

Garry Alder. *British India's Northern Frontier, 1865–95: A Study in Imperial Policy*. London: Longmans, 1963.

——. *Beyond Bokhara: The Life of William Moorcroft, Asian Explorer and Pioneer, Veterinary Surgeon 1767–1825*. London: Century, 1985.

Hamid Algar. *Religion and State in Iran, 1785–1906*. Berkeley: University of California Press, 1969.

——. 'Religious Forces in Eighteenth and Nineteenth Century Iran'. In *The Cambridge History of Iran: From Nadir Shah to the Islamic Republic*, edited by P. Avery, G. Hambly and C. Melville, Cambridge: Cambridge University Press, 1991, 705–31.

Nigel Allan. 'Defining Place and People in Afghanistan'. *Post-Soviet Geography and Economics* 42, no. 8 (2001): 545–60.

M.S. Anderson. *The Eastern Question, 1774–1923: A Study in International Relations*. London: Macmillan, 1966.

Ewan Anderson and Nancy Hatch Dupree, eds. *The Cultural Basis of Afghan Nationalism*. London: Pinter, 1990.

Sergie Andreyev. 'History and Doctrine of the Rawshani Movement'. Doctoral Thesis, University of Oxford, 1997.

Sarah Ansari. *Sufi Saints and State Power: The Pirs of Sind, 1843–1947*. Cambridge: Cambridge University Press, 1992.

Hans Antlon and Stein Tonnesson, eds. *Asian Forms of the Nation*. Richmond, Surrey: Curzon Press, 1996.

Arjun Appadurai. 'Introduction: Commodities and the Politics of Value'. In *The Social Life of Things: Commodities in Cultural Perspective*, edited by A. Appadurai, Cambridge: Cambridge University Press, 1986, 3–63.

Said Amir Arjomand. *The Shadow of God and the Hidden Imam: Religion, Political Order, and Societal Change in Shi'ite Iran from the Beginning to 1890.* Chicago: University of Chicago Press, 1984.

——. 'Introduction: Shi'ism, Authority, and Political Culture'. In *Authority and Political Culture in Shi'ism*, edited by S.A. Arjomand and Albany, NY: State University of New York Press, 1988, 1–24.

Peter Avery. 'Nadir Shah and the Afsharid Legacy'. In *The Cambridge History of Iran: From Nadir Shah to the Islamic Republic*, edited by P. Avery, G. Hambly and C. Melville, Cambridge: Cambridge University Press, 1991, 1–62.

Michael Axelworthy. *The Sword of Persia: Nader Shah, from Tribal Warrior to Conquering Tyrant.* London: I.B. Tauris, 2006.

Kathryn Babayan. *Mystics, Monarchs and Messiahs: Cultural Landscapes in Early Modern Iran, Harvard Middle Eastern Monographs.* Cambridge, MA: Harvard University Press, 2002.

Lal Baha. *N.-W.F.P. Administration under British Rule, 1901–1919, Historical Studies (Muslim India) Series.* Islamabad: National Commission on Historical and Cultural Research, 1978.

S.R. Bakshi. 'Elphinstone's Mission to Kabul'. *Journal of Indian History* 45, no. 2 (1967): 605–13.

Anil Chandra Banerjee. *Anglo-Sikh Relations: Chapters from J.D. Cunningham's 'History of the Sikhs'.* Calcutta: A. Mukherjee & Co., Ltd., 1949.

——. *The Khalsa Raj.* New Delhi: Abhinav Publications, 1985.

Indu Banga. 'Formation of the Sikh State, 1765–1845'. In *Five Punjabi Centuries: Polity, Economy, Society and Culture, C. 1500–1990*, edited by I. Banga, New Delhi: Manohar, 1997, 84–111.

Thomas Barfield. 'Tribe and State Relations: The Inner Asian Perspective'. In *Tribes and State Formation in the Middle East*, edited by P.S. Khoury and J. Kostiner, Berkeley: University of California Press, 1990, 153–84.

——. 'Problems in Establishing Legitimacy in Afghanistan'. *Iranian Studies* 37, no. 2 (2004): 263–93.

R.B. Barnett. *North India between Empires: Awadh, the Mughals and the British, 1720–1801.* Berkeley: University of California Press, 1980.

Ward Barrett. 'World Bullion Flows, 1450–1800'. In *The Rise of Merchant Empires: Long-Distance Trade in the Early Modern World, 1350–1750*, edited by J. Tracy, Cambridge: Cambridge University Press, 1990, 224–54.

Ian J. Barrow. *Making History, Drawing Territory: British Mapping in India, C. 1756–1905.* New Delhi: Oxford University Press, 2003.

Fredrik Barth. *Political Leadership Among Swat Pathans.* London: Athlone Press, 1959.

——. 'Introduction'. In *Ethnic Groups and Boundaries: The Social Organization of Culture Difference*, edited by F. Barth, London: Allen & Unwin, 1969.

——. 'Pathan Identity and Its Maintenance'. In *Ethnic Groups and Boundaries: The Social Organization of Cultural Difference*, edited by F. Barth, London: George Allen & Unwin, 1969, 117–34.

W. Barthold. *An Historical Georgraphy of Iran.* Princeton: Princeton University Press, 1984.

C.A. Bayly. 'Age of Hiatus: The North Indian Economy and Society, 1830–50'. In *Indian Society and the Beginnings of Modernization*, edited by C.H. Philips and M.D. Wainwright, London: SOAS, 1976, 83–102.

——. 'The Origins of Swadeshi: Cloth and Indian Society, 1700–1930'. In *The Social Life of Things: Commodities in Cultural Perspective*, edited by A. Appadurai, Cambridge: Cambridge University Press, 1986, 285–322.

——. 'India and West Asia, C. 1700–1830'. *Asian Affairs* 19, no. 1 (1988): 3–20.

——. *Imperial Meridian: The British Empire and the World, 1780–1830*. London: Longman, 1989.

——. 'Beating the Boundaries: South Asian History, C. 1700–1850'. In *South Asia and World Capitalism*, edited by S. Bose, New Delhi: Oxford University Press, 1990, 27–39.

——. 'Knowing the Country: Empire and Information in India'. *Modern Asian Studies* 27, no. 1 (1993): 3–43.

——. 'The British Military-Fiscal State and Indigenous Resistance: India 1750–1820'. In *The Imperial State at War: Britain from 1689 to 1815*, edited by L. Stone, London: Routledge, 1994, 322–54.

——. '"Archaic" and "Modern" Globalization in the Eurasian and African Arena, Ca. 1750–1850'. In *Globalization in World History*, edited by A.G. Hopkins, New York: W.W. Norton & Company, 2002, 45–72.

——. *Empire and Information*. New Delhi: Cambridge University Press, 2002.

——. *Rulers, Townsmen and Bazaars: Northern Indian Society in the Age of British Expansion, 1770–1870*. 2nd ed. New Delhi: Oxford University Press, 2003.

——. *The Birth of the Modern World, 1780–1914*. Oxford: Blackwell Publishing, 2004.

C.A. Bayly and Susan Bayly. 'Eighteenth Century State Forms and the Economy'. In *Arrested Development in India: The Historical Dimension*, edited by C. Dewey, New Delhi: Manohar, 1988, 66–90.

Susan Bayly. *Caste, Society and Politics in India from the Eighteenth Century to the Modern Age*, edited by G. Johnson, C.A. Bayly and J. Richards, *The New Cambridge History of India*. Cambridge: Cambridge University Press, 1999.

George D. Bearce. 'Lord William Bentinck: The Application of Liberalism to India'. *The Journal of Modern History* 28, no. 3 (1956): 234–46.

Ashgar Bilgrami. *Afghanistan and British India, 1793–1907*. New Delhi: New Sterling Publishers Ltd., 1972.

Jeremy Black. *A Military Revolution? Military Change and European Society*. Basingstoke: Macmillan Education, 1991.

——. 'Gibbon and International Relations'. In *Edward Gibbon and Empire*, edited by R. McKitterick and R. Quinault, Cambridge: Cambridge University Press, 1997, 217–46.

Ian Blanchard. *Russia's Age of Silver*. London: Routledge, 1989.

D.A. Brading. 'Mexican Silver-Mining in the Eighteenth Century: The Revival of Zacatecas'. *The Hispanic American Historical Review* 50, no. 4 (1970): 665–81.

D.A. Brading and Harry E. Cross. 'Colonial Silver Mining: Mexico and Peru'. *The Hispanic American Historical Review* 52, no. 4 (1972): 545–79.

Fernand Braudel. *Capitalism and Material Life, 1400–1800*. Translated by M. Kochan. London: Weidenfeld & Nicolson, 1973.

Y. Bregel. 'Turko-Mongolian Influences in Central Asia'. In *Turko-Persian in Historical Perpective.*, edited by R.L. Canfield, Cambridge: Cambridge University Press, 1991.

J.W. Burrow, Rosamond McKitterick and Roland Quinault. 'Epilogue'. In *Edward Gibbon and Empire*, edited by R. McKitterick and R. Quinault, Cambridge: Cambridge University Press, 1997, 333–41.

P.J. Cain and A.G. Hopkins. *British Imperialism: Innovation and Expansion, 1688–1914*. 2nd ed. London: Longman, 2000.

O. Caroe. *The Pathans.* London: Macmillan & Co. Ltd., 1962.

James Caron. 'Afghanistan Historiography and Pashtun Islam: Modernization Theory's Afterimage'. *History Compass* 5, no. 2 (2007): 314–29.

Partha Chatterjee. *Nationalist Thought and the Colonial World: A Derivative Discourse.* London: Zed Books, 1986.

K.N. Chaudhuri. 'India's Foreign Trade and the Cessation of the East India Company's Trading Activities, 1828–40'. In *Trade and Finance in Colonial India*, edited by A. Siddiqi, New Delhi: Oxford University Press, 1995, 290–320.

——. *The Trading World of Asia and the East India Company.* Cambridge: Cambridge University Press, 1978.

R.D. Choksey. *Mountstuart Elphinstone: The Indian Years, 1795–1827.* Bombay: Popular Prakashan, 1971.

Glushan Lall Chopra. *The Panjab as a Sovereign State.* 2nd ed. Hoshiarpur, India: Vishveshvaranand Vedic Research Institute Press, 1960.

Peter Christensen. 'The Qajar State'. In *Contributions to Islamic Studies: Iran, Afghanistan and Pakistan*, edited by C. Braae and K. Ferdinand, Aarhus: Aarhus University Press, 1987, 4–58.

R.O. Christensen. 'Tribesmen, Government and Political Economy on the North-West Frontier'. In *Arrested Development in India: The Historical Dimension*, edited by C. Dewey, New Delhi: Manohar, 1988, 170–87.

Winston Churchill. *The Story of the Malakand Field Force: An Episode of Frontier War.* London: Cooper, 1989.

Graham Clarke, 'Blood, Territory and National Identity in Himalayan States', In *Asian Forms of the Nation*, edited by S. Tonneson and H. Antlov, London: Curzon, 1996, 205–36.

Bernard Cohn. *Colonialism and Its Forms of Knowledge: The British in India*, edited by S. Ortner, N. Dirks and G. Eley, *Princeton Studies in Culture/Power/History.* Princeton: Princeton University Press, 1996.

——. 'Recruitment and Training of British Civil Servants in India, 1600–1860'. In *Asian Bureaucratic Systems Emergent from the British Imperial Tradition*, edited by R. Braibanti, Durham N.C.: Duke University Press, 1966, 87–140.

Linda Colley. *Britons: Forging the Nation*, New Haven: Yale University Press, 1992.

Linda Colley. *Captives: The Story of Britain's Pursuit of Empire and How Its Soldiers and Civilians Were Held Captive by the Dream of Global Supremacy, 1600–1850.* London: Pantheon Books, 2003.

Jean Comaroff. 'The Empire's Old Clothes: Fashioning the Colonial Subject'. In *Cross-Cultural Consumption: Global Markets, Local Realities*, edited by D. Howes, London: Routledge, 1996, 19–38.

John Comaroff. 'Governmentality, Materiality, Legality, Modernity: On the Colonial State in Africa'. In *African Modernities: Entangled Meanings in Current Debates*, edited by Jan-Georg Deutsch, Peter Probst and Heike Schmidt, Oxford: James Currey, 2002.

Frederick Cooper. *Colonialism in Question: Theory, Knowledge, History.* Berkeley, CA: University of California Press, 2005.

Robert D. Crews. *For Prophet and Tsar: Islam and Empire in Russia and Central Asia.* Cambridge, MA: Harvard University Press, 2006.

Philip Curtin. *Cross-Cultural Trade in World History.* Cambridge: Cambridge University Press, 1984.

Rohan D'Souza. 'Crisis Before the Fall: Some Speculations on the Decline of the Ottomans, Safavids and Mughals'. *Social Scientist* 30, no. 9/10 (2002): 3–30.

S.F. Dale. 'Indo-Russian Trade in the 18th Century'. In *South Asia and World Capitalism*, edited by S. Bose, New Delhi: Oxford University Press, 1990, 140–56.

——. *Indian Merchants and Eurasian Trade, 1600–1750*. Cambridge: Cambridge University Press, 1994.

Dayal Dass. *Charles Metcalfe and British Administration in India*. New Delhi: Criterion Publications, 1988.

Nicholas Dirks. 'Colonial Histories and Native Informants: Biography of an Archive'. In *Orientalism and the Post-Colonial Predicament: Perspectives on South Asia*, edited by C.A. Breckenridge and P. Van der Veer, Philadelphia: University of Pennsylvania Press, 1993, 273–313.

——. *Castes of Mind: Colonialism and the Making of Modern India*. Princeton: Princeton University Press, 2001.

——. *The Scandal of Empire: India and the Creation of Imperial Britain*. Cambridge, Mass.: Belknap Press, 2006.

Robert Dodgshon. *From Chiefs to Landlords: Social and Economic Change in the Western Highlands and Islands, C. 1493–1820*. Edinburgh: Edinburgh University Press, 1998.

Hastings Donnan and Thomas M. Wilson. *Borders: Frontiers of Identity, Nation and State*. Oxford: Berg, 1999.

Paul Dresch. *Tribes, Government, and History in Yemen*. Oxford: Clarendon Press, 1993.

Louis Dupree. *Afghanistan*. 2nd ed. Princeton: Princeton University Press, 1980.

——. 'Tribal Warfare in Afghanistan and Pakistan: A Reflection of the Segmentary Lineage System'. In *Islam in Tribal Societies: From the Atlas to the Indus*, edited by A. Ahmed and D.M. Hart, London: Routledge & Kegan Paul, 1984, 266–86.

Richard Eaton. *The Rise of Islam and the Bengal Frontier, 1204–1760*. 3rd ed. New Delhi: Oxford University Press, 2002.

Emily Eden. *Up the Country: Letter Written to Her Sister from the Upper Provinces of India*. London: Curzon Press, 1978.

Matthew Edney. *Mapping an Empire: The Geographical Construction of British India, 1765–1843*. Chicago: The University of Chicago Press, 1990.

David Edwards. 'Charismatic Leadership and Political Process'. *Central Asian Survey* 5, no. 3–4 (1986): 273–99.

——. 'The Evolution of Shi'i Political Dissent in Afghanistan'. In *Shi'ism and Political Protests*, edited by J.R.I. Cole and N. Keddie, New Haven: Yale University Press, 1986, 201–29.

——. *Heroes of the Age: Moral Fault Lines on the Afghan Frontier*. Berkeley: University of California Press, 1996.

Paul English. 'The Traditional City of Herat, Afghanistan'. In *From Medina to Metropolis: Heritage and Change in the near Eastern City*, edited by L.C. Brown, Princeton, NJ: Darwin Press, 1973, 73–90.

Martin Ewans. *Afghanistan: A Short History of Its People and Politics*. New York: Harper Collins Publishers, 2002.

K. Ferdinand. 'Nomad Expansion and Commerce in Afghanistan'. *Folk* 4 (1962): 123–59.

Michael Fisher. *Indirect Rule in India: Residents and the Residency System*. New Delhi: Oxford University Press, 1991.

——. 'The Office of Akhbar Nawis: The Transition from Mughal to British Forms'. *Modern Asian Studies* 27, no. 1 (1993): 45–82.

Anne Lincoln Fitzpatrick. *The Great Russian Fair: Nizhnii Novgorod, 1840–90*, St. Antony's/Macmillan Series. Basingstoke: Macmillan, 1990.

Arnold Fletcher. *Afghanistan: Highway of Conquest.* Ithaca: Cornell University Press, 1965.

Dennis Owen Flynn. 'Cycles of Silver: Global Economic Unity Through the Mid-Eighteenth Century'. *Journal of World History* 13, no. 2 (2002): 391–427.

Andre Gunder Frank. *Reorient: Global Economy in the Asian Age.* Berkeley: University of California Press, 1998.

W.K. Fraser-Tyler. *Afghanistan: A Study of Political Developments in Central Asia.* London: Oxford Univesity Press, 1950.

Marc Gaborieau. 'The *Jihad* of Sayyid Ahmad Barelwi on the North West Frontier: The Last Echo of the Middle Ages? Or a Prefiguration of Modern South Asia'. In *Sufis, Sultans and Feudal Orders: Professor Nurul Hasan Commemoration Volume,* edited by M. Haidar, New Delhi: Manohar, 2004, 23–44.

John S. Galbraith. 'The "Turbulent Frontier" As a Factor in British Expansion'. *Comparative Studies in Society and History* 2, no. 2 (1960): 150–68.

John Gallagher and Ronald Robinson. 'The Imperialism of Free Trade'. *The Economic History Review* 6, no. 1 (1953): 1–15.

Yuri V. Gankovsky. 'The Durrani Empire: Taxes and Tax System'. In *Afghanistan: Past and Present,* Moscow: Social Sciences Today, USSR Academy of Sciences, 1981, 76–99.

Heinz Gaube. *Iranian Cities.* New York: New York University Press, 1979.

Paul Georg Geiss. *Pre-Tsarist and Tsarist Central Asia: Communal Commitment and Political Order in Change.* London: Routledge Curzon, 2003.

Ernest Gellner. *Muslim Society.* Cambridge: Cambridge University Press, 1981.

——. 'Tribalism and State in the Middle East'. In *Tribes and State Formation in the Middle East,* edited by P.S. Khoury and J. Kostiner, Berkeley: University of California Press, 1990, 109–26.

Ashraf Ghani. 'Islam and Statebuilding in a Tribal Society'. *Modern Asian Studies* 12, no. 2 (1978): 269–84.

Dilip Kumar Ghose. *England and Afghanistan: A Phase in Their Relations.* Calcutta: World Press Private Ltd., 1960.

Michael Gilsenan. *Lords of the Lebanese Marches: Violence and Narrative in an Arab Society.* London: I.B. Tauris, 1996.

Bernt Glatzer. 'War and Boundaries in Afghanistan: Significance and Relativity of Local and Social Boundaries'. *Weld des Islams* 41, no. 3 (2001): 379–99.

P.B. Golden. *An Introduction to the Turkic Peoples. Ethnogenesis and State Formation in Medieval and Early Modern Eurasia and the Middle East.* Wiesbaden: Otto Harrassowitz, 1992.

Jos Gommans. *The Rise of the Indo-Afghan Empire.* New Delhi: Oxford University Press, 1999.

——. 'Indian Warfare and Afghan Innovation During the Eighteenth Century'. In *Warfare and Weaponry in South Asia, 1000–1800,* edited by J. Gommans and D.H.A. Kolff, New Delhi: Oxford University Press, 2001, 365–86.

——. *Mughal Warfare: Indian Frontiers and High Roads to Empire, 1500–1700.* London: Routledge, 2002.

Jos Gommans and Dirk H.A. Kolff. 'Introduction'. In *Warfare and Weaponry in South Asia 1000–1800,* edited by J. Gommans and D.H.A. Kolff, New Delhi: Oxford University Press, 2001, 1–44.

——. eds. *Warfare and Weaponry in South Asia, 1000–1800, Themes in Indian History.* New Delhi: Oxford University Press, 2001.

R. Gopalakrishnan. *The Geography and Politics of Afghanistan.* New Delhi: Concept Publishing Company, 1982.

Steward Gordon, ed. *Robes and Honour: Khil'at in Pre-Colonial India and Colonial India*. New Delhi: Oxford University Press, 2003.

——. 'Legitimacy and Loyalty in Some Successor States of the Eighteenth Century'. In *Kingship and Authority in South Asia*, edited by J.F. Richards, New Delhi: Oxford University Press, 1998, 327–47.

G. Grassmuck, L. Adamec & F.J. Irwin, ed. *Afghanistan: Some New Approaches*. Ann Arbor: University of Michigan Press, 1969.

Rose Greaves. 'Iranian Relations with Great Britain and British India'. In *The Cambridge History of Iran: From Nadir Shah to the Islamic Republic*, edited by C. Melville, Cambridge: Cambridge University Press, 1991, 374–425.

V. Gregorian. *The Emergence of Modern Afghanistan*. Stanford: Stanford University Press, 1969.

Derek Gregory. *The Colonial Present: Afghanistan, Palestine and Iraq*. Oxford: Blackwell Publishing, 2004.

J.S. Grewal. 'Business Communities of Punjab'. In *Business Communities of India: A Historical Perspective*, edited by D. Tripathi, New Delhi: Manohar, 1984, 209–24.

——. *The Sikhs of the Punjab,* edited by G. Johnson, C.A. Bayly and J.F. Richards, *The New Cambridge History of India*. Cambridge: Cambridge University Press, 1998.

Charles Grey. *European Adventurers of Northern India 1785–1849*. Lahore: Punjab Government, 1929.

G.E. von Grunebaum. 'The Structure of the Muslim Town'. In *Islam: Essays in the Nature and Growth of a Cultural Tradition*, London: Routledge & Kegan Paul Ltd., 1961, 141–58.

Ranajit Guha. *A Rule of Property for Bengal: An Essay on the Idea of Permanent Settlement, Le Monde D'outre-Mer Passe Et Present. Primiere Serie: Etudes Xix*. Paris: Mouton & Co., 1963.

Zalmay Gulzad. *External Influences and the Development of the Afghan State in the 19th Century*. New York: Peter Long, 1994.

Hari Ram Gupta. *History of the Sikhs: The Sikh Lion of Lahore (Maharaja Ranjit Singh, 1799–1839)*. Vol. 5. New Delhi: Munshiram Manharlal Publishers Pvt Ltd., 1991.

Jati Ram Gupta. 'Trade and Commerce in the Punjab under Ranjit Singh'. In *Maharaja Ranjit Singh: Politics, Society and Economy*, edited by F. Singh and A.C. Arora, Patiala: Punjabi University Publication Bureau, 1984, 186–204.

William Habberton. 'Anglo-Russian Relations Concerning Afghanistan 1837–1907'. *Illinois Studies in the Social Sciences* 21, no. 4 (1937): 1–102.

Rob Hager. 'State, Tribe and Empire in Afghan Inter-Polity Relations'. In *The Conflict of Tribe and State in Iran and Afghanistan*, edited by R. Tapper, London: Croom Helm, 1983, 83–118.

Charles Joseph Hall. 'The Maharaja's Account Books. State and Society under the Sikhs: 1799–1849'. Doctoral Thesis, University of Illinois, 1981.

G. Hambly. 'Iran During the Reigns of Fath Ali Shah and Muhammad Shah'. In *The Cambridge History of Iran: From Nadir Shah to the Islamic Republic*, edited by C. Melville, Cambridge: Cambridge University Press, 1991, 144–73.

Shah Mahmoud Hanifi. 'Inter-Regional Trade and Colonial State Formation in 19th Century Afghanistan'. Doctoral Thesis, University of Michigan, 2001.

——. 'Impoverishing a Colonial Frontier: Cash, Credit and Debt in Nineteenth Century Afghanistan'. *Iranian Studies* 37, no. 2 (2004): 199–218.

Bikrama Jit Hasrat. *Anglo-Sikh Relations, 1799–1849: A Reappraisal of the Rise and Fall of the Sikhs*. Hoshiarpur, India: V.V. Research Institute Press, 1968.

——. *Life and Times of Ranjit Singh: A Saga of Benevolent Despotism*. Hoshiapur Punjab, India: V.V. Research Institute Press, 1977.

Milan Hauner. 'One Man against the Empire: The Faqir of Ipi and the British in Central Asia on the Eve of and During the Second World War'. *Journal of contemporary history* 16, no. 1 (1981): 183–212.

Marshall Hodgson. *The Venture of Islam: Gunpowder Empires and Modern Times.* Vol. III. Chicago: University of Chicago Press, 1974.

Mary Holdsworth. *Turkestan in the Nineteenth Century: A Brief History of the Khanates of Bukhara, Kokand and Khiva.* Oxford: Central Asian Research Center, 1959.

P.M. Holt. *The Mahdist State in the Sudan, 1881–1898: A Study of Its Origins, Development and Overthrow.* 2nd ed. Oxford: Oxford University Press, 1979.

B.D. Hopkins. 'The Myth of the "Great Game": The Anglo-Sikh Alliance and Rivalry'. *Centre for South Asian Studies Occasional Paper, University of Cambridge,* no. 5 (2004).

——. 'The Transformation of the Kingdom of Kabul into the State of Afghanistan, C. 1793–1842'. Doctoral thesis, University of Cambridge, 2005.

——. 'Race, Sex and Slavery: "Forced Labour" In Central Asia and Afghanistan in the Early Nineteenth Century'. *Modern Asian Studies* 42, no. 4 (2008): 629–72.

——. 'The Bounds of Identity: The Goldsmid Mission and the Delineation of the Perso-Afghan Border in the Nineteenth Century'. *Journal of Global History* 2, no. 2 (2007): 233–54.

Peter Hopkirk. *The Great Game: On Secret Service in High Asia.* London: John Murray, 1990.

Albert Hourani and S.M. Stern. *Islamic City. Papers on Islamic History.* Oxford: Cassirer, 1970.

Caroline Humphrey and David Sneath, eds. *The End of Nomadism? Society, State and the Environment in Inner Asia.* Cambridge: The White Horse Press, 1999.

Robert Huttenback. *British Relations with Sind 1799–1843: An Anatomy of Imperialism.* Berkeley: University of California Press, 1962.

Anthony Hyman. 'Nationalism in Afghanistan'. *International Journal of Middle East Studies* 34, no. 2 (2002): 299–315.

Michael Ignatieff. *Empire Lite: Nation-Building in Bosnia, Kosovo and Afghanistan.* London: Vintage, 2003.

Ronald Inden. 'Orientalist Constructions of India'. *Modern Asian Studies* 20, no. 3 (1986): 401–46.

Edward Ingram. *The Beginning of the Great Game in Asia, 1828–1834.* Oxford: Claredon Press, 1979.

——. *Commitment to Empire: Prophecies of the Great Game, 1797–1800.* Oxford: Claredon Press, 1981.

——. *In Defence of British India: Great Britain in the Middle East, 1775–1842.* London: Cass, 1984.

——. *Britain's Persian Connection, 1798–1828.* Oxford: Claredon Press, 1992.

——. 'India and the North-West Frontier: The First Afghan War'. In *Great Powers and Little Wars: Limits of Power,* edited by J. Errington and H. Ion, New York: Praeger, 1992.

Eugene Irschick. *Dialogue and History: Constructing South India 1796–1895.* Berkeley: University of California Press, 1994.

Alfred Janata. 'Afghanistan: The Ethnic Dimension'. In *The Cultural Basis of Afghan Nationalism,* edited by E. Anderson and N.H. Dupree, London: Pinter Publishers, 1990, 60–70.

Hans Christian Johansen, *Shipping and Trade between the Baltic Area and Western Europe 1784–95.* Odense: Odense University Press, 1983.

Erach Rustam Kapadia. 'The Diplomatic Career of Sir Claude Wade: A Study of British Relations with the Sikhs and Afghans, July 1823 to March 1840'. M. A. Thesis, University of London, 1938.

Michael Kaser. 'Economic Continuities in Albania's Turbulent History'. *Europe-Asia Studies* 53, no. 4 (2001): 627–37.

Mulla Muhsin Fayd Kashani. 'The Kingly Mirror, in Two Seventeenth Century Tracts on Kingship'. In *Authority and Political Culture in Shi'ism*, edited by S.A. Arjomand, Albany: State University of New York Press, 1988, 269–84.

Firoozeh Kashani-Sabet. *Frontier Fictions: Shaping the Iranian Nation, 1804–1946*. Princeton: Princeton University Press, 1999.

Fayz Muhammad Katib. *Siraj Al-Tavarikh*. 2 vols. Tehran: Mu'assasah-'i Mutala'at va Intisharat-i Balkh, Hijra 1372 (1993/1994).

Firuz Kazemzadeh. *Russia and Britain in Persia, 1864–1914: A Study in Imperialism*. New Haven: Yale University Press, 1967.

John Keay. *When Men and Mountains Meet: The Explorers of the Western Himalayas, 1820–75*. New Delhi: Harper Collins, 1977. Reprint, 2000.

Ibn Khaldun. *The Muqaddimah: An Introduction to History*. Translated by F. Rosenthal. 3 vols, *Bollingen Series*. New York: Pantheon Books, 1958.

N.A. Khalfin. 'Indian Missions in Russia in the Late Nineteenth Century and British Historiography of International Relations in Asia'. *Modern Asian Studies* 21, no. 4 (1987): 639–46.

Ijaz Khan. 'Afghanistan: A Geopolitical Study'. *Central Asian Survey* 17, no. 2 (1998): 489–502.

M. Khan. *Anglo-Afghan Relations, 1798–1898: A Chapter in the Great Game in Central Asia*. Peshawar: Universal Book Agency, 1963.

Muhammad Hayat Khan. *Afghanistan and Its Inhabitants*. Translated by H. Priestly. 2nd ed. Lahore: Sang-e-Meel Publications, 1999.

Rudyard Kipling. *Kim, Penguin Popular Classics*. London: Penguin Books, 1994.

Dirk H.A. Kolff. *Naukar, Rajput and Sepoy: The Ethnohistory of the Military Labour Market in Hindustan, 1450–1850*. Cambridge: Cambridge University Press, 1990.

Igor Kopytoff. 'The Internal African Frontier: Cultural Conservatism and Ethnic Innovation'. In *Frontier and Borderlands: Anthropological Perspectives*, edited by M. Rosler and T. Wendl, Frankfurt am Main: Peter Lang, 1999, 31–44.

P. Kuhn. *Soulstealers: The Chinese Sorcery Scare of 1768*. Cambridge, MA: Harvard University Press, 1990.

Adam Kuper. *The Invention of Primitive Society*. London: Routledge, 1988.

Jean-Marie LaFont. *Fauj-I-Khas: Maharaja Ranjit Singh and His French Officers*. Amritsar: Guru Nanak Dev University, 2002.

Mohan Lal. *Life of the Amir Dost Mohammed Khan of Kabul*. Oxford: Oxford University Press, 1978.

A.K.S. Lambton. 'Persian Trade under the Early Qajars'. In *Islam and the Trade of Asia*, edited by D.S. Richards, Oxford: Burno Cassirer, 1970.

———. 'The Tribal Resurgence and the Decline of the Bureaucracy in 18th Century Persia'. In *Studies in 18th Century Islamic History*, edited by T. Naff and R. Owen, Carbondale: Southern Illinois University Press, 1977.

Ira Lapidus. 'Islamic Revival and Modernity: The Contemporary Movements and the Historical Paradigms'. *Journal of the Economic and Social History of the Orient* 40, no. 4 (1997): 444–60.

———. 'Muslim Cities and Islamic Societies'. In *Middle Eastern Cities: A Symposium on Ancient, Islamic, and Contemporary Middle Eastern Urbanism*, edited by I. Lapidus, Berkeley: University of California Press, 1969, 47–79.

Jonathan Lee. *The Ancient Supremacy: Bukhara, Afghanistan and the Battle for Balkh, 1731–1901*. Leiden: E.J. Brill, 1996.

E.R. Leech. *Political Systems of Highland Burma: A Study of Kachin Social Structure*, edited by J. Woodburn. 5th ed. *London School of Economics Monographs on Social Anthropology.* London: The Athlone Press, 1964.

David Lelyveld. 'Colonial Knowledge and the Fate of Hindustani'. *Comparative Studies in Society and History* 35, no. 4 (1993): 665–82.

Scott Levi. 'India, Russia and the Eighteenth Century Transformation of the Central Asian Caravan Trade'. *Journal of Economic and Social History of the Orient* 42, no. 4 (1999): 519–48.

——. *The Indian Trade Diaspora in Central Asia and Its Trade 1550–1900*, edited by N.d. Cosmo, D. Deweese and C. Humphrey, *Brill's Inner Asian Library.* Leiden: Brill, 2002.

Charles Lindholm. *Generosity and Jealousy: The Swat Pukhtun of Northern Pakistan.* New York: Columbia University Press, 1982.

——, ed. *Frontier Perspectives: Essays in Comparative Anthropology.* Karachi: Oxford University Press, 1996.

——. 'Kinship Structure and Political Authority: The Middle East and Central Asia'. In *Frontier Perspectives*, edited by C. Lindholm, Karachi: Oxford University Press, 1996, 147–71.

Charles Lindholm and Cherry Lindholm. 'Marriage as Warfare'. *Natural History* 88, no. 8 (1979): 11–21.

Ken Lizzio. 'Embodying History: A Naqshbandi Shaikh in Afghanistan'. *Central Asian Survey* 22, no. 2/3 (2004): 163–86.

David Ludden. 'India's Development Regime'. In *Colonialism and Culture*, edited by N. Dirks, Ann Arbor: The University of Michigan Press, 1992, 247–88.

——. 'Orientalist Empiricism: Transformation of Colonial Knowledge'. In *Orientalism and the Postcolonial Predicament*, edited by C.A. Breckenridge and P. van der Veer, Philadelphia: University of Pennsylvania Press, 1993, 250–78.

Ben Macintyre. *Josiah the Great: The True Story of the Man Who Would Be King.* London: Harper Collins, 2004.

Patrick Arthur Macrory. *Kabul Catastrophe: The Invasion and Retreat 1839–1842.* Oxford: Oxford University Press, 1986. Reprint, 2002.

Mohammad-Dja'far Mahdjoub. 'The Evolution of Popular Eulogy of the Imams among the Shi'a'. In *Authority and Political Culture in Shi'ism*, edited by S.A. Arjomand, Albany: State University of New York Press, 1988, 54–79.

Mulla Muhammad Baqir Majlisi. 'The Fountainhead of Life (Extracts), in Two Seventeenth Century Tracts on Kingship'. In *Authority and Political Culture in Shi'ism*, edited by S.A. Arjomand, Albany: State University of New York Press, 1988, 284–99.

Claude Markovits. *The Global World of Indian Merchants, 1750–1947: Traders of Sind from Bukhara to Panama.* Cambridge: Cambridge University Press, 2000.

P.J. Marshall. 'British Expansion in India in the 18th Century: A Historical Revision'. *History* 60, no. 198 (1975): 28–43.

——. 'Economic and Political Expansion: The Case of Oudh, 1765–1804'. *Modern Asian Studies* 9, no. 4 (1975): 465–82.

P.J. Marshall. *Problems of Empire: Britain and India, 1757–1813*, edited by P. Tuck. VI vols., Vol. II, *The East India Company: 1600–1858.* London: Routledge, 1968. Reprint, 1998.

Michelle Maskiell. 'Consuming Kashmir: Shawls and Empires, 1500–2000'. *Journal of World History* 13, no. 1 (2002): 27–65.

Saloni Mathur. 'History and Anthropology in South Asia'. *Annual Review of Anthropology* 29, (2000): 89–106.

Ina Baghdiantz McCabe. *The Shah's Silk for Europe's Silver: The Eurasian Trade of the Julfa Armenians in Safavid Iran and India, 1530–1750*. Atlanta: Scholars Press, 1999.

Robert McChesney. *Waqf in Central Asia*. Princeton: Princeton University Press, 1991.

———. *Central Asia: Foundations of Change, The Leon B. Poullada Memorial Lecture Series*. Princeton: The Darwin Press, Inc., 1996.

Martha McLaren. *British India and British Scotland, 1780–1830: Career Building, Empire Building, and a Scottish School of Though on Indian Governance*. Akron: University of Akron Press, 2001.

Barbara Metcalf. *Islamic Revival in British India: Deoband 1860–1900*. Princeton: Princeton University Press, 1982.

Thomas Metcalf. *Ideologies of the Raj*, edited by G. Johnson, C.A. Bayly and J.F. Richards, *The New Cambridge History of India*. Cambridge: Cambridge University Press, 1994.

Karl Meyer and Shareen Brysac. *Tournament of Shadows: The Great Game and the Race for Empire in Asia*. London: Abacus, 1999.

Bernardo A. Michael. 'When Soldiers and Statesmen Meet: 'Ethnographic Moments' on the Frontiers of Empire, 1800–1815'. In *Khil'at in Pre-Colonial and Colonial India*, edited by S. Gordon, New Delhi: Oxford University Press, 2003, 80–94.

Margaret Ann Mills. *Oral Narrative in Afghanistan: The Individual Tradition*. New York: Garland, 1990.

———. *Rhetorics and Politics in Afghan Traditional Storytelling*. Philadelphia: University of Pennsylvania Press, 1991.

Gail Minault. 'The Emperor's Old Clothes: Robing and Sovereignty in Late Mughal and Early British India'. In *Robes of Honour: Khil'at in Pre-Colonial and Colonial India*, edited by S. Gordon, New Delhi: Oxford University Press, 2003, 125–39.

N. Misdaq. 'Traditional Leadership in Afghan Society and the Issue of National Unity'. *Central Asian Survey* 9, no. 4 (1990): 109–112.

Pirouz Mojtahed-Zadeh. *Small Players of the Great Game: The Settlement of Iran's Eastern Borderlands and the Creation of Afghanistan*. London: Routledge, 2004.

Gerald Morgan. *Anglo-Russian Rivalry in Central Asia*. London: Cass, 1981.

G. Morgenstierne. 'Afghan.' In *The Encyclopaedia of Islam*, edited by H.A.R. Gibb, J.H. Kramers, E. Levi-Provencal and J. Schacht, London: Luzac & Co., 1960, 217–20.

Sayed Askar Mousavi. *The Hazaras of Afghanistan: An Historical, Cultural, Economic and Political Study*. London: Curzon, 1998.

Robert Nichols. *Settling the Frontier: Law, Land and Society in the Peshawar Valley, 1500–1900*. Oxford: Oxford University Press, 2001.

P. Nightingale. *Trade and Empire in Western India, 1784–1806*. Cambridge: Cambridge University Press, 1970.

Christine Noelle. 'The Anti-Wahabi Reaction in Nineteenth Century Afghanistan'. *The Muslim World* 85, no. 1–2 (1995): 23–48.

———. *State and Tribe in Nineteenth Century Afghanistan: The Reign of Amir Dost Muhammad Khan, 1826–1863*. London: Curzon, 1997.

J.A. Norris. *The First Afghan War, 1838–1842*. Cambridge: Cambridge University Press, 1967.

Asta Olesen. *Islam and Politics in Afghanistan, Nordic Institute of Asian Studies Monographs*. London: Curzon Press, 1995.

———. 'The Political Use of Islam in Afghanistan During the Reign of Amir Abdur Rahman (1880–1901)'. In *Contributions to Islamic Studies*, edited by C. Braae and K. Ferdinand, Aarhus: Aarhus University Press, 1987, 59–114.

D.N. Panigrahi. *Charles Metcalfe in India: Ideas and Administration*. Delhi: Munshiram Manoharlal, 1968.

Geoffrey Parker. *The Military Revolution: Military Innovation and the Rise of the West.* Cambridge: Cambridge University Press, 1988.

Peter Parkes. 'Alternative Social Structures Foster Relations in the Hindu Kush: Milk Kinship Allegiance in Frontier Mountain Kingdoms of Northern Pakistan'. *Comparative Studies in Society and History* 43, no. 1 (2001): 4–36.

Norbert Peabody. 'Tod's *Rajast'han* and the Boundaries of Imperial Rule in Nineteenth Century India'. *Modern Asian Studies* 30, no. 1 (1996): 185–220.

M.N. Pearson. 'Asia and World Precious Metal Flows in the Early Modern Period'. In *Evolution of the World Economy, Precious Metals and India,* edited by J. McGuire, P. Bertola and P. Reeves, New Delhi: Oxford University Press, 2001, 21–58.

Douglas Peers. *Between Mars and Mammon: Colonial Armies and the Garrison State in Early Nineteenth-Century India International Library of Historical Studies.* London: Tauris Academic Studies, 1995.

——. 'Colonial Knowledge and the Military in India, 1780–1860'. *The Journal of Imperial and Commonwealth History* 33, no. 2 (2005): 157–80.

J.R. Perry. 'The Zand Dynasty'. In *The Cambridge History of Iran,* edited by P. Avery, G. Hambly and C. Melville, Cambridge: Cambridge University Press, 1991, 63–103.

Rudolph Peters. *Jihad in Classical and Modern Islam: A Reader.* Princeton: Markus Wiener Publishers, 1996.

C.H. Philips, ed. *The Correspondence of Lord William Cavendish Bentinck, Governor General of India 1828–1835.* 2 vols. Oxford: Oxford University Press, 1977.

——. *The East India Company, 1784–1834.* 2nd ed. London: Routledge, 1998.

Hassan Poladi. *The Hazaras.* Stockton, CA: Mughal Publishing Co., 1989.

Kenneth Pomeranz. *The Great Divergence: China, Europe and the Making of the Modern World Economy.* Princeton: Princeton University Press, 2000.

Kenneth Pomeranz and Steven Topik. 'The World That Trade Created: Society, Culture and the World Economy, 1400-the Present'. In *Sources and Studies in World History,* edited by K. Reilly, New York: M.E. Sharpe, 1999.

Avril Powell. *Muslims and Missionaries in Pre-Mutiny India.* Vol. 7, *London Studies on South Asia.* London: Curzon Press, 1993.

Om Prakash. 'Global Precious Metal Flows and India, 1500–1750'. In *Evolution of the World Economy, Precious Metals and India,* edited by J. McGuire, P. Bertola and P. Reeves, New Delhi: Oxford University Press, 2001, 59–76.

John Prevas. *Xenophon's March: Into the Lair of the Persian Lion.* Cambridge, Mass.: Da Capo Press, 2002.

Serafin D. Quiason. *English 'Country Trade' With the Philippines, 1644–1765.* Quezon City: University of the Philippines Press, 1966.

Roland Quinault. 'Winston Churchill and Gibbon'. In *Edward Gibbon and Empire,* edited by R. McKitterick and R. Quinault, Cambridge: Cambridge University Press, 1997, 317–32.

Kapil Raj. 'When Human Travellers Become Instruments: The Indo-British Exploration of Central Asia in the Nineteenth Century'. In *Instruments, Travel and Science: Itineraries of Precision from the Seventeenth to the Twentieth Century,* edited by M.-N. Bourguet, C. Licoppe and H.O. Sibum, London: Routledge, 2002, 156–88.

Angelo Rasanayagam. *Afghanistan: A Modern History.* London: I.B. Tauris Publishers, 2003.

Ahmed Rashid. *Taliban: Militant Islam, Oil and Fundamentalism in Central Asia.* New Haven: Yale Nota Bene, 2000.

R.K. Ray. 'Asian Capital in the Age of European Domination: The Rise of the Bazaar, 1800–1914'. *Modern Asian Studies* 29, no. 3 (1995): 449–554.

Jane Rendall. 'Scottish Orientalism: From Robertson to James Mill'. *The Historical Journal* 25, no. 2 (1982): 43–69.

D.S. Richards. *Islam and the Trade of Asia.* Oxford: Bruno Cassirer, 1970.

———. *The Savage Frontier: A History of the Anglo-Afghan Wars.* London: Macmillan, 1990.

J.F. Richards. 'Introduction'. In *Kingship and Authority in South Asia*, edited by J.F. Richards, New Delhi: Oxford University Press, 1998, 1–12.

Janet Rizvi. *Transhimalayan Caravans: Merchant Princes and Peasant Traders in Ladakh, Oxford India Paperbacks.* New Delhi: Oxford University Press, 2001.

S.A.A. Rizvi. *History of Sufism in India.* 2 vols. New Delhi: Munshiram Manoharlal, 1983.

Saiyad Athar Abbas Rizvi. *Shah Wali-Allah and His Times: A Study of Eighteenth Century Islam, Politics and Society in India.* Canberra: Ma'rifat Publishing House, 1980.

Francis Robinson. 'Perso-Islamic Culture in India from the 17th Century to the Early 20th Century'. In *Turko-Persia in Historical Perspective*, edited by R. Canfield, Cambridge: Cambridge University Press, 1991, 104–31.

Lawrence Rosen. *The Culture of Islam: Changing Aspects of Contemporary Muslim Life.* Chicago: University of Chicago Press, 2002.

B. Rosenberg. 'Oral Sermons and Oral Narratives'. In *Folklore: Perfomance and Communication*, edited by B.-A. Goldstein, Hague: Mouton, 1975, 75–103.

M. Rossabi. 'The "Decline" of the Central Asian Caravan Trade'. In *The Rise of Merchant Empires*, edited by J.D. Tracy, Cambridge: Cambridge University Press, 1990.

———. 'Trade Routes in Inner Asia'. In *Cambridge History of Early Inner Asia*, edited by D. Sinor, Cambridge: Cambridge University Press, 1990.

Dietmar Rothermund. 'Problems of India's Arrested Economic Growth under British Rule'. In *Arrested Development in India: The Historical Dimension*, edited by C. Dewey, New Delhi: Manohar, 1988, 3–11.

Olivier Roy. *Islam and Resistance in Afghanistan.* Cambridge: Cambridge University Press, 1986.

———. 'Sufism in the Afghan Resistance'. *Central Asian Studies* 3, no. 4 (1983): 61–79.

———. 'The Origins of the Islamist Movement in Afghanistan'. *Central Asian Survey* 3, no. 2 (1984): 117–28.

Veena Sachdeva. 'Agrarian Production and Distribution in the Late Eighteenth Century'. In *Five Punjab Centuries: Polity, Economy, Society and Culture, C. 1500–1990*, edited by I. Banga, New Delhi: Manohar, 1997, 285–306.

Edward Said. *Orientalism.* London: Penguin, 1995, 2003.

P.C. Salzman. 'Tribal Chiefs as Middlemen: The Politics of Encapsulation'. *Anthropological Quarterly* 47, no. 2 (1974): 203–10.

William Schurz. *The Manila Galleon.* New York: E.P. Dutton, 1959. Reprint, 1939.

O. Semikhnenko. 'Central Asia'. In *Macmillan Encyclopaedia of World Slavery*, edited by J.C. Miller, New York: Macmillan Reference, 1998, 173–4.

Sudipta Sen. *Empire of Free Trade: The East India Company and the Making of the Colonial Marketplace, Critical Histories.* Philadelphia: University of Pennsylvania Press, 1998.

M. Nazif Shahrani. 'Local Knowledge of Islam and Social Discourse in Afghanistan and Turkestan in the Modern Period'. In *Turko-Persian in Historical Perspective*, edited by R. Canfield, Cambridge: Cambridge University Press, 1991, 161–85.

M. Nazif Shahrani and Robert Canfield, eds. *Revolutions and Rebellions in Afghanistan: Anthropological Perspectives.* Berkeley: University of California Press, 1984.

G.D. Sharma. 'The Marwaris: Economic Foundations of an Indian Capitalist Community'. In *Business Communities of India: A Historical Perspective*, edited by D. Tripathi, New Delhi: Manohar, 1984, 185–208.

R.R. Sharma. 'Some Aspects of Export and Import Trade under Ranjit Singh in the Light of Potedar Collection, Churu'. In *Maharaja Ranjit Singh: Politics, Society and Economy*, edited by F. Singh and A.C. Arora, Patiala: Punjabi University Publication Bureau, 1984, 233–6.

Asiya Siddiqi, ed. *Trade and Finance in Colonial India, 1750–1860*. Oxford: Oxford University Press, 1995.

Bhagat Singh. *Maharaja Ranjit Singh and His Times*. New Delhi: Sehgal Publishers Service, 1990.

——. 'Trade and Commerce under Maharaja Ranjit Singh'. In *Maharaja Ranjit Singh: Politics, Society and Economy*, edited by F. Singh and A.C. Arora, Patiala: Punjabi University Publication Bureau, 1984, 173–85.

Fauja Singh. 'Diplomatic Code of Ranjit Singh'. In *The Khalsa and the Punjab: Studies in Sikh History to the Nineteenth Century*, edited by H. Banerjee, New Delhi: Tulika, 2002, 86–92.

Ganda Singh. *Ahmad Shah Durrani: Father of Modern Afghanistan*. New York: Asia Publishing House, 1959.

David Sneath. *The Headless State: Aristocratic Order, Kinship Society and Misrepresentations of Nomadic Inner Asia*. New York: Columbia University Press, 2007.

Aidan Southall. 'The Segmentary State in Africa and Asia'. *Comparative Studies in Society and History* 30, no. 1 (1988): 52–82.

N. Steensgaard. *The Asian Trade Revolution of the Seventeenth Century: The East India Companies and the Decline of the Caravan Trade*. Chicago: University of Chicago Press, 1974.

Burton Stein. 'The Segmentary State in South Indian History'. In *Realm and Region in Traditional India*, edited by R.G. Fox, New Delhi: Vikas, 1977.

——. 'State Formation and Economy Reconsidered'. *Modern Asian Studies* 19, no. 3 (1985): 387–413.

S.M. Stern. 'The Constitution of the Islamic City'. In *The Islamic City*, edited by A. Hourani and S.M. Stern, Oxford: Buno Cassirer, 1970, 25–50.

George W. Stocking, Jr. *Victorian anthropology*. New York: The Free Press, 1987.

Eric Stokes. *The English Utilitarians and India*. New Delhi: Oxford University Press, 1959.

John Strong. 'Russia's Plans for an Invasion of India in 1801'. *Canadian Slavonic Papers* vii (1965): 114–26.

Percy Sykes. *A History of Afghanistan*. Vol. 2. London: MacMillan & Co., Ltd., 1940.

——. 'Holier Than Thou: Islam in Three Tribal Societies'. In *Islam in Tribal Societies: From the Atlas to the Indus*, edited by A. Ahmed and D.M. Hart, London: Routledge & Kegan Paul, 1984, 244–65.

——. 'The Tribes in 18th and 19th Century Iran'. In *The Cambridge History of Iran: From Nadir Shah to the Islamic Republic*, edited by P. Avery, C. Melville and G. Hambly, Cambridge: Cambridge University Press, 1991.

Richard Tapper. 'Ethnic Identities and Social Categories in Iran and Afghanistan'. In *History and Ethnicity*, edited by E. Tonkin, M. McDonald and M. Chapman, London: Routledge, 1989, 232–46.

G.P. Tate. *The Kingdom of Afghanistan: A Historical Sketch*. New Delhi: D.K. Publishing House, 1973.

John J. TePaske. 'New World Silver, Castille and the Philippines, 1590–1800'. In *Precious Metals in the Later Medieval and Early Modern Worlds*, edited by J.F. Richards, Durham, N.C.: Caroline Academic Press, 1983, 425–46.

Thomas Timberg. *The Marwaris: From Traders to Industrialists.* New Delhi: Vikas Publishing, 1978.

Thomas A. Timberg. 'Hiatus and Incubator: Indigenous Trade and Traders, 1837–1857'. In *Trade and Finance in Colonial India, 1750–1860,* edited by A. Siddiqi, New Delhi: Oxford University Press, 1995, 250–64.

James Tod. *Annals and Antiquities of Rajast'han, or the Central and Western Rajpoot States of India.* 2 vols. London: Smith, 1829–32.

J. Tracy, ed. *The Rise of Merchant Empires.* Cambridge: Cambridge University Press, 1990.

——, ed. *The Political Economy of Merchant Empires, Studies in Comparative Early Modern History.* Cambridge: Cambridge University Press, 1991.

Ernest Tucker. 'Explaining Nadir Shah: Kingship and Royal Legitimacy in Muhammad Kazim Marvi's Tarikh-I Alam-Ara-Yi Nadiri'. *Iranian Studies* 26, no. 1–2 (1993): 95–118.

——. 'Nadir Shah and the Ja'fari Madhhab Reconsidered'. *Iranian Studies* 27, no. 1–4 (1994): 163–80.

Unknown. 'The Borderlands of Soviet Central Asia: Afghanistan'. *Central Asian Review* 4, no. 2 (1956): 161–201.

Birendra Varma. *English East India Company and the Afghans, 1757–1800.* Calcutta: Punthi Pustak, 1968.

——. *From Delhi to Tehran: A Study of British Diplomatic Moves in North-Western India, Afghanistan and Persia, 1772–1803.* Patna: Janaki Prakashan, 1980.

Martha Vassar. 'Panoptican in Poona: An Essay on Foucault and Colonialism'. *Cultural anthropology* 10, no. 1 (1995): 85–98.

Mikhail Volodarsky. 'The Russians in Afghanistan in the 1830s'. *Central Asian Survey* 3, no. 1 (1984): 63–86.

Kim Wagner. *Thuggee: Banditry and the British in Early Nineteenth Century India,* edited by R. Drayton and M. Vaughan, *Cambridge Imperial and Post-Colonial Studies.* Basingstoke: Palgrave Macmillan, 2007.

Phillip Wagoner. 'Precolonial Intellectuals and the Production of Colonial Knowledge'. *Comparative Studies in Society and History* 45, no. 4 (2003): 783–814.

Immanuel Wallerstien. *The Modern World-System.* New York: Academic Press, 1974.

Gabriel Warburg. 'Mahdism and Islamism in Sudan'. *International Journal of Middle East Studies* 27, no. 2 (1995): 219–36.

David Washbrook. 'India, 1818–1860: The Two Faces of Colonialism'. In *Oxford History of the British Empire,* edited by W.R. Louis, A. Porter and A. Low, Oxford: Oxford University Press, 1999, 395–421.

——. 'Progress and Problems: South Asian Economic and Social History, C. 1720–1860'. *Modern Asian Studies* 22, no. 1 (1988): 57–96.

——. 'South Asia, the World System, and World Capitalism'. In *South Asia and World Capitalism,* edited by S. Bose, New Delhi: Oxford University Press, 1990, 40–84.

James L.A. Webb. 'The Horse and Slave Trade between the Western Sahara and Senegambia'. *The Journal of African History* 34, no. 2 (1993): 221–46.

Gordon Whitteridge. *Charles Masson of Afghanistan: Explorer, Archaeologist, Numismatist and Intelligence Agent.* 2nd ed. Bangkok: Orchid Press, 2002.

Andre Wink. *Land and Sovereignty in India: Agrarian Society and Politics under the Eighteenth Century Maratha Svarajya.* Cambridge: Cambridge University Press, 1986.

Thongchai Winichakul, 'Maps and the Formation of the Geo-Body of Siam', In *Asian Forms of the Nation,* edited by S. Tonneson and H. Antlov, London: Curzon, 1996, 67–90.

Anand Yang. 'A Conversation of Rumors: The Language of Popular 'Mentalites' in Late Nineteenth-Century Colonial India'. *Journal of Social History* 20, no. 3 (1987): 485–505.

M.E. Yapp. 'The Revolutions of 1841–1842 in Afghanistan'. *Bulletin of the School of Oriental and African Studies* 27, no. 2 (1964): 333–81.

——. 'British Policy in the Persian Gulf'. In *The Persian Gulf States: A General Survey*, edited by A. Cottrell, C.E. Bosworth, R.M. Burrell, K. McLachlan and R.M. Savory, Baltimore: The Johns Hopkins University Press, 1980, 70–100.

——. *Strategies of British India: Britain, Iran and Afghanistan 1798–1850*. Oxford: Claredon Press, 1980.

——. 'Tribes in the Khyber, 1838–1842'. In *The Conflict of Tribe and State in Iran and Afghanistan*, edited by R. Tapper, London: Croom Helm, 1983, 150–91.

M.E. Yapp. 'British Perceptions of the Russian Threat to India'. *Modern Asian Studies* 21, no. 4 (1987): 647–65.

——. 'The Legend of the Great Game'. *Proceedings of the British Academy* 111 (2000): 179–98.

Index

Abdur Rahman Khan (r. 1880–1901), 5, 11, 86, 107, 164, 174–5
Afghan civil war (1818–26), 4, 83, 104–5, 140, 145, 157, 160
(1978–2001), 164, 175
Afghan rulers, *see individual names*
Afghan-Sikh conflict, *see* Sikh
Age of Reform (1828–1835), 38
agriculture, 30, 94
  areas/regions, 25, 52
  goods, 138, 149, 154
  population, 31
  productivity, 53, 72, 113, 149–50, 155–7
  surplus, 30, 113, 149–50
  wealth, 53, 97, 138, 151, 153, 155
Ahmad Shah Abdali/Durrani (r. 1747–1773), 82–3, 94–6, 103–4, 107
  coronation of, *see* coronation
  election by jirga, 88, 103
  invasions of north India, 120
  rise to power, 3
Ahmed, Akbar, 31
Allard, Jean-Francois, 73
Amherst, William Pitt, 131
amīr, 95, 104
  amīr al-mu'minīn, 77, 88, 106
  Amir of Bukhara, 97, 139, 140, 142
  Amirs of Sind, 39, 48, 54, 55, 157
An Account of the Kingdom of Caubul (1815), 13–15, 32
anthropology, 12
  structural functionalism, 26, 31
archive(s), 13–14, 42
  colonial, 5, 38, 46, 165
  creation, 7, 17
Armenian, 118, 127, 140, 145
  merchants, 117–18, 127
  Orthodox clergy, 46
army
  of the Indus, 8, 65, 122
  of Retribution, 69, 82, 146
Auckland, Lord (George Eden, 1784–1849), 45, 54–6, 58, 65–7, 128
Avitabile, Paolo, 64, 73

Badakhshan, 5, 143
Balkans, 6, 114, 170
Balkh, 142
Bamian valley, 144
Barakzai, 57, 75, 83, 98, 103, 104–5
Barth, Frederik, 31
Bayly, C. A., 22, 68
bazaars, 42, 98, 119–20, 122, 130, 137–8
  bazaaris, 151
  Bukhara, 139
  gossip, 7, 43
  Herat, 154
  Kabul, 48, 49, 69, 145–8, 161
  Kandahar, 156
  Kunduz, 143
  Multan, 158
  rumour, 42, 43, 70, 113
  Shikarpur, 157–8
  trade, 151
Bentinck, Lord William Henry Cavendish (1774–1839), 38, 40, 41, 46–7, 51, 53
Bolan, *see* passes
Bombay, 117, 122, 124, 129, 147, 156
  customs house, 124
  Governor, 15, 47, *see also* Clare
  merchants, 48, 50, 122
  prices, 48, 155
borders, *see* frontiers
boundaries, 29, 49, 169
buffer, 61, 166
  state, 36, 54, 56, 61, 108–9
  strategy, 36
Bukhara, 137–42
  Alexander Burnes' travels to, 44, 62
  centre of learning, 99–100
  Dost Muhammad's escape to, 65
  merchant community, 119, 121, 125, 127, 154, 156
  money of, 117, 126–7, 145
  rulers, 106, 139–40
  Russian relations with, 49, 126
  'tolerance', 145

Bukhara – *continued*
  trade, 137–42, 144: bullion, *see* bullion;
    gold tillas, 125, 127; value of, 97,
    147, 151; with Russia, *see* Russia
bullion, 117, 119, 122, 124–8, 151, 161
  see also silver
bureaucracy, 17, 53, 59, 89–90, 140
Burnes, Alexander, 4, 44–5
  Cabool, 16
  death, 67
  description of Lohanis, 121–2, 147
  mission to Kabul, 48, 49, 50, 56, 58, 64–5
  survey of the Indus, 48, 54
  Travels into Bokhara, 16, 100, 141
  writings, 16, 43

Cabool: Being a personal narrative, see
  Burnes
Campbell, William, 71, 74
caravans, 5, 29, 122, 137–59, 166–7
  caravanserais, 141, 152, 153, 154
  cities, 10, 137–59, *see also individual
    names*
  commerce/trade, 10, 49, 110–11, 115,
    117, 136–7
  duties, 97–8
  kâfilas, 97, 101, 119–20; kafilabashi,
    148, 159
  Lohani, 147–9
  merchants, 42, 118, 119, 126
Central Asia, 134, 151–2, 161
  Anglo-Russian rivalry, *see* Great Game;
    Russia
  markets, 47–50, 115–19, 121–3, 126–7,
    see also individual cities' names
  political traditions, *see* Nadir Shah;
    Persia, Timurid
  Russian policies towards, 126
  trade, 125–6, 130–1, 136–42, 156–9
China, 40, 117, 124–6, 141, 143
Chinese Turkistan, 125, 132, 137, 139, 143
cities, *see individual names*
  corridor, 110–59
  nodal, 115, 121, 123, 137, 152, 167
Clare, Lord (John FitzGibbon,
  1792–1851), 47
colonial knowledge, 11–33
  effect on British understandings, 36,
    37, 40
  see also Elphinstone

Conolly, Arthur (1807–1842), 38, 42,
  146, 152
consumption, 110, 115, 116, 127–9, 134
  centres of, 138, 144
  cultures, 132
  patterns of, 80, 128, 130–3
  silver, 117, 124, 125
  sumptuary patterns, 10, 155, 167
containment, 78, 109, 111, 112
  Sikh, 51, 165–6
  strategy, 6, 61, 165, 169
coronation
  Ahmad Shah Durrani, 96
  Dost Muhammad Khan, 88, 106
  Nadir Shah, 92–3
Court, Claude-Auguste (1793–1861),
  73, 154, 155
credit, 113, 116–21, 124, 138
  Company, 50
  networks, 166
  systems, 50, 140, 141, 158, 159
customs, 29, 88, 101
  see also tradition

dacoit, *see* thuggee
dependency, 39, 115, 130, 161
depression (north Indian), 112, 116, 124
deserters, 46, 72, 74–5
  see also mercenaries
Dicks, Robert, 74
Dil brothers (Pur Dil Khan, Kohan Dil Khan
  and Rahim Dil Khan, r. 1817–39), *see
  also* Kandahar
Dost Muhammad Khan (r. 1826–39), 9,
  25, 58, 62, 144, 146, 160–1
  Alexander Burnes' mission to, 50, 64
  court of, 44, 132
  defeat of Shah Shuja, 56–7
  exile, 69, 82
  family of, 57, 63, 75, 78, 105, 148
  legitimacy, 68, 78, 83, 88, 90, 98, 105–7
  mercenaries in employ of, 45, 71, 73–4
  reception of Russian agent, 59
  relations with: Bukhara, 142; corrsepond-
    ence/relations with EIC, 45, 56, 62,
    79, 97; Mir Murad Beg, 143, Ranjit
    Singh, 55–9, 75–8, 105, 148, 161
  titles, 88, 104, *see also* amīr al-mu'minīn
  treatment of subjects, 89, 121, 128,
    146–9

Durand Line, 18
Durrani Empire (1747–1818), 86–8, 163
   collapse, 3, 75, 111
   foundation, 91
   rulers, 30
   territories, 25
   see also Ahmad Shah Abdali
duties, *see* caravans, taxes, trade

East India Company (EIC), 9, 71
   archives of, *see* archives
   conquest of South Asia, 71, 95
   Dutch (VOC), 125
   information order of, *see* information,
      order
   intelligence, *see* information,
      intelligence
   personnel, 46, 119
   role in South Asian economy,
      115–17
   ecology, 30–1, 112, 150
   see also social ecology
Edinburgh, 15, 21
Ellenborough, Earl of (Edward Law,
      1790–1871), 40
Elphinstone, Mountstuart
   descriptions of Afghanistan, 82, 94–5,
      100, 103–4, 125
   education, 14–15, 21
   episteme, 14–33, 37, 46, 82–4
   History of India, 15
   mission to Kabul, 4, 7, 13, 21, 43, 46,
      62, 68–9, 149
   papers and reports, 13–15, 42–4
   reception at Peshawar, 131
   'servant of the exotic', 15–17, 31
   see also An Account of the Kingdom of
      Caubul

fanatics, 77
Fast, Mr, 73, 74
Fath Khan, 104, 105
Fauj-i Ain, *see* Punjab
Fauj-i Khas, *see* Punjab
fault lines, 82, 86, 90, 107, 163,
      165–6
finance, 3, 110, 157, 158
   Ahmed Shah Abdali's, 120
   Dost Muhammad Khan's, 120, 132,
      134, 147, 148

East India Company's, 38, 115, 122,
      127, 146
   Nadir Shah's, 94, 127
   networks, 123, *see also* credit
   Ranjit Singh's, 48, 54
   state, 71
   see also military fiscalism
First Afghan War (1839–42), 17–18,
      28–9, 40, 65–70, 108, 155
   effect of, 50, 85
First Opium War (1839–42), 40,
      66, 124
Firuzuddin, 153
'fiscal colony', 84, 109, 114, 169
fitna, 62, 72, 74, 81
Forster, George, (c. 1752–1791), 46, 145,
      150, 152–3, 154, 156
Forward School of Indian defence,
      39–41, 68, 142
   strategic vision, 47, 50–1, 56, 63, 79
   uses of intelligence, 44
   views of, 54–5, 134
free trade, *see* trade
French
   British fears of incursions by, 4
   defeat, of Napoleon, 74
   demand for goods, 132
   officers, 56, 73–4, *see also individual*
      names Forster Napoleonic, 72–4
frontiers, 2, 4, 10, 19, 21, 33, 60, 62,
      157, 166
   administration of, 28, 32, 114, 134
   Afghan-Sikh, 77
   bifurcation of, 39–40, 47, 50
   defence of, 34, 36, 45, 47, 54, 69, 72,
      see also Forward School
   'effect', 149–50
   external/political, 40, 51, 64, 79–80, 142
   internal/territorial, 39, 51, 52, 53, 64,
      79–80
   Persian, 63, 65, 79, 153
   tribal uprisings along, 18
   tribes, 29, 32
fruits, 113, 128, 144–5, 154

Gangetic Plain, 11, 81, 163
genealogy, 25–7, 31
   idiom of (tribal), 21, 25–7, 77, 93, 99,
      100–5, 136
   kinship, 25–7, 31, 33

genealogy – *continued*
  lineage, 25–7, 29, 100, 102
  segmentary, 25, 33
Georgian, 117, 145
Gerard, Dr. James, (1793–1835), 62, 119, 145, 152
Ghilzai Pashtuns, 121, 123, 140, 148
Gibbon, Edward, 20
gifts, 128, 130–1, 132
globalization, 6–7, 10
'God's Shadow on Earth', 92–3
Gomal, *see* passes
governance, 18, 24, 57, 115, 157, 169
  Afghan, 66
  British, 18, 68, 124
  institutions of, 88, 89, 91
  laissez-faire, 49, 161
  norms, 24, 52, 91, 110, 162
  philosophies of, 37–9, 59
  tools of, 41
  tribal, 85, 88
governmentality, 38, 50, 79, 161
Governor-General, *see individual names*
Great Game, 4, 8, 34–60, 80–1, 165
'gunpowder empires', 3, 87, 110, 134, 166

hamsāya, 100
Hari Rud, 30
  River, 153
  valley, 113, 128, 138, 155
Harlan, Josiah (1799–1871), 73, 74, 143
Hazaras, 5, 6, 16, 23, 100–1, 144
Hazrat Ali shrine, *see* Mazar-i Sharif
'hegemonic text', 14
Herat, 137, 138, 150, 152–5, 160
  British policies towards, 36, 43, 63–6, 79
  centre of learning, 99, 153
  Persian policies towards, 56–8, 63–6, 74–5, 156, 166
  rulers of, 3, 104, 151, 160–1
hierarchy of civilizations, 14, 20
highlands, *see* Scotland
hindki, 116–21
Hindu Kush, 5, 28, 37, 40, 46, 49, 68, 149
horses, 10, 129, 150, 155, 161
  Company stud, 15
  trade, 161
Hume, David, 14
hundi, 117, 119

imaginative framework, 7, 35
imaginative power, 60
imaginative universe, 37
Imam, 92–3
  Imamate, 88, 92
  Reza Shrine, 151–2; *see also* Meshad
indigo, 141, 147, 154
Indus, 41–3, 45, 141, 158, 160
  Army of, *see* 'army'
  'closure of', 142
  navigation of, 44, 47, 51
  'opening of', 4, 39, 51, 54
  Plain, 5, 157
  River, 4, 8, 47
  Scheme, 38, 40, 42, 43, 46–50, 58, 122, 128, 130, 134
informants, 22–3
  indigenous, 43
information
  indigenous, 113
  orders, 13, 21, 35, 41–5, 68, 79:
    bureaucratization of, 37;
    construction of, 15, 22;
    contestation of, 18
  panics, 68
  see also intelligence
Ingram, Edward, 35–6
insurance, 118, 120
intelligence, 17, 19, 57, 59–60, 73, 108
  commercial, 48, 113, 130
  failure, 69, 78
  networks, 17, 22
  see also information
internalization of plunder, *see* plunder
International Security Assistance Force (ISAF), 1
Iran, *see* Persia
Islam, 86–8, 98–102, 105–7, 153
  dār al-Islām, 134, 159
  norms of, 58, 76–8, 90, 167
  political order, 163
  Shi'a, 90, 92–6
  Sunni, 95, 139–40
  see also legitimacy, ulamā

jāgīr, 48, 71
  see also 'tiyūl'
Jalalabad, 64, 68, 69, 149
  British retreat to, 68
  Dost Muhammad's control of, 105

Jamrud, 63–4
Jews, 117–18, 140, 145, 150, 152, 154
jihād, 58, 76
  against the Sikhs, 58, 76–8, 105–6,
    121, 148
jirga, 88–9

Kabul
  British: invasion of, 65–7, 82; relations
    with, 13–16, 21–2, 28, 39–58;
    retreat from, 67–70, 80, 120; *see
    also* Dost Muhammad Khan;
    Elphinstone, Burnes
  centre of government, 99
  Company news-writers in, 16, 22–3,
    43, 50, 106
  court of, 64–5, *see also* Dost
    Muhammad Khan
  economy of, 121–2, 127–9, 141–2,
    144–8, *see also* bazaar, trade
  Kingdom of, 15, 21–2, 28, 69, 165, 173
  Ranjit Singh's ambitions towards, 56,
    63–4
  ruler, *see* Dost Muhammad Khan
  Russian activities towards, 64–5
  trade, 117, *see also* bazaar
kâfila, see caravan
Kāfir, see Nuristanee
Kandahar
  British occupation, 67, 69
  Company news-writer in, 43
  Durrani heartland, 3, 71, 155
  rulers, 57, 83, 105
  Shuja's defeat near (1834), 57
  trade, 148, 150–1, 154, 155–6, *see also*
    bazaar
Karamat Ali, 22, 43
Kashmir, 52, 75
  shawls, 131–3, 141, 143, 147,
    154, 167
Khalsa Dal, *see* Sikh
Khalsa Raj, *see* Sikh
khan, 19, 28–30, 95
khanates
  Central Asian, 49, 140
  Khiva, 151
khattris, see merchant
khel, 9, 175
khil'at, 130–1, 132, 148
khirqa-i mubaraka, 106

Khiva, 49, 140, 142, 151–2
  merchants, 49, 151
Khorasan, *see* Herat, Meshad
  Multan's trade with, 158–9
Khulum, 137, 138, 142, 143–4, 157
khutba, 77, 106
Khyber, *see* passes
Kim, see Kipling
kingship, 91–2, 103, 105, 132
  Afghan, 74, 98, 107–8
  Savafid, 95, 106
kinship, *see* genealogy
Kipling, Rudyard, 4, 37
Kunduz, 46, 117, 137, 138, 142–4

Ladakh, 125, 132
Lahore, 52, 53–6, 67, 70, 73–5, 118, 150
  darbār, 45, 48, 53–4, 66
legitimacy, 68, 85–90, 98–109
  Islamic, *see* Islam
  legitimization, 78, 90–1, 93–5, 105–7,
    163
  political, 9–10, 23–6, 33, 37–9, 75–7,
    174–5
  royal, 28, 102–7, *see also* royalism
  tribal, 23, 25–6, 143, *see also* tribe
  see also normative order
Levant, 6, 114, 170
Lindholm, Charles, 31
loans, 118, 119, 120, 140, 146, 148
Lohanis (*powindahs*), 48, 121–3, 140,
    147–9, 158–9
  see also caravan
Lord, Percival Barton (P. B., 1808–40),
    46, 141, 143
Ludiana, 44–5, 57
  exile in, 57, 59, 65, 69, 82, *see also*
    individual names

Macartney, Lt. John, 21–2, 25, 33
Mackeson, Lt. Frederick (1807–53), 57
Macnaghten, William (1793–1841), 44,
    45, 49, 53, 58, 66
madrasas, 100, 101
Makhzan-i Afghani (Neamat Ullah
    Harawi), 20
Malcolm, Sir John (1769–1833), 15–16
Manila galleon, 125
'man on the spot', 44, 80
maps, 21–3, 24

Marathas, 94–5, 129
marginalization, 84, 110, 134, 165, 168
marwaris, see merchant
Masson, Charles (a.k.a. John Lewis,
    1800–53), 16–17
  Dost Muhammad's coronation, *see*
    coronation
  genealogies, 26
  Kabul news-writer, 43–5
  opinion of Mullahs, 100–1
  reports of caravan traffic, 147
Mazar-i Sharif, 100, 138, 142–3, 151
  Hazrat Ali shrine, 100, 143, 151
mercenaries, 10, 70–5, 129
  Afghan, 70–2
  European, 62
  export of, 116, 161
  Russian, 45, 74
  see also individual names, military
    labour market
merchants, 39, 48, 116–21, 140–1
  Afghan, 49
  bankers, 99, 123, 146, 153, 158
  Bombay, 48, 50, 122
  Central Asian, 126, 154, *see also*
    Central Asia
  extortion of, 97
  Indian, 130
  khattris, 116
  Khivan, 49, 151
  marwaris, 116
  Multani, 116–18
  networks, 113–14, 116–23,
    136–7
  Russian, 49
  Shikarpuri, 123, 127, 146,
    155, 156
Meshad, 150–2, 154
Metcalfe, Charles (1785–1846), 16, 41,
    45, 47, 54–5
  see also Forward School
Mexico, 124–5
Meyendorf, Baron von, *see* Russia
mian, 89, 100–1
military
  fiscalism, 52, 62, 71, 74, 89, 115
  labour market, 62, 70–5, 80, 81,
    129–30
  revolution, 71–6, 80, 129
Minto, Lord (Gilbert Elliot, 1751–1814), 15

Mir Izzat Ullah, 97, 127
Mir Murad Beg, 46, 101, 142
Mithankot, 48, 50, 122
  see also Indus Scheme
Mohan Lal, 144
monarch, 68, 75, 93–4, 97, 102–5
  'dispensary', 94
  monarchy, 24, 87–90, 95–6, 107
Moorcroft, William (1767–1825),
    46, 97
  death of, 129
  journals, 16–17
  report of the battle of Nowshera, 73–4
  'servant of the exotic', 15–6
Mughals, 3, 70, 115, 132
  authority, 52, 94
  concepts of information, 41
  Empire, 71, 110, 123, 127
  norms, 91–2, 128–31
  state form, 52, 96, *see also* state
Mullah, *see ulamā*
Multan, 77, 138, 148, 157–9
  bankers, 116–18, 123, 128, 140, 156,
    see also merchants
  trade, 121–2, 154, 158–9
munshis, 22, 144
  see also Mohan Lal

Nadir Shah (1688–1747), 91, 92–4,
    95, 127
nation, 82, 84–5, 104, 174
  Afghan, 5
  national community, 83
  state, 35
Navigation Treaty, *see* treaty
negotiation, 54, 57, 71, 76
Nesselrode, Count Karl Robert (1780–
    1862), 46
news-writers, 16, 17, 22, 43, 50, 106
  see also, Charles Masson, Karamit Ali,
    Mohan Lal
Nizhnii Novgorod, 121, 122, 126,
    141, 151
normative categories, 77
normative edifice, 88
normative orders, 27–8, 38, 83–7,
    98–107
  see also legitimacy
  Timurid, *see also* Timurid, 93
North West Frontier Province, 4, 25

Nowshera, battle of, 73–4, 76, 105
  see also William Moorcroft
Nuristanees, 5

'official mind', 12–13, 32–5, 38, 45, 68,
  108, 165
  see also archive, information order
opium, 124, 125, 130, 153, 175
'oriental despotism', 23, 38
Oxus River, 5, 49, 139, 142

paramountcy, 5, 8, 61–70, 91, 99
  Afghan, 49, 71
  British, 4, 39–40, 48, 50–9, 79, 164
  economic, 112, 144
  Hastings' declaration of (1818), 71
  political, 48, 129, 134, 149
  royal, 28, 95–7, *see also* royalism
  Sikh, 75
pashtûnwâlî, 19, 27–30, 98–9, 102–3, 105
  see also tarbûrwâlî
passes
  Bolan, 156, 157
  Gomal, 122, 148–9, 157
  Khyber, 134, 149, *see also* Jamrud,
    Sikhs, tribes
Payinda Khan, 104
performative identity, 27–8, 31
peripheralization, 87, 114, 155, 162, 170
Persia, 3, 58
  British mission in, 63
  court of, 132
  decadence, 20
  envoy to Kabul, 65
  expansionism, 61, 152–3, 156, 160–1
  Iran, 25, 93
  language, 90
  merchants, 117, 126
  political legacies, 90–8, 106,
    108
  Qajars, 36, 63, 92, 132, 160
  Russian influence over, 35, 40, 47, 56,
    63–6, 78–9, 155: siege of Herat, 57,
    58, 63, 74–5
  slaves, 140, 151
  Strategy, 36
  titles, 103–4, 106, 151
  trade, 94, 118, 123–4, 126–7, 137,
    142, 160
  see also Safavids

Peshawar, 25, 75–9, 102, 105, 138,
  149–50
  Afghan-Sikh hostilities over, 45,
    48, 56–9, 63–6, *see also* Dost
    Muhammad Khan, Sikhs
  centre of learning, 99–100
  Elphinstone mission to, 13, 15, 17, 22,
    26, *see also* Elphinstone
  sardârs, 83
  Sayyid Ahmed Barelwi's rule over, *see*
    Sayyid Ahmed Barelwi
  vale of, 113, 128, 138, 155
plunder, 90–8, 126–7, 133–4, 151,
  163–4
  internalization of, 10, 112, 150, 155
  opportunities for (lack of), 105, 107,
    114, 116
  'plundering polity', 3, 87, 143, 163–4
  political economy of, 85, 111, 114
  raids, 30, 83, 96, 112
  sources of, 120
Pottinger, Henry (1789–1856), 55
prestige, 36, 39, 42, 46, 69–70
  loss of, 50, 59, 98
proto-state, *see* state
Punjab, 50–9, 61–2, 66
  administration of, 39, 48, 52–4, 150
  British conquest of, 80
  containment of, *see* containment
  economy of, 53–4
  French officers in, 72–5
  military, 165: Fauj-i Ain, 53, Fauj-i
    Khas, 73, 105; *Khalsa Dal*, 51–2,
    53; *see also* labour market

Qajar, *see* Persia
qaum, 9, 175
qazî, see ulamâ
Qizilbash, 90, 93, 99, 105, 145
Quetta, 101, 118, 138, 156–7

Ranjit Singh, 39, 104, 163
  ambitions of, 45–6, 47–9, 51–6, 62–4,
    70, 75–6, 79–80
  British relations with, *see* Sikh
  death of, 66
  Punjab kingdom, 50–9, 61, 72, 95
  Russians, communications with, 45–6
  see also Dost Muhammad Khan,
    Lahore, Punjab, Sikhs

Ravenshaw, Edward, 42, 50
rawaj, 27–8
religious authority, 88, 92, 100–1, 107,
    142–3 *see also* ulamā
revenue, 66, 96–8, 119, 141, 149
    demands, 110, 115–16, 126, 127
    settlements, 70, 115
    sources, 80, 111, 144, 159
    see also military fiscalism, taxes
rivers, 49
    navigation, 44, 47–8, 49, 51
    steam, 47, 119, 128
    traffic, 38–9, 149
    see also individual names
royalism, 85–6, 102–5, 107
rumour, 36, 41–3, 46, 67, 78
    see also bazaar, information, intelligence
Russia
    agents, 4, 45–6
    Anglo-Russian rivalry, 108–9, 139, 166,
        see also Great Game
    army of, 74–5
    Empire, 8, 34
    expansion into Central Asia, 34–7, 49,
        151, *see also* Central Asia
    influence over Persia, *see* Persia
    Meyendorf, mission to Bukhara, 126, 140
    trade, 121–2, *see also* Central Asia
    trade fair, *see* 'Nizhnii Novgorod'

Saddozai, 28, 49, 83, 98, 103–7
    monarch, 68
    sardārs, 64
Safavids, 3, 87, 91–7, 103, 105–6, 107
    Empire, 9, 71, 89, 123, 163
    norms, 106, 132
    shah, 104
    state, 88
    see also Persia
sayyids, 89, 100–1, 149
Sayyid Ahmed Barelwi, 56, 76–8, 101–2,
    105
Sayyid Muheen Shah, 122, 130, 146
Scotland, 18–20
    highlands, 26, 29, 32, 139
    Scottish Enlightenment, 14–16, 21
    Scottish paisleys, 132
sedentary
    merchant groups, 123
    societies, 92

segmentary, *see* genealogy
sepoys, 49, 66, 71, 129, 168
Shah Mahmud (r. 1800–1803, 1809–
    1818, Herat 1818–1829), 83, 97,
    104, 153, 161
Shah Shuja ul-Mulk (r. 1803–9, 1839–41),
    56–7, 65–8
    attempts to regain throne, 28, 49, 63,
        75, 105
    British support of, 79–80, 107
    defeat of, 54, 74, 160, *see also* Dost
        Muhammad Khan
    Elphinstone's mission to the court of,
        see Elphinstone
    exile, *see* Ludiana
Shahzadeh Kamram (r. 1829–41), 104,
    151, 153–6, 161
sharīa, 88, 99, 101, 139–40
    duty rate, 97, 146, 156, *see also* taxes
Shikarpur, 157–8
    merchants, *see* merchants
    Ranjit's ambitions for, *see*
        Ranjit Singh
    trade, 122, 154, 157–8
Sikh
    Anglo-Sikh alliance, 50–9, 61–81,
        rivalry, 109, 134, 158, 165
    Afghan-Sikh conflict, 47–81, 102,
        105–6, *see also* Dost Muhammad
        Khan, Kabul, Peshawar, Ranjit Singh
silver, 124–7, 154, 158
    American, 124–5, 145, 160
    Company ban on import to India
        (1765), 130
    famine, 53, 124, 126
    see also bullion
Sind, 4, 38, 40, 47–8, 54–6, 76,
    117
    amirs of, *see* amīr
    British policies toward, 76–7, 80
    cities of, 51, 62, 156, 157
    Ranjit Singh's ambitions toward,
        see Ranjit Singh
slavery, 38
    in: Bukhara (Russian slaves), 140;
        Herat, 155; Khiva, 49, 151
    trade, 114, 140
Smith, Adam, 14
social ecology, 5–6, 84–7
    see also ecology, social formations

social formations, 9, 87, 160, 172–3
  alternate, 25, 168
  alternative, 84–5, 86, 87, 175
society
  civil, 83–4
  political, 23, 83–4, 132, 133
sovereignty, *see* state
state
  ethnographic, 21
  failure, 172, 175
  proto, 52, 77, 85–6, 87–90
  sovereignty, 21–4, 38, 56, 66, 90, 95,
      97, 139, 172, 174
  successor, 3, 22, 41–2, 52–3, 68, 79–80,
      95, 111, 115, 129, 163
  suzerainty, 3, 24, 95, 108, 144
  Weberian, 8, 24, 83–5, 163–4, 173
steam navigation, *see* river
structural functionalism, *see* anthropology
subsidy, 37, 96
  policy, 28–9, 87, 114, 169, 175
  subsidiary alliance, 52, 57, 66, 79
  tribal, 12, 28–9
  ulamā, 89
Sudan, 6, 114, 170
Sufi
  orders, 92, 102
  Sufism, 101
Sultan Muhammad Khan, 75–6, 78
  see also Peshawar *sardārs*
sumptuary patterns, *see* 'consumption'
Sutlej River, 39, 40, 53
  'closure of', 72

Tacitus, 7, 20
Tajiks, 5, 6, 23, 155
Taliban, 164, 173, 175
tarbûrwâlî, 27–8
  see also pashtûnwâlî
ṭarīqat, 9, 101, 102, 175
  see also Sufi orders
tax(es), 30, 48, 98, 118, 120, 128, 143,
      147, 150, 154, 156
  farming, 71, 97, 116
  land taxes, 96, 149
  receipts, 130, 147, 148, 160,
      167
  revenue, 124, 154
  taxation, 39, 132, 152, 155, 159
  see also duties, revenue

territory
  territoriality, 21–3, 84–5
  territorialization, 24–5, 169
thuggee, 40, 129–30
Timurid, 128–9
  Empire, 154
  legacies, 91, 93
  norms, 93, 132, *see also* legitimacy,
      normative order
  Tuqay-Timurids, 106, *see also* Bukhara
tiyūl, 71, 97
trade, 110–162
  British policy, 47–50, *see also* Indus
      Scheme
  fairs, 48, *see also* Mithankot, Nizhnii
      Novgorod
  free, 37–8, 40, 47, 50, 60
  patterns, 80
  tolls, 64, *see also* caravans, duties
  transit, 167
traditions, 28–9, 90
  documenting, 69
  intellectual, 20
  leadership patterns, 28–9
  literate, 101
  martial, 27, 62, 72
  Persianate, 92–6, 101
  political, 77, 91–2, 115, 139, 169, *see
      also* legitimacy, normative orders
Travels into Bokhara, *see* Burnes
treaty, 13
  of Amritsar, 52
  Navigation Treaty, 48
  Tri-Partite Treaty, 66, 80
  of Turkmanchai, 79
Trebeck, George, (1800–1825), 46
Trevelyan, George, 36, 42, 50
tribe
  Abdali, 3, 91, 103
  alternative social formation, 23–4
  colonial understandings of, 18–21
  community, 27–8
  Durrani, 4, 26–7, 85–9, 91, 103–5
  genealogy, 26
  Khyber, 19, 28–9, 64
  language of legitimacy, 68, 77, 85–90,
      92, 99, 163–4, *see also* legitimacy,
      normative order
  leadership in, 29
  structures, 30–1

tribe – *continued*
 tribalization, 20–1, 31, 94
 tribal kingdom, 85, 87–90, 108
 Turkic, 92–6
Tri-Partite Treaty, *see* treaty

ulamā, 89–90, 92, 99, 101, 140, 142–3
 Mullah, 74, 100–1
 qazī, 89
urbanization, 98, 108, 138–9, 167
Uzbek, 5, 23, 143
 see also Mir Murad Beg

Ventura, Jean-Baptiste, 73
Vitkevich, Ivan Viktoriovich, 45, 59, 65

Wade, Claude Martin, (1794–1861), 43,
 44–5, 100, 128
 resident at the Lahore durbar, 48, 51,
 55, 66, 73, 74
Wahabi, 76–8
Weberian state, *see* state

yaghistan, 1
yamboo (silver ignot), 125
Yapp, Malcolm (M. E.), 36
Yarkand, 46, 125, 137, 139
Yusufzai, 76, 101–2

Zeman Shah (r. 1793–1800), 70, 75,
 83, 104